Interstitial Private Law

Interstitial Private Law

Edited by

SAMUEL L. BRAY
Notre Dame Law School

JOHN C.P. GOLDBERG
Harvard Law School

PAUL B. MILLER
Notre Dame Law School

HENRY E. SMITH
Harvard Law School

OXFORD
UNIVERSITY PRESS

OXFORD
UNIVERSITY PRESS

Oxford University Press is a department of the University of Oxford. It furthers the University's objective of excellence in research, scholarship, and education by publishing worldwide. Oxford is a registered trade mark of Oxford University Press in the UK and certain other countries.

Published in the United States of America by Oxford University Press
198 Madison Avenue, New York, NY 10016, United States of America.

Library of Congress Cataloging-in-Publication Data
Names: Bray, Samuel L., editor. | Goldberg, John C. P., 1961– editor. |
Miller, Paul B. (Law teacher), editor. | Smith, Henry E., editor.
Title: Interstitial private law / [edited by] Samuel L. Bray,
John C.P. Goldberg, Paul B. Miller, Henry E. Smith.
Description: New York : Oxford University Press, 2024. |
Includes bibliographical references and index. |
Identifiers: LCCN 2024023099 | ISBN 9780197783627 (hardback) |
ISBN 9780197783641 (updf) | ISBN 9780197783634 (epub) | ISBN 9780197783658 (online)
Subjects: LCSH: Civil law—United States. | Equity—United States. |
Equity pleading and procedure—United States. | Estoppel—United States.
Classification: LCC KF385 .I55 2024 | DDC 346.73—dc23/eng/20240528
LC record available at https://lccn.loc.gov/2024023099

DOI: 10.1093/oso/9780197783627.001.0001

Printed by Marquis Book Printing, Canada

Note to Readers
This publication is designed to provide accurate and authoritative information in regard to the subject matter covered. It is based upon sources believed to be accurate and reliable and is intended to be current as of the time it was written. It is sold with the understanding that the publisher is not engaged in rendering legal, accounting, or other professional services. If legal advice or other expert assistance is required, the services of a competent professional person should be sought. Also, to confirm that the information has not been affected or changed by recent developments, traditional legal research techniques should be used, including checking primary sources where appropriate.

(Based on the Declaration of Principles jointly adopted by a Committee of the American Bar Association and a Committee of Publishers and Associations.)

For our families
—SB, JG, PBM, and HS

Contents

Acknowledgments

This book is the fruit of a workshop convened at the Notre Dame Rome Global Gateway in November 2022, having been delayed for two years due to the pandemic. We are grateful for the financial support for the workshop from the Notre Dame Program on Private Law and the Harvard Law School Project on the Foundations of Private Law. We are also grateful to Anna Ricigliano and Alicia Sachau of Notre Dame for their kind hospitality and logistical assistance in support of the workshop in Rome. We would also like to thank Jamie Berezin of Oxford University Press as well as the press for supporting the publication of this volume.

Contributors

Samuel L. Bray, John N. Mathews Professor of Law, Notre Dame Law School

Nicolas Cornell, Professor of Law, University of Michigan Law School

Courtney M. Cox, Associate Professor of Law, Fordham University School of Law

Christopher Essert, Associate Professor of Law, University of Toronto Faculty of Law

Mark P. Gergen, Robert and Joann Burch D.P. Professor of Tax Law and Policy, UC Berkeley School of Law

Andrew S. Gold, Professor of Law, UC Irvine School of Law

John C.P. Goldberg, Carter Professor of General Jurisprudence, Harvard Law School

Ben McFarlane, Professor of English Law, University of Oxford Faculty of Law, and Fellow of St. John's College, Oxford

Paul B. Miller, Robert and Marion Short Professor of Law and Associate Dean for International and Graduate Programs, Notre Dame Law School

James Penner, Kwa Geok Choo Professor of Property Law, National University of Singapore Faculty of Law

Carol M. Rose, Gordon Bradford Tweedy Professor of Law Emeritus of Law and Organization, Yale Law School and Professor of Law Emerita; and Lohse Chair in Water and Natural Resources Emerita, University of Arizona James E. Rogers College of Law

Zoë Sinel, Associate Professor of Law, Western University Faculty of Law

Henry E. Smith, Fessenden Professor of Law, Harvard Law School

Benjamin C. Zipursky, Professor and James H. Quinn '49 Chair in Legal Ethics, Fordham University School of Law

Introduction

Why Interstitial Private Law?

Henry E. Smith

The notion of interstices plays an important role in many fields, from the physical sciences and medicine to art and engineering. In architecture, a frequent source of metaphors for law, interstitial spaces and structures are ubiquitous and pose fundamental questions of design. How much space should exist between structures to accommodate utilities or to permit flexibility in redesign and remodeling at a future date? At what cost should space be devoted to the interstitial? How should one structure be connected to another where they come together at interfaces? Are there structures that are so basic (even foundational) that they serve to connect what would otherwise be disparate elements in a structure? Are there devices that can be used and reused to deal with compression and tension located at such interfaces or running throughout structures from top to bottom, and do they have anything in common?

This volume takes up similar questions in private law. The starting point for us is private law itself: inquiring into the interstitial in private law requires us to take seriously the idea that there is something for doctrines, principles, and the like to be "between." That is, there is such a thing as private law, and its structures are interesting and important enough to present problems of the interstitial. By the same token, if private law were one formless mush, there would be no room for anything that might be termed "interstitial."

The interstices of private law arise because there is such a thing as private law, and it has an interesting and important form or structure. This is not to be equated with the "formalism" of old.[1] Different areas of private law—contract, tort, property, restitution, as well as family law, intellectual property, organizational law, and the like—are distinct and need to relate to each other. Moreover, it may well be that their loose connections—importantly connected but leaving some play in the joints—allow such systems to change over time and to possess the required dynamism to respond to changing conditions. These areas may have some kind of mutual border, or they may overlap—or they may have gaps with a more elaborate interface. There may be cross-cutting principles that

[1] Paul B. Miller, *The New Formalism in Private Law*, 66 Am. J. Jurisprudence 175 (2021).

Henry E. Smith, *Introduction* In: *Interstitial Private Law*. Edited by: Samuel L. Bray, John C.P. Goldberg, Paul B. Miller, and Henry E. Smith, Oxford University Press. © Oxford University Press 2024.
DOI: 10.1093/oso/9780197783627.001.0001

weave the different areas of private law together. One possible source for such principles is equity; another might be positive morality. Different areas of private law and areas within areas of private law may or may not be unified through various themes or threads that weave them together. Precisely what this means and how it happens is not self-evident. Concepts may show up in more than one area of law, especially those relating to intent or state of mind, and one needs to ask whether they are serving the same function or a similar function—and for that matter how much they do or do not diverge in their basic meanings.

Before turning to how to address the interstitial in private law, it is worth pausing to reflect on why it has been so hard to notice. To begin with, post-Realist legal thought in the United States espouses skepticism about private law, including its structure and doctrines, making the interstitial virtually invisible. The whole idea of law itself through its systematicity serving a guiding function (rather than, for example, providing a list of incentives for behavior), is something that points toward the importance of interstitial law. More generally, an interest in the interstitial requires one to take internal perspectives on the law seriously. Unless one asks about the perspective of a participant or delves into the law's self-understanding, it will be difficult to inquire into interstitial private law. Again, the interstitial is part of the structure of private law, and that structure is amenable to an internalist approach. Which is not to say one cannot have interesting functional (or external) things to say about interstitial private law. Indeed, we might ask how the structures at the interfaces of private law and the connective tissue that weaves private law together (if it does) make the law more efficient, fair, or useful.

Another related reason for the interstitial not to receive its due is an overall reductionist tendency in legal theory. If law is reduced to a set of results or its effect on social welfare, a focus on interstitial law will not present itself as a compelling subject of study. This is especially true if law's effects are considered incidental to its character and structures or as emanating directly from social or political conditions, thus sidelining the law as a distinctive institution to be taken seriously—at least partially—on its own terms. Even internal perspectives that focus on foundations can overlook the interstitial. One might even say that interstitial private law is most at home with mid-level theorizing.[2] More generally, private law faces the problem of how its guidance at the level of individual persons—their duties in tort or their powers to form contracts with others—relates to bigger features of the social order, like distributive fairness, concentrations of political and economic power, the promotion of political freedom, and a culture of the rule of law. Different parts of private law might

[2] Stephen A. Smith, *Intermediate and Comprehensive Justifications for Legal Rules*, *in* Justifying Private Rights 63 (Simone Degeling, Michael J.R. Crawford & Nicholas Tiverios eds., 2020); *see also* Miller, *supra* note 1, at 105.

contribute differently and more or less directly to such emergent features at the societal level.[3] Although a landowner's invocation of trespass law might look unfair on a given occasion, a law of trespass might contribute to personal autonomy and economic efficiency, and even protect the weak against the strong.

Skepticism about private law and pervasive reductionism have not only effaced private law, or at least its structures. Such skepticism has relatedly led to changes in the way private law subjects are taught, at least in the United States. Each private law course has received less airtime in the first-year curriculum as schools have moved from year-long courses to semester courses, and from six or five hours to four or even three (if not outright abandonment). As private law courses are condensed, it is natural for teachers to seek to teach the "core" of each subject. Thus, contracts courses rarely deal with assignment and delegation or with third-party beneficiaries. These are topics that relate contracts to analogous questions in property and torts. Areas like theft and fraud that relate torts and property are downplayed, as is the transactional process in property itself. The list could go on. Even major aspects of the private law and its roots, from equity to concepts associated with Roman law or the natural law tradition seem not only less natural but are less visible in the first place. Moreover, whatever their source, concepts that could weave the areas together like privity are those that come in for special skepticism. And all of this is yet another step along the road to assimilating one area to another. The Death of Contract or the Contractification of Property are but two such visions.[4]

This is not our vision. The authors of the chapters in this volume take private law seriously and approach the interstitial in private law from a variety of angles. In keeping with the primary definition of the interstitial, three chapters focus on the space between areas of law. **Nicolas Cornell** explores how problems that arise between areas of law like contract and tort may be treated inconsistently across the divide, especially when another interstitial space—that between private and public law—is also at stake. For example, public officials might owe a duty to individual citizens under contract law but not according to tort law—all of which calls for an explanation in substantive terms, such as the difference between control of behavior ex ante and redressing injury ex post. Likewise, **James Penner** takes up pervasive questions often thought to implicate substantive law or even metaphysical entities—the attribution of the acts of one actor to another. Instead, Penner argues that although private law across its areas has no unitary approach, it does present an array of concrete attribution rules that occupy this important space in private law in different ways. In her chapter, **Carol M. Rose** takes up another major interface in private (and public) law—that between custom

[3] Andrew S. Gold & Henry E. Smith, *Sizing Up Private Law*, 70 UTLJ 489 (2020).

[4] Grant Gilmore, The Death of Contract (1974); Thomas C. Grey, *The Disintegration of Property*, *in* NOMOS XXII: Property 69 (J. Roland Pennock & John W. Chapman eds., 1980).

and the law. These two normative systems are intertwined, sometimes for the better—and sometimes very much for the worse, as with the history of racially restrictive covenants in the United States. The relation of law and custom can be one of convergence or separation. In the case of racially restrictive covenants, such covenants and racially discriminatory customs coevolved and reinforced each other until the covenants become unenforceable on constitutional grounds, when custom persisted without its legal support.

Relatedly, the law sometimes employs doctrines and principles to shape the space between areas of law. This modulation of the interstitial often cuts across many areas of the law. **Samuel L. Bray** devotes his chapter to the family of equitable maxims or principles dealing with what equity will not do. Because equitable intervention is a powerful tool that, if overused, threatens the stability of law, part of equity's traditional self-conception was a notion of self-restraint. Thus, doctrines providing that, for example, equity will not protect personal rights, will not punish, and will not protect political rights have come to the fore more or less at various times to keep equity in its role as a supplement—itself interstitial in a sense—rather than as a usurper of law. **Andrew S. Gold** explores how differentiation of private law fields can be valuable for many reasons, some of which are substantive. Thus, principles may tell us which field governs in cases of overlap, and the resulting interface may show a degree of modularity: the interfaces between private law fields are constrained and stylized such that each field can operate more (but not completely) independently of the other. This makes the system easier to navigate and promotes the rule of law, but it also may give relationships fostered by individual fields of law the room they need to thrive. **Ben McFarlane** shows how equity itself performs a modular interstitial role by supplementing (and not correcting) primary legal rules that endow parties with certain powers. Equitable estoppel and restitution both mitigate problems that arise from such rules when they produce unjust results, without thereby creating genuine exceptions to the rules.

Equity is not the only device the law employs that cuts across legal areas. Some concepts can be seen as common to multiple areas and thus to be playing a role in how one area relates to another. Some such concepts arise from common problems faced in multiple areas. **Courtney M. Cox** offers a methodological caution in the identification of such concepts. Contract, tort, and property all face something one is inclined to call deception, but Cox demonstrates the risks in employing the wrong notion of deception to identify this commonality. Cox does so by analyzing the prelegal notion of deception and using this analysis to question whether the prototypical legal response to "deception," namely the tort of deceit, is really about deception at all. Another key concept common to multiple areas of law that reflects an important social phenomenon is consent, the topic of the chapter by **Mark P. Gergen**. Consent is familiarly a major feature of criminal and tort law. But, as Gergen shows, we can detect that the same concept of consent is at work in contract and property as long as we are sensitive to the object of consent. In those areas, consent is directed to legal obligations and contractual terms rather than being about what people have in mind. And, indeed, mental states are important in more than one area of law. **John C.P. Goldberg** and **Benjamin C. Zipursky** take the concept of recklessness as a case study of how a concept familiar from criminal law makes sporadic appearances in tort law. It does this in two very different ways: first as a lower bound for malice in areas like defamation and fraud, and as an upper bound beyond which liability will attach more automatically for creating unjustified dangers. Sometimes a proper appreciation of the interstitial depends on a better understanding of its surroundings. **Zoë Sinel** shows how long-standing controversies and confusions over the collateral source rule rest on a misconstrual of the compensation principle. The collateral source rule prevents the introduction of evidence at trial that would show that a plaintiff seeking damages stands to recover from the plaintiff's insurer as well. Many see this rule as preventing double recovery, which would be a kind of windfall for the plaintiff in violation of the compensation principle. Sinel shows that a proper interpretation of the compensation principle sees it as correcting wrongful transactions, rather than wrongful losses, thus making collateral insurance payments not overlapping with damages sought in court after all.

Attention to the interstitial dovetails with taking the law's internal structure seriously in normative terms. Some of this structure is common across areas of law and so holds them together, in a kind of interstitial function. **Christopher Essert** argues that the incidents of rights, liberties, and powers should not be seen in reductive or deflationary terms but rather as being built up as the realization of moral ideas. These combine in different ways in various areas of law but provide common themes that contribute to the overall coherence of private law. Thus, rights relating to personality and property, as well as powers, exhibit structure that ultimately reflects a consistent set of justificatory considerations. Focusing on the concept of personality, **Paul B. Miller** shows that the common law has developed one that, although not as explicit as its analogue in the civilian tradition, is just as primordial. The concept of personality, he argues, is essential to the structure and organization of all private law and serves a modulating function that qualifies as interstitial in a deep and pervasive sense.

Interstitial private law puts many suppressed questions in legal theory back on the table. These include the significance of system for law, the nature of legal concepts, the relation of the parts of private law to each other and to the law as a whole, the public law-private law distinction, the nature of form and function, and internal and external perspectives on the law. There are few aspects of private law not touched by the interstitial.

Because of interstitial law's pervasiveness and its deeper centrality to private law, a sustained examination of this phenomenon points to a path out of our current impasse in legal theory. Modern legal theory is often about the law's purposes on the one hand and the results of disputes on the other. Private law falls into the yawning gap between results and ultimate reasons. Perhaps one lesson of this volume is that the more closely we look at private law and how it bridges this gap, the more we see how law's response to the interstitial shows up all over private law itself. This should not be surprising because private law is not some kind of uniform protoplasm and is instead a kaleidoscopically evolving set of loosely joined structures that serve important social functions. By attending to the interstices of private law—where they are, why they arise, and how private law deals with them—we can improve our understanding of private law itself. That is what the volume sets out to do.

1

Equity Will Not . . .

*Samuel L. Bray**

I. Introduction

Equity used to have a lot of doctrines that were phrased as limits. "Equity will not do this" and "equity does not do that." The most prominent, at least in the nineteenth- and twentieth-century American sources, were the following:[1]

1. Equity will not enjoin a crime.
2. Equity will not enjoin a criminal proceeding.
3. Equity will not punish.
4. Equity will not enjoin a libel.
5. Equity will not protect a personal right.
6. Equity will not protect a political right.

The "equity will not" doctrines are the subject of this chapter. It analyzes the formal structure of these doctrines (i.e., rule-exception) and their functions, especially how they shape access to equity and help to preserve equity's legitimacy. This chapter also briefly considers their current status, suggesting that most are still in use today, and concludes by arguing that they have enduring functions, even if their traditional scope may need to be adjusted.

On first glance, some readers will find these doctrines antiquated. The mere existence of these doctrines is premised on the assumption that there is something called equity. Yet even those who embrace equity may be surprised, for these doctrines offer apparently categorical rules for what equity does; these doctrines imply that equity is not all discretion and case-by-case flexibility. And

* I am grateful for criticisms from Aditya Bamzai and Aaron-Andrew Bruhl, as well as criticisms on earlier iterations of this chapter from Richard Re and attendees of the Notre Dame Remedies Roundtable, the Harvard Private Law Workshop, the Bolch Institute Federal Courts Workshop, and the Interstitial Private Law conference. I am also grateful to Joshua Getzler for a formative conversation on a walk in Oxford several years ago.

[1] Others include "equity does not concern itself with trivial matters," "equity does not aid doubtful rights," "equity does not favor forfeitures," "equity will not suffer a wrong to be without a remedy," and so on. In addition, some of the equitable maxims can be phrased negatively, such as "equity does not aid those who slumber on their rights."

Samuel L. Bray, *Equity Will Not . . .* In: *Interstitial Private Law.* Edited by: Samuel L. Bray, John C.P. Goldberg, Paul B. Miller, and Henry E. Smith, Oxford University Press. © Oxford University Press 2024.
DOI: 10.1093/oso/9780197783627.003.0001

perhaps most surprising of all is the notion that equity does not protect "personal rights" or "political rights"—since the protection of civil rights has been one of the good and great uses of equitable remedies over the last century.[2]

There is thus an understandable sense of distance between our standpoint today and the "equity will not" doctrines. Yet these reasons the doctrines seem antiquated have different degrees of validity. The idea that equity has disappeared is no longer tenable, and the equity revival in the United States has been underway for a quarter century.[3] Nor is it true that equity lacks rules and has only case-by-case judgments.[4]

More valid is the concern that the traditional limitations are in tension with remedies given in some of the leading political and civil rights cases of the last century, including *Baker v. Carr* and *Brown v. Board of Education II*. Yet on inspection this tension is both less real and more complex than it may seem. Many civil rights are protected by federal statutes that expressly authorize equitable relief,[5] and that authorization overrides background rules like the "equity will not" doctrines. Moreover, there has been a substitution effect, especially in election law, where the rise of equitable remedies has coincided with the disappearance of older remedies, such as damages, for violation of the right to vote.[6] A full accounting for the changes in the protection of political rights would show both gains and losses.

And no matter how surprised scholars may be at the invocation of the "equity will not" doctrines, they do remain in use in the courts. Like objects in a rearview mirror, these doctrines are closer than they appear. Yet almost no recent scholarship has considered them.[7] And they bear consideration, because they touch on two of the enduring questions about equity.

The first question is which cases should go to equity. Given that equity is a secondary system,[8] a perennial issue is the need for sorting rules that will determine

[2] *See, e.g.*, Brown v. Board of Education, 349 U.S. 294 (1955) (*Brown II*).

[3] For recent examples of the surge in attention to equity in US legal scholarship, *see* Owen W. Gallogly, *Equity's Constitutional Source*, 132 Yale L.J. 1213 (2023); Riley T. Keenan, *Functional Federal Equity*, 74 Ala. L. Rev. 879 (2023); Henry E. Smith, *Equity as Meta-Law*, 130 Yale L.J. 1050 (2021); and Symposium, *The Nature of the Federal Equity Power*, 97 Notre Dame L. Rev. 1763 (2022).

[4] *See generally* Mark P. Gergen, John M. Golden & Henry E. Smith, *The Supreme Court's Accidental Revolution? The Test for Permanent Injunctions*, 112 Colum. L. Rev. 203 (2012).

[5] *See* 42 U.S.C.A. § 1983 (authorizing a "suit in equity").

[6] *See* Derek T. Muller, *The Democracy Ratchet*, 94 Ind. L.J. 451, 485 (2019).

[7] The recent discussions of these doctrines are found in Aditya Bamzai & Samuel L. Bray, *Debs and the Federal Equity Jurisdiction*, 98 Notre Dame L. Rev. 699, 709–16 (2022); and Samuel L. Bray, *Punitive Damages Against Trustees?*, *in* Research Handbook on Fiduciary Law 201, 211–14 (D. Gordon Smith & Andrew S. Gold eds., 2018) (discussing "equity will not punish").

[8] *See generally* Samuel L. Bray & Paul B. Miller, *Getting into Equity*, 97 Notre Dame L. Rev. 1763 (2022); Smith, *supra* note 3.

which cases get routed over to that system. The "equity will not" doctrines are some of the traditional sorting rules. We could discard *these* sorting rules, but as long as equity is to be a secondary system, as long as it is to be "meta-law,"[9] we cannot do without sorting rules.

The second question is about the legitimacy of equity. Equity has always fostered fears, and not just hopes. Those fears are due to its powers of command and control, its suppleness, and its aversion to some of the traditional limits on state power such as the jury. One of the existential questions for equity, in recurring episodes for more than four hundred years,[10] is what legitimating conditions allow the exercise of these powers. It is not random which areas are demarcated and marked out of bounds by the "equity will not" doctrines. They are areas that, at least historically, have been minefields for equity, places where the chancellor could tread only at his own risk.

The "equity will not" doctrines are therefore worthy of consideration in a volume on interstitial private law for two reasons. First, they bound the interventions of equity across all the domains of private and public law. Second, equity is already an interstitial aspect of the law, smoothing seams and patching holes. The "equity will not" doctrines help keep it that way. These doctrines instruct equity not to act in areas in which legal doctrines and remedies are typically sufficient—that is, they instruct equity not to act in these areas, because they are not actually interstices at all, but are squarely covered by law. That leaves equity free to husband its resources and train its attention on the places where the ordinary operation of law does not achieve justice.[11]

The remainder of this chapter proceeds as follows. Part II lists the "equity will not" doctrines and briefly summarizes their operation and justification. Part III discusses the primary exceptions to these doctrines. Part IV asks whether these doctrines are really rules at all. Part V sketches their current status in the law of the United States. Part VI analyzes the two critical functions of the "equity will not" doctrines: they regulate access to equity, and they are meant to ensure the legitimating conditions for equitable intervention. Part VII concludes.

[9] *See* Smith, *supra* note 3.

[10] *See, e.g.*, J.H. Baker, *The Common Lawyers and the Chancery: 1616*, 4 Irish Jurist 368 (new series) (1969) (seventeenth century); Stanley N. Katz, *The Politics of Law in Colonial America: Controversies over Chancery Courts and Equity Law in the Eighteenth Century*, *in* Law in American History 257 (Donald Fleming & Bernard Bailyn eds., 1971) (eighteenth century); Samuel L. Bray, *Notes on the American Reception*, *in* Equity and Law: Fusion and Fission 31 (John C.P. Goldberg, Henry E. Smith & P.G. Turner eds., 2019) (twenty-first century).

[11] *See generally* Bray & Miller, *supra* note 8; Smith, *supra* note 3.

II. A Catalog of the "Equity Will Not" Doctrines

There are many things equity was not in the habit of doing, and some of these were expressed in a certain formula: "equity will not x." This part will briefly introduce the most common uses of that formula.

1. *Equity will not enjoin a crime.* That is, if an act is proscribed by the criminal law, then the chancellor will not issue an injunction against that act. This proposition is found in a number of the nineteenth- and twentieth-century treatises.[12]

The justifications given were several. First, if equity could punish crimes, it would be recovering a criminal jurisdiction that it lost centuries ago when the Star Chamber was eliminated. Second, to allow equity to enjoin crimes, and then punish disobedience with contempt, would be to tolerate an end run around the procedural protections of a criminal trial, including the jury. Third, equity does not need to restrain crimes, because there is already an adequate "remedy" for a violation of the criminal law (a criminal prosecution).

The growth of industry in the nineteenth-century United States led both to greater use of injunctions against nuisances and also to greater use of criminal penalties for nuisances. There were various ways of reconciling this new state of affairs with "equity will not enjoin a crime," but the most common was to say that equity would enjoin crimes, but it would not enjoin them simply *because* they were crimes. That is, equity would not "follow the (criminal) law," and instead there needed to be some other recognized basis for a suit in equity.[13] That resolution dissipated much of the rule's force, making it more of a reminder that some basis for equitable jurisdiction was needed.[14]

2. *Equity will not enjoin a criminal proceeding.* The criminal proceedings that equity will not enjoin may be trials, but also grand jury proceedings and

[12] *E.g.*, Henry L. McClintock, Handbook of the Principles of Equity 443 (2d ed. 1948); John Norton Pomeroy, A Treatise on Equity Jurisprudence § 1347, at 949–50 (5th ed., Spencer W. Symons ed., 1944) ("Injunction is never granted merely to restrain criminal acts; crimes are confided to the criminal courts, and the remedy by indictment and persecution is deemed to be adequate."); 2 Joseph Story, Commentaries on Equity Pleadings and the Incidents Thereto § 817, at 627 (1838) (describing as a ground for a defensive plea to a bill of discovery that "the cause is not of such a character, as the Court will aid by discovery; as if the cause . . . be of a criminal nature"). Pomeroy's treatise immediately adds: "There are, however, certain species of torts, in respect to each of which, as a class, it is settled that the legal remedy is generally inadequate, so that equity will generally interfere to prevent the wrong by injunction." Pomeroy, *supra*, § 1347, at 950.

[13] *See generally* Bray & Miller, *supra* note 8.

[14] For a recent example, *see* Cnty. of Cedar v. Thelen, 305 Neb. 351, 359, 940 N.W.2d 521, 527–28 (2020) ("There is a well-recognized exception to the general rule that enforcement of criminal laws provides an adequate remedy, namely, that where a more complete remedy is afforded by injunction than by criminal prosecution, a court of equity may, at the instance of properly constituted authorities, afford relief by injunction in order to protect the public welfare." (footnotes omitted)).

investigations that might lead to an indictment. This doctrine, too, is widely noted in nineteenth- and twentieth-century equity cases and treatises.[15]

This is sometimes given as a corollary of "equity will not enjoin a crime," but it is not logically entailed and has a different basis. For a start, strictly speaking, equity does not enjoin civil proceedings either. A chancellor who issues an "anti-suit injunction" is not enjoining what another court is doing, but rather is enjoining a party from litigating in that other court.[16] So the question answered by this proposition is something like whether equity will enjoin a prosecutor to prevent a likely or already-in-progress prosecution. And the answer given by this doctrine is no.[17]

The standard justification is that whatever arguments the equity plaintiff/criminal defendant wanted to make could be made in the criminal trial. In other words, for someone who is charged with a crime or likely to be charged with a crime, there is an adequate remedy at law.

For federal courts, reluctance to enjoin a state criminal proceeding is usually described, following *Younger v. Harris*,[18] as "*Younger* abstention." In that decision, Justice Black was clear that one basis for the holding was the doctrine that equity would not enjoin a criminal proceeding.[19] Under our Constitution, Justice Black said, that doctrine serves as a protection for federalism, because it constrains federal courts from enjoining state prosecutions.[20] In other words, *Younger* does not present itself as establishing a new "*Younger* abstention," but instead as applying a traditional limitation on equitable jurisdiction. Indeed, this very pairing of "equity will not enjoin a criminal proceeding" with federalism was already present in earlier cases.[21]

This federal reticence to enjoin a criminal proceeding is most marked for state criminal proceedings (consistent with *Younger*).[22] Even so, this doctrine

15 McClintock, *supra* note 12, § 173, at 469–70 (noting the widely stated principle that "equity has no jurisdiction to enjoin prosecutions under statutes or ordinances creating criminal offences," while also noting an increasing number of such injunctions, with the usual ground being "that there will be an irreparable injury to the property rights of the plaintiff suing in equity"); Story, *supra* note 12, § 3222, at 262–63 (describing as a ground for a defensive plea to a bill of discovery that "the cause is not of such a character, as the Court will aid by discovery; as if the cause . . . be of a criminal nature"); *see also, e.g.*, Paulk v. City of Sycamore, 104 Ga. 24 (1898).

16 *See* Whole Woman's Health v. Jackson, 142 S. Ct. 522, 532 (2021) (relying on *Ex parte Young*).

17 The Supreme Court has developed an exception for bad-faith prosecution. *See* Dombrowski v. Pfister, 380 U.S. 479, 489–90 (1965) (reversing the district court's dismissal of the complaint as failing "to allege sufficient irreparable injury to justify equitable relief" because the plaintiffs "have attacked the good faith of the [defendant officials] in enforcing the statutes").

18 401 U.S. 37 (1971).

19 *Id.* at 43 (referring to "the basic doctrine of equity jurisprudence that courts of equity . . . should not act to restrain a criminal prosecution").

20 *Id.* at 43–44.

21 *See* Stefanelli v. Minard, 342 U.S. 117, 120 (1951) ("The maxim that equity will not enjoin a criminal prosecution summarizes centuries of weighty experience in Anglo-American law. It is impressively reinforced when not merely the relations between coordinate courts but between coordinate political authorities are in issue.").

22 *See* Kellen Funk, *Equity's Federalism*, 97 Notre Dame L. Rev. 2057 (2022).

can be deployed by a federal court to avoid entanglement with federal criminal proceedings.[23]

3. Equity will not punish. Related expressions are that equity will not impose a penalty, and that equity abhors a forfeiture. This doctrine does not bar a certain action—enjoining crimes, enjoining criminal proceedings—but it instead bars actions that have a certain kind of motive or significance: punishing. This proposition is also found in the nineteenth- and twentieth-century treatises.[24] And the leading contemporary equity treatise endorses the point: "Punishment through monetary awards or otherwise is contrary to the basis and purpose of equity."[25]

This does not mean that equity avoids imposing negative consequences. It would certainly *feel* like punishment if a person were enjoined, and then held in contempt, and then committed to the Fleet. But as the oft-quoted saying goes, the contemnor "carries the keys of his prison in his own pocket."[26] Equity is not marking out the measure of the punishment and imposing it, but is instead trying to reform and correct the conscience of the contemnor. That aim is different than punishing. It might actually lead to *greater* negative consequences than punishment would, but it can also lead to *smaller* ones—it is operating with a forward-looking logic of correction and not a backward-looking logic of punishment.[27]

4. Equity will not enjoin a libel or slander. This proposition is declared as early as 1742,[28] and it was widely endorsed in nineteenth- and twentieth-century cases and treatises.[29] There are exceptions for trade libel and also for injunctions to prohibit libel or slander that has already been adjudicated by a court of law.

Two justifications are commonly given. One is that freedom of speech is eroded by prior restraints, and that an injunction against a libel or slander is exactly such a restraint. The other justification is that a person who has been libeled or slandered has an adequate remedy in a suit for damages.[30] Throughout

[23] Trump v. United States, No. 22-13005, 2022 WL 4366684, at *9 (11th Cir. September 21, 2022) (quoting Douglas v. City of Jeannette, 319 U.S. 157, 163 (1943)).

[24] *See, e.g.*, Walter Ashburner, Principles of Equity 53 (1902) ("A court of equity has no punitive jurisdiction. It never fined or imprisoned a wrongdoer except as part of its process."); *see also* Bush v. Gaffney, 84 S.W.2d 759, 764 (Tex. Civ. App. 1935) ("A court of equity is a court of conscience, but not a forum of vengeance. It will make restitution, but not reprisals. It will fill full the measure of compensation, but will not overflow it with vindictive damages.").

[25] J.D. Heydon, M.J. Leeming & P.G. Turner, Meagher, Gummow & Lehane's Equity: Doctrines and Remedies § 23-595, at 865 (5th ed. 2015).

[26] Gompers v. Buck's Stove & Range Co., 221 U.S. 418, 440 (1911).

[27] *See generally* Bray, note 7.

[28] *See* Michael I. Meyerson, *The Neglected History of the Prior Restraint Doctrine: Rediscovering the Link Between the First Amendment and the Separation of Powers*, 34 Ind. L. Rev. 295, 310 (2001) ("As early as 1742, it was ruled in the *St. James's Evening Post Case*, that the courts of equity had no jurisdiction over claims of libel and slander: 'For whether it is a libel against the publick or private persons, the only method is to proceed at law.'" (quoting Roach v. Garvan, 26 Eng. Rep. 683, 683 (1742)).

[29] *See, e.g.*, Brandreth v. Lance, 8 Paige Ch. 24 (Chancery Ct. of N.Y. 1839) (Walworth, Ch.).

[30] For recent examples, *see* Metro. Opera Ass'n, Inc. v. Loc. 100, Hotel Emps. & Rest. Emps. Int'l Union, 239 F.3d 172, 177 (2d Cir. 2001) ("The holding in *American Malting* rests in large part on

the twentieth century the prohibition on equity's enjoining a libel or slander was widely cited, and it was a way to connect the growing protection for the freedom of speech with traditional equitable doctrine.[31]

5. *Equity will not protect a personal right.* The leading case, often considered the originating case for this proposition, is *Gee v. Prichard*, an English Chancery decision in 1818.[32] In *Gee*, Lord Chancellor Eldon issued an injunction stopping a man from publishing his stepmother's letters. Equity would not protect a mere personal right, the chancellor said, but the stepmother had a proprietary interest in her letters, and that could support equity's intervention.[33] In the century after *Gee*, the proposition that equity would not protect personal rights was widely embraced, and one critic said, "The doctrine finds support in most of the text books on equity and in innumerable *dicta* of judges."[34]

The usual justification given was that equity was unneeded because tort law and criminal law were sufficient to protect the person. As William Walsh wrote in 1930, "In the usual cases of torts arising from violations of purely personal rights the reasons for denying relief in equity are clear. It is obvious that the injunction is not needed to restrain threatened assaults, disturbances of the peace, and other petty interferences with the person. The criminal law and the police afford all the relief required in such cases. It is clear that injunctions in negligence cases would be absurd."[35]

This doctrine was roundly criticized by the Legal Realists,[36] and Zechariah Chafee recounted the "determined onslaught" by Louis Brandeis, Samuel Warren, and Roscoe Pound "on the oft-repeated doctrine that equity protects only rights of property."[37]

6. *Equity will not protect a political right.* Political rights include the right to vote and the right to hold office. These are traditionally distinguished from civil rights on the grounds that political rights pertain to the polity (and thus may

the principle that injunctions are limited to rights that are without an adequate remedy at law, and because ordinarily libels may be remedied by damages, equity will not enjoin a libel absent extraordinary circumstances."); Balboa Island Vill. Inn, Inc. v. Lemen, 40 Cal. 4th 1141, 1174, 156 P.3d 339, 361–62 (2007) (Werdegar, J., concurring and dissenting), *as modified* (Apr. 26, 2007).

31 On the beginnings of the modern protection for freedom of speech and the shift to a neutrality paradigm in the late 1950s and early 1960s, *see generally* Jud Campbell, *The Emergence of Neutrality*, 131 Yale L.J. 782 (2022).

32 36 Eng. Rep. 670 (Ch. 1818).

33 For discussion, see Bamzai & Bray, *supra* note 7.

34 Joseph R. Long, *Equitable Jurisdiction to Protect Personal Rights*, 33 Yale L.J. 115, 116 (1923) (citing Spence, Kerr & Bispham).

35 William F. Walsh, A Treatise on Equity § 50, at 259 (1930); *see also, e.g.*, Chappell v. Stewart, 82 Md. 323, 33 A. 542, 543 (1896), *dismissed*, 169 U.S. 733 (1898); Angelus v. Sullivan, 246 F. 54, 64 (2d Cir. 1917).

36 *See, e.g.*, Roscoe Pound, *Equitable Relief Against Defamation and Injuries to Personality*, 29 Harv. L. Rev. 640 (1916).

37 Zechariah Chafee, Jr., *The Progress of the Law, 1919–1920*, 34 Harv. L. Rev. 388, 407 (1921).

be restricted to citizens of the polity).[38] This doctrine, too, was widely stated in nineteenth- and twentieth-century cases and secondary sources.[39] It was sometimes expressed in terms of equity not resolving a political question.[40]

Now it seems unimaginable that equity would not protect political rights, since we are used to injunctions being the default remedy in cases involving the right to vote. But in the heyday of this maxim, there was much more robust use of damages for denial of the right to vote,[41] and quo warranto and mandamus would be used in cases about the right to hold office.[42] In federal courts, the turning point was *Baker v. Carr*,[43] which was then followed by various federal statutes expressly authorizing injunctions for violations of voting rights.[44] Nevertheless, it remains the case that courts seem particularly sensitive about equitable involvement in elections,[45] and this sensitivity overlaps with equity's aversion to deciding political questions.

III. Two Exceptions

The "equity will not" doctrines are presented as rules but not as absolute ones.[46] There are exceptions, and the two primary ones are about statutes and property.

The first exception is that the "equity will not" doctrines give way if there is an express authorization of equity's involvement by the legislature.[47] This is especially important because of the growth of statues in the twentieth century, including statutes that authorize equitable remedies in circumstances that would otherwise lie in a zone of what equity will not do.

[38] For discussion of the core cases and points of contestation at Reconstruction, *see* Mark Tushnet, *The Politics of Equality in Constitutional Law: The Equal Protection Clause, Dr. Du Bois, and Charles Hamilton Houston*, 74 J. AM. HIST. 884, 885–88 (1987).

[39] *See, e.g.*, Rockefeller v. Hogue, 246 Ark. 712, 721–24 (1969) (Fogelman J. concurring); *Equity–Jurisdiction—Political Rights; Injunction to Protect*, 30 HARV. L. REV. 397 (1917) ("The overwhelming weight of judicial authority is to the effect that courts of equity will not protect those political rights which do not involve civil rights.").

[40] *Cf.* STORY, *supra* note 12, § 817, at 627 (noting that one ground for a defensive plea to a bill of discovery is "that the subject of the suit is of a political nature").

[41] *See, e.g.*, Nixon v. Herndon, 273 U.S. 536, 540 (1927) ("The objection that the subject-matter of the suit is political is little more than a play upon words. Of course the petition concerns political action but it alleges and seeks to recover for private damage. That private damage may be caused by such political action and may be recovered for in suit at law hardly has been doubted for over two hundred years. . . .").

[42] On the continuing use of mandamus in election litigation, *see generally* Derek T. Muller, *Election Subversion and the Writ of Mandamus*, 65 WILLIAM & MARY L. REV. 327 (2023).

[43] 369 U.S. 186 (1962).

[44] *E.g.*, 52 U.S.C.A. § 10101(c) (West).

[45] *See, e.g.*, Purcell v. Gonzalez, 549 U.S. 1 (2006) (per curiam). For critique, *see, e.g.*, Richard L. Hasen, *Reining in the* Purcell *Principle*, 43 FLA. ST. U. L. REV. 427 (2016).

[46] See Part IV.

[47] *See, e.g.*, See In re Sawyer, 124 U.S. 200, 210 (1888) ("The office and jurisdiction of a court of equity, unless enlarged by express statute, are limited to the protection of rights of property.").

The property exception requires more discussion. It is very common, so much so that it is often put into the formulation of the rule itself. Courts and commentators will say, for example, that "equity will not enjoin a criminal proceeding, except to protect property."[48] Or "equity will not protect a political right, because no property rights are involved."[49] And so on. This exception is traceable back to *Gee v. Prichard*,[50] and it emerges at the same time the courts are talking about equity not enjoining crimes or protecting personal rights.

This exception immediately raises the question of what counts as property. It has never been restricted to real property, for in *Gee* the property interest that allowed Lord Chancellor Eldon to continue the interim injunction was the plaintiff's interest in the letters she had written to her stepson. Over time, the trend was to expand the property that could support equity's intervention. In *International News Service v. Associated Press*,[51] for instance, the Supreme Court said, "The rule that a court of equity concerns itself only in the protection of property rights treats any civil right of a pecuniary nature as a property right; and the right to acquire property by honest labor or the conduct of a lawful business is as much entitled to protection as the right to guard property already acquired."[52] Given this expansion, it is more precise to refer to "the proprietary-interest exception."[53]

The proprietary-interest exception has been highly controversial. It was a favorite target of Roscoe Pound and other Legal Realists, who argued that the exception showed an irrational attachment to property rights. Their critique was sometimes put in terms of equity's bias for capital over labor. But the exception was also critiqued as a doctrine that once made sense but became outdated. As

[48] *See, e.g.*, Truax v. Raich, 239 U.S. 33, 37–38 (1915) ("It is also settled that while a court of equity, generally speaking, has no jurisdiction over the prosecution, the punishment, or the pardon of crimes or misdemeanors, a distinction obtains, and equitable jurisdiction exists to restrain criminal prosecutions under unconstitutional enactments, when the prevention of such prosecutions is essential to the safeguarding of rights of property." (citations and internal quotation marks omitted)); POMEROY, *supra* note 12, § 1361b, at 978 ("Criminal proceedings will never be enjoined, except where there is an attempt to enforce a law which is unconstitutional and void and the enforcement will result in irreparable injury to vested property rights." (brackets and citations omitted)); *see also* Charles Warren, *Federal and State Court Interference*, 43 HARV. L. REV. 345, 377 (1930) ("[T]he equitable jurisdiction of the federal courts, in these cases of injunctions against state law officials to restrain enforcement of alleged unconstitutional statutes, is based on the effect of such enforcement upon property rights. . . .").

[49] MCCLINTOCK, *supra* note 12, § 166, at 451 ("Ordinarily, equity will not grant injunctions to protect the political rights of individuals either because no property rights are involved or because of the difficulty of granting relief; sometimes it has been held that equity has no jurisdiction over the subject-matter of political rights.").

[50] 36 Eng. Rep. 670 (Ch. 1818); *see* Bamzai & Bray, *supra* note 7, at 714–16.

[51] 248 U.S. 215 (1918).

[52] *Id.* at 236.

[53] *Cf.* Bamzai & Bray, *supra* note 7, at 704 & n. 20 (using "property right" and "proprietary interest" interchangeably).

Roscoe Pound wrote, "We must remember that in 1818 the jurisdiction of equity to enjoin trespasses on land was not yet well developed and the whole subject of equity jurisdiction over torts was backward because of the unsatisfactory mode of trial."[54]

There have also been defenders of the proprietary-interest exception. Aditya Bamzai and I have argued that there are at least two good functions served by this exception. First, it is critical to preserving equity's freedom of movement.[55] At first, it may seem like a straightjacket, but recall that a proprietary interest is the basis for an *exception* to what equity will not do; a proprietary interest *allows* equity to work. Without that exception, the growth of tort law and criminal law in the late nineteenth and early twentieth centuries would have dramatically eroded equity's role. There would be no *Ex parte Young*[56] and no *International News Service v. Associated Press*.[57]

Second, the exception serves an "equity-focusing role." As Aditya and I have written,

> the property connection has the effect of focusing the exercise of the federal equity power. In this way the property connection in equity works much like modern standing doctrine. Modern standing doctrine helps to focus the dispute, ensuring that there are proper parties, that the bounds of the case fit those parties, and that the exercise of power is appropriate to the judicial function. The specificity encouraged by the property exception works in the same way. The property interest ensures the plaintiff has a tie to the dispute, it guides the court as to the scope of the dispute, and it encourages responsible use of the federal equity power. And if the property connection is stricter and narrower than Article III standing, then that is consistent with how the Supreme Court treats the requirements of equity as additional to and in some sense stricter than those of Article III.[58]

To these functions could be added a third. Equity can work preventively, jumping in to preserve the status quo during litigation.[59] This can be good, because it prevents one party from destroying the court's basis for vindicating the other party. But it has the disadvantage of drawing the court into the parties' dispute at

54 Pound, *supra* note 36, at 643.
55 *See* Bamzai & Bray, *supra* note 7.
56 209 U.S. 123 (1908).
57 248 U.S. 215 (1918).
58 Bamzai & Bray, *supra* note 7; *see also* William Baude & Samuel L. Bray, *Proper Parties, Proper Relief*, 137 HARV. L. REV. 153 (2023).
59 *See, e.g.*, University of Texas v. Camenisch, 451 U.S. 390, 395 (1981) ("The purpose of a preliminary injunction is merely to preserve the relative positions of the parties until a trial on the merits can be held.").

an earlier stage: perhaps A has not yet had her rights violated by B, but the court is already being asked to control B's conduct. That kind of early adjudication can turn out to be unnecessary—if the court had merely stayed out of the dispute, perhaps it would have gone away, or perhaps the parties would have remained in relatively passive hostility.

But here there is a difference between property rights (whether real, personal, or intellectual) and most personal rights. If there is a festering disagreement about who controls property, then everyone's ability to use it is impeded, and no one has an incentive to invest in it.[60] Property, as a thing in the world,[61] is still there, but the field lies fallow. By contrast, when there is a festering disagreement about personal rights, it is easier for the individuals involved to simply move outside of each other's orbits. (One of the largest exceptions might be disputes between employers and employees, or between employees, but these are covered by statutes regulating discrimination and harassment.)

Thus disagreements between people about personal rights and property rights are different, because the former can more often be handled with "live and let live," while the latter are more likely to require clarity in order to encourage, or at least not discourage, investment.[62]

IV. An Aside: Are These Doctrines Rules?

The "equity will not" doctrines are phrased as rules. They say that equity will not do something. They are not exactly prescriptive rules: "equity shall not" or "equity must not." But they describe what equity does not do, and that description is meant to have a kind of normative force.

The idea of a description having such normative force is not limited to law. When a person commits an egregious social blunder, and someone else says, "That simply isn't done," it is no contradiction to note that the thing that supposedly "isn't done" *was just done*. Is and ought are not always so cleanly separable when it comes to rules for conduct, whether social or legal.

And so even though they are phrased as descriptions of what equity will not do, these are not mere descriptions. Nor are they straightforwardly rulish.

Each of the "equity will not" doctrines has a domain. For some, the boundaries of that domain may be fairly clear (e.g., "equity will not enjoin criminal proceedings"). But for others, the boundary is a concept that is flexible and subject to characterization. A leading example is "equity will not punish." *Punishment*

60 *See* Samuel L. Bray, *Preventive Adjudication*, 77 U. Chi. L. Rev. 1275, 1310–14 (2010).
61 *See* Henry E. Smith, *Property as the Law of Things*, 125 Harv. L. Rev. 1691 (2012).
62 *See* Bray, *supra* note 60.

cannot simply mean "adverse consequences," as noted, for everything that equity does to a losing party may be experienced as a punishment or penalty.[63] So the concept must be more complex, and it draws not only on the defendant's experience of the equitable remedy but also on whether the adverse consequence is meant to punish.[64]

V. The Current Status

The fate of the "equity will not" doctrines largely tracks the fate of equity in the consciousness of the judiciary and the federal courts. By that I mean a pattern of stringent critique, apparent abandonment, and surprising survival.

In the early twentieth century, the criticisms of the "equity will not" doctrines by Roscoe Pound and others were sharp.[65] In the middle of the twentieth century, some courts rejected one or more of these doctrines.[66] Even where these doctrines were not expressly rejected, they began to be invoked less frequently. Nevertheless, just as the obituary has been written for numerous equitable doctrines,[67] the death of the "equity will not" doctrines may have been announced prematurely. Courts continue to endorse and rely on them, and in some states they are even codified. There is recent support for most of these doctrines, albeit with the traditional exceptions.

1. Equity will not enjoin a crime. This doctrine was endorsed in a recent decision of the Nebraska Supreme Court.[68] It is also codified in California, and the statute was the basis of a 2017 decision by the California Supreme Court that denied an injunction against a crime as an intrusion on prosecutorial discretion.[69] Nevertheless, it is also the case that courts routinely enjoin crimes without any litigant raising this doctrine.

[63] *See* United States v. Bolton, 496 F. Supp. 3d 146, 163–64 (D.D.C. 2020) ("Though the result might feel like a punishment to Bolton, a constructive trust is an equitable remedy. And equity does not punish.").

[64] *See* Bray, *supra* note 7.

[65] *See* sources cited, *supra* notes 36–37.

[66] *E.g.*, Orloff v. Los Angeles Turf Club, 30 Cal. 2d 110, 117, 180 P.2d 321, 325 (1947) ("On principle it is difficult to find any sound reason for the enunciation of a broad principle that equity will not protect personal rights.").

[67] *E.g.*, Douglas Laycock, The Death of the Irreparable Injury Rule (1991).

[68] *See* Cnty. of Cedar v. Thelen, 305 Neb. 351, 358, 940 N.W.2d 521, 527 (2020) ("Because equity, as a general rule, has no criminal jurisdiction, equity will not interfere to punish crime."). The court expressed the doctrine with its traditional limitation: "where acts complained of are in violation of the criminal law, courts of equity will not, on that ground alone, interfere by injunction to prevent their commission, as courts of equity will not exercise their power for the purpose of enforcing criminal laws. Because equity, as a general rule, has no criminal jurisdiction, equity will not interfere to punish crime. Something more than a violation of the law is required to justify the exercise of equity's powers." *Id.* at 357–58 (footnotes omitted).

[69] Leider v. Lewis, 2 Cal. 5th 1121 (2017).

2. *Equity will not enjoin a criminal proceeding.* A striking recent example is the Eleventh Circuit's decision in a case involving former President Trump. The district court had asserted equitable jurisdiction to halt the Department of Justice's investigative use of documents seized from former President Trump's residence at Mar-a-Lago. But the appellate court reversed. The assertion of equitable jurisdiction, the appellate court said, was inconsistent with the "familiar rule that courts of equity do not ordinarily restrain criminal prosecutions."[70] Some state courts also continue to apply the doctrine that equity will not enjoin a criminal proceeding. For example, in a recent case the Georgia Supreme Court unanimously held that an injunction that would protect the plaintiffs from arrest or prosecution "squarely implicates the administration of criminal law and, thus, is improper."[71]

3. *Equity will not punish.* In a recent decision about the Securities & Exchange Commission's statutory authority to seek restitutionary remedies, the US Supreme Court reiterated that equity cannot punish.[72] In the Court's words, "equity never 'lends its aid to enforce a forfeiture or penalty.'"[73] That is consistent with the Court's cases on the Seventh Amendment, which have emphasized that punitive remedies need to be routed through the jury.[74] At the same time, it should be noted that one of the traditional implications of "equity will not punish" is that there are no punitive damages in equity. That in turn means no punitive damages for equitable claims such as breach of fiduciary duty by a trustee. But that corollary of "equity will not punish" has been eroded in some jurisdictions.[75]

4. *Equity will not enjoin a libel or slander.* This continues to be the blackletter law in numerous jurisdictions, albeit with the traditional exceptions (e.g., injunctions against trade libel, injunctions against speech already held to be libelous or slanderous). For example, the Delaware Court of Chancery recently said, "[T]he general rule continues to be that a court of equity will not issue an injunction against future defamatory speech. Actions for defamation belong in the law courts, not Chancery."[76] Numerous other cases have

70 Trump v. United States, No. 22-13005, 2022 WL 4366684, at *9 (11th Cir. Sept. 21, 2022) (quoting Douglas v. City of Jeannette, 319 U.S. 157, 163 (1943)). The court noted the bad-faith exception from Younger and Dombrowski. *See id.* at *9, note 4.

71 GeorgiaCarry.org v. Atlanta Botanical Garden, Inc., 299 Ga. 26, 31, 785 S.E. 2d 874, 879 (2016) (citing, among other cases, a previous Georgia Supreme Court case stating that "equity will not enjoin a criminal prosecution solely to prevent such a prosecution" (alteration, citation, and internal quotation marks omitted).

72 Liu v. Sec. & Exch. Comm'n, 140 S. Ct. 1936, 1941 (2020).

73 *Id.* (quoting Marshall v. Vicksburg, 15 Wall. 146, 149 (1873)).

74 *See, e.g.*, Sec. & Exch. Comm'n v. Jarkesy, No. 22-859, 2024 WL 3187811, at *8 (U.S. June 27, 2024); Tull v. United States, 481 U.S. 412 (1987).

75 *See* Bray, *supra* note 7.

76 Preston Hollow Cap. LLC v. Nuveen LLC, 216 A.3d 1, 12 (Del. Ch. 2019) (citation and internal quotation marks omitted)).

explored this principle, and one of the leading cases is by former Judge Becker of the US Court of Appeals for the Third Circuit.[77] Yet the broader picture is mixed, with many courts still relying on this principle, but others rejecting or ignoring it.[78]

5. *Equity will not protect a personal right.* I have not found recent cases relying on this doctrine. Whether there is much change in outcomes is less clear, however, because this doctrine overlapped with the requirement of "no adequate remedy at law,"[79] and courts continue to invoke that doctrine.[80]

6. *Equity will not protect a political right.* Recent cases relying on this doctrine are less common, but there are still some. For example, an Illinois appellate court declined to enjoin the use of public funds for a referendum on a state constitutional amendment.[81] Among the controlling authorities the court relied on was *Fletcher v. City of Paris*,[82] which in part declined to enjoin the holding of an election because "[e]quity will not interfere in a case affecting only the enjoyment of political rights."[83] And the Georgia Court of Appeals reiterated what it called "the rule regarding political questions," namely: "Elections belong to the political branch of the government, and courts of equity will not interfere to protect a *purely* political right."[84]

The relative silence of the courts about equity not protecting personal and political rights doctrine is consistent with the view that these doctrines have been largely discarded. Yet it is not clear that they have been squarely considered in recent years and rejected, as opposed to being ignored. At least in most cases

[77] Kramer v. Thompson, 947 F.2d 666, 669–80 (3d Cir. 1991) (Becker, J.); *see also* Metro. Opera Ass'n, Inc. v. Loc. 100, Hotel Emps. & Rest. Emps. Int'l Union, 239 F.3d 172, 177 (2d Cir. 2001) (Walker, C.J.) ("[C]ourts have long held that equity will not enjoin a libel. Indeed, for almost a century the Second Circuit has subscribed to the majority view that, absent extraordinary circumstances, injunctions should not ordinarily issue in defamation cases." (citations omitted)).

[78] *Cf.* Eugene Volokh, *Anti-Libel Injunctions*, 168 U. PA. L. REV. 73, 90 (2019) ("Many past cases do say that 'equity will not enjoin a libel,' but that was a descriptive claim, describing a rule that no longer applies in many states."); Lowery v. Redmond, No. W202100611COAR3CV, 2022 WL 1618218, at *4 (Tenn. Ct. App. May 23, 2022) (concluding "it is unclear whether Tennessee law provides that a request for an injunction enjoining speech is clearly sufficient to invoke the chancery court's jurisdiction").

[79] *See, e.g.*, Chappell v. Stewart, 82 Md. 323, 33 A.542, 543 (1896), *dismissed*, 169 U.S. 733 (1898).

[80] *See, e.g.*, Samuel L. Bray, *The System of Equitable Remedies*, 3 U.C.L.A. L. REV. 530, 550 (2016) ("[D]espite vigorous scholarly criticism, seemingly every jurisdiction in American law still pays at least lip service to the 'no adequate remedy at law' requirement for equitable remedies."); *see also id.* at 535–36, 544, 550 n. 86, 580–81; *but see* LAYCOCK, *supra* note 67.

[81] Sachen v. Illinois State Bd. of Elections, 2022 IL App. (4th) 220470, 22, *appeal denied*, No. 128882, 2022 WL 4473739, at *4–5 (Ill. Sept. 20, 2022).

[82] 377 Ill. 89, 98, 35 N.E.2d 329, 329 (1941)).

[83] Sachen, 2022 IL App. (4th) 220470, 22 (*quoting* Fletcher v. City of Paris, 377 Ill. 89, 98, 35 N.E. 2d 329, 329 (1941)).

[84] Airport Auth. of City of St. Marys v. City of St. Marys, 297 Ga. App. 645, 647, 678 S.E. 2d 103, 105–06 (2009) (internal quotation marks and citation omitted); *cf.* Macy v. Oklahoma City Sch. Dist. No. 89, 1998 OK 58 n.3, 961 P.2d 804, 808 ("This court has stated on several occasions that a court of equity will not enforce a political right.").

involving civil or political rights, an injunction will be supported by statutory authorization, which means the background "equity will not" principle is not applicable, even by the lights of the traditional doctrine.

VI. Two Functions

The "equity will not" doctrines serve two functions: they regulate access to equity, and they preserve the conditions of equity's legitimacy.

First, the "equity will not" doctrines help to sort which cases go to equity. Access to equity is not straightforward. At law, we can speak of a "cause of action," which has elements that if met will entitle the plaintiff to relief. But that concept is foreign to equity. Instead, equity requires that the plaintiff present a grievance, which is a narrative about how the existing legal processes will be unable to achieve justice in her particular case.[85] And along with that grievance, the plaintiff needs to show that the redress sought is the sort of thing that equity is in the habit of doing.[86]

The "equity will not" doctrines are located in this context, and they adjust and reinforce it in three ways.

First, the "equity will not" doctrines help to describe, by a process of exclusion, the sorts of things that equity is in the habit of doing. Once you apply the "equity will not" doctrines, if they do not knock out the plaintiff's requested intervention, then there is a greater likelihood that it is the sort of thing equity *does* do. In other words, equity isn't just one discrete case after another, always resisting amalgamation and never coming to a true consolidation. Its work can be summarized in principles that are higher than the particular case. And the "equity will not" doctrines are examples of those principles.

Second, the virtue and vice of equity's access system is its indefiniteness. That crucial quality is one reason (along with remedial tailoring) that equity is considered "flexible." It can grasp a one-off case that cannot be captured by a legal rule, as Aristotle described so many centuries ago.[87] Yet the vice of that indefiniteness is that everything seems up for grabs. If equitable intervention is always possible, that would mean that broad, open-textured consideration of all the circumstances, which is so characteristic of equity, could be insisted on by one party or the other in every case. That burden would be more than any court

[85] *See generally* Bray & Miller, *supra* note 8.

[86] *See* Jones v. Parker, 163 Mass. 564, 566, 40 N.E. 1044, 1045 (1895) (Holmes, J.) (asking "whether a decree for specific performance would not call on the court to do more than it is in the habit of undertaking").

[87] *See* ARISTOTLE, NICHOMACHEAN ETHICS V.14, at 1137b 12–16 (C.D.C. Reeve trans., 2014).

could bear. The "equity will not" doctrines narrow the space in which equity's open-textured analysis is available.

Third, the "equity will not" doctrines regulate access to equity in ways that implicitly, but unmistakably, keep equity secondary. When courts and scholars in the past tried to justify the "equity will not" doctrines, the refrain was that equity would not act because equity did not need to act. Equity did not need to enjoin a crime, because a crime could be prosecuted. Equity did not need to enjoin a criminal proceeding, because any motivations for equity to act could be raised as defenses in the criminal trial. Equity did not need to protect personal or political rights, because would-be suitors in equity had other adequate means of redress. And so on. The "equity will not" principles are often categorical judgments about the availability of an adequate remedy.

In short, the "equity will not" doctrines are devices for keeping equity from acting gratuitously, from getting in the way of law, from spending its resources where they are not needed. In the past, they helped distinguish equity from other areas of law, preventing friction or jurisdictional competition. This was especially true for criminal law and also for tort law during its nascence.[88] More recently the principle that "equity will not enjoin a criminal proceeding" has been invoked to prevent competition between the federal and state courts,[89] and it continues to be used to prevent equity from eroding the procedural protections of the criminal law[90] and interfering with the investigative process.[91]

The other function of these doctrines is that they preserve the conditions that ensure equity's legitimacy. Equity has always been controversial. In the United States, it was controversial at the Founding, at the time of the labor injunctions, at the time of the civil rights structural injunctions, and now at the time of national injunctions. Precisely because of its extraordinary powers, and its greater reliance on discretionary considerations, equity has tended to be the most pro- *and* the most anti-Bickelian part of the common law systems. Equity is where American judges are most likely to overshoot, risking blowback from political actors and institutions, and it is also where those judges have most frequently used the available brakes to avoid overshooting.

These brakes include the "equity will not" doctrines. They have traditionally kept equity back from particularly sensitive areas, areas that are especially risky to the chancellor's self-preservation. These include crimes, civil rights, and political questions. For example, the principle that "equity will not protect political

[88] On the value of distinguishing equity and tort, *see* John C.P. Goldberg & Henry E. Smith, *Wrongful Fusion: Equity and Tort*, in EQUITY AND LAW: FUSION AND FISSION, note 10, 309.

[89] *See, e.g.*, Younger v. Harris, 401 U.S. 37 (1971).

[90] *See, e.g.*, Leider v. Lewis, 2 Cal. 5th 1121 (2017).

[91] Trump v. United States, No. 22-13005, 2022 WL 4366684, at *9 (11th Cir. September 21, 2022).

rights" once kept the federal courts out of political redistricting and even today is one of the headwaters for the modern political question doctrine.[92] Of course some of this same work can be done by the requirement of "no adequate remedy at law"; the "equity will not" doctrines can be seen as devices for directing the courts in how to read the adequacy of legal remedies.

Moreover, this legitimating function would seem to explain the statutory exception built in to many of the "equity will not" doctrines. If equity is concerned about overstepping—including, for example, by intervening in political questions—then that concern is substantially ameliorated if the legislature has authorized equity to act.

To be sure, a contemporary observer may detect in the "equity will not" doctrines a whiff of cowardice. Is equity playing possum, or at the very least devaluing civil and political rights by refusing to protect them (absent statutory authorization)? One can certainly point to cases that support this characterization.[93] Yet in other cases, equity declined to protect civil and political rights, not because they were unimportant, but because they were so important that they needed to be routed through the jury.

In effect, then, the "equity will not" doctrines are analogous to equitable abstention doctrines,[94] keeping the court out of situations that are more likely to involve political controversy or more likely to be seen as circumventions of the law's procedural protections. The difficult normative question is whether these equitable abstention doctrines, or other ones, are what we need.

VII. Conclusion

The "equity will not" doctrines structure equity's interventions. They help sort the cases that go to equity, keeping equity interstitial. And they steer equity toward the kinds of cases that are less likely to throw its legitimacy into doubt. These doctrines were rejected by scholars a century ago, and in recent decades scholars—but not courts—have wholly ignored them. But *something* will serve these functions.

[92] *See* John Harrison, *The Political Question Doctrines*, 67 AM. U. L. REV. 457, 487–92 (2017).

[93] *E.g.*, Giles v. Harris, 189 U.S. 475 (1903) (per Holmes, J.). For discussion of the case and its reception, *see* Richard H. Pildes, *Democracy, Anti-Democracy, and the Canon*, 17 CONST. COMMENT. 295 (2000); Samuel Brenner, Note, *"Airbrushed Out of the Constitutional Canon": The Evolving Understanding of* Giles v. Harris, *1903–1925*, 107 MICH. L. REV. 853 (2009).

[94] It is not an accident that many of the federal abstention doctrines that are still used were developed in equity (*e.g.*, Pullman, Burford, Younger). For further discussion, *see* Lael Weinberger, *Frankfurter, Abstention Doctrine, and the Development of Modern Federalism: A History and Three Futures*, 8&7 U. CHI. L. REV. 1737 (2020).

This chapter therefore goes right to the edge of the normative question: Are these the right sorting and legitimating devices for equity today? Then the chapter balks. Because I am not sure how to answer that question. I am not sure what the alternatives are. We are still in the early stages of the equity revival in the United States, but if it continues to flourish, this question will become more pressing.

2
Duties Owed to the Public

Nicolas Cornell

I. The Problem

Private law concerns relations that exist between private persons. Unlike regulatory law, criminal law, constitutional law, etc.—which are fundamentally structured in terms of a relation between the citizen and the state—private law is formally structured as relating each of us to each other. Whether in contract or tort, property or restitution, private law is about the claims that you have on me, the duties that I owe to you, and the instances when I wrong you.

A complexity arises, however, at the interstices between public and private law. The relation between two private individuals—private law's fundamental concern—may be shaped or mediated by one person's obligations to the state or to the public-at-large. What are we to say about cases in which I owe a duty to the public-at-large and you are a member of the public-at-large? Can that create a relationship between you and me that is properly cognized as a matter of private law?

This question cuts across all the core areas of private law. The ways that private law handles the question do not always appear consistent—or, perhaps more accurately, can appear downright contradictory. In short, despite the fact that public duty is a cross-cutting concept, its interpretation often appears problematically siloed.

The inconsistency is especially evident in situations where essentially similar public duties potentially implicate different areas of private law—factual situations at the interstices of contract and tort, or contract and property, etc. Here, at these intersection points, one finds different areas of private law seemingly arriving at flatly contradictory understandings of public duties. In other words, the problem is interstitial in two ways—it concerns both the boundary spaces between public law and private law and those spaces at the intersection of different fields of private law.

This chapter begins by laying out some of these tensions and contradictions, focusing particularly on four doctrines in contract, tort, and property. It then considers various ways of trying to reconcile these conflicting doctrines. Although the initial problems are narrow and doctrinal, the underlying issue is

Nicolas Cornell, *Duties Owed to the Public* In: *Interstitial Private Law*. Edited by: Samuel L. Bray, John C.P. Goldberg, Paul B. Miller, and Henry E. Smith, Oxford University Press. © Oxford University Press 2024.
DOI: 10.1093/oso/9780197783627.003.0002

not. It derives from a fundamental question about what it means to relate to one another, bilaterally, while being co-citizens within a shared political community. What do I owe to you when you are a member of the public-at-large?

II. Two Cases/Doctrines

To see the problem, we begin with two cases—one contract law, another tort law.

First, consider *Gray v. Martino*.[1] Defendant had diamonds and jewelry stolen. A police officer entered into an oral contract with the defendant in which she agreed to pay him $500 if he could procure for her the names and addresses of the thieves. He then worked with the police authorities, and the diamonds and jewelry were recovered. He sued to enforce the agreement. The New Jersey Supreme Court concluded that the agreement lacked consideration because the officer was simply doing his public duty. The court regarded "the dominant and conspicuous inquiry" to be, "Was the plaintiff, during the period of this transaction, a public officer, charged with the enforcement of the law?"[2] Concluding that he was, the Court held, "The services he rendered, in this instance, must be presumed to have been rendered in pursuance of that public duty, and for its performance he was not entitled to receive a special *quid pro quo*."[3] The contract lacked consideration because the police officer owed a preexisting legal duty to pursue the criminal. There was nothing that could be exchanged as part of a *quid pro quo*; there was no bargained-for legal detriment when a police officer was simply doing his job. Other legal-duty-rule cases reach similar results about promised rewards for public officials.[4]

Now consider *Washington v. Jefferson County Jail*.[5] A South Carolina inmate, serving time for auto theft, managed to escape from a work detail by stealing a vehicle. The inmate made his way to Washington's home, where he broke in, changed clothes, and stole Washington's car, all while Washington was in the house. Washington sued various corrections officials employed by the state, alleging that they had failed to supervise the inmate properly, enabling his escape. The South Carolina court dismissed the suit, applying the so-called public duty rule, which was concisely explained: "Under the public duty rule, public officials are generally not held liable to individuals for negligence in discharging public duties because the duty is owed to the public at large and not to any one

[1] 103 A. 24 (N.J. 1918).

[2] *Id.* at 25.

[3] *Id.*

[4] As noted in *Corbin on Contracts* § 7.11: "This principle has been held applicable to sheriffs, constables, and other police officers, to polygraph operators, to guardians, and even to attorneys and corporate officers" (collecting cases).

[5] 523 S.E. 2d 204 (S.C. Ct. App. 1999).

individual."[6] The court determined that, just as "police officers owe a duty of care to the public at large and not to any one individual," so too "those who maintain custody of prisoners or inmates do so for the protection of the public and are, therefore, not liable to individuals for damages caused by an escaped inmate under the public duty rule."[7] In other words, the public officials may have had a general duty to prevent the inmate from escaping and committing further thefts, but they did not owe that duty to Washington. This is a standard application of tort law's public duty rule.[8]

These cases are in tension. In *Gray*, the police officer's duty is understood to be owed to the victim of the theft. Had there not been a duty owed to the victim, then the agreement would not lack consideration. But, in *Washington*, the court says that the corrections officials did not owe a duty to the victim, only a duty to the public-at-large. One might think that perhaps this general duty to the public-at-large might explain the preexisting duty in *Gray*. But what matters for consideration is whether a preexisting legal duty was owed *to the promisor*.[9] A legal duty owed to some third party does not preclude consideration.[10] That makes sense because unless performance was already owed to the promisor, the promisor acquires something new as consideration—namely, a duty owed to them.[11] Thus, in applying consideration doctrine to invalidate rewards and side agreements with public officials, the law says that public officials owe their legal duties to individual members of the public. But, in applying the public duty rule to tort actions, the law says that public officials do not owe their duties to individual members of the public.

The tension here has a further dimension. In most jurisdictions, the public duty rule is subject to exceptions. The most common—in some ways a corollary of the rule itself—is that the rule does not apply when a public official has acquired a "special duty" to an individual member of the public. That is, although

6 *Id.* at 206.

7 *Id.* at 207.

8 Thomas Cooley offers a canonical statement of the rule: "In order that a public officer shall be liable to an individual in tort, it is necessary that the officer shall have violated some legal duty owing by him to such individual, as a result of which violation the individual has suffered damage. For the mere failure of an officer to perform a public duty owing by him to the public at large, as for example, the duty of a legislator to act honestly, or of an executive officer to enforce the law, no action lies by an individual." A TREATISE ON THE LAW OF TORTS 144 (1930).

9 *See* RESTATEMENT (SECOND) OF CONTRACTS § 73 cmt. d (ALI 1981) ("[T]he tendency of the law has been simply to hold that performance of contractual duty can be consideration if the duty is not owed to the promisor.").

10 "Consideration is not insufficient because of the fact . . . that the party giving the consideration is then bound by a contractual or quasi-contractual duty to a third person to perform the act or forbearance given or promised as consideration . . ." RESTATEMENT (FIRST) OF CONTRACTS § 84(d) (ALI 1932).

11 "The fact that A might have satisfied his duty to B and his separate duty to C by performing one and the same act is quite immaterial and shows no identity in the *legal relations*." Arthur Corbin, *Does a Pre-Existing Duty Defeat Consideration?—Recent Noteworthy Decisions*, 27 YALE L.J. 362 (1918).

public duties are generally owed to the public-at-large and not to individuals, certain special circumstances can create a duty to an individual citizen. Jurisdictions differ in their characterizations of how such special duties can arise, but the most widely accepted basis for a special duty is where a government official makes promises or explicit assurances to an individual. The idea is that, although police officers' duty to protect against crime is owed only to the public-at-large, when a police officer is apprised of a particular threat and offers explicit assurances of protection—for example, to a witness who will testify at trial—then there exists a duty to protect that is owed to that individual.

The public duty rule thus says, not only that officials' duties are owed to the public-at-large rather than individuals, but also that duties to individuals can arise by way of explicit assurances or concerted undertakings. But, in contract cases applying the legal duty rule—like *Gray v. Martino*—the very thing denied is that something new, over and above what was already owed, can be added to the preexisting legal duty. The tension, then, is not just about the basic understanding, with contract law apparently regarding public duties as owed to individuals and tort law apparently regarding public duties as owed to the public-at-large rather than individuals. Making matters worse, contract law says that where there exists a public duty, no further legal obligation can be undertaken, and yet tort law says that is precisely what sometimes happens. The tension thus concerns both the basic understanding of public duties and also the malleability of that default.[12]

III. Two More Cases/Doctrines

Consider another pair of cases, this time at the interstices of contract and property.

In *H.R. Moch Co. v. Rensselaer Water Co.*,[13] the city of Rensselaer hired the Rensselaer Water Company to supply water to the city. The company promised to furnish water for streets and sewers, public buildings, and fire hydrants. While this contract was in effect, a fire broke out in Rensselaer, which spread

[12] I've described the tension here by focusing on the duties of public officials, where it is especially vivid. The same tension arguably inheres in contract and tort law's orientation toward ordinary citizens' duties to abide by criminal and regulatory law. Within contract law, a promise to comply with one's existing statutory duties would generally not count as consideration. *See, e.g.*, Houston v. United States Bank Home Mortgage Wisconsin Servicing, 505 Fed. Appx. 543 (6th Cir. 2012) 549–50 (bank's promise to engage in loss mitigation as an alternative to foreclosure was not consideration because a statutory provision, which did not afford a private right of action, required loss mitigation). But in tort law, only statutes that are intended to protect a specific class of persons are understood to give rise to a cause of action or to negligence per se. *See* Restatement (Second) of Torts § 288, § 874A (ALI 1979).

[13] 159 N.E. 896 (N.Y. 1928).

to the warehouse of H.R. Moch Company, destroying the warehouse and all that was inside it. Moch sued the water company, alleging that the company had failed to provide water to the fire hydrants in accordance with its contract, allowing the fire to spread and destroy the warehouse. The New York Court of Appeals, in an opinion by then-Judge Cardozo, rejected the plaintiff's complaint. Acknowledging that "[i]n a broad sense" the contract was "for the benefit of the public," Cardozo emphasized that "[m]ore than this . . . must be shown to give a right of action to a member of the public not formally a party."[14] Here, the contract to furnish water had "in view a benefit to the public that is incidental rather than immediate, an assumption of duty to the city and not to its inhabitants."[15] Moch could not sue for breach because the water company's duties were owed only to the city, not individual citizens.[16] Consistent with this well-known decision, members of the public are not generally regarded as third-party beneficiaries who can enforce government contracts. If anything, the rules permitting a third-party contract enforcement are applied more stringently than normal in the context of government contracts.[17] A contractual duty to provide water to public hydrants—or some similar service—is not owed to individual members of the public.

Compare the decision in *Anderson v. W.R. Grace & Co.*,[18] one piece of the litigation made famous by the book *A Civil Action*.[19] Residents of Woburn, Massachusetts, alleged that the defendant corporation had contaminated the groundwater in East Woburn. Two municipal wells drew water from the affected aquifer. As a result of the contamination of the municipality's wells, the plaintiffs were allegedly exposed to chemicals that caused serious illnesses, including leukemia. Among the plaintiffs' causes of action was nuisance. This complaint sounded in public nuisance because the allegation was not that the defendants had interfered with plaintiffs' private property but rather that the defendants had interfered with public property.[20] The defendants attempted to argue that,

[14] Moch, *supra* note 13, at 897.

[15] *Id.*

[16] Accord German Alliance Insurance Co. v. Home Water Supply Co., 226 U.S. 220 (1912).

[17] *See, e.g.*, Cooper v. Charter Communications Entertainments I LLC, 760 F.3d 103 (1st Cir. 2014) 109: "Because government contracts by their very nature tend to benefit the public, Massachusetts courts apply a presumption against finding third-party liability in assessing those contracts . . . ." Notably, both the First and Second Restatements contained separate provisions for third-party beneficiaries of government contracts. Restatement (First) of Contracts § 145 (ALI 1932); Restatement (Second) of Contracts § 313 (ALI 1981). Somewhat overstating the case law, Justice Scalia wrote, "the modern jurisprudence permitting intended beneficiaries to sue does not generally apply to contracts between a private party and the government." Armstrong v. Exceptional Child Center, 575 U.S. 320, 332 (2015).

[18] 628 F. Supp. 1219 (D. Mass. 1986).

[19] Jonathan Harr, A Civil Action (1995).

[20] "The right to be free of contamination to the municipal water supply is clearly a 'right common to the general public,' thus interference with that right would be a public nuisance." Anderson, *supra* note 18, at 1233.

as private individuals, the plaintiffs could not bring an action based on a right of the public-at-large—that such actions must be brought by public officials. The court rejected that argument. It explained that, in public nuisance cases, "when a plaintiff has sustained 'special or peculiar damage,' he or she may maintain an individual action."[21] Because the plaintiffs had alleged such special injuries, the court concluded that they had the standing to maintain a public nuisance action and to seek damages for their injuries. The plaintiffs were limited to seeking compensatory damages—injunction and abatement expenses were not judged to be within their purview as private citizens—but their complaint was permitted to proceed. The case typifies public nuisance, which allows particularly injured citizens to sue based on rights of the public-at-large, rights in something like a water supply.[22]

The tension should be apparent. In *Moch*, the defendant had a duty to provide water to the public hydrants. The court determined that this duty was owed to the municipality, not the individual citizens. The injured plaintiff could not point to the breach of that duty and seek redress for its resulting injuries. In *Anderson*, the defendant had a duty not to contaminate the public well water. This duty, likewise, was owed to the municipality. But the plaintiffs were allowed to bring a cause of action based on the breach of that duty and to pursue damages to compensate their injuries resulting from the breach.[23]

The difference cannot be explained by the fact that, in *Moch*, the plaintiff suffered only property loss, whereas in *Anderson*, the injuries were to physical health. Even physical injury does not generally enable citizens to bring private claims as third-party beneficiaries of government contracts.[24] And, conversely, property loss is a classic "special injury" for the purposes of public nuisance standing.[25]

There does not appear to be a unified conception across contract law and property law of what it means for the public-at-large to be a rightholder. A public well providing water to the community is one thing; a public contract to provide

[21] *Id.*

[22] *See* RESTATEMENT (SECOND) OF TORTS § 821C (ALI 1979).

[23] To add a further dimension, some jurisdictions might even allow a citizen to sue in unjust enrichment where there has been a breach of a public duty, like a duty not to pollute a water supply. *See* Branch v. Mobil Oil Corp., 778 F. Supp. 35 (W.D. Okla. 1991).

[24] For example, in Bootay v. KBR Inc., 437 Fed. Appx. 140 (3d Cir. 2011), a court dismissed an Army veteran's complaint against a company with which the Army Corps of Engineers had contracted. The veteran alleged that the company had caused his exposure to sodium dichromate, which had left him with serious health issues and totally disabled, but the court found that, even if there were "a duty under the contract to perform an environmental assessment, that duty extended only to USACE, as KBR's customer, and not every single soldier." *Id.* at 145 (n. 8).

[25] *See, e.g.*, Cottman v. Lochner, 278 P. 71 (Wyo. 1929) (loss of five head of sheep). Even losses of future profits can sometimes be the basis for standing to sue for public nuisance. *See* Iveson v. Moore, 91 Eng. Rep. 1224 (1699) (loss of profits from colliery); Hampton v. North Carolina Pulp Co., 27 S.E. 2d 538 (N.C. 1943) (loss of commercial fishermen's catch).

water to the community is another. There's no reason that it has to be that way. Beneficiaries of government contracts could be afforded standing in the fashion of public nuisance, that is, wherever they suffer a "special" injury. Or, alternately, public nuisance suits could be restricted to cases in which the government has expressed an intent to convey the standing to enforce its rights, that is, in the fashion of third-party contract beneficiaries. Instead, contract law and property law just seem to lack a consistent framework for understanding duties owed to the public-at-large—as exposed by these cases in the interstices.[26]

IV. Anti-Formalism

One response to these apparent tensions would be to conclude that the doctrinal explanations are not to be taken seriously—that they are merely cover for various policy objectives. Although courts frame these doctrines in terms of whether a duty is "owed to the individual" or "owed only to the public-at-large," such formulations are not explanatory—they are, at best, conclusory. We should not be surprised, the thought goes, that they seem to be in tension with one another because the decisions are actually driven by various and divergent policy considerations.

This anti-doctrinal response may seem especially plausible for two reasons. First, each of these doctrines might be dismissed as fringe—hardly the essence of contract, tort, or property law respectively. Second, there are policy considerations that are readily apparent in each context that might be driving the outcomes.

Consider each doctrine in turn. The preexisting duty rule in contract law is hardly uncontroversial. The entire doctrine of consideration, from which it derives, is often considered problematic.[27] And the preexisting duty rule has been perhaps its most criticized aspect. The rule has been largely abandoned with respect to its most significant application, contractual modifications. Its continued application to public duty cases like *Gray v. Martino* is, one might think, misguided because those cases can be explained on other grounds. Public policy against bribery and corruption should dictate that public officials do not receive extra compensation for performing their duties. It is this fact—and nothing

[26] For another example of this same tension, consider scenarios in which public officials elicit contractual promises from developers to create areas of public access. *See, e.g., New Yorkers Got Broken Promises. Developers Got 20 Million Sq. Ft.*, N.Y. TIMES, July 21, 2023. If the developer blocks access, are they liable to members of the public who suffer special injury? Practically speaking, the scenario resembles paradigmatic public nuisances cases—blocking access to a public right-of-way or public park. Why should contract law treat it differently?

[27] *See, e.g.*, CHARLES FRIED, CONTRACT AS PROMISE (1981) 35.

about the structure of public duties per se—that explains the unenforceability of agreements to reward public officials.

The public duty rule in tort might also be dismissed as illusory formalism. For one thing, the rule might be regarded as at the periphery of tort law—the core of which concerns the relation of one person with another. More importantly, the doctrine might be regarded as simply a confused formulation of sovereign immunity. On this view, decisions are driven not by considerations about the structure of duty but rather by policy considerations about when the state and its officials should and should not face liability. In support of this contention, it might be pointed out that the doctrine arose under the somewhat anomalous situation where municipalities lacked the sovereign immunity held by state and federal government. And it might be further pointed out that courts in states that have waived sovereign immunity have sometimes interpreted that waiver as implicitly abrogating the public duty doctrine.[28] From this vantage point, it looks like the rule has less to do with the structure of public duties and more to do with policy considerations around government liability.

Similarly, third-party beneficiary rules in contract law are often regarded as peculiar, exceptional, or even unjustified. Their application to government contracts may be considered especially idiosyncratic. And there is a special policy concern at play: the price of government contracting. The potential of facing liability to individual citizens would drive up the prices charged by government contractors. In *Moch*, Cardozo notes, "A promisor will not be deemed to have had in mind the assumption of a risk so overwhelming for any trivial reward."[29] So, here too, perhaps the results have less to do with the formal structure of duties and more to do with public policy.

Lastly, public nuisance is regularly understood to be anomalous. Although private citizens have long held the standing to sue for public nuisance when they suffered distinctive injury, this standing might be a conflation of private nuisance—a tort and genuine concern of private law—and public law. Here is how Prosser put the point:

> There are . . . two kinds of nuisance, which are quite unrelated . . . A private nuisance is narrowly restricted to the invasion of the use or enjoyment of land. It is only a tort, and the remedy for it lies exclusively with the individual whose rights have been disturbed. A public nuisance is a catch-all low-grade criminal offence, consisting in the interference with the rights of the community at large. . . Although as in the case of other crimes, the normal remedy is in the hands of the state, a public nuisance may also be a private one, when it interferes

[28] *See, e.g.*, Adams v. State, 555 P. 2d 235 (Alaska 1976).
[29] Moch, *supra* note 13, at 898.

> with private land. The seeds of confusion were sown when courts began to hold that a tort action would lie even for a purely public nuisance if the plaintiff had suffered "particular damage."[30]

On this view, public nuisance is not truly a matter of private law at all—its tort-like qualities are the result of a historical confusion. The continued existence of private suits for public nuisance can be explained on policy grounds, as allowing citizens to function as private attorneys general, akin to *qui tam* actions or American antitrust actions.[31] Yet again, formal ideas about the structure of public rights and duties might just be a distraction.

Although there is probably some truth in each of these thoughts, I do not think that we should be satisfied by them. First, many reconceptualizations in terms of public policy have been explicitly rejected by courts. It is one thing to say that a case like *Gray v. Martino* is actually a matter of public policy, even if the stated rationale is the preexisting duty rule. The two justifications are compatible, and the court's adoption of one explanation should not preclude thinking that the other undergirds the result. It is quite another to say that public policy is driving decisions when courts have been invited to adopt public law justifications and have declined that invitation. For example, many courts have explicitly rejected the idea that the public duty rule reduces to a form of sovereign immunity, with most courts that confront the issue concluding that it persists even after a state waives immunity.[32] Similarly, in public nuisance actions, the question of whether private parties are acting as private attorneys general often arises directly, and courts often reject it explicitly.[33] That conclusion is implicit in the *Anderson* court's refusal to let the plaintiffs seek abatement, which it regarded as a matter for public officials. Perhaps courts are mistaken about what they are doing, but they seem to regard these cases as involving genuine issues of traditional private law.

More importantly, there is a basic question here: When someone owes a duty to the public-at-large, how do they stand with respect to individual members of the public? To deny that there is any general answer to that question—to think that there are only ad hoc policy considerations at play—would seem to imperil

30 William Prosser, *Private Action for Public Nuisance*, 52 Virginia L. Rev. 997, 999 (1966).

31 *See, e.g.*, NAACP v. AcuSport Inc., 271 F. Supp. 2d 435, 497 (EDNY 2003) ("A private party bringing an action for public nuisance is acting as a *de facto* private attorney general, suing on behalf of itself as well as the public.").

32 For a particularly clear discussion and a survey of jurisdictions, see the Illinois Supreme Court's discussion in Coleman v. E. Joliet Fire Protection Dist., 46 N.E. 3d 741 (Ill. 2016), which concludes "The public duty rule is not the equivalent of any type of sovereign immunity," at 45.

33 *See, e.g.*, the divided opinions in Miotke v. Spokane, 678 P. 2d 803 (Wash. 1984), in which the Washington Supreme Court fractured over whether to award attorney fees on a private attorney general theory, with the plurality awarding fees for the injunctive phase of the litigation but not the entire litigation.

all talk of rights and duties in private law. If appeals to rights and duties are just covert policymaking in this context, why not think that is true throughout private law? Shallow realists might be happy to go that far, but I am not.

It might appear that one can distinguish these cases by virtue of the presence of the public-at-large. These cases—the thought would go—are understandably a matter of policy considerations precisely because they involve the public directly. They are thus categorically different from the rest of private law. But that is misleading. Private law regularly concerns our relations with each other under some description. It asks what I owe you as a promisee, as a landowner, as someone who has invited your trust, etc. There's no reason why the law should not be able to ask—and answer—what I owe to you as a member of the public-at-large. The answer could be nothing: that legally owing you anything requires more. But it would be quite peculiar to think that this is simply a question to which private law has no general answer at all.

Finally, one reason to resist wholesale skepticism about the role played by an idea of duties owed to the public-at-large is that such a blanket rejection of the doctrinal explanation is simply unnecessary. Even if these doctrines are in tension with one another, one need not cast them all aside at once. It makes far more sense to take as many of the doctrines at face value as one can, explaining away only those doctrines that cannot be reconciled with a general theoretical framework. The remainder of this chapter pursues variations of such an approach.

V. Collective Duties Only

One coherent understanding would be that duties owed to the public-at-large do nothing between private individuals. They are only owed to the collective. Public duties, on this view, relate an individual to the public-at-large, but they do not (directly at least) structure the relationship between one private individual and another. Tort law's public duty rule basically has the correct understanding.

This view appears compatible with the thought that certain special circumstances might generate individualized duties to individual citizens. The "special duty" exception to the public duty rule would be understood not as enforcing (exceptionally) the public duty, but rather as the facts giving rise to an independent and individualized duty. Similarly, where the government intends for individuals to be able to sue privately, that too will be allowed (assuming they satisfy basic standing requirements): thus the rights of third-party beneficiaries under government contracts where clearly intended. But, absent a specifically generated right to the individual, duties are owed only to the public-at-large, not to the individual.

This understanding appears incompatible with the preexisting duty rule's application to public officials (*Gray*) or with the private actions for public nuisance (*Anderson*). But these might be explained away in the modes already described. Contracts with public officials can be void as against public policy, not based on a preexisting duty analysis. Private standing for public nuisance can be dismissed as a historical anomaly or confusion, which persists only as a weird form of private attorney general. With these doctrines cast aside, there is no barrier to saying that duties owed to the public are owed only to the public-at-large, not individuals. Many theorists may find this position to be the most amenable.

There are, however, reasons not to be terribly sanguine about it. Doctrines like those in *Gray v. Martino* and *Anderson* did not come out of nowhere. Rather, they reflect a natural understanding of what it means to be owed to something as part of a collective. A police officer's duty to investigate crimes is not something that has nothing to do with us—akin to a contract between two strangers. It is hardly surprising that courts, when confronted with the question, concluded that police officers owed a preexisting duty to individual members of the public offering a reward. Similarly, we intuitively grasp that the roads, waterways, reservoirs, and so on are, in some sense, ours. If a company contaminates your municipality's water supply, you are apt to regard that as destroying something that is yours—your water. The contamination would not be something between two strangers, akin to Poland Springs breaching its supply contract with your grocer. When it's your public water supply, you would be among those directly aggrieved. Whatever their difficulties, the preexisting duty rule and private suits for public nuisance both tap into that intuitive idea: we each have a direct stake in public duties.

In contrast, saying that a duty is owed only to the public-at-large and not to any individuals should, to my mind, strike us a bit perplexing. One can readily understand how duties might be owed to the king, not to private citizens. But the public-at-large is different—it's a composite of the citizens themselves, not some separate person. How can a duty be owed to that, without being owed to any individual whatsoever?

By way of analogy, imagine that a kindergarten teacher brought a platter of cookies to his classroom. All day, every time any student reached for a cookie, the teacher pulled the platter away and explained, "those are not for you, they are for the class." We would find the teacher's behavior bizarre and perhaps even incoherent. Note that the statement, "they are for the class," makes perfect sense if it is deployed to fend off a student trying to jump the gun or to take more than his fair share. What is incoherent is invoking it with respect to each and every student. If the cookies are for the class, then it makes no sense to say that no student may have one. The class is not some entity altogether separate from the individual students. Likewise, the public-at-large is not some entity entirely separate from the citizens.[34] Yet, in the context of the public duty rule in torts and the third-party beneficiary doctrine for government contracts, this is more or less what courts say to each and every plaintiff: "Those rights are not for you, they are for the public-at-large." Even if we think this conclusion ultimately correct, we should recognize its paradoxical quality.[35]

Of course, the cookie analogy has its limitations. Cookies are material goods, the value of which comes through consumption. Rights, in contrast, convey a kind of decision-making authority. This difference matters because, whereas the class cannot consume cookies without individual students consuming cookies, a collective might exercise authority to decide a question without any individual having the authority to decide. This is a critical point to which I will return. For now, observe simply that the categorical proposition that duties owed to the public-at-large are not owed to any individual should hardly be a place to which theorists gravitate eagerly.[36] It's a puzzling idea that appears at odds with basic egalitarian and democratic commitments; it treats the public-at-large as conceptually akin to a separate person like a king.

VI. Public Duties as Duties to Each

Rather than say that duties to the public-at-large are not owed to individual citizens, one might adopt the opposite position. That is, one might say that, generally, a duty owed to the public is owed to each citizen. This would fit with contract law's conception of a preexisting duty, as in *Gray v. Martino*. To a lesser degree, it would also fit with public nuisance law (though the special injury requirement would still need explanation).

Such a conception is starkly at odds with the public duty rule in torts, but, as already noted, the public duty rule might be explained as a muddled form of sovereign immunity. And it also seems to be in tension with the limited third-party enforcement of government contracts, but that too might be explained away as problematic.

The bigger issue—of which these doctrinal tensions are arguably just small examples—is that understanding all public duties as owed to individual members

[34] Some might see an important disanalogy here—that, by virtue of something about political communities, the public-at-large is its own distinct entity in a way that a kindergarten class is not. Whatever difference there might be here, I don't think that it is doing decisive work. Imagine a state that said that no one may consume the corn grown with public funds because the corn belongs to the public-at-large, not individuals. That would introduce the same incoherence.

[35] Occasionally, the public duty rule is skeptically labeled the "duty to all, duty to no one" doctrine. *See, e.g.*, Adams, *supra* note 28, at 241.

[36] Compare Stewart v. Schmieder, 386 So. 2d 1351, 1358 (La. 1980): "the mere fact that a duty is of a public nature, and benefits the general public, does not require a conclusion that the city cannot be found liable for the breach of that duty."

of the public seems to be at odds with our broader commitments regarding public governance. Decisions about public policy are collective; individuals don't get to make them unilaterally. If you have a duty not to trespass on a parcel of state-owned land, I can't give you permission to enter. If you have a statutory duty not to release pollutants at a rate above certain parts per million, I don't get to decide that you get an exception—or, for that matter, that you are *not* entitled to an exception. In this light, it's hardly surprising that private individuals generally don't get to enforce government contracts. The duties do not correspond to private entitlements in this sense. Any conception of public duties as owed to each of us must confront that reality.

VII. Misfeasance/Nonfeasance

One might appeal to the distinction between misfeasance and nonfeasance to navigate the puzzle about public duties. This distinction may seem to map onto the paradigmatic cases of liability and absence of liability. Many tort cases invoking the public duty rule involve allegations that public officials failed to perform affirmative duties to aid or to enforce the law properly, and the refusal to impose liability in tort law may appear to fit with tort law's general refusal to impose liability in failure-to-aid cases.[37] In contrast, many public nuisance cases involve a defendant who has affirmatively done something—contaminated a public well, blocked a public highway, etc.—and that may appear to fit with private law's standard liability for wrongful interference with others. A distinction between *Moch* and *Anderson*, for example, is that the defendant in *Moch* failed to provide water to the hydrants, whereas the defendant in *Anderson* affirmatively contaminated the water.

But there are problems with invoking the distinction between misfeasance and nonfeasance as a meaningful explanation of the doctrine. Courts that reject liability to individual citizens presumably do conceptualize breach of public duty to be a kind of nonfeasance with respect to individuals. But, for the most part, that only begs the question. What is needed is not an account of whether there is a duty—something to which the misfeasance/nonfeasance distinction can be informative—but rather an account of to whom the duty is owed.

37. Some courts even characterize the contours of the rule in these terms. *See, e.g.*, Moore v. Murphy, 119 N.W. 2d 759, 760 (Iowa 1963) ("an officer or employee of a county is not personally liable for acts of nonfeasance in connection with his duties as such employee, but is liable for acts of misfeasance which occur while in the performance of his duties."). *But see* Commerce & Indus. Ins. Co. v. City of Toledo, 543 N.E. 2d 1188, 1194 (Ohio 1989) ("The applicability of the public duty rule does not depend upon whether the allegations against the municipality may be characterized as nonfeasance or as misfeasance."). *See also* Jean W. v. Commonwealth, 610 N.E. 2d 305 (Mass. 1993).

To see the point, consider the public contract cases. Breach of contract is not nonfeasance with respect to the promisee. So the lack of liability in a case like *Moch* cannot be explained simply on the grounds that defendant's failure to provide water was, per se, nonfeasance rather than misfeasance. It was indisputably misfeasance *with respect to the public-at-large*; it is only conceivably nonfeasance *with respect to the plaintiff*. That seems to be how courts like *Moch* understand government contracts—as promises to the public-at-large, but not to the citizens.[38] But then the application of the misfeasance/nonfeasance distinction depends upon, rather than explains, the treatment of individuals vis-à-vis the public. The important question is whether the public-at-large excludes or includes the plaintiff.

Once one appreciates the point, it is unsurprising that the misfeasance/nonfeasance distinction does not fully explain even the relevant tort cases. There are public duty cases rejecting liability even for affirmative interference by public officials.[39] And there are public nuisance cases arising from the defendant's failure to perform affirmative actions.[40] Many persons owe some affirmative legal duties to the public-at-large; the thorny question is when those duties are also owed to individual members of the public. The struggle in commonwealth countries to develop a coherent tort of misfeasance in public office is a testament to the problem.[41]

Any explanation that revolves around the misfeasance/nonfeasance distinction thus doesn't appear capable of answering the fundamental question: how to conceptualize the metaphysical relation between individual citizens and the public-at-large. If they were wholly separate entities, then duties to the public would simply not be owed to individuals; if they were completely identifiable, then duties to the public would constitute duties owed to individuals. The question is essentially about the nature of the public-at-large. The misfeasance/nonfeasance distinction does not purport to address this question; it concerns the nature of actions and duties. So, however fundamental the distinction may be to

[38] At least, for the purposes of enforcement. For the purposes of consideration, courts go the other way.

[39] *See, e.g.*, Cheriee Gazette v. City of Pontiac, 41 F.3d 1061 (6th Cir. 1994) (police affirmatively lied); Curtis v County of Cook, 456 N.E. 2d 116 (Ill. 1983) (city erected signpost into which car crashed); Long v. Soderquist, 467 N.E. 2d 1153 (Ill. 1984) (police officer instructed plaintiffs to remain in location where they were then injured).

[40] Consider cases involving a defendant whose vehicle collides with an animal; the driver may be liable for failing to clear the obstruction from the public road. *See, e.g.*, Hardy v. Brooks, 118 S.E. 2d 492 (Ga. Ct. App. 1961). Similarly, landowners may be liable in public nuisance for dangerous structures or substances on their property, even when the problem was created by a third party or by natural causes. *See* Restatement (Second) of Torts § 839 cmt. d.

[41] For discussions of the puzzles this tort generates, *see* John Murphy, *Misfeasance in a Public Office: A Tort Law Misfit?*, 32 Oxford J.L.S. 51 (2012); Mark Aronson, *Misfeasance in Public Office: A Very Peculiar Tort*, 35 Melbourne Univ. L. Rev. 1 (2011.

structuring private law generally, it doesn't seem equipped to address this particular question.

VIII. In Rem/In Personam

The contrast between the decisions in *Moch* and *Anderson* might suggest yet another story. In that pair, there are different outcomes depending on whether it is a public water source or a public contract to provide water. That is, the law apparently treats the duties owed to the public-at-large—and the corresponding rights of the public-at-large—differently if the duties and rights are those of property or those of contract.[42]

Although that might look like a technical distinction, there could be reasons why it should matter here. Property rights, after all, are rights in rem. And, as such, they involve everyone in an important way. Property rights address the world.[43] That a piece of land—or a road or a well—is not ours means that we have certain duties with respect to it. Property rights are, in this way, everyone's business. Contract rights are different, paradigmatic rights in personam. They create or alter duties only as between the parties to the contract. Contract rights are not everyone's business. Framed this way, a public well is a concern of everyone in the community in a way that a public contract to supply water is not.[44]

Of course, this distinction pertains to the way in which each individual is *bound* by duties. It is not about each individual being *owed* duties. But perhaps it might generate an argument in that direction. I imagine two forms that such an argument might take.

First, one might think that, as a matter of fairness, one who is bound by duties has a kind of claim against others who breach those same duties.[45] Each citizen in Woburn owed a duty not to contaminate the town wells. Perhaps that offers a basis for thinking that those citizens have standing to hold accountable the company that violates that same duty. In contrast, the citizens of Rensselaer had no duties to provide water to hydrants. Perhaps they have less claim to enforce such duties by which they were not themselves bound.

Second, one might think that because everyone is bound by property, there is a difference in the overall information costs in allowing private enforcement. Formally, everyone already knows the contours of property rights, which

[42] *See also supra* note 26.

[43] *See* Felix Cohen, *Dialogue on Private Property*, 9 RUTGERS L. REV. 357, 374 (1954).

[44] The idea might also explain the public duty rule cases as long as the duties of public officials are conceptualized as contractual.

[45] *See* H.L.A. Hart, *Are There Natural Rights?*, 64 PHILOSOPHICAL REV. 175, 185 (1955).

are designed to be public, standardized, and clearly demarcated.[46] Private enforcement of property rights would not force those creating the rights to consider and inform persons who they would not have otherwise. In contrast, the prospect of enforcement of government contracts by individual citizens who were not parties to the contract formation might force the contracting parties to approach the creation of rights quite differently. What they create would not just be a matter of them and their negotiating partner, with the understandings and interpretations that they share. Contract rights and duties would have to be crafted in a way that would account for anyone's reasonable understanding. Given this difference in informational burdens, perhaps public property rights should be treated differently from public contract rights.

While these are both intriguing thoughts, I don't see that the basic puzzle can be explained in these terms. For one thing, the above arguments face significant problems. With respect to the argument from fairness, although it is true that members of the public are not burdened by the duties of performance under a government contract (they don't have a duty to provide water to hydrants), they are still burdened by the contract insofar as they are members—perhaps taxpayers—of the public that is giving consideration for the performance. Moreover, everyone is under the duty not to take payment from the government for a service without providing that service. With respect to the information cost argument, while we should be concerned about the information costs to third parties when they would be bound by duties (as they are with property rights), it's less clear why the information costs to third parties should be a reason to preclude them from a set of rights. Unknown and unchosen burdens are a problem; unknown and unchosen benefits are not. Moreover, it's just doubtful that information costs are doing real explanatory work here. Widespread citizen enforcement would, undoubtedly, reshape government contracts, but that's because of the increased liability itself—as Cardozo says—not because of increased information costs, which would pale in comparison.

More generally, any explanation that appeals to the in rem/in personam distinction—like appeal to the misfeasance/nonfeasance distinction—ultimately just seems inapt for addressing the foundational question: What's the conceptual relationship between private individuals and the public-at-large? If a duty is owed to the public-at-large, is it owed to me? The property/contract divide doesn't address this question directly. To the extent that I'm a member of the public-at-large, it would seem superficially that my status as "a public landowner" and as a "public contract-promisee" should run parallel. Perhaps there is

[46] *Cf.* Thomas W. Merrill & Henry E. Smith, *The Property/Contract Interface*, 101 Columbia L. Rev. 773, 793 (2001): "The unique advantage of in rem rights . . . is that they conserve on information costs relative to in personam rights in situations where the number of potential claimants to resources is large, and the resource in question can be defined at relatively low cost."

something about the structure of a political community such that property rights and contract rights operate differently. But the explanation should not be only about the nature of the rights; it must also be at least partly about the nature of the political community itself.

IX. Control and Benefit

Let me offer one final possible explanation: the public-at-large is a separate entity from individual citizens in one respect and not in another, and, as a result, duties are "owed to" individual citizens in one respect and not in another. Famously, a political community is a kind of will of its own, apart from a mere aggregation of the individuals within it. This is Rousseau's "general will" or Kant's "omnilateral will." On a view like this, the will of the public-at-large is not mine to determine unilaterally. At the same time, the public-at-large is not just an altogether separate entity akin to another person. This is so in two respects. First, its will is, in some sense, still the will of the members. The general will is importantly mine even though I don't get to determine it unilaterally. Second, the public-at-large has no material interests untethered to the material interests of its members. Even if the public-at-large has a well-being that is not simply reducible to the well-being of its members (a controversial claim), it's clear that the well-being of the public-at-large cannot exist apart from the well-being of its members.

To the extent that something like this conception is correct (and I think that it is), then it may shed some light on why, in private law contexts, individual citizens sometimes can, and sometimes cannot, enforce the rights of the public-at-large. Individual citizens are not entitled to determine the collective will unilaterally. As a result, where recognition of a private cause of action would effectively award that kind of private control, it is not appropriate. The duties are not owed to individuals in the sense of their having that kind of control. But, at the same time, it would be a mistake to say that the duties aren't owed to individual citizens in any sense. Citizens do not relate to public duties as they relate, for example, to a promise made to a stranger. First, the rightholder—the public-at-large—is them; the collective will is their will. And, second, they are the material beneficiaries of these duties. Use of the public roads cannot be for the public-at-large yet not for any individuals any more than a plate of cookies can be for the kindergarten class and yet not for any of the kindergarteners. Thus, where recognition of a private cause of action would not give unilateral control but rather would respond ex post to an injury caused by a breach of duty, then it is appropriate and natural.

This difference between exercise of control and ex post injury might thus seem to explain the variable treatment of public duties in private law. Because private causes of action are sometimes primarily an exercise of the rightholder's normative control and are sometimes primarily an ex post remedial response to the injuries resulting from a duty's breach, private individual actions are neither always nor never fitting. When a cause of action would arrogate to an individual control over a duty owed to the public-at-large, then it is precluded. When a cause of action merely vindicates or remedies an injury from breach of a public duty, then it is allowed.

The separation between control and benefits is, of course, familiar to private law—it is the foundation of the law of trusts. One way to frame the proposed explanation is that duties owed to the public-at-large are held in a kind of public trust. There is something illuminating in that characterization, and its widespread adoption would probably be an advance. But it can also be a little misleading. In a normal trust relation, the will of the trustee is fully distinct from the will of the beneficiary—the beneficiary is subject to the choices of an external other who acts on his behalf. But, in the public context, the general will is, in an important sense, the will of the individual.[47] When the general will is violated, it is a violation of their will. So citizens are rightholders in an important way that beneficiaries of a normal trust are not. Still, the trust imagery may be helpful—it reflects the sense in which individual harm matters legally and yet individuals do not have unilateral control.

The doctrine does not perfectly align with this explanation, but it does seem to reflect it in some important ways. Consider first the preexisting duty cases involving public officials, like *Gray v. Martino*. The issue here seems to be a matter of control. The citizen who offers a reward attempts, through the mechanism of contract, to obtain a kind of private influence over the action of the public official. There is a consideration problem because the duties were already owed to the citizens. True, the private citizen did not have unilateral control over the performance of those duties, but the duty was already owed to them and in a form that would preclude obtaining unilateral control.

In contrast, the special-injury requirement for public nuisance actions is plausibly designed to ensure that individuals who have suffered harm—not merely the loss of a rightholder's typical control—have access to a remedy. Private citizens don't get to police the public roads and waters; that's the role of the state. Allowing an individual who has not suffered any distinctive injury to sue would effectively enable such private control. The injury that we all suffer alike is to be responded to—whether through prosecution or a choice not to prosecute—by us all together.[48] But when an individual suffers a distinctive material injury from a

[47] The point might be illustrated by contrasting American law's conception of the relation between Native Americans and the federal government, which is explicitly described in terms of a trust relation. If every citizen were in that position, the special rules of Federal Indian Law would be unnecessary.

[48] Courts applying public trust doctrine have sometimes imposed a similar special injury requirement. *See, e.g.*, Koehler v. Century of Progress, 188 N.E. 445 (Ill. 1933); Kopelman v. Board of Public

breach and seeks retrospective compensation, that is not an exercise of unilateral control. Rather it is appropriate ex post compensation because the individual suffered a transgression against something that was, in an important way, theirs. The plaintiffs in *Anderson* weren't attempting to police the use of Woburn's well; they were asserting a grievance based on a fait accompli. Quite unlike the pre-existing duty rule cases, which are primarily about ex ante control, the public nuisance cases seem aimed ex post compensation for material injury.[49] This explanation also fits with the disfavor that public nuisance law shows towards injunctive relief for private plaintiffs, as seen in *Anderson*. Though willing to recognize ex post injuries, the courts do not regard the duty as owed to individuals for the purpose of ex ante control.[50]

The public duty rule in torts is somewhat harder to square with this conception. The rule often looks to be based on a straightforward inference that because a duty is owed to the public-at-large, there cannot be an individual grievance based upon its breach. As a categorical claim, that proposition is hard to justify. In practice, however, the rule comes with lots of exceptions. One way to characterize the rule-in-practice is that it insulates discretionary actions and judgment calls of public officials from liability, while not eliminating liability where public officials were committed to a course of action.[51] Some courts even explicitly describe the public duty rule as applying only to discretionary duties as opposed to ministerial duties.[52] That framing seems consistent with conceptualizing the public duty rule as ensuring that tort law does not give private individuals control over public officials. Rather than a blanket denial that public duties are owed to individuals, the public duty rule might thus be more akin to the operation of the business judgment rule in corporate law—it insulates certain discretionary judgments from liability, not because there aren't duties owed, but for the sake of the agency relation itself.[53] The special-duty exception might be understood in these terms as well. When a public official commits to a course of conduct, protecting or rescuing a particular person, the transformative element is not that they have thereby created a duty where there was none before, but rather that

Works, 276 A. 2d 56 (Md. 1971). This seems to reflect a recognition even within public trust doctrine that it is not an ordinary trust relation.

49 This may count against private suits having preclusive effect on subsequent public enforcement.

50 The availability of abatement in private suits for public presents some complication here. But I think that abatement can still be regarded as an ex post response.

51 Compare the discretionary function exception under the Federal Tort Claims Act. The FTCA waives sovereign immunity, so the point is not that public duties are, as a general conceptual matter, not owed to individuals. Rather, the idea is that ex post remedies should not turn into ex ante control.

52 *See* Adams v. Schneider, 124 N.E. 718 (Ind. 1919).

53 Notice that corporate law could have said that managers owe their duties to the corporation-at-large, not to any individual shareholders. But the business judgment rule has seemed a better approach.

they are then precluded from appealing to their official discretion. So, while the public duty rule is not typically described in these terms, it seems plausible that the rule instantiates a principle that individuals don't get to determine or second-guess official action unilaterally, but that, where there is no question of discretion on the table, individuals may sue for the material injuries that they suffer.[54]

This leaves only the third-party beneficiary rules for government contracts, as exemplified by *Moch*. Enforcing a contract might look like a kind of rightholder control, and perhaps the unreceptiveness toward citizen enforcement is motivated by that understanding. But if citizens were to have only an unvested (as is typical for third-party beneficiaries) power to enforce government contracts where breach caused a special injury to them, that would look consistent with the conception sketched. Citizens would not be getting a form of ex ante control; the law would merely be recognizing a kind of material injury ex post. It's hard to see the rationale for denying such recovery purely on the grounds that there was nothing owed to them. Indeed, the trust image seems especially potent here. The origins of third-party beneficiary rules are enmeshed with trust ideas,[55] and the strongest case for third-party standing seems to be where the promise is somehow acting on behalf of the third party in making the contract. This is true of government contracts. A paradoxical feature of the cases involving government contracts is that standing is often denied because citizens are neither donee beneficiaries nor creditor beneficiaries.[56] Citizens are denied standing because the performance is *more strongly* owed to them: they are not mere gift recipients or creditors of the state—they are the state. It seems far more coherent to recognize individual citizens as beneficiaries of government contracts such that they can sue when they suffer a special material injury.

That conclusion, however, threatens to create immense potential liability and to drive the costs of public contracts prohibitively high. But, to the extent that is a concern, the public-at-large might affirmatively contract into less onerous remedial schemes in order to obtain cheaper government contracts.[57] A way to understand the present disfavor toward third-party actions enforcing government contracts may be as a kind of default implied term—that we assume the government meant to limit the remedial options available. While somewhat unsatisfying, that strikes me as a better explanation than a conceptual claim that the public contract duties are simply not owed to individual citizens. The warehouse

[54] The puzzling tort of misfeasance in public office might also be seen as grasping toward a liability for official misconduct without attributing any kind of private control over official actions.

[55] *See* Anthony Jon Waters, *The Property in the Promise: A Study of the Third Party Beneficiary Rule*, 98 Harvard L. Rev. 1109, 1113 (1985).

[56] *See, e.g.*, Martinez v. Socomá Companies, 521 P. 2d 841 (Cal. 1974).

[57] The best argument offered in *Martinez*, *id.*, is that the government limited the available remedies.

owner in *Moch* is situated much like the public well users in *Anderson*; in both cases, the duty in question was owed to them in roughly the same sense.

Undoubtedly this understanding—according to which public duties are not owed to individuals for the purpose of exerting ex ante control but are owed to individuals for the purposes of compensating injuries ex post—is somewhat revisionary. But it has the potential to offer a unified, cross-cutting account of what it means for duties to be owed to the public-at-large, something that has eluded the disparate areas of private law operating independently.

3
This Is a Chapter about Deception

*Courtney M. Cox**

I. Introduction

This chapter is less direct than others in this volume, as perhaps befitting a chapter about deception. But I'll refrain from such mischief at least momentarily and lay my cards on the table: Unlike other chapters, this chapter is *not* about the interstitial function of the chosen concept—here, deception. Instead, it is a cautionary *methodological* tale about the choice and application of interstitial concepts. And to tell it, I will apply a philosophical analysis of deception to a pair of *questions* about a single, siloed example from tort law—that of deceit—rather than compare or consider the workings of this concept across boundaries. Please do not be fooled: this is not a chapter about that tort. It is still a chapter about deception and what it can teach us about our use of interstitial concepts in private law.

Of course, the methodological point—and the caution—is related to the function that interstitial concepts like deception serve, and how they serve it. And so, while I won't provide a full analysis (or defense) of the interstitial function of deception, some brief remarks at the outset are appropriate.

Interstitial concepts serve different functions. Some serve as foundational building blocks of other legal concepts. Others create domains that cut across private law silos. Deception arguably does both: Deception serves as a foundational building block of other legal concepts, like fraud, which is often defined in terms of deception.[1] And, related, deception arguably creates a cross-cutting domain—the so-called law of deception.

These are important functions. Such domains can trigger special procedural requirements and, once entered, often involve standard suites of private law concepts. In deception's case, the effect is far-reaching: Laws addressing

* I thank Bruce Cox, Deborah Denno, Janet Freilich, Andrew Gold, Mark Greenberg, Paul Miller, Seana Shiffrin, Henry Smith, Lior Strahilevitz, Murray Tipping, Steven Weise, Benjamin Zipursky, the editors and other authors in this volume, participants at the UCLA Legal Theory Workshop, Fordham's librarians, and my research assistants.

[1] *E.g.*, *Fraud*, Black's Law Dictionary (11th ed. 2019) (quoting John Willard, A Treatise on Equity Jurisprudence 147 (Platt Potter ed., 1879)).

Courtney M. Cox, *This Is a Chapter about Deception* In: *Interstitial Private Law*. Edited by: Samuel L. Bray, John C.P. Goldberg, Paul B. Miller, and Henry E. Smith, Oxford University Press. © Oxford University Press 2024. DOI: 10.1093/oso/9780197783627.003.0003

deception and its close cousin, misrepresentation, appear in nearly every corner of private law, from the tort of deceit to contract's fraudulent inducement to copyright's factual estoppel doctrine. And they are usually accompanied by procedural hurdles, like heightened pleading requirements, and structured by a standard suite of substantive concepts that includes misrepresentation, materiality, and reliance.[2]

More importantly, judges who are otherwise minimalist—deciding cases incrementally within traditional private law silos—can become maximalists within a domain once identified, aiming to make the domain consistent across silos. Such interstitial concepts thus stand to have greater systemic effects than cabined ones. Or at least, so some commentators have suggested.[3]

Despite this cross-cutting function, the literature is largely siloed—that is, focused on deception in particular contexts, like false advertising, securities, or contract.[4] But some theorists have begun theorizing deception, and close cousins like lies and misrepresentation, between the traditional silos.[5] Such work might seem overdue: in a world swimming with lies and misinformation, getting our collective heads around the legal regulation of lies and deception grows increasingly urgent.

But before we can theorize, we must identify the object of theorizing. That is, what is "deception"?

This question has provided endless fodder for philosophers but received comparatively little attention from lawyers.[6] Then, why should it? We all know, or think we know, what "deception" means: to be deceived is, roughly, to be duped.[7] And the legal concept appears parasitic on, if not directly invoking, this pre-legal concept with which we're all familiar.[8] Since we have a rough idea of

[2] *E.g.*, Fed. R. Civ. P. 9(b); Derry v. Peek [1889] 14 App. Cas. 337, 380; David A. Hoffman, *The Best Puffery Article Ever*, 91 Iowa L. Rev. 1395, 1402 (2006); John C.P. Goldberg & Benjamin C. Zipursky, *The Fraud-on-the-Market Tort*, 66 Vand. L. Rev. 1755, 1756 (2013); Cathay Y.N. Smith, *Truth, Lies, and Copyright*, 20 Nev. L.J. 201, 221 (2019).

[3] Saul Levmore, *A Theory of Deception and Then of Common Law Categories*, 85 Tex. L. Rev. 1359, 1380–81 (2007); *cf.* Jeremy Waldron, *"Transcendental Nonsense" and System in the Law*, 100 Colum. L. Rev. 16, 24–26 (2000).

[4] Courtney M. Cox, *Legitimizing Lies*, 90 Geo. Wash. L. Rev. 297, 306–07 (2022) (summarizing literature).

[5] Seana Valentine Shiffrin, Speech Matters: On Lying, Morality, and the Law (2014); Gregory Klass, *The Law of Deception: A Research Agenda*, 89 U. Colo. L. Rev. 707, 715 (2018); Cox, *supra* note 4; *see also* Richard Craswell, *Taking Information Seriously: Misrepresentation and Nondisclosure in Contract Law and Elsewhere*, 92 Va. L. Rev. 565, 594–607 (2006); Levmore, *Theory*, supra note 3.

[6] Shiffrin, Speech Matters, *supra* note 5; Klass, *Law of Deception*, *supra* note 5; and Stuart P. Green, Lying, Cheating, and Stealing: A Moral Theory of White-Collar Crime (2006) are notable exceptions.

[7] John C.P. Goldberg, Anthony J. Sebok & Benjamin C. Zipursky, *The Place of Reliance in Fraud*, 48 Ariz. L. Rev. 1001, 1004–06, n. 4, 1020 (2006); Goldberg & Zipursky, *supra* note 2, at 1758, 1761.

[8] *Deception*, Black's, *supra* note 1; *see also infra* Part II and note 18.

what deception is, why get more specific in the manner of philosophers? What a tedious distraction.

And yet. Tedious or not, it is critical how we specify the object of inquiry—especially for concepts, like deception, that create or stand to create such cross-cutting domains. Conceptual groundwork not only determines the cases deemed relevant, but also the connections made. And so too, the path of the law—if it is in fact true that interstitial concepts can function in this manner, causing judges and those who guide them to become maximalists within an area of law once identified.[9]

So, that is the goal of this chapter: conceptual housekeeping in service of a methodological point. I begin with what deception is, before turning to why it matters. Unlike other chapters, I won't offer a cross-cutting analysis of deception's interstitial function beyond these brief remarks. Instead, I use the so-called law of deception's leading example—the tort of deceit—to tell a cautionary methodological tale about our choice and use of interstitial concepts.

Again, please do not be tricked. My point is not about the single siloed example. And while I motivate the questions I raise about it—convincingly, I hope!—I do not answer them here.[10] My point is rather about our ability to ask the questions, and how our use of interstitial concepts might limit our ability to see them.

II. What Is Deception?

The natural first question is this: What is "deception"? The answer may seem obvious, so obvious that some deception theorists don't bother to ask.[11] Most working on deception have a clear sense of the cases they are interested in, and many of them clearly involve deception.[12] We could just start there, and allow the law to guide us by examining what *the law* regards as deception—"legal deception"—and then see if the law has any consistency in its treatment of "legal deception," when it's permitted or when not and what kind of harms come from it.[13]

There are many ways to skin a cat, and those approaches have proven fruitful.[14] But one reason it may seem obvious what deception is—particularly

[9] *E.g.*, Levmore, *Theory*, *supra* note 3; Saul Levmore, *Judging Deception*, 74 U. Chi. L. Rev. 1779, 1792 (2007).

[10] I plan to elsewhere.

[11] *E.g.*, Levmore, *Theory*, *supra* note 3.

[12] *Id.*

[13] Gregory Klass, *Meaning, Purpose, and Cause in the Law of Deception*, 100 Geo. L.J. 449, 450 (2012) (developing framework for how "laws of deception determine their regulatory objects"—i.e., "identify[] behavior informationally significant enough to merit legal attention"); *cf.* Craswell, *supra* note 5, at 601.

[14] *E.g.*, *id.*

given that the law turns out *not* to be consistent in its treatment of deceptive acts[15]—is that we have pre-legal concepts of deception. Deception is unlike other legal concepts, say property or intellectual property, where it's debatable whether we have something approaching a clear pre-legal concept independent of legal regimes.[16] And even if some pre-legal concepts diverge from their legal analog so dramatically that the pre-legal concept is not only irrelevant but perhaps distinctively unhelpful,[17] deception is not one of them: legal usage of deception generally draws on the pre-legal concept.[18] One might even say that *legal* deception is at most, to borrow John Gardner's term, "legally shaped"—that is, it is "legally created only on the back of an attempt at legal recognition of [the] extra-legal" concept.[19]

So, it would seem worth at least one attempt at beginning at the beginning, with the pre-legal concept, and seeing where it takes us.

That said, our aim is ultimately *legal* theory, and so we can afford to be a little rough and ready. My aim in this section is thus a *working* definition, or more accurately, clusters of definitions. We need not resolve any philosophical debates about what, *exactly*, constitutes the necessary and sufficient conditions for deception. It will be enough to have a competent working definition, or definitions (plural), to grasp our subject and its conceptual fault lines.

A. Some Working Definitions

Deception is commonly defined as follows:

(D0) A *deceives* B when A [intentionally] causes B to have a false belief.[20]

But this simple definition leaves much unanswered. There are important clarifications it omits, including about A's beliefs, A's intentions, how B comes to have the false belief, and how A's beliefs and intentions relate to B's false belief (if at all).

15 Cox, *supra* note 4, at 309–12, 367–70; Hoffman, *supra* note 2, at 1405.

16 *Cf.* Letter from Thomas Jefferson to Isaac McPherson (August 13, 1813), *in* 13 Thomas Jefferson, The Writings of Thomas Jefferson 326, 333–35 (Andrew A. Lipscomb ed., 1905).

17 *E.g.*, Stephen A. Smith, *The Deed, Not the Motive: Fiduciary Law without Loyalty*, Contract, Status, and Fiduciary Law 213, 220–21 (Paul B. Miller & Andrew S. Gold eds., 2016).

18 For example, Black's definition might be seen as an imprecise version of the working definitions introduced in Part II.A. *Deception*, Black's, *supra* note 1 (defining deception as "1. The act of deliberately causing someone to believe that something is true when the actor knows it to be false. 2. A trick intended to make a person believe something untrue.").

19 John Gardner, Torts and Other Wrongs 344–45 (2019).

20 *Cf. Deception*, Black's, *supra* note 1; Klass, *Law of Deception*, *supra* note 5, at 711; Shiffrin, Speech Matters, *supra* note 5, at 19–21.

I could proceed by working through incremental improvements on D0, as is often done in philosophical literature. But I understand lawyers are an impatient bunch—I am also one—and so instead I'll put some alternative definitions on the table and then explain the changes from D0 and the reasons for them in what follows.

(D1) A *deceives* B as to P when A, intending for B to conclude that P (or something in the vicinity of P), acts so as to cause B to conclude that P (or something in the vicinity of P), where P is false, and A has the relevant beliefs as to P.

(D2) A *deceives* B as to P when A, intending to communicate or imply to B that P (or something in the vicinity of P), acts so as to cause B to conclude that P (or something in the vicinity of P), where P is false, and A has the relevant beliefs as to P.

where "A has the relevant beliefs as to P" is given by one or some combination of the following:

(B1) A believes that P is false.
(B2) A doesn't believe that P is true.
(B3) A doesn't believe that P is false.
(B4) A believes that P is true.

We could take any of these as our core definition of deception. Philosophers might argue over which alternative is better, but we needn't let that detain us. I'll refer back to these—and their distinctions—in Part III.

Something to note at the outset is that these definitions don't say anything about whether the deception—or the intent, or action, or result—is *wrongful*. One might sensibly use moral valence as a limitation, to make the field of study more manageable, particularly if the object of theorizing is how the law can *regulate* or *limit* the bad instances of the act. Others have used this approach to make good progress on design problems related to such laws.[21]

I do not adopt this limit for two reasons. First, it's not necessary for our purposes. And second, there are interesting things to be uncovered by not assuming as much.[22] To quote another deception theorist, "it is the fact that deception is sometimes acceptable and sometimes not that makes the subject interesting."[23]

[21] Klass, *Law of Deception*, *supra* note 5; Klass, *Meaning*, *supra* note 13.

[22] Cox, *supra* note 4; Janet Freilich, *Prophetic Patents*, 53 U.C. Davis L. Rev. 663 (2019); Brief of *The Onion* as Amicus Curiae in support of Petitioner, Novak v. City of Parma, No. 22-293 (S. Ct.), *cert. denied*, 143 S. Ct. 773 (February 21, 2023) [hereinafter Onion Amicus].

[23] Levmore, *Theory*, *supra* note 3, at 1359, 1366.

But you might think that even a neutrally described concept needs to at least accord with the negative connotation generally ascribed to it.[24] That is, you might think that, in deciding between some narrower definition X and some broader definition Y, you should stick with the narrower X if expanding to Y only adds "innocent" behavior. Those inclined to this view are likely to prefer some combination of (D1) and/or (D2) with (B1) and/or (B2), and to see (D2) with (B3) and (B4) as outside the core concept of deception. If this is you, I encourage you to note it now, for reference when we turn to Part III.

B. B's False Belief

Perhaps the only point on which nearly everyone agrees is that deception involves the imparting of false belief(s). One way to think about beliefs, including false beliefs, is to take the content of beliefs to be propositional. That is, the objects of belief are propositions—claims that can be either true or false.[25] Philosophers often describe a belief of B's thus: "B believes that P," where P is some proposition (e.g., "it's raining"). If P is true—if it is in fact raining—then B has a true belief. And if P is not true, then B has a false belief. And so, to say that B has a false belief is simply to say that there is some proposition, P, which B thinks is true but is actually false.

An important problem in laws dealing with misrepresentation is the need to interpret what proposition has been represented so that it can be determined whether that proposition is true. That is, for any alleged misrepresentation, we need to know, *inter alia*:

1. What is the content of the alleged misrepresentation—i.e., what is P?
2. Is P a proposition (i.e., the kind of thing that *could* be true or false)?[26]
3. Is P true or false?

The same seems true for deception. To determine whether B has a false belief, we need to know:

1. What does B believe—i.e., what is P?
2. Is P a proposition (i.e., the kind of thing that *could* be true or false)?
3. Is P true or false?

[24] Thomas L. Carson, Lying and Deception: Theory and Practice 47 (2010).
[25] This isn't clearly true, but it is a standard reading that will serve our purposes.
[26] The law usually expresses the requirement that a misrepresentation be a proposition by requiring a misrepresentation "of fact."

The significance of propositions to both misrepresentations and deception creates a host of interpretative design problems for the law, which Gregory Klass has helpfully begun elucidating.[27]

But, you might wonder, why spell out "B believes P, where P is false" if we know that determining whether "B has a false belief" requires determining both the content of B's belief and whether it's false? The answer is that doing so enables us to evaluate whether B's false belief relates in important ways to what A has done. When we ask whether A has deceived B—whether, following D0, A has caused B to have a false belief—we need to know whether the false belief that B has is one that was *caused* by A. And if you agree with the inclusion of "intentionally" in D0, then we further need to know whether the false belief that B has is one that was *intentionally caused* by A. But to do all this, we need to identify the content of the false belief so that we can evaluate whether *that* belief was brought about by something A has done. By saying "A has caused B to believe P, and P is false," we are able to break our inquiry into its component parts more clearly: Does B believe P? And if so, did A cause B to believe that P? Did A intend to cause B to believe that P (as opposed to say, intending to cause B to believe that Q)? And is P false?

But there's a difficulty: deception might not be strictly propositional. As Carson explains:

> Suppose that I intend to bring it about that you are confused and have certain false beliefs. I know that what I am doing will cause you to have a number of false beliefs, but I do not have a very clear view of which false beliefs I am likely to cause you. So, there is no particular false proposition [P] that I intend to cause you to believe. Should we count this as deception?[28]

Carson argues that whether this counts as deception will depend on whether we can "specify what the deception is *about*."[29] I am inclined to agree. That is, to count as deception, A must intend to cause B to have false beliefs about *something* (e.g., the election) even if A doesn't intend for B to falsely believe a particular *proposition* (e.g., "Some people in Chicago voted twice.").[30] By contrast, A does *not* deceive B when A intends only to cause B to have "many false beliefs so that B will be confused and unable to act in a certain situation," but A has "no idea of what those false beliefs are about."[31] In this latter situation, A might *confuse* B,

27 *E.g.*, Klass, *Law of Deception*, *supra* note 5.
28 CARSON, *supra* note 24, at 49.
29 *Id.*
30 *Id.*
31 *Id.* (cleaned up to use A and B).

but it would be strange to say that A *deceived* B "because there's nothing she has deceived B *about*."[32]

For this reason, I'm inclined to agree with Carson that deception is a *tripartite* relationship. That is, it isn't "A deceives B" simpliciter, but "A deceives B *as to*" something. And also that for A to deceive B, it isn't necessary that B come to believe a particular proposition P (where P is false), only that B come to believe something related to the subject matter of P (where that is also false). There's probably a more elegant way to cash this out, but for our working definitions D1 and D2, I have revised D0 from a definition of "A deceives B" simpliciter to "A deceives B *as to P*" and changed "B has a false belief" to "B believes P (or something in the vicinity of P)."

In short, these changes emphasize that, for there to be deception, B must come to have a belief, P; P must be false; and P must relate to other aspects of deception in important ways, causally and otherwise.

C. Causing False Beliefs in the Right Way

Note that the requirement of false belief just discussed entails a success condition: for A to deceive B as to P, it must be the case that A actually causes B to believe P. But it is generally thought that A must cause B to have that belief *in the right way*. This is why D0's "causes B *to have* a false belief" has been modified to "cause[s] B *to conclude*" in D1 and D2.[33]

What is the right way? It's easiest to understand this by considering alternative methods for causing B to have a false belief that would not count as deception. Suppose an evil scientist stimulates your brain with electrodes, to plant a belief that "it's raining." Assuming it's not raining, has he deceived you? On most accounts, no. He has not operated on your reasoning capacities in the correct way.

But what if he stimulates your brain so you *perceive* rain—that is, he stimulates your brain so that you hear the sound of rain and see water on the window that's not there—and you conclude, based on your perceptions, that "it's raining." Has he deceived you? It would seem he has, much as if he had had his assistant simulate the attributes of rain by spraying water and playing a white noise recording on hidden speakers—and you, seeing water and hearing rain, had concluded "it's raining."

What these examples show is that deception is not a one-sided affair. For B to be deceived by A, B is not totally inert: B must incorporate the

[32] *Id.* (cleaned up to use A and B).
[33] *Cf.* Goldberg, Sebok & Zipursky, *Reliance*, *supra* note 7, at 1012, n. 37.

information presented by A (be it in the form of simulated rain or in the form of a lie) and choose whether to adopt (or maintain[34]) a belief based on it. B's belief must be an inference from the perception caused by A, or a belief in what is communicated by A.

I will pause here to observe that this *causing in the right way* that forms part of the pre-legal concept of deception has an analogy in the legal elements of the related tort of deceit, namely, *reliance*.[35] For A to commit the tort of deceit against B, it is not enough for A to communicate to B some falsehood; B must come to believe that falsehood as a result of A's communication. Of course, legal reliance is more than mere epistemic reliance: To state a claim for deceit, B must not only rely on A's misrepresentation as input into the *epistemic* process of *concluding* that P. Rather, B must also then rely on the conclusion that P as an input into *practical* deliberations over whether to ψ, where choosing to ψ would be to B's detriment. Whatever the disvalue of false beliefs, merely being put in a poorer *epistemic* position is generally insufficient for the legal concept of reliance.

But I digress. The important point is that our pre-legal concept requires that B's false belief be caused in the right way, and this is what I hope to communicate by using the phrase "B *concludes* that P" in D1 and D2.

Before moving on, I want to say one more thing about the causal mechanism: By pointing out its necessity, I make no claim about whether B is conscious of this process.[36] We often accept the testimony of others without reflecting upon whether we should, just as we make inferences based on our sensory perceptions without consciously connecting "sounds like rain" to "is raining." And since I make no claim about this, one might wonder whether the distinction I began with at the outset truly matters: What is the difference between implanting the belief directly through the manipulation of neurons and presenting B with some stimuli that causes B to subconsciously reach the conclusion that P? I don't have a ready answer to this question, but observe that it's worth pondering, especially for those who wish to better understand the pre-legal *causal mechanism* and its analogous legal concept of *reliance*, and especially in an age of technology designed to operate on our rational faculties in just this subconscious manner.

34 SHIFFRIN, SPEECH MATTERS, *supra* note 5, at 19–20.

35 Goldberg, Sebok & Zipursky, *Reliance*, *supra* note 7.

36 To wit: I thought I worked out the evil scientist example myself, but it also appears in Carson's discussion of Mahon. CARSON, *supra* note 24, at 50–51; James Mahon, *A Definition of Deceiving*, 21 INT'L J. APP. PHIL. 181, 185, 188–90 (2007) (citing Gary Fuller, *Other-Deception*, 7 SW. J. PHIL. 23 (1976)).

D. A's Intent

The methods of deception are bounded only by imagination. A can deceive B through direct lies ("The town isn't planning to build a road through here.") or by mere misleading ("There is no improper relationship."). A can deceive B through loaded questions ("Have you stopped cheating on your spouse?"), or through omissions in contexts where silence has meaning.

These methods need not be verbal. Deceptive methods include acts calculated to convey false impressions, like wearing a disguise, faking an injury before a referee, or "answering" your phone to avoid small talk.

Because the methods of deception appear limitless, there's often thought a need to distinguish between situations where A's actions give rise to a mistaken inference, and those where A's actions *deceive*. Consider:

> A keeps an umbrella in her office. Suppose A uses it to walk home in the rain Monday evening. Tuesday morning, A brings the umbrella back to the office, and her colleague B sees A carrying it. B knows that A pays close attention to the forecast and mistakenly infers that A has brought the umbrella because it is likely to rain.[37]

Here, A's actions cause B to have a false belief (about either the likelihood of rain, or A's beliefs about the likelihood of rain). But it's not clear that A has *deceived* B.

Examples like these have motivated theorists to suggest various limitations when developing an account of deception. Two such limitations concern A's mental states.[38] The first is that A must have the requisite sort of intent, usually characterized as an intent to deceive. The second is that A must themselves have the relevant sort of belief with respect to P. I will address intent first; I will turn to A's beliefs in the next section.

What's the requisite sort of intent? It's often thought that the relevant intent is that A must intend *to deceive* B.[39] Indeed, such intent will be present in many cases of interest to deception theorists.[40]

But this kind of intent—intent to deceive—will be missing in some clear cases of deception. This is true whether the intent is simply to deceive, or more generally, to "influence B's mental contents."[41] Consider the reluctant perjurer: A is a mobster who lies on the stand to avoid retaliation, but does not intend to deceive

[37] Klass, *Law of Deception*, *supra* note 5, at 712 (cleaned up to use A and B).
[38] *Id.* at 713 (using example to motivate a third limitation to "*wrongfully* caus[ing] a false belief in another") (emphasis added).
[39] Carson, *supra* note 24.
[40] *E.g.*, Levmore, *Theory*, *supra* note 3.
[41] Shiffrin, Speech Matters, *supra* note 5, at 21.

the jury—he even hopes the jury *won't* believe him.[42] Alas, incredulously and just his luck, juror B is gullible and believes A's lies. Has A deceived B? I think the clear answer is yes.

What makes this a clear case of deception? It's not that A intends to deceive. It's that A intends to state, imply, or give a particular impression as to P. Usually, when an actor intends to communicate or imply (by speech or action) that P, they also intend for their audience to then believe that P. But perhaps, as with lying, there are exceptions, and the reluctant perjurer is again one of them. One can deceive without intending to deceive—without intending to impart a false belief—in those cases where one intends to communicate a falsehood without the aim of being believed and yet is believed anyways. That is what happens in the case of the reluctant perjurer who encounters a gullible juror—the reluctantly successful perjurer. It also explains why the umbrella mistake is not deception: A doesn't intend to communicate or imply anything, to anyone, by returning her umbrella to work.

This is the sort of intent and case I aim to capture by making the change from D1's "intending for B to conclude that P . . ." to D2's "intending to communicate or imply to B that P . . . ."[43]

E. A's Beliefs

A final limitation arises with respect to A's beliefs as to P, again with an eye to distinguishing between cases of mistake and deception. Consider the case of the misinformed:

> A is told something that is false. A believes what he is told and repeats it to B, thereby causing B to believe it. In reporting this to B, A is not trying to bring it about that B believes anything that A does not believe to be true.[44]

Does A deceive B?

Carson recognizes that linguistic intuitions might differ. He writes, "Some people think that it makes sense to describe this as a case in which I deceived you 'albeit without intending to do so.'"[45] Others, by contrast, prefer to use the

[42] CARSON, *supra* note 24, at 20 (using example in analysis of "lying").

[43] Another way to accommodate the reluctant perjurer is to add a rider to recognize a second sort of deception that occurs when A frustrates B's epistemic expectations that A "will not permit or facilitate ... a false impression of the facts." SHIFFRIN, SPEECH MATTERS, *supra* note 5, at 21.

[44] CARSON, *supra* note 24, at 47 (cleaned up to use A and B).

[45] *Id.*

term "mislead" to mark the distinction between intentionally and unintentionally causing another to have a false belief.[46]

For his part, Carson believes that we should not count this case as one of deception because "[t]he negative evaluative connotations of the term 'deception' are inappropriate if we hold that there can be completely unintentional deception (for which people are often blameless)."[47]

The simple way of making the distinction—whether one uses the labels "deception" and "inadvertent deception" or "deceive" and "mislead"—is to add a condition specifying A's beliefs with respect to P:

(B1) A believes that P is false.
(B2) A doesn't believe that P is true.
(B3) A doesn't believe that P is false.
(B4) A believes that P is true.

Carson would exclude cases where A believes P is true (B4), and perhaps cases where A does not believe that P is false (B3), from the concept of deception. He bases this exclusion on the negative evaluative connotation of the term. As to (B1) and (B2), Carson doesn't see a principled basis to distinguish between them, at least not on the basis of ordinary language; and instead suggests proceeding with "narrower" (B1) and "broader" (B2) concepts of deception.[48]

I don't have strong intuitions about this case but am inclined to remain neutral for now. I am just as interested in when unintentional deception is wrongful as when knowing deception is not.[49] And I don't think the evaluative connotations are as clear-cut as Carson suggests: online misinformation and conspiracies—spread between believers—suggests the negative connotation is appropriate in at least some (B4) cases.[50]

But we need not resolve which is the best *philosophical* position today. It's enough to simply recognize the conceptual distinctions in identifying potential activities of interest.

III. Who Cares

So what? So far you have skimmed (or skipped!) half a dozen pages of dense prose, and very little of it has been about the law. On the one hand, this is to be

[46] *Id.*
[47] *Id.*
[48] *Id.* at 48.
[49] *Cf.* Seana Shiffrin, *Learning about Deception from Lawyers*, 93 Aristotelian Soc'y Supplementary Volume 69, 71–72 (2019).
[50] *Id.*

expected: you are, after all, reading "a chapter about deception" in a volume on theory. On the other hand, this is a volume on *legal* theory, and so, you might feel you have been tricked into reading philosophy. What is the point?

One reason to begin with a *pre-legal* concept rather than jumping straight to the legal concepts is that it enables us to ask how the law targets or tracks that pre-legal object. This mode of proceeding is obviously useful to clients, on a practical level, when the pre-legal object in question is a tangible object—like a horse. It allows lawyers to identify laws and regulations of interest, and to draw connections between them, that will guide decisions about what you need to do if you have a horse or a horse business.[51] The same can be said for an abstract object, like the pre-legal concept of deception. For deception is key to parody, and *The Onion* needs to know what liability is created by their craft—and especially whether it's obvious that it's "obvious that parodists cannot be prosecuted for telling a joke with a straight face."[52]

This mode of proceeding can also generate insights for theorists. For one, not all deception is bad, even though it is still, analytically, *very much deception*. Sometimes the law allows it and sometimes not. But the law on this score is perplexing and its shadow unclear. The law even legitimizes some deceptive lies and is not above resorting to euphemisms when it does.[53] And so, the difficulties encountered by parodic deceivers—and investigative journalists and civil rights advocates and even lawyers—is part of what makes "the law of deception" so endlessly fascinating in a way that "the law of the horse" is perhaps not.

But I have begun waging that battle elsewhere, about the value of deception and the breadth of the law's response to it.[54] Here, I turn my sights instead to a second, perhaps more important point to be made about interstitial theorizing on deception and the so-called law of deception.

The point is this: beginning with the pre-legal concept of deception allows us to better assess the relevant legal concepts and what parts of the so-called law of deception are really about. For I'm no longer convinced they are about deception, and we risk unnecessarily tying our hands by supposing otherwise.

I here focus on only one example, the tort of deceit. But as the leading example of the "law of deception," it is illustrative of the danger: if we risk unnecessarily tying our hands here, where else might we run astray if "deception" creates a cross-cutting domain?

51 *E.g., Equine* (Hodgson Russ LLP) <https://perma.cc/FGB8-RHN8> accessed March 30, 2023.

52 Onion Amicus, *supra* note 22, at 15. Unfortunately, as this case on qualified immunity shows, it is apparently not obvious that it is obvious that it is obvious. Novak v. City of Parma, 932 F.3d 421 (2019) (denying motion to dismiss), 33 F.4th 296 (2022) (granting summary judgment), *cert denied*, 143 S. Ct. 773 (2023).

53 Another term for lies. Cox, *supra* note 4, at 299, 323–36, 369–70.

54 *Id.*

A. Deceit Is Not Deception

Deceit is usually thought to be about deception. This association is unsurprising. The ancient tort shares a name with the pre-legal concept. And deception theorists (myself included) have reinforced the connection: the common law tort is usually listed first as a quintessential example of "the law of deception"[55] or of "lying-related causes of action."[56]

But armed with the pre-legal concept, it becomes apparent that deceit and deception are not the same. I begin with an observation by John Goldberg, Anthony Sebok, and Benjamin Zipursky, that reliance plays a central role in common-law fraud—the modern label for the tort of deceit.[57] Throughout, I use "deceit" to refer to that tort, and "deception" to the pre-legal concept(s) discussed in Part II.

Reliance is a common element of the tort of deceit. For example, the Second Restatement describes the tort of deceit (under the name "fraudulent misrepresentation") as follows:

> One who fraudulently makes a misrepresentation of fact, opinion, intention or law for the purpose of inducing another to act or to refrain from action *in reliance upon it*, is subject to liability to the other in deceit for pecuniary loss caused to him *by his justifiable reliance upon* the misrepresentation.[58]

Note that "reliance" appears twice.

Unfortunately, the term "reliance" frequently goes undefined. But we can begin with what it is not. It is not "just the label" for causation in deceit claims, or an "excessive-liability filter," "tempting" though it may be to suppose.[59] "The easiest way to appreciate this point is to observe that even if a misrepresentation actually harms a victim, the victim has no claim for deceit if she does not rely upon it."[60] This is true even where the misrepresentation not only causes the loss, but also causes the victim's actions that led to her loss. For example, where A makes misrepresentations to B, and on that basis, B causes C to act to her detriment,

[55] *E.g.*, Thomas L. Eovaldi, *The Market for Consumer Product Evaluations: An Analysis and a Proposal*, 79 Nw. U. L. Rev. 1235, 1235 (1984); Goldberg, Sebok & Zipursky, *Reliance*, *supra* note 7, at 1023–26; Klass, *Law of Deception*, *supra* note 5, at 707.

[56] *E.g.*, Cox, *supra* note 4, at 314; *see also* Goldberg, Sebok & Zipursky, *Reliance*, *supra* note 7, at 1003, 1015.

[57] Goldberg, Sebok & Zipursky, *Reliance*, *supra* note 7.

[58] Restatement (Second) of Torts § 525 (1965) (emphasis added); *accord* Restatement (Third) of Torts: Liability for Economic Harm § 9 (2020).

[59] Goldberg, Sebok & Zipursky, *Reliance*, *supra* note 7, at 1002; Goldberg & Zipursky, *supra* note 2, at 1760.

[60] Goldberg & Zipursky, *supra* note 2, at 1760; *see also* Goldberg, Sebok & Zipursky, *Reliance*, *supra* note 7, at 1002.

C generally cannot recover against A in deceit (whatever other recourse she might have) because she did not *rely* on A's misrepresentations.[61]

Of course, just because reliance isn't a causal filter doesn't mean it has a central role. Reliance might still play second fiddle to misrepresentation, narrowing claims for deceit to a specific subset of cases where the plaintiff was harmed by misrepresentations *made to them*. Such limitations are common in the law governing lies, especially given First Amendment and practical considerations.

But Goldberg, Sebok, and Zipursky think otherwise. They argue that reliance isn't a filter, and that the wrong of deceit isn't, at its core, about misrepresentation. Reliance is key to understanding what that wrong is.

They begin by observing that when a plaintiff brings a claim for deceit—rather than for some other misrepresentation-based harm—he complains of having been "deceived into making a detrimental choice that he would not otherwise have made."[62] Reliance is necessary to make this showing: to be duped, it's not enough to allege that the defendant made a misrepresentation. Rather, the misrepresentation must interfere in the plaintiff's decision-making process. That is, a plaintiff must allege that they believed the misrepresentation and then acted upon it. For example, a plaintiff did not rely in purchasing a fake painting where she simply wrote a check at the request of her son-in-law (who had chosen the painting based on defendant-seller's misrepresentations).[63]

By contrast, where reliance is not required, "the crux" of such complaints is usually "*not* that she had been deceived."[64] Rather, "the gist" of such reliance-free misrepresentation-based complaints is that the misrepresentation set off a causal chain that harmed the plaintiff, *not* that the defendant's acts were a "wrongful interference" with the plaintiff's "decisional capacity."[65]

So reliance matters to deceit—indeed, is central to it—because it amounts to the allegation that the defendant wrongfully interfered with the plaintiff's decisional autonomy.

The argument up to this point likely sounds a lot like an argument that deceit is in fact about deception and not something else. But this is only because it's an argument that the wrong of deceit isn't principally about lies, or misrepresentations. But if not misrepresentations, then what? Deception seems like the obvious candidate. And so Goldberg, Sebok, and Zipursky conclude: "To commit fraud . . . is to violate a relational legal directive that enjoins the making

61 Goldberg & Zipursky, *supra* note 2, at 1760; *see also* Goldberg, Sebok & Zipursky, *Reliance*, *supra* note 7, at 1002.

62 Goldberg, Sebok & Zipursky, *Reliance*, *supra* note 7, at 1023.

63 Rosen v. Spanierman, 894 F.2d 28, 30, 33–34 (2d Cir. 1990).

64 Goldberg, Sebok & Zipursky, *Reliance*, *supra* note 7, 1022–24 (discussing Langridge v. Levy (1837) 2 M&W 519, 150 Eng. Rep. 863; Randi W. v. Muroc Joint Unified Sch. Dist., 929 P.2d 582 (Cal. 1997)).

65 Goldberg, Sebok & Zipursky, *Reliance*, *supra* note 7, at 1022.

of a misrepresentation of fact *for the purpose of deceiving another* into making a choice that is to the other's detriment."[66]

But we should only conclude this if reliance is about being deceived. And it is not.

To see this about reliance, note that deception, like misrepresentation, is also not enough to show reliance. Suppose A is selling a house, and talks to B who comes to the open house. A tells B "the Green Line extension will have a station nearby," which is false and A knows it. B believes A, concluding that P: the Green Line extension will have a station nearby. But no matter: B was just a busy-body not planning to purchase and doesn't buy the house.

On our analysis of Part II, A has deceived B as to P. But has B *relied* on A's misrepresentation? No. B may be deceived as to P. But B has not incorporated P into her decision-making process about whether to take some further action. B was not going to buy the house, regardless of whether P was true.

Perhaps that's not enough to show that reliance is not about being deceived: B did not act in the last example and so could not have relied in acting to their detriment. So consider another case, where B is not only deceived, but does what A wants. Suppose, as before, A is selling a house and makes the false claim to B about the Green Line extension. This time, B *is* a prospective buyer. Once again, B believes A, concluding that P: the Green Line extension will soon be built nearby. But B doesn't care about public transportation, or its effect on the value of the house: she hates the environment and is filthy rich. B, not caring about price, outbids other buyers through an automatic, uncapped escalation clause; the final price is of course inflated, since most of those who bid are willing to pay more for the feature they (falsely) believe exists.

On our analysis of Part II, A has deceived B as to P. But B did not rely on P because—even though B was deceived, B did what A wanted, and the misrepresentation caused B to overpay—P did not feature in B's decision-making. And so, B cannot be said to have relied on P, regardless of what B believed as to P.[67] The wrong is not complete (even if B might have other modes of recourse).

But wait! Perhaps the problem is that we're confusing reliance with causation, much as the courts occasionally do. Let's consider two final examples to see the distinction, one with deception and reliance but no causation, and the other with deception and causation but no reliance.

First, consider the case where B relies on a false belief imparted by A, but B's reliance doesn't cause her to act to her detriment. Suppose the same facts as

[66] *Id.* at 1012.

[67] Tyler v. Turner Ctr. Sys., 147 A.287, 288–89 (Vt. 1929) (no reliance where plaintiff learned of deception before completing transaction); Gridley v. Sayre & Fisher Co., 409 F. Supp. 1266, 1273–74 (D.S.D. 1976) (no reliance where plaintiffs had already decided to act before hearing defendant's misrepresentations).

before—A deceives B as to P—but this time, B *does* care about public transportation and its effect on home values. B takes this into consideration and decides to bid. Now, reliance is satisfied: B decides to bid in reliance upon P. The wrong is nearly complete; her decisional autonomy has been interfered with. But before B can place a bid, someone outbids her. And so B's reliance on A's misrepresentation does not cause damage. That is, here we have reliance without causation. The deception interfered with B's decision-making process, leading her to a detrimental decision; happily the fates intervened to prevent her from acting, breaking the causal chain.

Contrast this with a case where deception does cause B to act to her detriment, but without reliance. Suppose as before that A makes misrepresentations as to P (the Green Line extension) at an open house. The open house is attended by B and her mother C, who is planning to buy a home for B as a gift. C smiles when she hears of the Green Line extension—she loves eco-friendly transportation—but doesn't weigh in on whether to purchase; that is B's decision alone, and, in any event, transport is nice but not a reason for choosing this apartment over an identical one the next stop up. But B sees her mother's smile and, taking it as a good omen (her mother hardly ever smiles), decides she wants the house. A and B settle on a price—which again is inflated by A's misrepresentations to other bidders—and C whips out her checkbook. They all raise a glass of champagne to celebrate.

On our analysis of Part II, A deceived C as to P. Such deception caused C to act to her detriment in buying the house: Had A not deceived C, C would not have smiled, B would not have decided she wanted the home, and C would not have bought it. And this decision to buy the property resulted in C's pecuniary loss: overpaying for the property. But C cannot be said to have relied on P, because P did not factor into C's decision-making.[68]

What I hope these examples show is that reliance is not merely believing the substance of a defendant's falsehood. It is something more. And so just as A does not commit deceit merely by making a misrepresentation, A does not commit deceit merely by deceiving B. The deception must interfere with B's decision-making process. Just as reliance shows deceit is not about harmful misrepresentations, reliance shows that deceit is not about harmful deceptions.

This interference, not the deception, is why reliance has such a central place in deceit: it is not just believing the falsehood—being deceived—but *relying* upon that falsehood *in the decision-making process*. And it's this interference with the decision-making process that Goldberg, Sebok, and Zipursky rightfully point out is the wrong of common law deceit.

[68] This example is based on Rosen v. Spanierman, 894 F.2d 28, 33–34 (2d Cir. 1990), discussed in Goldberg, Sebok & Zipursky, *Reliance*, *supra* note 7, at 1005. *See also* Gridley, *supra* note 67, at 1273–74.

There's a name for such covert interference with another's decision-making: manipulation.[69] But deception is only one of its tools.[70]

B. What Is Deceit?

Still, you might wonder, what difference does it make to say that deceit is "about deception" or not? You might think that this is a purely semantic difference and that I am being pedantic: Deceit obviously has to do with deception, for even if it's about manipulation, it's about manipulation *by means of deception*. That's all I have managed to show. This "about" business is academic nonsense.

Or is it? Once you see that the core wrong of deceit isn't deception, but manipulation, you can sensibly ask: Why is manipulating using this method—interfering with decisional autonomy in *this* way—the object of the tort (if it is)? What is the basis for limiting deceit to interference using *false beliefs* rather than interfering with some other aspect of the reasoning process? Is the tort so limited? Should it be? Insisting that deceit isn't "about deception" opens the possibility that there may be a choice of two deceits, one narrow, limited to manipulation *by means of* deception, and one broad that does not contain this limit.

This chapter is not the place for a full defense of either claim: that deceit is about manipulation, or that there is a choice of two deceits. For one, the pre-legal concept of manipulation has proven more vexing to philosophers than the pre-legal concept of deception (if you can believe it). For another, this is a chapter about deception. But in this section, I hope to do what I can to motivate the potential existence of this choice. That is, I want to better motivate the questions: Are there two deceits to choose from? Which should we choose? What's stopping us?

To do so, I will first shore up the suggestion that deceit is really about manipulation. It turns out that viewing deceit through the lens of manipulation appears analytically powerful.[71] Then I will cast doubt on whether the tort's elements so understood are really *consistent* with a limitation to the pre-legal concept of deception explored in Part II.

[69] Daniel Susser, Beate Roessler & Helen Nissenbaum, *Technology, Autonomy, and Manipulation*, 8 INTERNET POL'Y REV. 1, 3 (2019).

[70] *Id.*; *see also* Daniel Susser, Beate Roessler & Helen Nissenbaum, *Online Manipulation: Hidden Influences in a Digital World*, 4 GEO. L. TECH. REV. 1 3, 21–22 (2019).

[71] It is also normatively powerful. Fraud is the worst precisely because it interferes with another's reasoning—because it is manipulative; *e.g.*, DANTE ALIGHIERI, THE DIVINE COMEDY (Clive James trans., 2013) canto XXXII, XXXIV. The same is often also said of lies. Christine M. Korsgaard, *The Right to Lie: Kant on Dealing with Evil*, 15 PHIL. & PUB. AFFS. 325, 325–27 (1986); Klass, *Law of Deception*, *supra* note 5, at 713–15 ("Although the law of deception, as I have defined it, captures more than lies, much of it can be justified by appeal to that rule.").

i. Deceit as Manipulation

What is manipulation? A thorough exploration would require another chapter, so for now, I'll borrow the concept of manipulation defended by Daniel Susser, Beate Roessler, and Helen Nissenbaum ("the SRN account").[72] On their view, manipulation is "hidden influence": "manipulating someone means intentionally and covertly influencing their decision-making, by targeting and exploiting their decision-making vulnerabilities."[73]

At the outset, I'll note this view of manipulation bears important affinities to deception. To see them, contrast "manipulation" with two related but distinct concepts: persuasion and coercion. The SRN account defines *persuasion* as an "attempt to influence someone by offering reasons they can think about and evaluate." And it defines *coercion* as "influenc[ing] someone by constraining their options, such that their only rational course of action is the one the coercer intends."[74]

On the SRN account, persuasion and coercion differ from manipulation in an important respect: both persuasion and coercion are "*forthright* forms of influence."[75] By contrast, manipulation is "hidden—we only learn that someone was trying to steer our decision-making after the fact, if we ever find out at all."[76]

The hidden nature of the influence is what might cause manipulation and deception to be readily confused. Both are appropriately described as "trickery."[77] Both make victims feel "played."[78] And both "disrupt[] our capacity for self-authorship" by interfering with our decision-making process without our knowledge.[79]

I'll observe that essentially the *same* phrases are used to describe the tort of deceit.[80] But the tort of deceit is not only described in a similar way as manipulation on the SRN account. The emphasis on covert *interference* with another's *decision-making*—that is, the emphasis on manipulation, rather than mere deception—appears throughout the other elements of deceit. Viewed this way,

72 Susser, Roessler & Nissenbaum, *Technology*, *supra* note 69, at 4.
73 *Id.* (emphasis omitted).
74 *Id.*
75 *Id.*
76 *Id.*
77 *Id.*
78 *Id.*
79 *Id.*
80 *E.g.*, JD James Construction v. PDP Landscaping, No. A-4903-18T3, 2020 WL 5587439, at *3 (N.J. Super. Ct. App. Div., September 18, 2020) ("trick"); Western Reserve Life Assur v. Graben, 233 S.W.3d 360, 376 (Tex. App. 2007) ("using cunning, deception, or artifice to cheat"); *see also* Goldberg, Sebok & Zipursky, *Reliance*, *supra* note 7, at 1011, 1020 ("trick," "dupe"); Goldberg & Zipursky, *supra* note 2, at 1761 ("interference with decisional autonomy").

elements like materiality and reasonableness that are sometimes thought of as "secondary" filters instead gain analytic importance.

Consider materiality first. Materiality is the limitation that for a misrepresentation "[t]o be actionable," it must be "of importance in determining the recipient's course of action at the time the representation is made."[81] Because immaterial lies are unlikely to cause harm, it's tempting to view materiality as yet another requirement that serves a "secondary role" as a filter whose "purpose is not to identify the legal wrongs, but to sort out the correct legal response to them."[82] On this view—the deceit-as-deception view—materiality is a filter that excludes claims based on trivial misrepresentations.

But if, as I suggest, deceit is about *manipulation*, and not merely deception, then the role of the materiality requirement becomes plain: the misrepresentation must be material—must be "of importance in determining a recipient's course of action"—if it's to influence that individual's decisions about their course of action. Otherwise, why would they rely on it? And so, if A makes a misrepresentation to B, but the misrepresentation is not material, it's unlikely that A is trying to manipulate B—that is, it's unlikely that A made the misrepresentation "for the purpose of inducing [B] to act or to refrain from action *in reliance upon it*."[83] For A can deceive B with an immaterial misrepresentation. But A cannot manipulate B with a misrepresentation unless it would affect the reasoning process. Materiality is about manipulation.

This lens also explains a puzzle that arises on the "filter" view of materiality. If materiality just excludes claims based on trivial misrepresentations, then why can a "trivial or even ridiculous" misrepresentation count as material if "the maker knows that the recipient, because of his own peculiarities, is likely to attach importance to it?"[84] That would be a poor filter indeed. But viewing deceit as manipulation, materiality is not a filter; it shows intent to manipulate. And this is the exact reasoning offered by the Second Restatement for recognizing "trivial or even ridiculous" misrepresentations as material.[85]

Now consider another element of deceit, the general rule that reliance must be *reasonable*. It's tempting, again, to view this requirement as serving the secondary role of filtering out frivolous claims, or imposing a kind of contributory negligence carve-out. If a clerk reading *The Onion*'s recent amicus believed it

[81] Restatement (Second), *supra* note 58, at § 525 cmt. e; *id.* at § 538; *accord* Restatement (Third), *supra* note 58, at § 9 cmt. d.

[82] Klass, *Meaning*, *supra* note 13, at 460.

[83] Restatement (Second), *supra* note 58, at § 525; *accord* Restatement (Third), *supra* note 58, at § 9.

[84] Restatement (Second), *supra* note 58, at § 538 cmt. f.

[85] *Id.*

"enjoys a daily readership of 4.3 trillion" and, in reliance on that belief and to their detriment, extolled to their boss that the "single most powerful and influential organization in human history" has weighed in, their boss might well reply, "*Tu stultus es.* You are dumb."[86] Such reliance would not be reasonable. And a claim on it would be foolish, appropriately excluded by a reasonableness filter.

But the reason the clerk's claim would be foolish isn't because the clerk is; and the clerk's stupidity is also not the reason the "reasonable reliance" requirement excludes his claim. It's because the fact that reliance would not be reasonable confirms that *The Onion* obviously did not intend to manipulate him in this manner. *The Onion* only intended to make him do a double take, to illustrate the value of deception in parody.

Recent research seems to confirm that this is, indeed, the correct function of the reasonableness requirement.[87] The reasonableness requirement is not about whether the victim was reasonable to have been deceived, but is descended from the intended reliance rule: the rule that, for a victim to recover, the putative tortfeasor must have *intended to for them to rely*—that is, to manipulate them.[88] Courts relaxed this rule to make it "tougher" on fraudsters, adopting in its place a justifiable reliance rule that served the same purpose while also enabling *unintended* victims to recover.[89] As Mark Gergen explains, usually where plaintiff's reliance is unreasonable, the defendant did not intend for him to rely on it.[90]

A fuller exploration of manipulation, and deceit as manipulation, must be left for another time. But at least on first pass, it seems that viewing deceit through the lens of *manipulation* rather than merely *deception* is likely to be explanatorily powerful, offering a more robust understanding of the tort's elements than viewing them as filters that just limit recourse to "harmful" deceptions. Rather, they support a finding that the victim has been manipulated—that "their decision . . . was not authentically theirs."[91]

ii. A Choice of Two Deceits

I return to the question I wanted to motivate: If deceit is plausibly about manipulation, does it matter the tool? That is, should the tort of deceit be understood (1) broadly, as manipulating another to their detriment—that is, the use of covert influence to cause harm; or (2) narrowly, as limited to cases where the defendant manipulates another to their detriment *by means of a deception*?

86 Coincidentally, this is *The Onion*'s motto. *See* Onion Amicus, *supra* note 22, at 1, 4.
87 Mark P. Gergen, *A Wrong Turn in the Law of Deceit*, 106 GEO. L.J. 555, 559 (2018).
88 *Id.*
89 *Id.* at 558.
90 *Id.* at 559.
91 Goldberg & Zipursky, *supra* note 2, at 1772–73.

The case for the narrower reading is obvious. There's the name of the ancient tort, for one. Then there's the frequent emphasis on the word "misrepresentation," including in the name of the modern tort and the opening clause of its description.[92] Pesky details, perhaps. But reliance might appear to favor the narrow view.[93] The narrow view seems to be the common reading.[94] And to the extent the common readings differ between a broad view and a narrow view, it's not over the line between the broad and narrow views of manipulation, but over whether the tort is really about deception or only misrepresentation.[95]

I trust I needn't belabor the point. The mountain of evidence and arguments favoring the narrow reading could swallow the chapter. The real question is this: Why bother contemplating the broader?

Let's begin with our pre-legal concept analyzed in Part II. I said that one of the only points about deception that nearly all agree upon is that, when A deceives B, A causes B to have false beliefs.[96] But equating falsehoods and false beliefs with misinformation that interferes with decisional autonomy is a dated and simplistic view of how "misinformation" works to subvert our individual and collective reasoning. This is true as a matter of both theory and practice.

As a matter of theory, the problem should have always been apparent. While deceptions are propositional-ish, misinformation is not. As Richard Craswell has argued, the "'quantized' or 'particle-based' view of information" mistakenly assumes that "all bits of information can be decomposed into its smallest particles or bits"—propositions—that can be either true or false.[97] But "information in the real world is more complex than the quantized view suggests": "it is not always possible to separate the true from the false, so even preventing misrepresentation often requires decisions about what bits of accurate information are worth giving up in order to get rid of the inaccurate bits."[98]

Craswell was focused on misrepresentations and disclosure. But the same could be said for deception: it's probably impossible to impart only false beliefs. But how should the law think about manipulation by *deception* when a mix of beliefs, both false and true, are imparted? What ratio of false-to-true

[92] RESTATEMENT (SECOND), *supra* note 58, at § 525; *accord* RESTATEMENT (THIRD), *supra* note 58, at § 9.

[93] Reliance might seem an odd fit for some types of manipulation, like using anxiety-provoking background music to rush a decision. But it fits with at least some nondeceptive ones: you can rely on a person's truthful representations to your detriment, without forming a false belief. These are sometimes characterized as deceptive omissions—but perhaps the simpler way to understand them is that they are manipulative truths. And so it may be that reliance favors narrowing, but of a different sort. (With thanks to Seana Shiffrin for asking whether reliance favors the narrow view.)

[94] *E.g.*, Goldberg, Sebok & Zipursky, *Reliance*, *supra* note 7, at 1012; GOLDBERG, SEBOK & ZIPURSKY, TEACHER'S MANUAL, TORT LAW: RESPONSIBILITIES AND REDRESS 408 (5th ed. 2021).

[95] *Cf.* Goldberg, Sebok & Zipursky, *Reliance*, *supra* note 7, at 1002–03.

[96] *See supra* Part II.B.

[97] Craswell, *supra* note 5, at 569.

[98] *Id.* at 570.

beliefs counts as "deception"? And assuming we could determine the relevant threshold, if some lesser ratio is important to the decision-making process—say, because of how the presentation focuses our attention on particular beliefs (true or not)—would the fact that it's not "deception" mean it isn't covered by deceit? How strange: I never knew philosophers could have such power.

There may well be a principled way to distinguish manipulation *by deception* from manipulation *by other means.* I don't claim there's not, only that it's not obvious there is. And to be sure, even without a principled basis, we could still use a rough working concept for the narrow reading of the tort. Afterall, vagueness hasn't stopped us from drawing legal lines before.

But if there's not a principled basis for distinguishing manipulation generally from manipulation by way of deception, this would seem to favor at least being *open* to the broader reading. And so the relevant question is this: Would the broader view be doctrinally foreclosed?

A full answer to that question requires a deeper dive into the tort of deceit than space allows. But at first pass, the answer seems to be no: the broader view is not only not doctrinally foreclosed; it appears that it may even be more consistent with the evolution of the tort and its equitable origins.[99]

Begin with the pesky detail, about how deceit usually invokes "misrepresentation." It's commonly complained that "fraud" and "misrepresentation" are inconsistently used, covering a range of behavior that seem to exceed their plain meaning.[100] But if you understand deceit as the wrong of manipulation—as not limited to the wrong of misrepresentations—then this looseness is a feature, not a bug.

For example, despite the language of misrepresentation, claims for misdirection—for "play[ing] on inferences other persons are likely to draw from facts or information to which they have access"—commonly sound in deceit.[101] And courts are not only unbothered by the absence of a misrepresentation; they offer "less doctrinal clarity about the elements of a misdirection claim" as a result.[102] This is unsurprising: manipulation by means other than misrepresentation will likely intersect differently with the elements of deceit.

The other elements also don't confine the tort to manipulation by way of deception. We can see this by comparing the elements with our analysis of the prelegal concept of deception.

Consider, for example, the requirement on A's beliefs with respect to P. There's some disagreement among philosophers about whether A deceives B as to P if

[99] Henry E. Smith, *Equity as Meta-Law*, 130 YALE L.J. 1050, 1065–66 (2021).

[100] Goldberg, Sebok & Zipursky, *Reliance*, *supra* note 7, at 1003; *cf.* Klass, *Meaning*, *supra* note 13, at 450–51, 454 n. 9, 464.

[101] Klass, *Meaning*, *supra* note 13, at 464.

[102] *Id.*

A believes P is true (B4) or doesn't believe P to be false (B3).[103] The dominant view seems to be that A does *not* deceive B as to P if A believes P is true; this may be a case of *misleading*, but not *deception*. Even more strongly, there are both broad and narrow dominant views: some believe that for A to deceive B as to P, A must not only lack a belief that P is true (B2), but affirmatively believe that P is false (B1).

If you agree with the dominant view—that for there to be a deception, (B1) or (B2) must apply—then there's a further case for seeing that deceit is not limited to manipulation by way of deception. For deceit doesn't always require a showing that the tortfeasor believed P to be false or even lacked confidence; it's sometimes enough that the tortfeasor not care, that he "knows that he does not have the basis for his representation that he states or implies."[104] (B3) As the Restatement's comments indicate, he might even believe that P is true (B4): "since knowledge implies a firm conviction, a misrepresentation of a fact so made as to assert that the maker knows it, is fraudulent if he is conscious that he has merely a belief in its existence and recognizes that there is a chance, more or less great, that the fact may not be as it is represented."[105]

You might be tempted to explain this away by suggesting that in such cases there are *two* misrepresentations—one as to P and one as to the strength of A's belief that P. And so, although A doesn't deceive B as to P because she believes P is true, she has deceived B as to the strength of her belief.[106] But this explanation doesn't quite capture the situation or comport with the Restatement's characterization: the Restatement does not require a showing that A *deceived* B about the strength of her belief, but rather that "the circumstances *justify* [B's] reliance upon A's supposed knowledge."[107] This makes sense: for even if B were deceived about the strength of A's belief that P, what ultimately interferes in B's decision-making is B's resulting belief that P, not B's belief about A's belief in P.[108] And so

[103] *See supra* Parts II.A, II.E.

[104] Restatement (Second), *supra* note 58, at § 526; *accord* Restatement (Third), *supra* note 58, at § 10.

[105] Restatement (Second), *supra* note 58, at § 526 cmt. e; *accord* Restatement (Third), *supra* note 58, at § 10.

[106] I don't believe intent is required (Part II.D), but if you do—that is, if you believe that to deceive B, A must intend to deceive B—then this move is unavailable: A has not deceived B as to the strength of A's belief that P, because A's intention is to get B to believe P and is indifferent as to what B believes about A's belief that P, provided B comes to believe P. Mahon, *supra* note 36, at 191.

[107] Restatement (Second), *supra* note 58, at § 526, cmt. e, Illustration 1 (emphasis added). Note that while misrepresentations as to A's knowledge or the basis of A's opinions are often imputed, it need not be shown B *relied* on representations (implied or otherwise) about the strength of A's knowledge that P; only that, given such circumstances, it would be *justifiable* for them to rely on A's claim that P.

[108] *Id.* ("A is subject to liability to B for the loss that B suffers through relying upon his statement [that P] if the circumstances justify [B's] reliance upon A's supposed personal knowledge [as to P]"); *accord* Restatement (Third), *supra* note 58, at § 10.

on the dominant view of deception, while A has manipulated B by stating that P, A hasn't deceived B *as to P* because she believes P is true.

Put differently, most contexts are warranting contexts, and assertions made in a warranting context implicitly invite reliance on the speaker's knowledge.[109] Does A *deceive* B when she asserts what she takes to be true, knowing B will probably believe her? That seems an inapt description. No, the more natural way—the dominant way—to describe this is that A *misled* B as to P—she was intentionally careless about B's beliefs as to P because she wanted him to believe that P.

We could descend further into the weeds by debating when and whether A's awareness of a mismatch between the strengths of A's beliefs and B's assumptions about A's beliefs should be characterized as deception. I will spare you.

The point is that there are broader and narrower concepts of deception. Suppose you were inclined to reject (B3) and (B4): that is, you think that A has not deceived B but only *misled* B where A doesn't believe P is false (B3) or where A believes P to be true (B4). If so, then it seems appropriate to say that A manipulated B by *misleading* B as to P—by being *careless* as to B's beliefs as to P—rather than by *deceiving* B as to P. You might appropriately say A tricked B into deciding something on the basis of P; but it would be weird to say A "tricked" B into *believing* that P, as A did not intend any such trick—she thought P was true. If you were not inclined to reject (B3) and (B4), then maybe you would count these as deception.

In any event, we are faced with a choice: concede a broader view of deception, or a broader view of deceit. The latter seems the more natural reading: deceit covers this scenario, whatever your views on deception.

The expansiveness of deceit should not be surprising. Deceit is designed to capture fraudsters. And while A might defend herself as having not *deceived* B as to P because she sincerely believed P was true, if she misled B as to P for purposes of *manipulating* B's decisions, for purposes of overriding B's decision-making process by demanding B believe P, it will hardly be a defense for A to insist she "truly believed" that P in the event that P should turn out to be false and to B's detriment.

So, at least on this cursory analysis, deceit already seems broader than manipulation by deception, especially if you were inclined to read deception narrowly. But even supposing the tort had not yet reached beyond deception, the evidence suggests the tort of deceit is designed to evolve with the fraudsters. For example, courts relaxed the intentional reliance rule to make it "tougher" for them.[110]

[109] CARSON, *supra* note 24, at 26–29; SHIFFRIN, SPEECH MATTERS, *supra* note 5, at 12–19; JENNIFER MATHER SAUL, LYING, MISLEADING, & WHAT IS SAID 10–12 (2012).

[110] Gergen, *supra* note 87, at 558.

Courts have suggested that "[f]raud is multiform and as such admits of no single, all-encompassing definition."[111] And courts have a history of making "the law of deceit ... available for use in emerging factual situations."[112] These features are consistent with the equitable approach to fraud, from which the common law tort is descended.[113]

Evolution here seems appropriate. "[D]eception and playing on people's desires and emotions have likely been the most common forms of manipulation in the past."[114] So it's not surprising that precedent concerning common law fraud would be dominated by cases involving manipulation by deception. But "there is reason to believe that exploiting cognitive biases and vulnerabilities is the most alarming problem confronting us today."[115] Manipulators no longer need to impart false beliefs. They have incredible and increasing power to "frame information in a way that disposes us to a certain interpretation of the facts," and "can strategically 'anchor' our frame of reference when evaluating the costs or benefits of some decision."[116] The science of how to do so grows increasingly advanced. Were fraudsters to leverage it, why wouldn't deceit evolve to match?

C. Interstitial Trickery

So, what do my questions about a single tort—deceit—have to do with interstitial theorizing? Saul Levmore has suggested that legal theorists affect the law "at least as much by grouping cases together as by arguing for particular results."[117] They do so by identifying concepts that cut across cases, and using those concepts to unite previously doctrinally unrelated cases in new categories. To the extent a new category seems useful, it may grow into a grouping picked up by judges, and once picked up by judges, judges "feel encouraged to be less than minimalist, as everything within the newly defined area is in play."[118] He predicted "deception" might be one such category, and he and other theorists have begun to rationalize the terrain from that vantage point.[119]

But as has probably grown evident, I'm concerned that by focusing on "deception," and grouping laws as "laws of deception," we risk encouraging the wrong kind of rationalization.

[111] McEwin v. Allstate Tex. Lloyds, 118 S.W.3d 811, 816 (Tex. App. 2003).

[112] Paula J. Dalley, *The Law of Deceit, 1790–1860: Continuity Amidst Change*, 39 Am. J. Legal Hist. 405, 441 (1995).

[113] *See* Smith, *supra* note 99, at 1130–31.

[114] Susser, Roessler & Nissenbaum, *Technology*, *supra* note 69, at 5.

[115] *Id.*

[116] *Id.*; *see also generally* Susser, Roessler & Nissenbaum, *Online*, *supra* note 70.

[117] Levmore, *Theory*, *supra* note 3, at 1382.

[118] *Id.*

[119] *Id.*; Klass, *Meaning*, *supra* note 13.

Return to the choice between the broad and narrow readings of deceit. Though I raise the question, I do not claim that the broad reading is the correct view. There are clear reasons to favor the narrower one: We do not have a clear concept of manipulation writ large. The doctrine talks in terms of misrepresentations and false beliefs. And perhaps most troubling, to the extent manipulation extends to exploiting weaknesses in our rationality through choice architecture, there's a danger that the category grows too expansive: choice architecture is inevitable.[120] The narrow view of deceit could be seen as an attempt to regulate that mess by focusing on *one* particular means of violating another's interest in not having others surreptitiously muck with their reasoning process, just as design defect and manufacturing defect focus on different means of violating another's interest in not being harmed by commercial products.[121] And so long as equity remains available as a second-order system, we needn't worry so much that the narrow view of deceit unduly ties the court's hands: courts could invoke the equitable doctrine of constructive fraud to catch manipulators who use tools beyond deception.[122]

But to see all this is to put deception in its proper place. The place of deception in fraud isn't at the core. It plays a secondary, limiting function, by focusing on aspects of choice architecture that are more likely to have been designed to surreptitiously muck with another's reasoning process. And it helps litigants articulate how they were harmed: one is more likely to recognize she's been duped by a false belief than by more advanced techniques of manipulation, and to understand the concept of manipulation by reflecting on its most basic form.

This leads to a larger point about taxonomy. Properly understood, even the narrow reading of deceit isn't appropriately characterized as a law of *deception*, but as a law of *manipulation* that addresses one way of manipulation, one way of covertly mucking with another's reasoning process.

Why does this matter? It's because of anchoring bias—the way our decision-making can be influenced by our starting point (or anchor)—which, ironically, is one of the very tools used by effective manipulators.[123] It goes back to Levmore's point about categories and the judicial if not legal drive to create consistency within them. When categorized as a "law of deception," it's easy to view deceit as about false beliefs, or even more narrowly, about the communication of particular false propositions.

And herein lies the danger with emphasizing the wrong interstitial concepts: the urge for consistency—and discomfort with messiness—then

[120] Cass R. Sunstein, *The Ethics of Nudging*, 32 YALE J. REG. 413, 420–21 (2015); *cf.* Klass, *Law of Deception*, *supra* note 5, at 713–15.

[121] Klass, *Meaning*, *supra* note 13, at 453–60.

[122] Smith, *supra* note 99, at 1078, 1130–31.

[123] Susser, Roessler & Nissenbaum, *Technology*, *supra* note 69, at 5.

pushes for a narrowing of not only the tort, but the entire domain, to generate consistent rules and principles by *focusing on propositions*.[124] But if, for example, that were to happen to equitable fraud, it couldn't serve the function described earlier.[125]

I don't claim that all laws identified as "laws of deception" are about this phenomenon, of mucking with the reasoning process rather than the veracity of our beliefs. And no deception theorist believes that the law of deception is necessarily "one big thing." But query whether some of the categories so identified—the different ways the law gets at the phenomenon, the different places the law invokes the word "deception"—might be more appropriately viewed with this manipulation lens.

That choice has consequences. The appropriate lens may change how shared elements, like misrepresentation, should be applied; and the mode of reasoning—loose or clear—that is appropriate in such cases. If deceit is about manipulation, then perhaps courts are right to refuse to bow to analytic clarity: they resist ceding power to the fraudsters. Insisting on clarity might rightly be viewed as one means of mucking with another's practical reasoning process.

These questions about deceit illustrate my methodological caution. As modern research on manipulation and choice architecture shows, the lens we choose—our use of interstitial concepts to create domains—matters. To borrow Levmore's analogy, it will affect the shape of the garden bed and so how we go about pruning it.

IV. Conclusion

So, what is deception? Unless you're a deception specialist, the answer may well be the same as if I had asked "what is a horse?": Who cares. The complexity of misinformation means theorists and courts should probably prioritize different interstitial concepts. But this was still a chapter about deception: namely, about how in choosing our conceptual focus, we stand to deceive ourselves.

[124] *Fraud*, BLACK'S, *supra* note 1 ("Thus 'fraud' at common law is a false statement . . . : fraud in equity has often been used as meaning unconscientious dealing—'although, I think, unfortunately,' a great equity lawyer has said." (quoting WILLIAM R. ANSON, PRINCIPLES OF THE LAW OF CONTRACT 263 (Arthur L. Corbin ed., 3d Am. ed., 1919))).

[125] See text accompanying *supra* notes 113, 122. *Cf.*, *e.g.*, Smith, *supra* note 99, at 1077 ("'Fraud is infinite' given the 'fertility of man's invention.'" (quoting JOSEPH STORY, COMMENTARIES ON EQUITY JURISPRUDENCE: AS ADMINISTERED IN ENGLAND AND AMERICA § 186, 212 (1836))); Smith, *supra* note 99, at 1087–88 (quoting and discussing Story's definition of constructive fraud), *with id.* at 1078 (characterizing constructive fraud as addressing "a larger set of *misrepresentations* [than legal fraud]" (emphasis added)); *see also Constructive Fraud*, BLACK'S, *supra* note 1 (defining constructive fraud and equitable fraud as "unintentional deception or misrepresentation that causes injury to another").

4

On the Form and Justification of Some Private Law Rights, Liberties, and Powers

*Christopher Essert**

I. By Way of Introduction

Rights, liberties, and powers are fundamental building blocks of private law. I take analysis of them to be interstitial in the sense that a proper understanding of them must operate across the various doctrinal divisions of private law rather than being confined to any of its proper parts. In what follows I will consider some of the formal characteristics of these so-called incidents but also some elements of their justification, and as things develop what will emerge will be something by way of an account of the relations between form and justification.

In contrast to a reductive or perhaps deflationary view of rights, liberties, and powers that is sometimes talked about in terms of contingently connected "bundles," I will suggest a way of thinking about these incidents as different aspects of a realization of abstract moral ideas. In other words, if we begin with some idea about how we ought morally to relate to one another and proceed to elaborate what that idea requires of us in the context of different sorts of interactions we might have, we might see how the incidents are understandable as various aspects of that. On this understanding, then, the incidents are importantly connected to each other in pervasive ways, as well as deeply embedded throughout private law—in a way that you might call "interstitial"—so that we can see that their justification ties together their various forms and their application within the different departments of private law.

II. Persons and Property

Outside of contract law—which I mostly leave to one side in what follows for reasons of expediency and my own expertise—private law entitlements can

* Thanks to the participants in this volume's workshop and especially to Sam Bray and John Goldberg for their comments.

Christopher Essert, *On the Form and Justification of Some Private Law Rights, Liberties, and Powers* In: *Interstitial Private Law*. Edited by: Samuel L. Bray, John C.P. Goldberg, Paul B. Miller, and Henry E. Smith, Oxford University Press.
 DOI: 10.1093/oso/9780197783627.003.0004

basically be divided into two groups. There are entitlements in respect of persons and entitlements in respect of property. I assume that anyone taking the time to read a chapter in a volume called *Interstitial Private Law* will have a grip on the basic idea of this distinction. Of course, going from the basic idea to a workable and defensible justificatory account of the distinction—an account that allows us to sort borderline cases and explain the grounds of that sorting—is not simple.[1] Luckily, for present purposes, the basic idea is sufficient. Into the personal category we can pretty uncontroversially put things like my right that you not hug or punch me, my liberty to hug or punch myself, and my power to consent to your hugging me or punching me. Similarly, into the property category we can put my right that you not eat my mango or sleep in my bed, my liberty to eat my mango or sleep in my bed, and my power to consent to your eating my mango or sleeping in my bed.

There is of course one very obvious difference between persons and property, and, as a matter of positive law at least we can describe it (if perhaps not really come to understand it) relatively simply. The difference is that my property is mine only contingently whereas my person is me (not mine!) necessarily. I have a power to sell, give, bequeath, or perhaps otherwise transfer (or "alienate") my mango to you, and, after exercising that power, instead of my having a liberty to eat the mango and a right that you not do so, you would have a liberty to eat the mango and a right that I not do so. But any such power is absent in respect of my person: while I have a power to consent to your punching me, I cannot transfer to you the right that you (or others) not punch me. I will have more to say about these dynamics, but we can set them aside for a moment and focus instead on the similarities between persons and property. The spare examples in the previous paragraph disclose that similarity pretty well: when it comes both to persons and property, private law protects (roughly) rights that others not use or touch, liberties to use or touch, and powers to consent to others' using or touching. Despite these formal similarities, I want to suggest some ways in which what is going on in these two cases is importantly different.

III. Liberties and Rights

In the familiar Hohfeldian sense, A has a liberty to *v* with respect to B when B has no right that A not *v*, when A would not wrong B by *v*ing.[2] Loosely, we might say that A is at liberty to *v* or, even more loosely, free to do so. But those looser

[1] For my own effort, *see* C. Essert, Property Law in the Society of Equals (2024).

[2] I will use uppercase Roman letters at the start of the alphabet (A, B, C . . .) to represent persons and lowercase Italic letters nearer the end of the alphabet (*v, w, x* . . .) to represent actions.

usages, we need to remember, elide one of Hohfeld's crucial points, that, as a matter of private law, liberties (like the other jural relations we'll come to) are relations between persons, so that just saying that A has a liberty to *v* is in an important sense an incomplete statement: we need to know with respect to whom it is that A has a liberty.[3] A might have a liberty to *v* with respect to B but not with respect to C: if *v*ing is eating C's mango or giving C a hug, it could easily be true that A would wrong C by *v*ing (supposing that C hasn't given A consent to *v*) but (now supposing A hasn't agreed otherwise) the very same act of *v*ing would not wrong B (or affect B at all). Questions of A's liberties with respect to B and with respect to C are separate questions, as a general matter. In the basic case, C has no right that A not eat B's mango, which means that A has a liberty vis-à-vis C to eat B's mango; more colloquially we might say that what A does with B's mango is none of C's business, legally. (And the same is true if we substitute D for A.)

The situation with rights is, from one point of view, essentially the converse of the situation with liberties. Again, in the Hohfeldian sense, A has a right that B not *v* when B is not at liberty to *v* with respect to A. We tend here to think and to say that B would be committing a (private) legal wrong against A were B to *v*. And the Hohfeldian lesson about the way in which jural relations are relations between private persons applies: whether or not A has a right against B in respect of B's *v*ing is juridically neither here nor there with respect to the question of whether or not A has a right against C or, for that matter, whether or not D has a right against B. In our present context, we are concerned with property rights and personal rights, and both of these kinds of rights are, for the most part, *in rem*, good against the world.[4] My entitlement to my own person means that I have a right against each and every other person that they not hug me or punch me, and if that mango is really mine, then my property in it means that I have a right against each and every other person that they not touch it or eat it. Still, the specifics of individual private law relations must be considered on a relation-by-relation basis. By default, A's property in the mango means that A has a right that B not eat the mango, and a right that C not eat the mango, and a right that D not eat the mango, and so on.[5] But as we have already seen, A also has a

[3] I assume basic familiarity with Hohfeldian concepts and take most of what he says that I rely on to be pretty uncontroversial. While again I doubt anyone reading *Interstitial Private Law* needs this reference, I ought to say that the terminology comes from W.N. Hohfeld, *Some Fundamental Legal Conceptions as Applied in Judicial Reasoning*, 23 YALE L.J. 16 (1913).

[4] There might be a different sense of *in rem* on which an entitlement is only *in rem* if it relates to a *res*, which is to say if it's a property right. On this view, although personal rights are good against the world, they are not, strictly speaking, *in rem*. I'm not unsympathetic to this thought, but here I follow the crowd in using *in rem* as simply synonymous with "good against the world." And personal rights of the sort I consider here are clearly *in rem* in that sense.

[5] How to do this—to understand an *in rem* right in terms of bilateral (person-to-person) relations—is an interesting question in property theory, but not one that will concern us here. For some discussion, *see* J.E. PENNER, THE IDEA OF PROPERTY IN LAW (1996), C. Essert, *The Office of Ownership*, 63 UTLJ 418 (2013); J.E. Penner, *On the Very Idea of Transmissible Rights*, *in*

power to consent to what would otherwise be an infringement of that right. If we suppose that A did so in respect of B, that would have no effect on A's right against C or D. (That is a lot of abstraction and letters to say something close to truistic: when I share my mango with you, that does not mean that I share it with the others; when I consent to your hugging me, I have not consented to anyone else's doing so.)

Now, as I said at the end of the previous section, setting the question of transfer or alienation to the side for a moment, private law seems to treat rights and liberties in respect of persons and in respect of property in essentially the same way, at least in the sense that their juridical form is very, very similar: I have a liberty (against you, against anyone else) to do what I want with my mango and I have a liberty (against you, against anyone else) to do what I want with my person; similarly, I have a right (against you) that you not take my mango and a right against you that you not punch me or hug me. Of course, for the full story, more needs to be said here, because our liberties are constrained by the rights of others: I do not, in fact, have a liberty to hit you in the face with my fist or my mango, since you have a right that I not hit you in the face with anything. Much of the work of tort law, and in particular the law of nuisance and negligence, consists in working out a set of rights and liberties for everyone that can be systematically realizable.[6] Still, the thought is that we tend to think about our rights to our persons and our rights to our property as formally rather similar. But this formal similarity might mask a deeper contrast.

IV. The State of Nature

I already mentioned one way in which our entitlements to persons and to property are different, when I talked about alienability or transferability. The mango that is mine today might be yours tomorrow. This is a specific instance of a broader phenomenon, which is typically discussed by saying something like that my personal rights are necessarily mine whereas my property rights are only contingently mine, or perhaps that my property rights are separable from me. Another instance of this same idea is that, while my rights to my person seem in an important and intuitive sense to be mine automatically, whatever property I have, I had to get from somewhere, whether that be buying it, or receiving it as

PHILOSOPHICAL FOUNDATIONS OF PROPERTY LAW 44 (James Penner & Henry Smith eds., 2013); C. Essert, *The Office of Ownership Revisited*, 70 UTLJ Supp. 2, 287 (2020); J.E. PENNER, PROPERTY RIGHTS: A RE-EXAMINATION (2020); ESSERT, *supra* note 1.

[6] For a different view, on which those rights are constituted independently of these areas of law, *see* E.J. WEINRIB, RECIPROCAL FREEDOM 89–92 (2022).

a gift, or (in a vanishingly small set of cases these days) acquiring it originally, in the sense of being the first person ever to have it as their own.

This adds up to our being able to say that, for every single piece of property, there has to be some specific event in virtue of which it became property. Generalizing, we can see that every single thing that is owned was once not owned. Now ask, what is the status of things before they are owned? Answering this question is the task of the kinds of state-of-nature thought experiments that are at the heart of the works of Grotius, Pufendorf, Locke, Kant, and others, which are so central to much of the development of liberalism and everything that follows from it. In these discussions, we ask a question like, how would things be if nobody owned anything? In asking these questions, of course, we are not committing to anything like the claim that there was or even could be a world in which nobody owned anything.[7] Rather we are using the state of nature as a tool for thinking, as an idea of reason (as Kant says), to help us think through moral questions that might have more practical relevance, like the questions with which we began this paragraph. In other words, one particularly vivid way to think about the moral status of owned and never-owned objects is to think about how things would be, morally, if nothing were owned.

There are basically two different answers that we see in the liberal tradition to the question of how things would be, morally, in a world where nobody owned anything. According to one answer, if nothing is anyone's, then everything is everyone's, in the sense that everyone has a right in respect of every other one's use. People usually call this a world in which everything is held "in common," but, following Pufendorf, I like to call it the positive community. According to the other picture, if nothing is anyone's, then everything is no one's. The normal name for this is "the commons," but since those two normal names are confusingly similar, again I follow Pufendorf and adopt his more clarifyingly contrastive name, the negative community.[8] I think these options are essentially exhaustive, as we can see with the Hofheldian terminology and, I guess, some basic logic. In our world, with property, the right that nobody eat this mango is held by someone, the owner. In the negative community, that right is held by no one. And in the positive community, it is held by everyone. And there's no other option outside the set {nobody, somebody, everybody}, right? So that means that the negative community and the positive community are the only viable options to imagine the moral situation in a world without property.[9]

[7] Indeed, for some, the point of the exercise is, in a sense, to show why there could never (morally) be such a world.

[8] S. von Pufendorf, The Law of Nature and Nations, IV.4 (1672).

[9] On this logic, private forms of co-ownership are instances of private ownership: in a world with a lot of people, there is no fundamentally important difference between one person owning something and two people owning that thing together. And, indeed, this is the common law's view.

For my part, it seems clear that the negative community is a better depiction of how things would be, morally, without property. For one thing, our actual positive law tends to treat unowned objects as if they were in a negative community: nobody commits a wrong by touching or using unowned objects. Rather, they are, for the most part, free for the using and, indeed, the taking. That is not conclusive, of course, but the fact that this is essentially the universal rule should not be dismissed out of hand. Moreover, and more directly, I just find it pretty implausible to think that, in a world without property, I would need the consent of each and every other person to take or use literally any object. But that is what the positive community picture requires: in its pure form, the positive community is a world in which each person has a right that each other person not take or use any object, and so any taking or use of any object requires the consent of the other members of the community. So merely picking up a mango that has fallen from a tree, or stacking up some rocks to make a shelter from the wind, or using a piece of driftwood as a flotation device while crossing a river would be prima facie wrongful. But these acts strike me as totally unobjectionable.

What is going on here, then? What is the appeal of the positive community? One thought must be that the positive community vindicates the idea that, absent a system of property, nobody has the right to *take* anything out of the common stock, which is to say that nobody has the right to deprive others of things. The examples I just offered are not instances of that. So perhaps the positive community might be understood as a world in which using is ok but taking is not. The problem with that view is that we lack a way to draw a comprehensive and systematically realizable line between taking and using. Every use deprives others of at least some competing uses—you cannot hold the mango or the rocks or the wood while I am moving them around—and some uses deprive others of the possibility of any other uses. So the intuition is a valuable one: there is a worry about how it can be permissible to deprive others of things. But the worry is comprehensible and addressable in the negative community. What we are really worried about when we worry about deprivation, I think, is making it wrongful for others to use things, that is, asserting a right to them.[10]

The negative community fully vindicates the idea that, in a world without property, we cannot assert a right to things. I cannot rightfully deprive you of the mango in the negative community since there is nothing wrong, in that world, with your simply coming to take the mango back when I put it down. I cannot, that is, make a claim of right, a legal claim, to prevent you from being able to

[10] One of the most famous critiques of property is the one Rousseau makes in the Second Discourse, the second part of which famously begins with this: "The first man who, having enclosed a piece of ground, to whom it occurred to say '*This is mine.*'" Rousseau here notices that it is the claim of right—the saying "this is mine"—that is the decisive moment, rather than the physical act, and in noticing that echoes the point here.

access the mango. The action, as it were, lies in the right: it is the claim of right, which can only arise within an institution of property, that allows for the possibility of deprivation and, at the same time, the possibility of the normal kinds of usings and takings we associate with things belonging to one another. That's true, in fact, even if you sign on to the positive community picture, as Locke taught us long ago.[11] So the motivation for the positive community view—that it's wrongful to take things—turns out to be a motivation that the negative community view can incorporate and address, without having to take on the implausible picture that the positive community generates. In other words, the negative community is a better characterization of the idea of reason that we are after.

Now set all that aside just for the moment, and ask the parallel, personal rights version of the question that we just asked about property rights. A question like, how would things be morally if we did not have a legal institution of personal rights (protected by torts of battery and so on)? A positive community view is close to absurd on its face: nobody thinks that our persons and bodies are naturally held in common by all, so that the hands I am using to type these sentences are in any sense "everyone's" and somehow I just have a kind of license to use them.[12] But—and here the contrast with property really comes out clearly—a negative community kind of view also does not seem very appealing. Nobody really thinks that our persons and bodies are naturally held as a commons so that we can freely use and take the persons and bodies of others. By contrast with the property situation, where we feel some anxiety about justifying property in part due to the way it seems artificial (in Hume's sense), many people share a pretty robust intuition according to which our persons are naturally the subject of some kinds of rights that are essentially held by ourselves. Indeed, many people take this intuition, or something like it, to be the basic starting point in political philosophy.

V. A Contrast between Persons and Property?

This last point suggests a kind of a contrast between property and personal entitlements in private law, the contrast that I gestured towards at the end of

[11] In paragraph 28 of the Second *Treatise*, Locke tells us that we need (and are thus permitted) to leave the commons and create property because, in the commons, "Man had starved, notwithstanding the Plenty God had given him," which is to say that, were every other person's consent required to use things, nobody would be able to use anything.

[12] This example invokes, for better or worse, Cohen's discussion of the "eyeball lottery" in Self-Ownership, Freedom, and Equality (1995). I will not get into the details of that discussion, though, because I want to avoid all talk of self-ownership. I am with those who think that the idea is confused in that it effaces the many important differences (many of which I am discussing in this chapter!) between personal and property rights while providing no additional benefit to us that cannot be gotten by the idea of a personal right not conceived of using any concept of ownership.

section II. Formally, as I have indicated here and there, these two classes of entitlements have a lot in common. We tend to be comfortable saying something like, as a matter of private law, it is up to me rather than anyone else what others can do to my person, and we cash that out in Hohfeldian terms by saying that I have a liberty to do what I like with my person and a right that others not interfere with my person, where the contents of those rights are specified by reference to a requirement that they be systematically realizable, that each of us have the same right in our persons as everyone else. (As I said already: my view is that it is the role of the common law of negligence to do this work.[13]) And, in parallel, we tend to be comfortable saying the same thing about property: when I own something—a mango, some land—it is up to me rather than anyone else what others can do with it. I also indicated that a major difference between the two classes is the fact that in the property case there is only a contingent connection between owner and thing owned, whereas in the personal case that connection is anything but contingent.

But the discussion so far points to a different contrast. What we just saw is that it seems like things would be quite different indeed when it comes to these two classes of entitlements in the state of nature: absent a law of property, we would have no rights over things at all, and the Hohfeldian status of such a world would be one of unconstrained liberties, whereas in the personal case, we tend to think that, absent a law of assault and battery and the like (a law for which we have no obvious idiomatic name beyond something like "the law of torts in respect of personal rights"), we would nevertheless still have (non-legal) rights of some sort in our persons. We tend to think, that is, that there are no natural rights in property but that there may be something like natural rights in our persons.[14]

Now, I am not super confident about the personal rights part of that claim. On the one hand, there is what I already said, to the effect that it seems that the moral situation in respect of our persons in a world without any legal rights would not be either the free-for-all equivalent of the negative community, in which my touching or using your person would not be a wrong, nor the equivalent of the positive community, in which all of our persons were held collectively. On the other hand, though, I doubt that we should understand our personal rights as fully determinate or really anywhere close to fully determinate in the state of nature. I think that we need a legal system to authoritatively render these rights

[13] I gesture toward something like this in C. Essert, *The Value of the Neighbour Relation*, *in* Private Law and Practical Reason: Essays on John Gardner's Private Law Theory 301 (Harris Psarras & Sandy Steel eds., 2023).

[14] Who's "we"? I understand that there are some people—"libertarians"? "Lockeans"?—who think that we have fully determinate and understandable pre-political rights of property. In part because of the arguments in the main text, I set such views aside here, except to notice that I share the skepticism of them articulated in, for instance, L. Murphy, *The Artificial Morality of Private Law: The Persistence of an Illusion*, 70 UTLJ 453 (2020).

determinate in the same way that we do for our property rights, because I think it is impossible a priori to know where the boundaries of my personal rights are: Does my right that you not interfere with my person include a right that you not interfere with my mental states? Does it prevent you from injuring me through your carelessness? Does it encompass rights of privacy, or in respect of the use of my image? Does it protect parts of my body that are separate from me? There are just as many such questions when it comes to our persons as there are when it comes to our property, and in both cases this is (I think) the core of the reason that we need institutions of private law: we need them to answer these questions in a way that is systematically realizable and consistent with our standing as equals. Let me expand on that briefly: when it comes to both cases, personal and property, we need to have private law institutions in order to allow us to relate in respect of these institutions' subject matters—persons and things—in ways that are consistent with our relating or standing as equals. Our social world and all the various activities big and small that make it up—from reading books to dancing the tango to playing baseball to shopping at the mall—are built on a foundation of legal rights (and liberties) to our persons and property. Without these institutions, then, we would not be able to live in the social world that we know and understand on morally acceptable terms, because we would have no grounds on which to structure the immense and indefinite interactions that make that social world up.

To recap the last few paragraphs, then, we can say the following. In the case of property, there seem to be solid grounds for thinking that, absent a legal institution of property, our moral relations in respect of property's subject matter would be very different: without property nobody can own anything. But when it comes to persons, the situation looks different. Absent a legal institution protecting personal rights, we might think, there is at least some sense in which those rights would still exist. An almost universal intuition is that we would have something that resembles rights to the control of our own persons even absent the law. So there is an asymmetry. On the other hand, though, we actually noted two symmetries between personal and legal property. The first is the formal one, where legal personal rights and legal property rights look formally the same (aside from alienability). The second is the fact that in both cases we need a legal institution to realize and protect the rights in question. In the personal case, I said, we need legal rights to our persons because the non-legal or pre-legal rights that we have are too indeterminate, among other things, and so we need the law to render them determinate by answering specific questions about their scope and boundaries and how they can be systematically realized. But the pre-legal right to personal integrity structures and constrains the legal institution. There are some things that the legal institution cannot say for it to be a realization of the pre-legal idea, for it to be doing the thing that it is meant to do.

When it comes to property, though, things are different. When we think about a world without property, we think of the negative community. I think the burden of a theory of property is to show how the negative community could not be a morally acceptable world. And I think a theory of property can show that.[15] Such a theory then shows how we need to leave the negative community and create an institution of property. But here the institution is much less constrained by the pre-legal moral situation than in the personal case. I said a moment ago that our social world is constituted in a way that gives us a need for an institution of property to be able to live in it on terms of equality. But that is not to say very much about the contents of that institution. And indeed, my view is that the range of permissible property institutions is going to be quite wide. And that means, in turn, that the space for emancipatory revision in property is actually quite wide, too.[16] Something like this is behind some of the political project of legal realism: once you see that there are no pre-political property rights, you can argue more aggressively about how our current property system is failing as a matter of justice. (Again note the contrast: people just do not tend to be inclined to say that, since there is so much economic injustice in our world, we should be redistributing the hands of the rich, or the manually advantaged.) But at the same time, the institution of property does play a certain distinctive role in social morality: it is an institution that is aimed at allowing us to relate as equals in respect of its subject matter. So while there is a very wide range of permissible alternatives, the range is not endless, and there are some kinds of things that are ruled out as possible institutions.

VI. Introducing Powers

Let us now take a rather abrupt turn and consider legal powers. Legal powers in private law are, roughly, those things that allow us to change our rights and liberties. We saw some examples earlier: I have the power to waive my right that you not hug me or my right that you not eat my mango, and when I do, you gain a liberty to hug me or eat my mango.

The distinctive thing about powers, of course, is the way in which they are, if you like, second order. That is, powers operate on rights and liberties and so they are conceptually dependent on them in the sense that you need the idea of a right or a liberty before you can have the idea of a power. You do not, to be clear, need

[15] I try to do so in ESSERT, supra note 1.

[16] So, unfortunately, is the space for the adoption of property institutions that encode and enforce various kinds of subordination. The idea that property is aimed at allowing egalitarian relations in respect of its subject matter rules out some things, but it also permits other institutions that stray far from their regulatory ideal, for instance, by allowing pervasive homelessness.

a right before you can have a power, as the case of property shows. Someone might not own anything at all and so have no rights in respect of property, while still having a power to acquire property. (And the same is true for contracts: you could be in a situation where you are party to no contracts at all, but you'd still have the power to participate in contract formation.) But to create a right is, in the relevant sense, to operate on a right.

The conceptual priority of rights over powers leads us to some interesting places, because the way that powers are what we might call an additional conceptual step beyond rights seems to press a question about what justifies our taking that step. That is, it seems to press a question about why we are able to have these powers. This is a question that has generated some interest, not just in legal theory, but in moral philosophy more generally.[17] There, the most prominent argument for the existence of normative powers (as they tend to be called outside the law) is Joseph Raz's. Raz argues that we have a normative power just when it is good for us to have one. There is some talk in the literature of how "it would be good that *p*, therefore *p*" is not a good argument. I am with Raz (and others) who think that, in the normative realm, this kind of argument has a lot more plausibility.[18] I will not defend that here, though, because the validity of the argument is not my concern; rather, I want to talk about how Raz's argument fits into the question with which I began this paragraph, the question of what you need, so to speak, to "get" from rights to powers.

On Raz's account, the existence of some right and an accompanying power—say the power to waive the right—are, strictly speaking, entirely separate matters. That is, to establish that A has a right that B not *v*, we ask and answer a specific kind of question. And *then*, to establish that A has a power to waive A's right that B not *v*, we ask and answer a different kind of question. Both questions are forms of a more basic question, a question about reasons: the first is a question about whether some aspect of A's well-being gives sufficient reasons to impose a duty not to *v* on B; the second is a question about whether there are sufficient reasons for A to have the power in question. But when you put the two questions like that side by side, you can see that there is no reason at all in principle to think that the two questions would have the same answer. I mean, sure, they might *tend* to go together, in the sense of a statistical correlation. But—and this is the point—they

[17] Let me just say one quick thing about the legal vs moral version of this question. Some scholars (e.g., Liam Murphy, whose views I discuss later) think that there is no interesting question about legal powers, since the answer to the question "why do we have legal powers?" is just "because the law says we do." But that kind of answer assumes a version of positivism that is not particularly illuminating in this kind of inquiry: I take it that we can demand an actual justification of our legal norms. There are other reasons that one might pull apart legal and moral powers (and in particular the ways in which they respectively relate to legal and moral rights), but I do not have the space to consider them here.

[18] Raz's most recent version of this argument is in chapter 7 of Joseph Raz, The Roots of Normativity (2022). Another well-known version is in Thomas Nagel, Concealment and Exposure & Other Essays 39–40 (2002).

are separate questions, and the existence of the power needs its own stand-alone argument; the existence of the right will not buy you anything in the currency of powers.

A different way to think about powers links powers and the rights to which they correspond much more closely. An exemplary recent instance of this way of thinking is Seana Shiffrin's argument about consent. On Shiffrin's view, we can argue for the existence of a power to consent in a kind of transcendental way, by noting that consent seems an ineliminable constituent of certain moral valuable and non-optional parts of the social world. Shiffrin writes:

> One *could* imagine a conception of autonomy without consent in which an agent exercised complete sovereignty over her body and other personal spaces, such as the home, but had no ability to share or transfer these powers to others. That is, the agent could not grant consent to others to exercise these powers in lieu of or alongside herself.

Here, I want to interject, Shiffrin is describing, with slightly different vocabulary, a world with rights and liberties but no powers. She goes on:

> Such a structure is imaginable but so impoverished as to be utterly implausible . . . . Rights of autonomous control that were inalienable to this degree would render (morally) impossible real forms of meaningful human relationships and the full definition and recognition of the self (not to mention making medical and dental care cumbersome, dangerous, and awfully painful). To forge meaningful relationships, embodied human beings must have the ability to interact within the same physical space, to share the use of property, and to touch one another. They must therefore be able to empower particular people.[19]

I think the idea here is something like this: if we think about *why* we have rights in our persons and property, the answer we quickly arrive it is that we need it to be up to us, at least sometimes, how others can act in respect of our persons and property. The argument in the last section was a gesture in this direction: creatures like us necessarily inhabit a social world in which a wide range of activities and relations is constituted by this kind of control over others' actions. But "this kind of control" would be woefully defective were our control limited to a toolbox containing just rights and liberties: we need to be able to exercise powers to allow others to do things that, absent the exercise of those powers, would violate our rights. The power to consent is then just as essential an element

[19] Seana Valentine Shiffrin, *Promising, Intimate Relations, and Conventionalism*, 117 Philosophical Rev. 481, 501–02 (2008).

of that control, of the idea of others' actions being up to us, as rights and liberties. And now note the contrast to Raz's view. There the justification of the right and the justification of the power are separate. Here, the right and the power both get their justification from the same source: the need to realize the relevant form of control over others' actions in respect of our persons or our property.[20] Both the right and the power are complementary constituent elements of the realization of that control.

Now, speaking slightly more generally, Shiffrin's argument about consent is helpful because it shows us a model of thinking about the various Hohfeldian incidents in private law. On this model, we understand the presence of various rights, liberties, and powers, as well as the relations among them, from the point of view of the relevant justificatory considerations. Shiffrin's defense of the power to consent depends on our understanding why we have control over our bodies and the role of consent in that understanding. It is worthwhile to say a little bit in more general terms about this way of thinking.

VII. Justificatory Accounts of Hohfeldian Incidents

Shiffrin's view of consent seems like an example of a view about private law incidents that focuses on the relations between persons that are constituted and regulated by private law. Like the Razian view, this view is normative through and through, in that it answers questions about what rights, liberties, and powers we have by reference to considerations about why we have (or might have) them, about what good they do. But where the Razian view has a broad and pluralistic account of that point, in that it allows for any number of reasons that the

[20] I want to emphasize, though, that I do see Shiffrin as giving an argument that does have, strictly speaking, two steps. That is, the right is still conceptually prior to the power, and you need to think of the right first to get the argument for the power. This is good because it fits with the idea that we began with, namely the idea that powers are second order in a more formal sense, that a power is a power *in respect of* a right or liberty. So you can conceive of rights and liberties without powers but not vice versa. So while I agree with Liam Murphy that a power to consent is very closely tied to the right to which it attaches, I disagree with his claim that consent is "not an example of a normative power at all." Murphy, *supra* note 14, at 71 says "It is not accurate to think of the right as a prohibition on boundary crossing to which we add a desirable normative power of consent. The ability to consent is part and parcel of what it is to be free." But Murphy's argument here makes sense only if we read that "add" in the first sentence in a kind of Razian way, as if the power's addition were a contingent matter that we could take or leave. But Shiffrin's argument shows how that is not the way to think of it, that, while the power is a conceptually distinct matter—again: you can have rights without powers but not powers without rights—the argument for it is a distinctive sort of argument, so that the step from right to power is very short indeed. That sort of view preserves the intuitive thought that consent is a power whose exercise must be communicated in the same way as the exercise of any other power—more on this later—but also allows us to accept Murphy's point in the second sentence, that the ability to consent is part of what it is to be free. But it is not the only part: the right is a part, too, and they are separate parts.

existence of a right or power might be good, this different view focusses on the ways in which rights, liberties, and powers constitute and structure relations among persons. Why that limited view? Because of the form of these relations. That is: when we talk about rights, liberties, and powers (at least in private law) we are talking about different kinds of normatively structured relations between persons. To say that I have a right that you not *v* is not to say anything about the badness of *v*ing in general, or even the badness of *v*ing to me. It is simply the claim that you would wrong me by *v*ing. And so the normative question becomes this: Why think *that*? That is, why think that there is some value in setting things up such that your *v*ing counts as a wrong against me?

Well, I think that is a question about the value of a certain kind of relation between you and me. We think something like this: because of the kinds of beings that you and I are, it is good that we relate in such a way that you cannot *v* without wronging me. Now that sounds abstract and odd, but of course once it is given a bit of particular content, it looks entirely familiar. Because of the kinds of beings that we are—more on that in a moment—we want a relation wherein you wrong me by (say) touching me harmfully or offensively. There is just something about us in virtue of which we tend to think that, prima facie, none of us can harmfully or offensively touch any other. Now there is a lot of handwaving there—about what kinds of beings we are, about what it is that grounds these thoughts. But, actually, that is not a problem, because different specific forms of this kind of relational account of the value of rights are going to fill things out differently to assuage the worry about handwaving. So some people are going to say that we need to have these sorts of relations because otherwise we could not be independent or autonomous or something like that. I tend to favor an interpretation that is even more explicitly relational: we need to have relations where I have rights against you and you have rights against me so that neither of us can dominate nor subordinate the other. Morally acceptable relations among moral equals in our social world require that we relate as equals. Without a right that you not touch me harmfully or offensively, we could not have relations of that sort, because the question of whether or not harmful or offensive touchings would take place would be settled by (morally arbitrary) questions of strength, speed, cunning, etc. In other words, the strong would be able to dominate the weak, and morality proscribes a world in which that is permitted. So, at a very high level, we have rights in our persons because we need rights in our persons to relate on morally acceptable terms (as equals).

But precisely the same considerations that justify our thinking we have these rights also justify our thinking that we have the liberties and powers that we tend to associate with them. That is, in a way, just a gloss on the Shiffrin argument that I discussed earlier. When we think about the role of private law in constituting our social world, we see that, in order to relate as equals, we need to have control over the permissibility of the actions of others when it comes to our persons and some stuff (the subject matter of property). And that control, to be fully realized, requires not just liberties to use our persons and our things along with rights that others not interfere with those uses. It also requires the capacity to permit others to do what is otherwise prohibited, since many—most?—of the things we do with our bodies and our property involve others' participation. So the same justificatory considerations that explain why we have rights to our persons and our property give us the explanation for the presence of the accompanying powers.[21]

VIII. Bundling and Unbundling

Now we can focus some of this talk onto the bundle of rights picture of property. Lots of people mean lots of different things when they talk about the bundle of rights, but for me its central claim is about the connection, or lack of connection, among rights, liberties, and powers. On the bundle view, as I understand it, to know whether or not A's ownership of some particular bit of the world includes, let's say, a right that B not *v*, a liberty against C to *w*, a power to waive a right that D not *x*, and so on, we need to ask entirely separate questions. That is, each incident, at least in principle, stands and falls on its own terms. On the bundle picture, there is, as James Penner puts it, "no 'internal' organizing principle which makes sense of that fact that certain [features of property] seem to go together."[22]

But that aspect of the bundle of rights picture seems very implausible once you look at the material through the kind of justificatory account that I have describing here.[23] To recap: we saw that, properly understood, we should see powers as so intimately connected to both personal rights and property rights that any justification of the rights is also a justification of the powers (even if there is some fancy transcendental maneuvering from one to the other of the sort we discussed in the last section). So to think that individual incidents of property ownership are to be justified individually is just to misunderstand the material in a deep and important way. One way to see this is by noticing how the argument about rights and powers I made earlier works in just the same way for personal

[21] As Ripstein notes (in PRIVATE WRONGS (2016)) exceptions to this case prove the rule. Minor children and the incapacitated can have personal rights without the accompanying powers, since the role of their rights is slightly different and does not require powers in the same way. Important as they are, I lack space here to discuss these more complex cases.

[22] PENNER, PROPERTY RIGHTS: A RE-EXAMINATION, *supra* note 5, at 4. Penner's account of the bundle-of-rights picture is surely in certain respects different than mine. In particular, his is more sophisticated that what I am working with here. But I think we share attention to the feature I describe in the text.

[23] For the same criticism of the bundle picture *see* RIPSTEIN, *supra* note 21, at 11.

rights and property rights, but hardly anyone wants to defend a bundle picture of the person.[24]

I take (one of) the central motivations for the bundle picture to be the claim that, as a matter of law, there's no such thing as pure "Blackstonian" dominion, that ownership of different kinds of resources involves different sets of Hohfeldian incidents, that ownership is often shared or incomplete. But those ideas do not necessitate the bundle picture at all. The contrasting view—the one that arises out of the justificatory account—says something like this: there is a kind of unifying overall structure to property that can be clearly (and, arguably, best) seen by attending to its justification. The point of property is to allow us to relate to each other as equals in respect of things.[25] And relating as equals in respect of things requires that we can have things as our own, that we can relate to each other through what I call the idea of yours and mine.[26] Having something as yours or mine involves having the capacity to tell others that they cannot use it (i.e., having a right to exclude them) and also the capacity to tell them that they can (i.e., having a power to waive that right). But having something as yours or mine does not require that these capacities be unlimited. It is perfectly plausible to talk about something being yours or mine in a context where our private law rights and powers over it are limited or constrained in various ways: indeed, it is more than plausible, since we talk about things being yours or mine all the time and there is no situation that exists in which those rights and powers are not limited in at least some ways. But on this view, the different sets of incidents that the law recognizes in different resources and different contexts can all plausibly be understood as instances of the same phenomenon, which is to say property, and we can understand each of the various sets as hanging together on that basis.

On the bundle view, by contrast, it is a coincidence that these incidents travel together, since there is nothing that really binds them together. In fact, when you think about the words that I used in that sentence, the bundle metaphor actually starts to look self-undermining. In the most extreme form of the bundle picture, people sometimes talk about property as a bundle of sticks. But a bundle of sticks is *bound* together by something, which is what makes it a *bundle* as opposed to a pile. The bundle picture has no account of what binds the bundle, except a deflationary account that sees the sticks as no more than merely contingently tied together by instrumental considerations. But to

[24] Ripstein makes this point: FORCE & FREEDOM: KANT'S LEGAL AND POLITICAL PHILOSOPHY 88 (2009). But for a defense of a bundle of rights theory of the person, *see* V. KURKI, A THEORY OF LEGAL PERSONHOOD (2019).

[25] I use the word "things" here for convenience, although I think it is not quite the best way to put this point: *see* ESSERT, *supra* note 1. On property and things, *see* Henry E. Smith, *Property as the Law of Things*, 125 HARVARD L. REV. 1691 (2021).

[26] *See* ESSERT, *supra* note 1.

identify property as a bundle as opposed to a pile (or, as Penner says, an aggregate) we need such an account. The justificatory story I offered might be just the thing. In other words, there is a grain of truth in the bundle story—different kinds of property ownership involve different kinds of combinations of Hohfeldian incidents, and which combination applies in which context is a matter of justification—but it lacks the conceptual resources to fully capture the importance and power of this grain. By seeing property from the top down, as it were, we can explain and understand the way in which these incidents do come in bundles, and why both normal non-legal thought and talk about property as well as almost all sensible justificatory discussions of the institution as a whole tend to operate at the level of the bundle taken as a whole rather than at the level of the individual incidents.

IX. Justification and Particular Questions

That is not to say that it is never a good idea to think about one or another of these incidents on its own. Go to back to powers once more. Across a wide array of private law contexts, a question comes up about what kinds of facts ground the exercise of a legal power; in particular, people often want to ask about the role of the subjective psychological states of a power-holder in the exercise of a power. They ask questions like this: Does the exercise of the power of consent depend on whether the consenter subjectively intends or desires the consented-to conduct? Similar questions arise in respect of the power to license entry to real property, the power to participate in contract formation, and many others. I think—and in past argued at some length—that we can answer these questions by attending to the fact that these are private law powers, and that the exercise of a private law power always involves at least two private parties. In all of the cases I just enumerated, for instance, the exercise of the power will change the legal situation not just for the power-holder but also for the other party to the interaction. That is, my exercising my power to grant you a license to enter my real property eliminates my right that you not enter—strictly speaking, by transforming into a "no-right"—and at the same time eliminates your duty not to enter by transforming it into a liberty (or, as we often say in this context, privilege). So the exercise of the power is not just about me, the power exerciser, but about you. Given this relational or symmetrical aspect of the exercise of a private law power, it seems clear to me that the facts that ground that exercise—the facts in virtue of which we can say that the power has, in fact, been exercised—need to be facts that are public as between us, in the sense of equally available to both of us to know. And our subjective mental states are not like that at all: we cannot know, really, what others are thinking, except by inferring based on what they do or say.

So the law tends to say that the exercise of these sorts of powers requires that we manifest a certain mental state.[27]

But even though we can make sense of the argument in the previous paragraph on its own terms, the careful reader will have noticed an implicit premise that ties that argument to the broader justificatory questions that have occupied most of this chapter. The idea that, since the exercise of the power affects both of us, we both need to have equal access to the facts that ground it depends on a premise about our equal standing in private law. We do not think that the facts that ground the exercise of my power to transfer ownership of my pet goldfish to you need to be available to the goldfish. Now, we can accept that premise based purely on something like an observation that it is a pretty inescapable part of private law. That is, anyone with any familiarity with private law can see that its self-understanding, as exemplified in its form, its core doctrines, and the decisions of its leading practitioners, includes a commitment to the equality, or equal standing, of the parties. And then the argument about powers can, like many other arguments about private law, be built on just that basis. In other words, we could say that, for legal powers in private law to be a part of private law properly understood, they need to be structured so that both parties to their exercise can have access to the facts that ground that exercise, while at the same time leaving a more basic justificatory question—if there is some good in private law so understood—open. I guess this is one way to read some of Ernest Weinrib's earlier work.[28] But of course we might say more, and it is here that the link between the argument about the way that powers work and the earlier part of the chapter arises. We *need* to relate to each other as equals because that is what political morality requires at its most basic, and private law allows us to relate as equals, so private law is a good, indeed necessary, thing. On this kind of view, the question about whether or not private law powers can be grounded on the subjective psychological states of the parties is not best understood as merely a kind of conceptual inquiry into how things look or what our intuitions are about particular cases, but something that follows inexorably from the most basic commitment of political morality.

X. By Way of Conclusion

What I hope to have shown here is the value of thinking about our private law institutions from the point of their institutional justification. That is, if we

[27] That paragraph summarizes the argument in my *Legal Powers in Private Law*, 21 Legal Theory 136 (2015).

[28] There are many strands of The Idea of Private Law (1996) in particular that have this form.

conceive of our institutions of personal rights or property rights as, in the first instance, realizations of abstract ideas required to allow us to live together as morality requires, we will see these institutions as structured by a set of relevant justificatory considerations. This top-down picture then sheds light on the individual questions about things like rights, liberties, and powers (in the same way that, although I've said nothing about it here, it sheds light on particular cases and controversies).

5

Consent across Private Law

*Mark P. Gergen**

I. Introduction

My task is to examine the concept of consent across all of private law. Happily the rules on consent as a defense in the Restatement of Torts to Intentional Persons provide a good framework. The authors were faced with the hard problem of writing rules that would be acceptable to a broad audience that could handle the fraught issue of determining consent to a sexual touching when consent is disputed. They solved this problem by going back to basics and defining actual consent as the mental state of being willing for a touching to occur plus the absence of vitiating circumstances (e.g., incapacity, duress, and mistake). This rule is supplemented by narrow rules on apparent consent and presumed consent. These rules are narrow because they treat a person as having consented (although they did not) to a boundary crossing for which actual consent generally is required.

This chapter extends this framework across all of private law by broadening the rules of actual, apparent, and presumed consent to cover any situation in which a person can choose or intend to exercise a legal power to confer a legal right, power, privilege or immunity on another person.[1] This task is fairly straightforward so long as one is clear about the object of consent, that is, about the object a person must consciously have in mind when they choose or intend to exercise a legal power. Clarity about the object of consent pays dividends. It shows that consent in private law has three broadly different types of objects. The object of consent can be to a broad type of human interaction (e.g., consent to an exchange or to make a gift); to a particular aspect of an interaction (e.g., consent to a particular type of touching or to a particular term of an agreement);

* I thank Ken Simons and participants in Conference of Interstitial Private Law for comments on drafts.

[1] Henceforth I will simply say exercise a legal power and drop the last qualification in the interest of concision. Some voluntary acts of will that exercise a legal power do not confer a legal right, power, privilege, or immunity upon another person and so are not aptly described as rules of consent. Examples include the rules on acquiring possession of property and making a will.

Mark P. Gergen, *Consent across Private Law* In: *Interstitial Private Law*. Edited by: Samuel L. Bray, John C.P. Goldberg, Paul B. Miller, and Henry E. Smith, Oxford University Press. © Oxford University Press 2024.
DOI: 10.1093/oso/9780197783627.003.0005

or to a legal formality (e.g., consent to a writing as an expression of terms of an agreement).

Consent is relational in several senses: consent is given from one person to another; consent is present or absent in relation to the object of consent; and, the rules on apparent consent and presumed consent in a particular legal context relate to the legal consequences that follow from finding apparent or presumed consent present or absent in the context. Apparent consent generally is given effect to protect a recipient's reliance on the appearance of consent while presumed consent generally is given effect to facilitate an interaction that a person is reasonably expected to welcome (or at least not object to) when it is impractical to obtain actual consent.

II. Consent in the Restatement of Intentional Torts to Persons

This section explains the materials on consent in the Restatement of Intentional Torts to Persons. I believe the Restatement makes a contribution to promoting analytical clarity in the law on a par with the materials on causation in the Restatement, Third, Torts: Liability for Physical Harm. Both Restatements promote analytical clarity by resolutely separating factual issues from normative issues as much as they can be separated. The authors of the Restatement had hard cases like the following in mind as they worked out these rules. **Case 1:** B touches A in a sexual way that would be highly offensive if A did not consent to the touching. B mistakenly believes A consented though A did not consent.[2]

Under the Restatement, conduct that would otherwise be a tort is not if there is either "actual consent," "apparent consent," or "presumed consent" to the conduct. Presumed consent is not possible in Case 1 so I put it to the side for now. Consent also requires the absence of vitiating circumstances (e.g., incapacity, duress, and mistake). I come back to this as well. The Restatement warns against using the term "implied consent," and strongly warns against stretching the term consent to cover cases of "implied-in-law consent" and "constructive consent."[3]

[2] *Cf.* Restatement, Third, Torts: Intentional Torts to Persons (Tent. Draft No. 6, April 26, 2021, § 18, comment f ("suppose E and F meet at a party; E asks F for a kiss: F responds by immediately grabbing E's genitals"); comment j, Illustration 10 ("Sexual boor Boris, on his first date with Pauline, suddenly kisses her fervently and continues to do so despite her repeated and clear verbal protests but ignores them because he believes her protests are insincere and that she actually consents").

[3] Restatement, Third, Torts: Intentional Torts to Persons (Tent. Draft No. 4), April 1, 2019, § 12, comment d.

Surely this is correct.[4] When A consents to a touching that would otherwise be a wrong against A, A may not complain without regard to A's actual interests in the matter because A consented to the touching. This is why Heidi Hurd describes "consent" as "moral magic."[5] Hurd is referring to actual consent. There is no magic in "apparent consent" or "presumed consent." These are given effect for other reasons that must be sufficiently strong to justify treating a person as having consented when they did not.

Actual consent is a conscious mental state. The Restatement describes the mental state as A "is willing" for B's act to occur.[6] Other possible descriptions are that A "chooses" for B's act to occur[7] or that A "intends" for B's act to occur.[8] Defining actual consent as a conscious mental state requires that the object of consent always be defined by reference to an object people can be expected to actually have in mind when they consent. Objects that do not satisfy this requirement of mental immediacy cannot be an object of consent. Legal enforceability cannot be a general object of consent required for contractual obligation because people who make contracts often do not have this object in mind. On the other hand, an exchange or a writing can be general objects of consent required for contractual obligation because people can be expected to have these objects in mind when they make contracts.

The Restatement defines the object of A's consent as B's conduct in touching A and the touching itself (the "otherwise tortious invasion").[9] The object of consent is defined in very particular terms as the conduct and touching A actually had in mind. A rule on scope of consent determines whether A's consent covers the conduct and touching that actually occurred. This rule requires that the conduct and touching not "substantially differ from the conduct a person was willing to permit."[10]

The Restatement defines "apparent consent" literally as apparent actual consent. The black-letter states: "Apparent consent exists if the actor reasonably

[4] DERYCK BEYLEVELD & ROGER BROWNSWORD, CONSENT IN THE LAW 61 (2007) (describing consent as a "non-substantive form of justification).

[5] Heidi M. Hurd, *The Moral Magic of Consent*, 2 LEGAL THEORY 121 (1996).

[6] RESTATEMENT, THIRD, TORTS: INTENTIONAL TORTS TO PERSONS (Tent. Draft No. 4), April 1, 2019, § 13 comment b.

[7] Kimberly Kessler Ferzan, *Clarifying Consent: Peter Westen's The Logic of Consent*, 25 LAW & PHILOSOPHY 193, 204 (2006) (explaining why "chooses" is better than the term "desires," which Westen sometimes uses to describe the mental state).

[8] Heidi M. Hurd, *The Moral Magic of Consent*, 2 LEGAL THEORY 121 (1996). Larry Alexander, *The Moral Magic of Consent II*, 2 LEGAL THEORY 165, 166 (1996), questions use of the term intent when consent is to another person's action on the ground that it is not possible for a person to intend someone else's act. In contract law and property law it is common to say a person intends to make a contract or to transfer property.

[9] RESTATEMENT, THIRD, TORTS: INTENTIONAL TORTS TO PERSONS (Tent. Draft No. 4), April 1, 2019, § 13, comment d.

[10] *Id.* § 14(a) and comment b.

believes that the other person actually consents to the conduct, without regard to whether the person does actually consent."[11] B must reasonably believe A has the state of mind of actual consent, for example, that A consciously is willing for B's act to occur. The rule on apparent consent does not cover a case in which B believes A has given no thought to the matter but that A would consent, if A did think about the matter.

"Presumed consent" is all that remains.[12] Under the Restatement, "Presumed consent exists if: (1) under prevailing social norms, the actor is justified in engaging in the conduct in the absence of the other person's actual or apparent consent, and (2) the actor has no reason to believe that the person would not have actually consented to the conduct if the actor had requested the person's consent."[13] This rule is why a salesperson knocking on a stranger's door during the daytime is not a trespass when there is no sign saying "no soliciting." And it is why providing physical assistance to an unconscious person in distress is not a battery.[14]

Under these rules consent cannot be used to explain the absence of liability in **Case 2**: "Tony enters a crowded bus and loudly shouts 'Keep your distance! Do not touch me.' Ben squeezes past Tony after the bus driver asks people to move to the back of the bus."[15] Tony's shout eliminates the possibility of actual, implied, and presumed consent. The Restatement handles this case with a special rule of nonliability "for minor contacts that are clearly socially justifiable."[16]

[11] *Id.* § 16(a). A criticism of the rule is that it does not require that A be responsible for the appearance of consent. *Id.*, comment c ("Apparent consent . . . need not be based on the words or affirmative conduct of the plaintiff.") Ben Zipursky provides an example: B hugs A, who looks like his wife, from behind at a party. The Reporter's Note collects authority on both sides of the question whether the plaintiff must be responsible for the appearance of consent. In contract law and property law, the consentor must be responsible for the appearance of consent. Another point of disagreement involving actual consent is over whether consent must be communicated to be effective. See text and notes at *infra* notes 19–21.

[12] In addition to rejecting concepts like implied-in-law consent and constructive consent, the Restatement makes a contribution by creating the concept of "presumed consent" and separating cases covered by this concept from cases covered by the concept of "apparent consent." RESTATEMENT, SECOND, TORTS § 892 lumps these cases together and tries to cover them by the concept of "apparent consent." For example, comment d of § 892 takes the position there is apparent consent to hunt on private law if the custom in the area is to permit the public to go hunting on private land.

Separating apparent consent and presumed consent clarifies that presumed consent requires both a normative decision that B's conduct is appropriate in the absence of consent and in addition that B have no reason to believe A would not consent if A was asked. The separation of apparent consent and presumed consent, and a change in social mores, may well change the result in Illustration 3 of § 892 of the SECOND RESTATEMENT: "A, a young man, is alone with B, a girl, in the moonlight. A proposes to kiss B. Although inwardly objecting, B says nothing and neither resists nor protests by any word gesture. A kisses B. A is not liable to B." Under the rules in the RESTATEMENT THIRD, there is apparent consent only if A reasonably believes B's silence and lack resistance means B is consciously willing to be kissed.

[13] *Id.* § 16(b).

[14] *Id.* § 17.

[15] *Id.* § 1, Illustration 7.

[16] *Id.* § 1, comment h.

The comment explains that "Only a small handful of cases will be affected by this special rule of nonliability, because other tort law doctrines (e.g., requirements of offensiveness or lack of consent) will usually preclude liability in cases similar to" the illustration involving Tony.[17] As you shall see, cases like this—where an act that conventionally connotes consent is treated as consent though the other party knows or has reason to know the actor does not consent—are ubiquitous in contract law. Indeed, tolerance for this result is the most distinctive feature of classical (Willistonian) contract law.

Increased sensitivity to sexual violence may explain why the Restatement takes the position that the concept of consent should not be stretched to cover Case 2. "No" means no consent. The comments further limit the rule on presumed consent by requiring that the touching represent a "minor" invasion of the interests of the person touched and that the circumstances make it unlikely that the person touched will have thought about the physical contact before it occurs. **Case 3**: E and F are on a third date and "E suddenly reaches out and holds F's hand for the first time." Consent is presumed if E had no reason to believe F would object.[18] Presumed consent is possible in Case 3 because the touching is minor and because the circumstances make it appropriate for E to hold F's hand even if E thinks F has given no thought to the matter.

The rules on apparent consent and presumed consent reflect the relational nature of consent. They generally focus on B's beliefs about A's state of mind (apparent consent) and what B knows about A's preferences (the second, negating element of presumed consent). On the other hand, the Restatement insists that actual consent is effective even if the consent is not communicated to the actor.[19] The Restatement, Second, Torts takes the same position and provides this illustration: **Case 4**: A pool owner invites any and all of her neighbors to swim in the pool. The owner's consent extends to a neighbor who swims in the pool unaware of the invitation.[20]

17 *Id.*

18 *Id.* § 16, comment d and Illustration 10. Under the Restatement Ben is liable for battery if he knowingly touches Tony. There is no additional requirement that Ben knowingly harm or offend Tony. This is referred to as a "dual intent" requirement. *See* Restatement, Third, Torts: Intentional Torts to Person (Tent. Draft No. 1), April 8, 2015, § 2, comment b (rejecting dual intent requirement). A simple dual intent requirement is objectionable because the rule would shield a boorish person who is unaware a touching is offensive from liability for battery because the boor does not know the touching is offensive. *Id.*, Illustration 11. An alternative formulation of the dual intent rule would require an intent to touch in a way that the actor should reasonably believe would be harmful or offensive. This rule would shield Ben from liability but not the boor. It is debatable whether the ad hoc rule of non-liability in the Restatement is superior to this form of a dual intent rule.

19 Restatement, Third, Torts: Intentional Torts to Persons (Tent. Draft No. 4), April 1, 2019, § 13, comment e.

20 Restatement, Second, Torts § 892, Illustration 1. The new Property Restatement keeps the result while taking the position that consent (it uses the term "permission") requires a communicative act, but that the permission need not be communicated to the entrant to be effective. Restatement, Fourth, Property (Tent. Draft No. 4), Preliminary Draft No. 4 (Sept. 12 2018),

In discussing this issue, the reporters of the Restatement of Intentional Torts to Persons note "[t]he view that consent requires communication is quite defensible in some legal contexts, such as contract law (insofar as consent underlies that field of law). But it does not therefore follow that tort law, with its distinctive goals and principles, should also employ a communicative conception of consent."[21] This point is true more generally. While the framework in the Restatement can be extended across all of private law the implementation of the framework and details vary across legal contexts. Other differences include whether apparent consent is given effect, whether and when consent may be presumed, and whether consent may be withdrawn.

The fundamental rule is that actual consent to a touching requires that A consciously be willing to be touched by B plus the absence of vitiating circumstances. Consent to a touching is an exercise of a legal power.[22] Generalizing this fundamental rule, actual consent to exercise a legal power requires that A consciously choose or intend whatever the law requires for the exercise of a legal power (the object of consent), plus the absence of vitiating circumstances. Rules with this general form appear across all of private law. The most important difference across legal contexts is the definition of what an actor is required to have in mind to exercise a legal power (the object of consent). A gift requires intent to make a gift and intent to do an act that the law treats as delivery. A contract often is said to require intent to make a promise as part of an exchange. And so on. One payoff from being clear that actual consent requires the actor have the object of consent in mind is that it invites close attention to the definition of what an actor must have in mind to exercise a legal power in a legal context.

Vol. 2, Division 1, Chapter 2, § 1, comments c and i. This explanation is consistent with the rule on gifts that delivery only requires the thing given (typically a deed of property) be out of the transferor's hand. The transferee need not be aware of this. The mailbox rule in contract law is similar.

[21] Restatement, Third, Torts: Intentional Torts to Persons (Tent. Draft No. 4), April 1, 2019, § 13, Reporter's Notes to comment e (and citing the philosophical and legal literature debating this issue).

[22] Heidi Hurd makes this point in The Moral Magic of Consent. H.L.A. Hart is credited with coining the term "power-conferring rule" to describe a type of legal rule that is not a command and does not impose a duty. H.L.A. Hart, The Concept of Law 27–28 (1951). Gregory Klass, *Three Pictures of Contract: Duty, Power, and Compound Rule*, 83 N.Y.U.L. Rev. 1726 (2008), has a thoughtful discussion of the problems of distinguishing rules that confer powers and rules that impose duties. He observes "power-creating laws have two characteristic features. First, the law must be designed in a way that underwrites an expectation of its purposive use—an expectation that persons will satisfy the law for the sake of the legal consequences. Second, that expectation must be the law's reason for attaching those legal consequences to acts of that type." *Id.* at 1741–42. Klass continues that "the clearest indication that a law is concerned with the purpose with which it is satisfied" is that a law's validity conditions "sort on purpose." *Id.* at 1743. He identifies four broad types of such validity conditions: "legal formalities; required nonconventional legal speech acts; legal-intent tests; and nonlinguistic proxies for legal purpose." *Id.*

The definition of vitiating circumstances and the legal effect of their presence also differs across legal contexts. The Restatement of Intentional Torts to Persons provides that legally effective consent requires capacity, absence of duress, and absence of mistake.[23] Misrepresentation can be added to the list for the Restatement treats misrepresentation as a species of mistake.[24] In other contexts, the equitable doctrines of undue influence and constructive fraud often are included among the list of vitiating circumstances.

The Restatement provides that duress and mistake vitiate consent to an act that would otherwise be an intentional tort only if the actor caused or knew of the duress or the mistake.[25] The law of restitution is different. An innocent recipient of a benefit can be required to make restitution if they do not have a change-of-position defense. This difference relates to the different legal consequences that flow from treating consent as ineffective in the two contexts. Obligation in restitution requires a defendant to do no more than return a benefit received. The obligation generally is not fault based. It is imposed to eliminate unjust enrichment. Liability in tort general entails an obligation to pay compensatory damages. The liability generally is fault based, either negligence or intent, though there are rules of strict liability. It is an intentional tort (battery) if B knows and does not disclose they have a sexually transmitted disease before having consensual sexual intercourse with A. A's mistake about the danger posed, and B's fault in failing to correct A's mistake, vitiate A's consent. On the other hand, it is not an intentional tort if B is unaware they have the disease. B might still be held liable for negligence if B failed to take reasonable precautions.[26]

III. Contract Law

There is widespread confusion about the place of consent in contract law. For example, Nate Oman argues in a recent paper that consent "is less normatively important to contract law than many contract law theories assume," and that no "single, normatively consistent vision of consent drives contract law."[27] Oman cannot see the place of consent in contract law because he assumes the object of consent in contract law must be to create legal relations. This cannot be the object of consent generally because people often do not have legal consequences

[23] Restatement, Third, Torts: Intentional Torts to Persons (Tent. Draft No. 4), April 1, 2019, § 15.

[24] *Id.* § 15, comment e correctly observes that misrepresentation is a subset of mistake. In a case of misrepresentation, A's mistake is induced by false or misleading information supplied to A by B.

[25] *Id.* § 15, comments d and e.

[26] *Id.* § 15, Illustrations 7 and 8.

[27] Nathan B. Oman, *Intent to Create Legal Relations and the Nature of Contractual Consent*, *in* Research Handbook of the Philosophy of Contract Law 1, 2 (Chen & Saprai eds., 2024).

in mind when they make a contract. The object of consent always must be something people have in mind.

The place of consent in contract law becomes apparent once one looks for rules with the same general form as the rule on consent in the Restatement of Torts to Intentional Persons. These are rules that condition a contractual obligation on an actor actually consciously choosing or intending some object, or on the appearance of actual consent. Contract law has multiple rules of this general form with different objects of consent. These objects include consent to an exchange, consent to a term, and consent to a writing as an expression of terms. These are not just different objects. They are different types of objects. An exchange is a general type of human interaction. A term is a particular aspect of an interaction. A writing is a legal form.

Consent to an exchange. Exchange, not promise, is the most basic object of consent in contract law. The Restatement, Second, Contracts is clear on the centrality of exchange to contract. It provides "the formation of a contract requires a bargain in which there is a manifestation of mutual assent to the exchange and a consideration."[28] The definition of consideration requires a promise made or a performance rendered as part of an exchange.[29] And an exchange can give rise to a contractual obligation in the absence of an express promise.[30] This is called an implied-in-fact contract.

The object of consent—to engage in an exchange—is general and social. **Case 5**: B was hired by A's neighbor to pull weeds. B mistakenly pulls weeds at A's house. A sees B as B is beginning to work and gives a thumb's up. **Case 6**: C transmits an offer of employment to D. D transmits an acceptance in response. The offer and acceptance have materially different terms. D begins work under C's oversight.

There is a contract in both cases based on actual or apparent consent to an exchange. Nothing more is required in the way of consent. In Case 5, B has in mind they will be paid for weeding and A has reason to know B has this in mind. This is all that it takes for there to be a contract. It is not necessary that B have in mind the exchange is with A. And it is not necessary that either A or B have in mind the price of weeding. In Case 6, all C and D need to have in mind for there to be a contract is that they are in an exchange relationship. That they have different terms in mind does not prevent formation of a contract.[31]

If I have not persuaded you yet, consider **Case 7**: E and F are in an intimate relationship. F renders a service to assist E in E's business. There is a contract if F intends an exchange (and not a gift), and if E should reasonably understand

[28] Restatement, Second, Contracts § 17.
[29] *Id.* § 71.
[30] *Id.* § 69.
[31] McGurn v. Bell Microproducts, Inc., 284 F.3d 86 (1st Cir. 2002).

this is F's intent. Contract law often fails to do justice in this type of case because people in long-term intimate relationships often think about their interactions in communitarian terms that do not conform to the legal categories of gift and exchange. As a consequence, F is unlikely to be able to satisfy the burden of proving E should have reasonably understood this was an exchange, and so F will be left with a possible claim in restitution.

What follows legally from consent to an exchange depends on how deeply people become engaged in the transaction, the terms each has in mind, the terms they actually or apparently consent to, and whether one or both transmits a writing to express terms. Generally, when people consent to an exchange there is an obligation to pay the market price for benefits received in the exchange. But sometimes even this is not true. If people have a different prices in mind, and neither apparently consents to the other's price, then a court will hold the contract fails because of a mutual misunderstanding, and a claim for benefits received will be in restitution.[32] If people are deeply engaged in a transaction, and one or both transmits a writing to express terms, a court is likely to find there is a contract and look to the writing(s) to define terms. Untangling this problem would take us beyond the realm of consent and into the legal intricacies of the common law mirror-image rule, the common law last-shot rule, and UCC § 2-207.

Consent to a term. A term can become part of a contract without consent. A term can become part of a contract by consent to a writing that contains the term or a term can be implied (either by presumed intent or by a default rule). A term can become part of a contract by consent only when people think and communicate about the term in making a contract. When a term does become part of a contract by consent, the object of consent is the particular term. One or both parties must intend the term to be part of the contract. If only one party intends a term to be part of the contract, then the term becomes part of the contract if the other party has reason to know of the first party's intent.

The rules of interpretation illustrate. Here the issue is the meaning attached by the parties to a term in a contract. The rules of interpretation in contract law precisely track the rules on actual and apparent consent in the Restatement of Intentional Torts to Persons. **Case 8:** G and H make a contract for the purchase and sale of "chicken." The term *chicken* is ambiguous and could be interpreted to mean either young chicken (broilers) or fowl (stewing chicken).[33] If G and H have the same type of chicken in mind, this is their contract. G and H actually consent.[34] If G has young chicken in mind, H has fowl in mind, and in the circumstances a reasonable person would think chicken means young chicken,

[32] Vickery v. Ritchie, 88 N.E. 835 (1909).
[33] Frigaliment Importing Co. v. B.N.S. Intern. Sales Corp., 190 F. Supp. 116 (S.D.N.Y. 1960).
[34] Restatement, Second, Contracts § 201(1).

then the contract is for young chicken.[35] G actually consents and H apparently consents. If G and H have different types of chicken in mind, and neither meaning is more reasonable in the circumstances, then there is no contract.[36] Both actual consent and apparent consent are lacking. In this case, either party may elect to enforce a contract on the other party's terms. There is actual consent by the party against whom the contract is enforced, which is all contract law requires.

Consent to a writing. When a person consents to a writing that expresses terms of an agreement, they are held to the terms of the writing even if they do not read the writing. This rule applies even if a party is unable to read the writing and even if the other party is aware of this.[37] Obviously, under the rule the object of consent is the writing. The object of consent is a legal formality. The rule is often referred to as the "duty-to-read" rule. This name suggests people are expected to read a writing to which the rule applies. If people really were expected to read contractual writings, then one could say there was apparent consent to a writing's terms. But people are not expected to read many types of contractual writings. Consumers are not expected to read form contracts. And it is well known that when businesses exchange form contracts business people often do not read each other's forms. A person cannot actually or apparently consent to a term in a writing they predictably do not read.

The duty-to-read rule works alongside the parol-evidence rule to give a person the power to use a writing to determine the terms of a contract by getting the other party to consent to the writing as an expression of terms. The duty-to-read rule makes a term in a writing part of a contract even though there is no actual agreement with respect to the term. The parol-evidence rule can exclude a term *not* in a writing from a contract, even though there may be an actual agreement on a term, when the term would normally be included in such a writing. Under both rules, the terms of a contract generally are determined by the writing the parties actually or apparently consent to as an expression of their agreement, and not by the parties' actual or apparent agreement.

A party who fails to ensure a writing conforms to their intent does so at their peril. Under classical (Willistonian) contract law this is at great peril for a party can be held to terms of a writing that do not conform to their intent even when the other party knows or has reason to know the writing does not conform to the first party's intent. **Case 9:** J and I sign a purchase and sale agreement for a home that does not include J's promise to I to have an ugly icehouse on adjacent land moved. Under classical contract law, the promise is unenforceable under

[35] *Id.* § 201(2)(b).
[36] *Id.* § 20(1).
[37] Morales v. Sun Constructors, Inc., 541 F.3d 218 (3d Cir. 2008).

the parol evidence rule even if J knows I believes the promise to be part of the agreement.[38]

Technically, this result is possible because a court is instructed not to consider the strength of the evidence that the parties intended the term to be part of the agreement in applying they rule. Instead a court asks if the term would ordinarily be in a writing such as the parties adopted, if it were part of the agreement.[39] Classical contract law also has the plain-meaning rule. The rule instructs a court to give effect to the plain meaning of an unambiguous term and not to consider evidence the parties' agreement was different.[40] Thus, under classical contract law it is not possible for parties to use the term "buy" to mean "sell." Modern contract law allows this.[41]

Classical contract law inherited rules from equity that provide a safety valve to prevent a person from exploiting another person's mistake regarding the content of a writing. For example, in Case 9 if the parties had instructed the drafter to include the promise to move the icehouse in the writing, and the drafter had failed to do so, then equity would intervene to correct the mistake by reforming the writing.[42]

This pattern was common before the merger of law and equity. A power-conferring rule in the law would require people to do a formal act (like execute a bond) to change their legal position. The object of consent under the legal rule was to do the formal act. Equity sometimes would operate as a safety valve to prevent injustice when people failed to comply with law's formalities.[43] Equity would look behind form to give effect to people's actual intent.

Modern contract law rejects the plain-meaning rule and the Willistonian version of the plain-meaning rule, changing the result in the original version of Case 9 if the court finds I believed the promise to move the icehouse to be part of the contract and J knew or should have known of this belief. The pattern is broadly similar to the rule on presumed consent in the Restatement of Intentional Torts

38 Mitchill v. Lath, 160 N.E. 646 (1928).

39 Under the modern (Corbinian) version of the rule a judge does consider the strength of the evidence of the alleged parol agreement. The different positions of Corbin and Williston on this point follow from their different views on the purpose of the rule. Williston thought the rule served a formal purpose while Corbin thought it served an evidentiary purpose. John D. Calamari & Joseph M. Perillo, *A Plea for a Uniform Parol Evidence Rule and Principles of Interpretation*, 42 IND. L.J. 333 (1967).

40 Steuart v. McChesney, 444 A.2d 659 (Pa. 1982). The case applies a particularly extreme version of the rule that requires a court to ignore almost all extrinsic evidence and to apply the semantic meaning of a term.

41 Compare RESTATEMENT, FIRST, CONTRACTS § 231, Illustration 2; and RESTATEMENT, SECOND, CONTRACTS § 212, Illustration 4.

42 Ace Drug Marts, Inc. v. Sterling, 502 S.W.2d 935 (Tex. Civ. App. 1973). *See also* Sisneros v. Citadel Broadcasting Co., 142 P.3d 34 (N.M. App. 2006). Rescission would also be available as a remedy if J noticed the mistake and failed to bring it to I's attention. Under modern tort law, this would also constitute fraudulent nondisclosure, exposing J to claims for compensatory and punitive damages.

43 Henry E. Smith, *Equity as Meta-Law*, 130 YALE L.J. 1050 (2021).

to Persons. The rule has two parts: "(1) under prevailing social norms, the actor is justified in engaging in the conduct in the absence of the other person's actual or apparent consent, and (2) the actor has no reason to believe that the person would not have actually consented to the conduct if the actor had requested the person's consent."[44] As for the first part of the rule, the law takes the position that a party to a contract may presume a writing the other party adopts as an expression of terms of a contract is definitive with respects to terms that are in the writing or that would normally be in such a writing.

As for the second part of the rule, modern contract law does not allow a party to stand on a writing if they know or have reason to know the writing does not reflect the other party's intent. Thus, the duty to read rule does not apply to hold the recipient of a writing to an unread term when the party presenting the writing knew or had reason to know the recipient objected to the term. This is likely to be explained in terms of the fraud exception to the duty-to-read rule, which is similar to the second part of the presumed consent rule. A difference is that the fraud exception only covers cases in which the recipient of a writing has thought about a term and communicated their objection to the term to the party presenting the writing.

The reasonable-expectations doctrine and the materially- alter rule in UCC § 2-207(2)(b) go further by requiring the party presenting the writing to anticipate the recipient's preferences, bringing contract law closer to the rule of presumed consent. The reasonable-expectations doctrine does not give effect to a term in a pre-prepared form where the company "has reason to believe that the party manifesting such assent would not do so if he knew that the writing contained a particular term."[45] The materially-alter rule does not give effect to a term if doing so would "result in surprise or hardship" to the recipient of the form.[46] However, relatively few US courts have adopted the reasonable-expectations doctrine. And most US courts have refused to apply § 2-207 to consumer form contracts, holding the statute only applies to cases in which there is a "battle of the forms" because each party sends a form and neither party adopts the other's form.[47]

US courts also have taken an expansive view on how a person can adopt a writing. Early cases involved tickets, claim checks, catalogs, bills of lading, and other documents that routinely accompanied a transaction. Recipients of such documents were treated as impliedly manifesting assent to a document if a reasonable person who received the document would understand it contained contract terms.[48] Shrinkwrap agreements are a modern variation on this problem.

[44] *Id.* § 16(b).
[45] Restatement, Second, Contracts § 211(3).
[46] UCC § 2-207, comment 4.
[47] DeFontes v. Dell, Inc., 984 A.2d 1081 (R.I. 2009)(describing this as majority position).
[48] *See, e.g.*, Maynard v. James, 146 A. 614, 65 A.L.R. 427 (Conn. 1929).

A purchaser of consumer goods is treated as assenting to a form that accompanies the goods, if a form tells a purchaser they can return the goods if they do not assent to its terms. The legal effectiveness of a shrinkwrap agreement cannot be explained as a matter of actual consent or apparent consent to a form within a box because it is unlikely that a purchaser who chooses not to return goods consciously thinks they are consenting to a form in the box. Presumed consent is a plausible ground for the rule because it is unlikely that a purchaser would actually decline to consent to the form, if asked.

IV. Property Law

Property law has many rules of consent.[49] This section briefly looks at the rules of consent in the law of abandonment and the law of gifts to show they can easily be fit within the general framework of the Restatement of Intentional Torts to Persons. As always, the main issue is identifying the object of consent under a rule. Private law also has a bevy of rules that work alongside rules of consent to determine when an owner who transfers property in a non-consensual transaction can recover the property (or its value) from a downstream possessor. These include rules on void and voidable title and rules that protect bona fide purchasers. These rules are not rules of consent. Typically they allocate a loss between two victims of transactions in which consent is absent or vitiated.[50]

Abandonment. Abandonment requires an act of relinquishment of possession of property and the intent to permanently part with the property. Intent can be actual, inferred, or presumed.[51] I would add that abandonment has the additional requirement that an owner intend other persons be able to acquire ownership of the property by taking possession. A person who puts a document with sensitive information in the trash is relinquishing possession of the property, but they do not intend that other people be able to acquire the document (and the information) by taking possession.[52] Once this is added the rule of intent in abandonment is appropriately described as a rule of consent. The object of consent in the law of abandonment can either be general or particular, depending on the circumstances.

[49] The law of bailment has extensive rules on consent. The property torts (conversion and trespass) are qualified by rules on consent.

[50] For example, if A obtains property from B by fraud, and then A sells the property to bona fide purchaser C, then the rule giving A voidable title to the property casts the loss on B. If A had stolen the property from B, then the rule giving A void title casts the loss on C.

[51] C&H Manufacturing, LLC v. Harlan County Industrial Development Authority, Inc., 600 S.W.3d 740, 747 (Ky. App. 2020).

[52] For a multi-jurisdiction survey of how courts handle this problem, *see* Saw, *The Law of Abandonment and the Passing of Property in Trash*, 23 SINGAPORE ACADEMY OF LAW JOURNAL 145 (2011).

The problem of consent in the law of abandonment is similar to the problem of consent in the law of battery in that the defendant is subject to liability in tort in the absence of consent. The problems differ in two respects. First, in possible cases of abandonment where an owner's intent to abandon property is at issue, the person in possession of the possibly abandoned property often has a stronger interest in being able to use the property than whatever interest the owner has in the property. Second, the person in possession often is not in communication with the owner, and so they cannot be expected to know the owner's actual preferences in the matter.

These differences explain why intent to abandon property is determined by applying an objective standard and strong presumptions. One such presumption is that relinquishment of possession for a relatively long period establishes an intent to abandon. Another presumption is that a commercial tenant is presumed to abandon equipment they leave behind when they turn over a lease to a new tenant in the same line of business.[53] These rules treat the object of consent as being general and social.

These presumptions are rebuttable. Intent to abandon is not found when a possessor actually knows or has reason to know an owner does not intend to abandon property. The object of consent is specific and individual in **Case 10:** B agrees to care for A's pet dog when A moves to California until A can find an apartment suitable for the dog. This arrangement unexpectedly stretches for two years. During this period A communicates with B regularly to get updates on the dog and A occasionally sends money to B to help cover expenses of caring for the dog. B predictably becomes deeply attached to the dog. A has not abandoned the dog. B could not reasonably believe A has consciously decided to part with the dog forever. Even if a long lapse of time creates a presumption of abandonment, B has reason to believe A would not actually choose to part with the dog forever, if A were asked.[54]

Gift. The rules on consent in the law of gifts are similar to the rules on consent in contract law. A major difference is that a gift of property generally requires actual intent to make a gift.[55] In addition, intent to make a gift of property must be proven by clear and convincing evidence.[56] **Case 11:** C and D are in an intimate relationship. C transfers $5,000 to D to assist D in D's business. The transfer will

[53] *Id.*

[54] Zephier v. Agate, 957 N.W.2d 866 (Minn. 2021).

[55] Intent to make a gift is presumed only in one very narrow case. An intent to make a gift in forgiveness of a loan is presumed when the debtor is the natural object of the creditor's bounty, and the creditor allows the statute of limitations to run on the gift. Because the debt is uncollectible after the statute of limitations runs, the primary effect of this rule is that the debtor does not incur income tax liability on cancellation of indebtedness income. RESTATEMENT, THIRD, PROPERTY: WILLS AND OTHER DONATIVE TRANSFERS, § 6.1, comment k.

[56] *See, e.g.*, Schultz v. Schultz, 637 S.W.2d 1 (1982); Oehler v. Falstrom, 273 Minn. 453, 142 N.W.2d 581 (1966).

be treated as an interest-free loan unless there is clear and convincing evidence C intended to make a gift.[57]

In Case 11, the transfer may be treated as a loan even if D reasonably believed C intended to make a gift. While this might seem harsh to D, reversing an apparently intended gift of money or property often does not leave the innocent recipient of an apparently intended gift much worse than they would have been had the gift not been made. The recipient is not liable for conversion because the transfer is treated as an interest-free loan. If the apparent gift is of property, then it is treated as a gratuitous bailment. The transferee is liable for conversion only if they refuse to return the property on demand.

When the issue of intent involves a gift's size, rather than intent to make a gift, different rules apply. **Case 12:** E makes a gift of real property to F by deed. E intends to give 1/4 of Blackacre to F. As a result of a mistake, the deed includes all of Blackacre. **Case 13:** G makes a gift of cash to H. G intends to transfer $1,000. As a result of a mistake, G transfers $10,000. The donor's remedy to correct the mistake is in the law of restitution in both cases.[58] One consequence is a donee has a change-of-position defense in Case 13. The defense is available if H reasonably believes G intended to make a gift of $10,000, and H spends the money in a way that would make it inequitable to require H to repay the money to G.[59] H would not have a change-of-position defense if they spent the money to pay a usual and necessary expense. H would have a change-of-position defense if they gave the money to charity or spent it on a vacation.

I see no good normative reason why the law protects the reliance interests of an innocent recipient of an apparent gift when an actor's mistake involves the size of a gift, but not when an actor's mistake involves creating a false impression of intent to make a gift. The likely explanation for the difference is that the different types of mistakes are handled in different places in the law. A mistake about the size of a gift is lumped together with other types of mistakes in the exercise of legal power and handled as a single problem in equity or in the law of restitution. A mistake in creating a false impression of intent to make a gift is handled in the law of gifts.

V. Consent's Cousins

This section addresses several rules that resemble rules of consent but with differences. Consent's cousins include intent-based rules of culpability, the

[57] Oehler v. Falstrom, 273 Minn. 453, 142 N.W.2d 581 (1966).

[58] *See* RESTATEMENT, THIRD, RESTITUTION AND UNJUST ENRICHMENT (2011), § 11, comment b, for illustrations.

[59] *Id.* § 65, comment c.

doctrine of waiver, and the doctrine of assumption of risk. The minimum requirement for a legal rule to be described as a rule of consent is that the rule must generally require an actor's actual consent, plus the absence of vitiating circumstances, for an actor to be held to whatever legal consequences follow from application of the rule. The doctrine of waiver does not satisfy this minimum requirement. An additional requirement for a legal rule to be described as a rule of consent is that the rule must govern an actor's exercise of a legal power. Rules of culpable intent require a voluntary act of will by an actor but they are not rules of consent because they do not govern the exercise of a legal power. In the nineteenth century, the doctrine of assumption of risk would not have been described as governing the exercise of a legal power because the doctrine generally covered cases in which an actor voluntarily put themselves in a position where a risk creator owed them no duty of care or only a limited duty of care. One strand of the modern doctrine may be described as a rule of consent.

Culpable intent. Kimberley Ferzan remarks on the strong family resemblance between consent and culpable intent in a recent paper on the defense of consent in criminal law.[60] Ferzan's paper is a review of Peter Westen's *The Logic of Consent.* Westen identifies four types of consent: factual attitudinal consent (i.e., actual consent), factual expressive consent (i.e., apparent consent), prescriptive intent (i.e., the absence of vitiating factors), and imputed consent (which covers presumed consent and more). Ferzan argues the core concept of consent is "prescriptive attitudinal consent,"[61] and observes "[t]his construct is far from foreign to the criminal law. Rather, the same factors that bear on whether an individual should be held responsible for a crime likewise determine whether prescriptive attitudinal consent exists. In each case, we are evaluating whether there is a voluntary choice by a responsible agent."[62]

The function of intent-based rules of culpability obviously differs from the function of rules of consent. Rules of consent govern the exercise of legal powers while intent-based rules of culpability govern conduct the law discourages. That said, Ferzen's concept of "prescriptive attitudinal consent" precisely corresponds to actual consent plus the absence of vitiating factors. In the nineteenth century, this would have been described as a voluntary act of will. Rules that either respond to or give effect to voluntary acts of will run throughout the law. They are so ubiquitous that nineteenth-century legal theorists tried to explain almost all of the law in terms of responding to or giving effect to voluntary

60 Kimberly Kessler Ferzan, *Clarifying Consent: Peter Westen's The Logic of Consent*, 25 Law & Philosophy 193 (2006). Heidi Hurd draws the same connection in *The Moral Magic of Consent.* In a later co-authored paper Ferzan and Westen describe factual attitudinal consent as "assent" and the absence of vitiating circumstances as necessary to establish consent. Kimberly Kessler Ferzan & Peter Westen, *How to Think (Like a Lawyer) about Rape*, 11 Crim. Law & Philos. 759 (2017).

61 Ferzan, *Clarifying Consent*, supra note 60, at 203.

62 *Id.* at 204.

acts of will.[63] Thus Roscoe Pound's Readings on the History and System of the Common Law prefaces a section on "Acts" by distinguishing "events," which are "occurrences which take place independently of the human will," and "acts," which "are subject to the control of the human will and flow therefrom." Pound then distinguishes between "[a]cts [that] have legal consequences because they interfere with interests . . . recognized and protected by law" and "acts [that] have legal consequences because such was the intention of the person or persons performing them."[64] The line Pound draws is precisely that between voluntary-act requirements for legal liability and voluntary-act requirements for the exercise of legal powers.

Waiver. The private law doctrine of waiver bears a strong family resemblance to the defense of consent in tort law. Both doctrines operate as a shield in the sense that "the consenting [or waiving] agent, A, is precluded from raising a complaint about the conduct of the recipient agent B."[65] Both doctrines have rules that allow consent or waiver to be retracted unless retraction would be unfair because B has changed her position in reliance on A's consent or waiver. The definition of waiver literally requires a voluntary act of will. A leading case explains "'waiver' has been defined to be the intentional relinquishment of a known right. It is voluntary and implies an election to dispense with something of value, or forego some advantage . . ."[66]

Waiver often involves actual, apparent, or presumed consent but waiver does not require actual, apparent, or presumed consent. **Case 14**: A secured creditor with a lien on a debtor's mobile home repeatedly takes late payments and forebears exercising its power to declare default and seize the collateral. The creditor will be held to have waived the right to declare default on a late payment. The creditor can retract the waiver, but it must give the debtor a reasonable opportunity to cure the default.

In Case 14 it is very unlikely that the creditor consciously decides to waive its power to declare default and seize the collateral in the event of a future default. If the creditor gives any thought to the matter, then she is likely to think she is choosing not to declare default at this point in part because she knows she has the power to declare default if the debtor does not do better in the future. If this is how a creditor is likely to think about the matter, then actual consent and apparent consent are off the table.

Presumed consent is the remaining possibility. While this is a stretch for the same reason that apparent consent is off the table, a finding of presumed consent should be definitively precluded by an anti-waiver clause. Recall this illustration

63 Roscoe Pound, *The Role of the Will in Law*, 68 Harv. L. Rev. 1 (1954).
64 Roscoe Pound, Readings on the History and System of the Common Law 453 (1921).
65 Deryck Beyleveld & Roger Brownsword, Consent in the Law 40 (2007).
66 Clark v. West, 86 N.E. 1 (1908).

in the Restatement of Intentional Torts to Persons: "Tony enters a crowded bus and loudly shouts 'Keep your distance! Do not touch me.' Ben squeezes past Tony after the bus driver asks people to move to the back of the bus."[67] Tony's statement makes it impossible to find actual, apparent, or presumed consent so the Restatement creates a special rule to deal with such cases. An anti-waiver clause in a written contract is a commonplace analogy to Tony's shout. The anti-waiver clause precludes finding presumed consent because it gives the debtor "reason to believe" the creditor would not consent to waiving the power to declare default, if the creditor was asked. Nevertheless "the weight of authority ... is that an 'anti-waiver' clause, like any other term of a contract, is itself subject to waiver ...."[68]

It follows that waiver is possible only when relinquishment of a right is not thought to require consent. Contract rights are waivable as a general matter while personal rights protected by intentional torts to persons are not waivable (i.e., relinquishment of the right requires consent), and this is so for obvious reasons involving the differences between the relative interests of the parties in the two legal contexts.[69] Intentional torts to persons generally protect core human interests in bodily integrity, individual autonomy, and psychological well-being. Meanwhile the duties imposed by these torts generally do not greatly impair the interests of other people. People can comply with what the tort of battery commands of them by not intentionally touching other people in ways that harm or offend.

The relative interests of the parties often are very different when a waiver of a contract right is involved. Contract rights often involve purely financial interests, which can be less important to people than the personal interests protected by tort law. Meanwhile the obligation imposed by a contract can significantly impair the interests of the obligor. In Case 14, waiver imposes a fairly modest financial loss on the creditor while it protects the debtor from being unhoused without being given notice and a reasonable opportunity to cure the default. When a person's interest in a contract right is sufficiently weighty, then the right is likely to be treated as non-waivable or to require express waiver.

Assumption of risk is an affirmative defense to a personal injury claim (negligence or strict liability). When courts talk about assumption of risk there always has been a voluntary act of will by the plaintiff that put the plaintiff in a position to be harmed by the defendant's tortious conduct. In the nineteenth century it would have been odd to describe assumption of the risk as an exercise of a legal power. In many assumption-of-risk cases, the plaintiff voluntarily chose to put themselves in a position in which the defendant owed them no duty of

67 *Id.* § 1, Illustration 7.

68 Westinghouse Credit Corp. v. Shelton, 645 F.2d 869 (1981).

69 As you would expect, property rights are subject to derogation without consent. This generally is governed by the doctrine of equitable estoppel and not the doctrine of waiver.

care or only a limited duty of care. **Case 15**: Pedestrian jaywalks on a busy street with many speeding drivers. It would be odd to say Pedestrian exercises a legal power to absolve the drivers from a duty of care they would otherwise owe him. Pedestrian is putting themselves in a position in which the drivers owe them no duty of care or only a limited duty of care.[70]

The development of the modern negligence action put the doctrine in a tenuous position. One reason for this is that many results under the traditional doctrine clearly seem wrong under modern negligence law. Prosser's famous critique of the doctrine exploits Case 15. The pedestrian, Prosser argued, "cannot by any stretch of the imagination be found to consent that the drivers shall not use care to watch out for him and avoid running him down. On the contrary, he is insisting that they shall."[71] Prosser's rhetorical point about the absence of consent turns on defining the object of consent as the risk "drivers shall not use care to watch out for him," and not the choice to jaywalk on a busy street. A nineteenth-century court would have said the choice was to jaywalk and assumption of risk was a consequence of the choice. The result of no recovery in Case 15 clearly seems wrong under modern principles of tort law, which expand the duty of care to require people to take precautions against other people's careless conduct (and even other people's unlawful conduct), replace contributory negligence with comparative fault, and cut back on rules of superseding cause.

The history of the doctrine is an example of the importance of how one defines the object of an actor's choice when a rule is conditioned on an actor's choice. In the nineteenth century, a worker was held to assume the risk of negligence of her coworkers when she entered the workplace.[72] The object of choice was entering the workplace. Bearing the risk of coworkers' negligence was a consequence that followed from a worker choosing to enter the workplace. By the mid-twentieth century the object of choice was redefined in terms of the assumed risk. The rule in the Restatement, Second, Torts requires that the "plaintiff knows of the existence of the risk and appreciates its unusual character."[73] This change in the definition of the object of choice significantly narrowed the scope of the defense.

70 In some traditional assumption of risk cases the plaintiff's choice is to encounter defendant's otherwise wrongful conduct. For example, sober adult A freely and knowingly chooses to go joyriding in a passenger car driven by obviously intoxicated driver D. It would be odd to say in this case that D did not breach a duty not to drive while drunk. It would be more appropriate to say A's choice renders the breach non-wrongful with respect to A. I thank John Goldberg for this point.

71 W.P. Prosser et al., Prosser & Keeton on the Law of Torts 485 (5th ed. 1984). Kenneth Simons, *Assumption of Risk and Consent in the Law of Torts: A Theory of Full Preference*, 67 B.U.L. Rev. 213, 226 (1987), makes this point.

72 *See, e.g.*, Boatman v. Miles, 199 P. 933 (1921). Fleming James observes "assumption of the risk developed in response to the general impulse of common law courts 'to insulate the employer as much as possible from bearing the human overhead which is the inevitable part of the cost-to someone-of the doing of industrial business.'" Fleming James Jr., *Assumption of the Risk*, 61 Yale L.J. 141, 154 (1951).

73 Restatement, Second, Torts § 496D. The rule is subjective. See comment c.

The modern form of the doctrine has several strands.[74] One strand covers the enforceability of express exculpatory terms.[75] This generally is referred to as express assumption of risk.[76] Express exculpatory terms are creatures of contract and consent is determined applying contract law. They are subject to public policy limitations.[77] A second strand covers cases in which a plaintiff chooses to expose themselves to a known risk.[78] The Restatement, Second, Torts refers to this as implied assumption of risk.[79] A third strand covers cases in which a plaintiff chooses to engage in an activity that by its nature involves conduct that might be unreasonable in other contexts. A leading case involves a young woman who chose to play in a rough, co-ed touch football game during the Super Bowl halftime. She was held to have assumed the risk of having her finger badly broken by another player knocking her down and stepping on her hand.[80] Most cases in this strand involve recreational sports. A difference between the third (recreational sports) strand and the second strand is that under the recreational-sports strand, the plaintiff need not know of the risk she assumes. The object of choice is to engage in the sport.

It is possible to describe the recreational-sports strand of the doctrine as a rule of consent. The object of choice is both immediate and general: the choice is to

[74] Many torts scholars believe that once the doctrine is cut back to eliminate wrong results there is no useful work left for the concept of assumption of risk to do in negligence law. THE RESTATEMENT, THIRD, TORTS: APPORTIONMENT OF LIABILITY, takes this position. A 1987 paper by Kenneth Simons pushes back against the abolitionists. Simons identifies a narrow class of cases in which a plaintiff's conscious choice to encounter a risk ought to absolve an actor from liability for tortuously creating the risk. These are cases in which the plaintiff would have chosen to encounter the risk even if the plaintiff had been given the option to engage in the same activity without encountering the risk. Simons, *Assumption of Risk and Consent*, *supra* note 71, at 218–21. For example, a passenger in a car urges the driver to speed. Simons would not describe his rule as a rule of consent because of "the uncertainty the risk will materialize." Simons, *Assumption of Risk and Consent*, *supra* note 71, at 248.

[75] These terms sometimes are referred to as waivers. I do not use this term because they are treated like other contract terms. Consent is required and the term cannot be unilaterally revoked.

[76] RESTATEMENT, SECOND, TORTS § 496A.

[77] The rules that govern express exculpatory terms are unlike most of contract law in that a person with a bargaining advantage is not permitted to exploit that advantage to obtain a term absolving them from negligence liability and strict liability for bodily harm. *See, e.g.*, Tunkl v. Regents of University of California, 383 P.2d 441 (Cal. 1963)(stating that among the factors that weigh against enforcing an exculpatory term are that the defendant "is engaged in performing a service of great importance to the public, which is often a matter of practical necessity for some members of the public," and that "as a result of the essential nature of the service, in the economic setting of the transaction, the [defendant] possesses a decisive advantage of bargaining strength ...")

[78] *See, e.g.*, Smollett v. Skayting Dev. Corp., 793 F.2d 547 (3rd Cir. 1986).

[79] RESTATEMENT, SECOND, TORTS § 496C. Some versions of implied assumption of risk require that a plaintiff's choice to encounter a risk be reasonable. Under these versions of the rule, an unreasonable choice to encounter a risk is treated as contributory negligence, which is only a partial bar to recovery in a comparative-fault system, while a reasonable choice to encounter a risk is treated as assumption of risk, which is a complete bar to recovery. *See, e.g.*, Smollett v. Skayting Dev. Corp., 793 F.2d 547 (3rd Cir. 1986). In some jurisdictions where assumption of risk has been completely merged into comparative fault, a share of responsibility may be assigned to a plaintiff who reasonably chooses to encounter a risk. *See* Kenneth Simons, *Reflections on Assumption of Risk*, 50 UCLA L. REV. 48, 490, and n. 26 (2002).

[80] Knight v. Jewett, 834 P.2d 696 (Cal. 1992). The court called this primary assumption of risk.

participate in a recreational sport that is commonly understood to involve a risk of physical injury. Whether this can be described as a choice to exercise a legal power turns on how you think about the duty of care under negligence law. If you think of the duty of care in abstract and general terms, then you might say that a person who chooses to participate in a recreational sport is choosing to change their legal (and moral) position with respect to other participants so the duty they owe each other is to play by the rules of the game (formal and informal). If you think of duties of care in specific and relational terms, then you might find it difficult to describe this choice as an exercise of a legal power. Instead you might say the choice to participate in a sport creates and defines the duty owed.

VI. Conclusion

I have a defined a rule of consent as a rule that conditions an actor's exercise of a legal power on an actor consciously choosing or intending to do something, or to permit another person to do something, plus an absence of vitiating circumstances. Rules of this general form are ubiquitous in private law. The most important difference in these rules is how the object of consent is defined. Other differences include whether apparent consent and presumed consent are effective, the definition of vitiating circumstances, whether consent may be withdrawn, and whether consent must be communicated.

6

Private Law's Choice of Private Law

*Andrew S. Gold**

I. Introduction

Interstitial private law takes different forms. This chapter considers the interstitial private law that operates along the boundaries of private law fields (contract, tort, fiduciary law), telling us which field should govern a dispute when more than one field is potentially in play.[1] This interstitial law would be of limited import if each private law field converged on the same answers. Yet that convergence is clearly lacking, and in practice, the principles of private law fields diverge significantly. It is these contexts of divergence that this chapter will address. In such cases, should the court apply contract law or tort law? Tort law or fiduciary law? Some combination thereof?

Various legal doctrines provide answers to these questions. As I will argue, however, there is a pattern to the interstitial law in this context: among other things, the law generally operates to prevent the distinctive norms of each private law field from being overwhelmed by the distinctive norms of other private law fields. When encroachments from a neighboring field like contract law are sufficiently threatening to the operation of, say, tort law, interstitial private law works to limit the risk.

A closer look at this interstitial private law suggests additional features. First, there appear to be multiple strategies for addressing conflicts across private law fields (rules, standards, safety valves, and more complex structures). Second, at least some of these strategies give private law fields a modular structure—at least to a degree—not just at the local level of individual doctrines, but writ large. At times, the law requires courts to see a dispute in solely tort law terms, fiduciary law terms, or contractual terms, with the consequence that legal reasoning does not need to consider the implications for adjacent private law fields. The

* I am grateful to Courtney Cox, Mark Gergen, Ben McFarlane, Paul Miller, Henry Smith, and Ben Zipursky for helpful suggestions. I am also thankful for comments from participants at the Interstitial Private Law conference held in Rome and co-hosted by Notre Dame Law School and Harvard Law School, and from participants at a talk at the UC Irvine School of Law. Any interstitial errors are my own.

1 One could readily have added property law to this list, particularly if we consider the law of nuisance or landlord-tenant law. I thank Carol Rose for noting this.

Andrew S. Gold, *Private Law's Choice of Private Law* In: *Interstitial Private Law*. Edited by: Samuel L. Bray, John C.P. Goldberg, Paul B. Miller, and Henry E. Smith, Oxford University Press. © Oxford University Press 2024.
DOI: 10.1093/oso/9780197783627.003.0006

resulting field-level modularity serves multiple functions. As would be expected, it cuts down on delineation costs and information costs. But it also protects and even encourages divergence between the principles that govern contract, tort, and fiduciary law. In other words, private law principles may not merely diverge when viewed across contract, tort, and fiduciary law. When viewed as a system, private law may even aim at divergence.

With this in mind, I will conclude by suggesting several other functions that are served by the modularity of tort, contract, and fiduciary law (and, thus, by the interstitial private law that helps produce this modularity). At the micro-level, private law concepts are modular themselves, and that modularity serves multiple ends. Among other things, it contributes to the intrinsic value of special relationships (legal or moral). When these concepts are reduced to the terms of neighboring fields—for example, when fiduciary loyalty is reduced to a contractual obligation and nothing more—something worthwhile is lost. Interstitial private law protects the integrity of private law fields as a way of protecting the integrity of the smaller-scale concepts within these fields, and as a way of protecting the distinctive relationships that those concepts help to constitute.

This chapter will begin with the descriptive. Part II of this chapter will offer a brief discussion of what it means for a private law field to overlap with its neighbors—that is, what it means to have a boundary case. Part III will then discuss the different ways that interstitial private law addresses boundary cases involving tort, contract, and fiduciary law. Part IV will discuss field-level consequences. In addition to the significance for individual cases (e.g., a plaintiff may win or lose depending on whether contract law or tort law principles prevail), interstitial private law may also help maintain the principles within a private law field as a whole, preserving those principles from dilution and differentiating each field from its neighbors.

Part V will then shift focus to justifications. This portion of the chapter will indicate how interstitial private law gives private law fields (contract, tort, fiduciary law) a modular structure. Notably, this field-level modularity may cut down on delineation costs for judges and information costs for private parties; it is easier to know which field's law applies and to know the content of that law. Other benefits might include an increase in a field's internal coherence, or, perhaps, an increase in autonomy due to variation across private law fields. Part VI will turn to micro-level benefits. For example, field-level modularity may help preserve small-scale modular structures within those fields (e.g., certain conceptions of how rights, duties, and wrongs interrelate). This small-scale modularity, in turn, could again cut down on delineation costs and information costs. Another possibility, however, is that this small-scale modularity has a different kind of value. Thus, a loyalty obligation with a particular kind of modularity may contribute to the value of special relationships. Were contract law obligations to encroach too much on fiduciary law, the value of fiduciary relationships might decrease because of a change in the kind of loyalty involved. Part VII will conclude.

II. A Note on Definitions

On the present account, the law that governs choices between private law fields is a component of private law, but it does not fall within any one private law field in isolation. It is interstitial in the sense that it falls between fields or across fields (or is not identified with any one field in particular when applied), telling us which field should govern in a given context and which field is subservient or inapplicable. Thus, it is not merely a question of tort law whether tort should take precedence over contract law.[2] That is a question that tort law may help to answer, but it is not built into tort law that it should occupy a hierarchy with contract law subservient to tort (or vice versa). Nor is it built into contract law. Moreover, in certain settings the law may switch between one private law field and another, as occurs when courts pierce the corporate veil. Whatever hierarchy exists in veil piercing cases, it is dynamic. While one can call veil piercing doctrine a part of tort law (in tort settings), or a part of corporate law, it is equally accurate to say that it is an area of law that governs the interaction between these two fields.

In some of these cases there is a definitional challenge, at least after the fact. A central strategy for addressing cases that intersect with multiple private law fields is to determine that a given legal problem falls within one private law subfield rather than another. For example, when a court states that a given dispute arises from a contract and therefore must be decided in contractual terms rather than fiduciary terms, it is claiming that there is no proper overlap between these two fields. Ex post, one might think that such cases are not true boundary cases, insofar as the court's answer gives us a per se rule that only one legal field governs. It may simply be a matter of contract law that this is a contract law question. Yet the choice to favor a particular private law field in this way is not always a foregone conclusion when the case at issue is a case of first impression. I will treat such cases as boundary cases to the extent they involve uncertain outcomes ex ante (or could plausibly be seen that way by courts of law). That is, I will consider a case to be a boundary case subject to interstitial private law if the court

[2] It will, on the other hand, sometimes be a question of tort law what subject matter it covers. Boundary disputes will sometimes be eliminated by a careful elucidation of a particular private law field's core principles, without reference to any neighboring fields or concerns with their overlap. This is not to say that such elucidation eliminates the boundary disputes altogether. *Cf.* John Gardner, *Breach of Contract as a Special Case*, *in* TORTS AND OTHER WRONGS 343 (2020) (suggesting that "the classic way of contrasting contract-law obligations and tort-law obligations can survive important boundary skirmishes," while noting that "there are never-ending borderline cases of everything").

could plausibly—whether or not correctly—have found a legal problem to fall within either of two private law subfields.

I recognize, however, that there will be some instances where I might find interstitial private law to be in operation and the reader might disagree. The possibility of disagreement is increased by the reality that this type of interstitial private law is rarely announced as such when applied. I am hopeful that divergent interpretations are limited, but the argument in this chapter can allow for at least some contested applications. Other cases are more obviously interstitial private law questions, as is true for corporate veil piercing or for the rules on contractual modifications to partnership loyalty. While the exact scope of the phenomenon is something on which reasonable minds can differ, the phenomenon itself is evident in a range of private law settings.

III. Some Inter-Field Examples

In assessing this type of interstitial private law, I will consider three pairs of field-level relations: contract and tort; contract and fiduciary law; and tort and fiduciary law. Other combinations are possible: one might include property law, for example. These three categories, however, are especially common contexts for boundary cases, and they will be discussed for illustrative purposes.

Contract and tort interactions have produced some of the most famous decisions in the tort law canon. *MacPherson v. Buick Motor Co.* is a classic example of tort law principles taking precedence over contract law principles.[3] As Judge Cardozo indicated, the obligations in this context find their source in law, not in contract.[4] Yet, express assumption of risk cases suggest a different angle. Here, multifactor tests and public policy play an important role, and the potential for a contract to modify the effects of tort law will vary by situation.[5] Notwithstanding the import of public policy and the various factors in play, it is at least sometimes possible for contract principles to prove decisive. Analysis of these cases is admittedly complex, for we might think that the application of contract principles in these cases is nothing more than a specialized example of tort law principles in action. Still, it is possible to interpret express assumption of risk doctrine as an example of courts allowing contract principles to take priority within tort law where the right circumstances are present.

[3] MacPherson v. Buick Motor Co., 217 N.Y. 382 (1916).

[4] *See id.* at 390.

[5] *See, e.g.*, Dalury v. S-K-I Ltd, 670 A.2d 795, 797–98 (Vt. 1995). For further analysis of contract and tort interactions, *see* Mark P Gergen, *Privity's Shadow: Exculpatory Terms in Extended Forms of Private Ordering*, 43 Fla. St. U.L. Rev. 1 (2015); John C.P. Goldberg & Henry E. Smith, *Wrongful Fusion: Equity and Tort*, *in* Equity and Law: Fusion and Fission 309, 319–20 (John C.P. Goldberg et al. eds., 2019).

The relation between contract law and fiduciary law is well-traveled territory, and the many interactions between these two fields have triggered a lasting series of interpretive and policy debates. There is added complexity here because doctrinal patterns are so inconsistent. Some fiduciary settings show little room for contractual modifications, and it is commonplace in fiduciary law that contracts cannot eliminate the duty of loyalty altogether. In corporate law, contracts that limit fiduciary duties have been held unenforceable.[6] Certain fiduciary relationships will even lose their status in a given category if they do not include a duty of loyalty. A purported trust without fiduciary loyalty is not a trust; a purported agency relation without fiduciary loyalty is not agency.[7]

On the other hand, there are many settings in which fiduciary obligations are subject to contractual modifications, sometimes in dramatic fashion. It is no longer the case, as Judge Cardozo once said in *Meinhard v. Salmon*, that equity will not countenance a "disintegrating erosion" of the fiduciary duty of loyalty.[8] In certain settings, loyalty actually can be completely eliminated by contract—this is a characteristic feature of the Delaware LLC.[9] In other fiduciary contexts, fiduciary loyalty may be modified up to a point. The Revised Uniform Partnership Act permits partners to identify certain categories of conduct that will not violate the duty of loyalty, so long as this is not "manifestly unreasonable."[10] And the Delaware corporate code permits some corporate opportunities to be taken by a fiduciary where these opportunities are set forth ex ante in the corporation's charter.[11]

Contract and fiduciary law also interact in other ways. For example, there are also cases in which contract principles entirely displace the operation of fiduciary law. A good illustration is *Nemec v. Shrader*.[12] There, the Delaware Supreme Court adopted the following rule:

> [W]here a dispute arises from obligations that are expressly addressed by contract, that dispute will be treated as a breach of contract claim. In that specific

[6] *See, e.g.*, Paramount Communications v. QVC Network, Inc., 637 A.2d 34, 51 (Del. 1994) ("To the extent that a contract, or a provision thereof, purports to require a board to act or not act in such a fashion as to limit the exercise of fiduciary duties, it is invalid and unenforceable.").

[7] For discussion, *see* Andrew S Gold, *The Fiduciary Duty of Loyalty, in* The Oxford Handbook of Fiduciary Law 397 (Evan Criddle et al eds., 2019). The feature is not inevitable, for a default fiduciary relationship like the Delaware LLC can have loyalty duties removed entirely while still retaining its relationship status as an LLC. It is an interesting question whether we should distinguish LLC cases (which involve statutes) from common law doctrines that address boundary policing.

[8] *See* Meinhard, 249 N.Y. at 464.

[9] *See* Delaware Limited Liability Company Act, §18-1101.

[10] *See* Revised Uniform Partnership Act, §103 (b)(3) (providing for identification of types or categories of activities that do not violate the duty of loyalty "if not manifestly unreasonable").

[11] *See* Delaware General Corporation Law, §122(17) (providing for renunciation in corporate charter of specified business opportunities).

[12] Nemec v. Shrader, 991 A.2d 1120 (Del. 2010).

context, any fiduciary claims arising out of the same facts that underlie the contract obligations would be foreclosed as superfluous.[13]

Thus, in a case like *Nemec*, contract prevails over fiduciary obligations.

Preferred shares suggest a variation on this approach. In the default situation, the courts have made it clear that the rights of preferred shareholders are entirely a matter of what the preferred contract provides. The covenant of good faith and fair dealing provides some protections here, but it is interpreted narrowly. If, however, the preferred shareholders find themselves in a position of vulnerability equivalent to the vulnerability of the common shares, fiduciary duties are triggered.[14] In effect, equity steps in when the risks of opportunism against the preferred are severe enough, and it uses fiduciary law as its mechanism to protect the preferred.

Contract and fiduciary law are not unique in this respect; tort and fiduciary law also have a complex relationship. It is an interesting question whether fiduciary breaches are ever a species of tort; I will assume for present purposes that they are not tortious.[15] Even if we adopt that starting point, tort law encroaches in striking ways on the guiding principles of some fiduciary fields. Yet a case can also be made that fiduciary law principles encroach on tort law.

In a tort case, the doctrine on piercing the corporate veil can be seen as an example of tort law principles taking precedence over corporate law's limited liability rule (although it can also be seen as equity taking precedence). Enterprise liability for sibling corporations and successor liability doctrines provide further examples. Still, there are also circumstances in which fiduciary principles take priority over tort law principles. Consider what John Goldberg and Benjamin Zipursky refer to as a "triangular tort" setting.[16] Triangular tort cases involve special relationships that may cut off duties of care that are ordinarily owed to third parties. Doctor-patient relationships, therapist-patient relationships, and lawyer-client relationships all implicate this concern. A leading example involves therapists and their patients. Suppose a therapist causes great harm to a patient's father by using hypnosis in a negligent way, resulting in false recovered memories of abuse by the patient's father.[17] Although the cases are split, courts have shown a general reluctance to find a breach of care owed to the father.[18]

[13] *See id.* at 1129.

[14] *See* Jedwab v. MGM Grand Hotels, Inc., 509 A.2d 584, 594 (Del. Ch. 1986).

[15] *See* John Gardner, *Torts and Other Wrongs*, *in* TORTS AND OTHER WRONGS 1, 5–6 (2020) (suggesting there are reasons to separate equitable wrongs from torts).

[16] *See* John C.P. Goldberg & Benjamin C. Zipursky, *Triangular Torts and Fiduciary Duties*, *in* CONTRACT, STATUS, AND FIDUCIARY LAW 239, 241 (Paul B. Miller & Andrew S. Gold eds., 2016).

[17] *See id.*

[18] *See id.* (noting the split and also the general tendency to find there is no duty of care owed to the third party).

Goldberg and Zipursky suggest that a judicial refusal to recognize the tort law duty of care in cases like this is justified by the loyalty duty that the professional owes to her patient.[19] If so, then this is apparently a case in which fiduciary principles—most notably, fiduciary loyalty obligations—take precedence over what would ordinarily be standard tort law principles on the duty of care.

While no single private law field takes precedence over the others, there are recognizable tendencies among the legal mechanisms involved. We should note that the legal approaches in these boundary cases—the techniques used in this sphere of interstitial law—take characteristic forms. Some cases adopt what we might call a jurisdictional strategy. *Nemec v. Shrader* is a good example, inasmuch as the court announces a rule that fiduciary principles simply do not apply where the rights at issue are grounded in contractual relations. Others use a threshold strategy—in these cases, one private law field may encroach on another's territory with impunity, but only up to a point. Multifactor balancing tests are another approach. Consider the balancing tests that are commonly used in express assumption of risk cases. And there is also a safety valve approach, one characteristic of at least some applications of equity.[20] In cases of corporate veil piercing, an equitable exception to the corporate entity is recognized on a case-by-case basis. Here, the norm is to allow corporate law principles to take precedence, but in egregious circumstances tort law principles will take over.

It is also worth noting another way that these approaches can be categorized. Some of what modularizes a private law field could be internal to that field; it is simply the elaboration of that field's content as such (for example, an elaboration of what a tort is may help set its boundaries).[21] This mechanism operates at the primary level. In other cases, however, what works to modularize private law fields is a type of meta-law—that is, a type of law about law. This mechanism operates at a secondary level (for example, consider a court that analyzes, from an overarching perspective, whether contract law or fiduciary law should prevail in particular settings of potential conflict). Finally, these two mechanisms may operate in tandem. Meta-law might operate to fix a legal field's domain by putting in place a primary level limit on a legal field's content (for example, if a court decides as a matter of law that fiduciary law should prevail over tort law in a

[19] *See id.* at 247 ("There is a qualitatively different kind of legal duty on one side of this imagined ledger, and it is the sort of duty that, given the present state of the law, requires courts to decline to recognize a duty on the other side."). In other words, taking seriously the professional's loyalty duty does not leave space for recognizing a duty of care to third parties.

[20] For helpful discussion of a safety valve approach to equity, *see* Henry E. Smith, *Equity as Meta-Law*, 130 YALE L.J. 1050 (2021). As indicated therein, equity as meta-law does not always operate through safety valves.

[21] Note, however, that a private law field's boundaries will not always be fully clarified—in some cases, a private law field could have a larger potential domain of application than its actual application. I thank Henry Smith for noting this possibility.

certain context, and then consequently makes an adjustment by limiting the tort law duty of care from within tort law).[22]

These variable approaches tell us something about the judicial approach to boundary-policing doctrines. Courts do not merely demarcate the separate domains and applicability of each private law field's doctrine by happenstance; they have sophisticated and sometimes quite distinctive mechanisms for doing so. This interstitial private law is not only applied across a range of intersecting doctrinal fields, it is apparently the product of careful design. Rules, standards, safety valves are all in play, and presumably, they are in use with the goal of accomplishing something. I will turn to that topic now.

IV. Differentiation of Legal Fields

As indicated, there is a general pattern of private law fields taking precedence over adjacent fields in a wide range of contexts, and then deferring to those adjacent fields in a wide range of other contexts. No one field dominates the others. That is an interesting pattern, but one might think that its primary significance is at the level of individual case outcomes. Interstitial private law makes it more likely that particular plaintiffs will win, or that particular remedies will be available to those plaintiffs. Yet there is also something else that interstitial law likely accomplishes: differentiation of one private law field from another, with the effect that each private law field is largely independent in its conceptual analysis from neighboring fields.

Perhaps the strongest evidence for this effect is the pattern we see in the theoretical literature. There is a certain kind of reductive theorizing that seeks to recharacterize a private law field in light of the concepts and principles that predominate in a neighboring field. Prominent examples are the scholarly efforts to reinterpret fiduciary law as contractual at base, or to reinterpret contract law as tortious in nature. These theories fail badly as long as significant doctrinal fit is required. Interstitial private law is one likely reason why these theories founder on the law, for it facilitates the emergence of doctrinal features in each private law field that are a mismatch for their neighboring fields. The result is that, as long as a moderate degree of doctrinal fit is required, it is very difficult to develop reductive theories of fiduciary law in terms of contract, or contract in terms of tort.[23]

[22] I am grateful to Henry Smith for suggesting these distinctions.

[23] For what may be the most striking failure, *see* GRANT GILMORE, THE DEATH OF CONTRACT (1974) (suggesting contract law would be absorbed by tort law). Another example is the effort to theorize fiduciary law in contractual terms. *Compare* Frank H. Easterbrook & Daniel R. Fischel, *Contract and Fiduciary Duty*, 36 J. L. & ECON. 425 (1993), *with* Lionel Smith, *Contract, Consent, and Fiduciary Relationships*, *in* CONTRACT, STATUS AND FIDUCIARY LAW 117 (Paul B. Miller & Andrew S. Gold eds., 2016).

Note that, in policing boundaries between private law fields, courts make it less likely that principles from one field will be applied as part of the reasoning within another field, and thus avoid blurring conceptual categories. Indeed, the mere decision that one field versus another should prevail underscores that these fields are doctrinally different. Courts send a signal to future decision makers that the doctrinal material under review has its own coherence, its own characteristic set of rights, duties, wrongs, and remedies. That does not guarantee that future courts will agree, but it reinforces a certain mode of thinking, one in which each field is taken to have its own characteristic structure of reasoning and its own characteristic doctrines.

Interstitial law also makes it less likely that a field's concepts will fall into desuetude, replaced by the standard working of another field's concepts. In the extreme case, the risks are obvious. If, for example, duties of loyalty were removed as a matter of course through contractual customization, or if tort duties of care were rendered ineffective across the board through liability waivers, the respective fiduciary and tort obligations might be unchanged but they would also be unused. Whether or not fiduciary loyalty obligations or tort law duties of care would then be diluted by contractual principles, they would presumably evolve in a different fashion, and in all likelihood their content would suffer as a result.

As John Gardner indicates, private law fields evolve:

> As areas of law take shape, they also take root. Each develops its own way of differentiating itself and its own related way of accounting for itself, a rationale, or more often a set of connected but partly competing rationales, for its own existence.[24]

That process of taking root, and the resultant doctrinal differentiation, would likely be jeopardized if private law did not find some way to keep each field separate from adjacent, potentially overlapping fields.

These effects are hard to prove definitively. Even absent this interstitial law, there are reasons why reductivism would be difficult to achieve, and why doctrinal differentiation would persist. For example, in cases where two fields clearly do not overlap—and, thus, no interstitial private law is involved—courts might settle into a mode of thinking that is uniquely characteristic of contract, tort, or fiduciary law. Separation of fields can originate in more than one way, and so can differentiation of legal content. It is plausible to think, however, that interstitial private law's boundary-policing rules are a contributing factor in maintaining the conceptual differences between private law fields.

24 *See* John Gardner, *Torts and Other Wrongs*, *in* TORTS AND OTHER WRONGS 24 (2020).

We should also bear in mind that sometimes an overlap between private law fields poses no particular risk to each of the fields involved, given the mode of interaction between them. For example, consider the case of tortious interference in contractual relations.[25] This is rather clearly a context in which both tort and contract intersect, but it is not clear why one field would have to interfere with the clarity, content, or goals of the other. In such cases, policing boundaries is seemingly unnecessary, or less necessary, than it might be in cases like those involving a contractual waiver of tort liability. Differentiation of contract and tort law content could still be important in these more innocuous cases of overlap between fields. Indeed, it could be important both to have the overlap and to have differentiation. It seems likely that some interstitial private law bridges private law fields and helps coordinate their interactions rather than differentiating them or policing their boundaries.[26]

Let us assume, however, that boundary-policing interstitial law does have a differentiating effect. This brings us to the question whether any of this is desirable, and, to be sure, it may not be. After all, the particular concepts that take root in a given private law field might be misguided, or at least inferior to the concepts that have taken root in a neighboring field (or, perhaps, inferior to the concepts available if we combine both fields together). With these doubts on the table, we can now turn to a different question. Both at the doctrinal level and at the theory level, the law's approach to the boundaries between private law fields is noteworthy, and, apparently, consequential—this interstitial law likely helps to differentiate tort from contract, contract from fiduciary law. Are there reasons for adopting doctrine that limits interactions between private law fields in this way? The next sections of this chapter will shed light on this topic.

V. The Modularity of Private Law Fields

Consider the way that these interstitial private law mechanisms create separation among private law fields. Sometimes it is tort, sometimes contract, sometimes fiduciary law, but in each instance a particular field emerges as the victor, and courts will often have little doubt as to which field it should be. Interstitial private law determines which field should apply in which sphere, and those

[25] Note also that there are occasional failures to address properly the interactions between private law fields. Cf. John C.P. Goldberg & Robert H. Sitkoff, *Torts and Estates: Remedying Wrongful Interference with Inheritance*, 65 STANFORD L. REV. 335 (2013).

[26] Corporate law may be a candidate example, although it is questionable whether it merits the "interstitial" label. For helpful discussion of how corporate law brings together principles from more primary private law fields, *see* Paul B. Miller, *Corporations*, *in* THE OXFORD HANDBOOK OF THE NEW PRIVATE LAW 341 (Andrew S. Gold et al. eds., 2020). I thank Paul Miller for emphasizing this additional role for interstitial private law.

private law fields that don't apply then largely drop out of the picture. One way of looking at this phenomenon is to see how it makes private law fields into modular components of a larger private law system. This modularity, in turn, offers several potential justifications for private law's boundary-policing doctrines.

What does it mean for a legal institution to be modular? On one leading definition of modularity: "It is that 'of a unit that is a component part of a larger system and yet possessed of its own structural and functional identity.' "[27] As a module, a legal institution may thus be a subpart of a hierarchically organized system.[28] When sufficiently complex, such systems have certain characteristic features. Complex systems are often "nearly decomposable" in Herbert Simon's sense, hiding information within components that interact with other components along stylized interfaces.[29] As he notes, when a system is nearly decomposable in this way, "interactions between the subsystems are weak but not negligible."[30] While it uses different terms, Simon's account of the "nearly decomposable" is another way of recognizing that complex systems can often be broken into modules to limit their complexity.

Modularity is a matter of degree,[31] and I do not wish to overstate the point. As should be evident, modularity operates in a variety of settings, not all of them legal, and not all of them artificial (consider the view that the human mind is modular). Legal systems can, however, make use of modularity, much as other complex systems do. To the extent that happens, there are a variety of benefits:

> If a set of interactions can be partitioned such that interaction is intense within modules and less intense across interfaces, a system can achieve the benefits of complexity without many of the costs. Cars are modular systems and are easier to design, make, service, and use because the component subsystems interact in stylized ways—for example the fuel injection and the brakes. Such systems

[27] *See* Werner Callebaut, *The Ubiquity of Modularity*, *in* Modularity: Understanding the Development and Evolution of Natural Complex Systems 8 (Werner Callebaut & Diego Rasskin-Gutman eds., 2005) (quoting L. Moss, *Deconstructing the gene and reconstructing molecular developmental systems*, *in* Cycles of Contingency: Developmental Systems and Evolution 91 (S. Oyama, P.E. Griffiths & R.D. Gray eds., 2001).

[28] On hierarchically organized systems, *see* Herbert A Simon, *The Architecture of Complexity*, 106 Proceedings of the American Philosophical Society 467, 468–69 (1962). As Simon makes clear, the term "hierarchy" is used in a loose sense.

[29] *See* Herbert A. Simon, The Sciences of the Artificial 197 (3rd ed. 1996). For application to legal institutions, *see* Henry E. Smith, *Property as the Law of Things*, 125 Harv. L. Rev. 1691, 1701–03 (2012).

[30] Simon, *supra* note 29, at 197.

[31] *See* Callebaut, *supra* note 27, at 6 (noting that modularity should be seen as a "gradual property"). *See also* Ted Sichelman & Henry E Smith, *A Network Model of Legal Relations*, 382 Phil. Transactions Royal Soc'y A 1 (2024).

> are more robust, easier to understand, and afford a range of flexibility in evolution and innovation.[32]

With appropriate adjustments, what works for cars can also work for legal institutions.

Granted, modularity is not always easy to achieve. It may be no coincidence that tort, contract, and fiduciary law each also have extralegal analogues. Breaking up complex systems into component parts is much easier if there are intuitive breaking points available. Drawing on Plato's *Phaedrus*, Carliss Baldwin and Kim Clark note the advantage of finding such breaking points:

> For human beings, the only way to manage a complex system or solve a complex problem is to break it up. In the breaking apart, it is best to look for points of natural division, dividing "the Idea at the joints, as nature directs, not breaking any limb in half as a bad carver might."[33]

Private law fields may not be broken up "as nature directs," but it helps that their boundaries are often recognizable from the perspective of conventional morality.[34]

Note, also, that this breaking up into component parts calls for some sort of interface between modules. As Baldwin and Clark also note:

> An interface is a preestablished way to resolve potential conflicts between interacting parts of a design. It is like a treaty between two or more subelements. To minimize conflict, the terms of these treaties—the detailed interface specifications—need to be set in advance and known by the parties.[35]

Interstitial private law fits this template quite nicely; indeed, it can be compared to a treaty between private law subfields.

Why should courts create field-level modules? In legal contexts, one of the primary benefits of modularity is that it cuts down on delineation costs for

[32] *See* Andrew S. Gold & Henry E. Smith, *Scaling Up Legal Relations*, *in* WESLEY HOHFELD A CENTURY LATER: EDITED WORK, SELECT PERSONAL PAPERS, AND ORIGINAL COMMENTARY 419, 432 (Shyamkrishna Balganesh, Ted Sichelman & Henry E. Smith eds., 2022).

[33] CARLISS Y. BALDWIN & KIM B. CLARK, 1 DESIGN RULES: THE POWER OF MODULARITY 64 (MIT 2000) (citing Plato, *Phaedrus*, 265D).

[34] Granted, one could imagine other easy breaking points. One might have a "law of the waterfront" or a "law of railroads." I thank Carol Rose for the examples.

[35] *See* BALDWIN & CLARK, *supra* note 33, at 73. Note that accessibility may be as important as simplicity when selecting breaking points. For further discussion of the accessibility issue, *see* Andrew S. Gold & Henry E. Smith, *Legal Concepts as a Deep Structure of the Law: Reinach's A Priori in Action*, *in* REINACH AND THE FOUNDATIONS OF PRIVATE LAW (Marietta Auer, Paul B. Miller, Henry E. Smith & James Toomey eds., forthcoming).

courts. For example, a thing-centered account of *in rem* rights is modular in a way that a Hohfeldian, bundle of rights picture tends not to be. This makes it much easier for courts to elaborate on legal rights and obligations in concrete cases. Such delineation cost benefits also suggest one reason why it makes sense to modularize a private law field like contract law or tort law. In figuring out the details of contract law, courts will only have to worry about limited settings in which the details of contract law will impinge on useful tort law doctrines; likewise, courts resolving tort law cases will usually not need to think through all of the contract law settings that their holding might influence.[36]

Another fundamental benefit is that modularity cuts down on information costs for regulated parties and transactional planners. This information cost worry should matter even for theorists who are not drawn to the overall economic perspective. It is a basic rule of law concern that private law concepts are accessible and not overly complex.[37] If private parties cannot readily tell if they should be navigating tort law versus fiduciary law norms, or contract law versus tort law norms—or even some muddled combination—then the information costs will be quite high. Given that the information costs will in some settings be high even in a single field (see, for example, the Hand Formula), a system of overlapping private law fields is a recipe for profound informational complexity.[38] In short, field-level modularity could be valuable for the standard delineation cost and information cost reasons, whether or not our starting point is an overall efficiency concern.

Still, field-level modularity is not only significant for delineation cost and information cost reasons.[39] This modularity also has implications for coherence purposes. As Gardner suggests, efforts to find a narrative coherence that cuts across private law fields may be counterproductive:

> Narrative coherence is not scalable. Growing indifferent to the established legal differences between torts and equitable wrongs, or becoming rationalistically fixated with harmonizing contract with tort, is apt to create an incomprehensible brouhaha: not a more unified narrative, not a bigger choice of narratives, but no narrative at all.[40]

36 Of particular concern is the way that concepts used in one field can have ripple effects in other fields where a version of the same concept reappears. On this type of systemic concern, *see* Jeremy Waldron, *"Transcendental Nonsense" and System in the Law*, 100 COLUM. L. REV. 16, 40 (2000). Some degree of modularity may cabin that risk.

37 *See* Andrew S. Gold & Henry E. Smith, *Sizing Up Private Law*, 70 U. TORONTO L.J. 489, 511–12 (2020).

38 For a suggestion that the separation of property, tort, and contract subsystems provides clarity-related benefits, *see* Henry E. Smith, *Modularity and Morality in the Law of Torts*, 4 J. TORT L. 1, 28 (2011).

39 *Cf.* Gardner, *supra* note 15, at 24 (discussing the way field-specific rationales take root).

40 *See id.* at 25.

If Gardner is right in this thesis, then an additional benefit of modularity could be that it helps avoid the incoherence that would result if private law fields were more unified.[41] The interstitial private law that governs boundary cases may actually preserve the disunity of private law, as an alternative to the incomprehensible results of convergence across fields. If narrative coherence is a desirable goal for legal systems, this suggests another justification for separating fields. Indeed, a further possibility emerges if we adopt a pluralist account like Hanoch Dagan's, which draws on autonomy principles to support variation across fields.[42]

Under the right circumstances, these goals could be sufficient to justify the boundary-policing doctrines in private law's interstices. That depends on how costly complexity is in a given setting, how redundant or not interstitial private law turns out to be, or how problematic, if at all, the legal doctrine is that develops in a given private law field. There may, however, be another family of justifications worth considering, one which emphasizes the interaction between mid-level and micro-level legal features.

Recall the discussion earlier of private law's differentiation. By allowing different private law principles to take root in each field, notice that field-level modularity could help preserve small-scale modular subsystems that are themselves a means to limit complexity. In addition, there could be intrinsically valuable features of small-scale private law relationships that are jeopardized when one private law field encroaches too much on another. For example, if a special relationship's intrinsic value is lost when fiduciary law is reduced to a contractual subject matter, then field-level modularity may have another justification; it may help differentiate fiduciary law from contract law in a way that retains the value in such special relationships. I will turn to these possibilities in the next section.

VI. Rethinking Modularity's Role

These reflections invite a reassessment of what modularity does for private law. First, private law's modularity is often recognized at the micro-level of deontological reasoning. Here, we see modularity instead at the mid-level of legal

[41] Interestingly, the resulting local coherence might also be a way for legal systems to make room for the intuition-based contradictions that sometimes exist in our personal lives. *See* Bernard Williams, *Conflicts of Values*, *in* MORAL LUCK 82 (1981) ("[T]he public order, if it is to carry conviction, and also not to flatten human experience, has to find ways in which it can be adequately related to private sentiment, which remains more 'intuitive' and open to conflict than public rules can be."). While interstitial private law may sometimes add unity to private law (cf. Zoë Sinel's chapter in this volume), it may also have the benefit of making private law less unified.

[42] *See* Hanoch Dagan, *Pluralism and Perfectionism in Private Law*, 112 COLUM. L. REV. 1409 (2012).

fields. Second, private law's modular structures are often justified by concerns with delineation costs and information costs. This is with good reason, but at this level we can see justifications of another type. As suggested, field-level modularity may help retain the narrative coherence of private law, or it may facilitate an autonomy-centered pluralism. These alternatives are not mutually exclusive. Many private law concepts and doctrines are multifunctional; private law's modularity could be multifunctional as well.[43]

There are, however, additional reasons why field-level modularity could be useful. Notably, field-level modularity can protect smaller-scale structures within each module. Recall the idea that modular components may be parts of hierarchically ordered systems. It is possible to think of private law's micro-level modular structures as components of a larger, mid-level system (e.g., the tort system or the contract system), a system which is in turn a modular component of a yet larger system (e.g., the private law system, or even the public law system). The field-level modularity of contract, tort, or fiduciary law may even serve to protect the micro-level modularity of private law rights and duties that are components of those field-level conceptual structures.[44]

This may once again offer delineation cost and information cost benefits, but in a different way (for we are now concerned with the simplicity and accessibility of smaller-scale subsystems rather than the simplicity and accessibility of the fields themselves). For example, Henry Smith has argued that the smaller-scale features of tort law—its bilateral structure, its notions of corrective justice, or its application of proximate cause—contribute modularity.[45] This small-scale modularity has information cost benefits, given the simplicity and accessibility of tort law's deontological concepts for potential litigants, and the way that it rules out otherwise relevant context. The legal concepts could also be easier for courts to apply, given their own familiarity with the concepts at issue. But the modularity of these structures is by no means guaranteed—at least not to the same degree—if tort law suffers encroachments from its neighbors. By limiting intrusions from other legal fields, field-level modularity could protect the integrity of these submodules, thus preserving the delineation cost and information cost benefits that they offer.

And this is not the only plausible justification for preserving smaller-scale modular structures. At the micro-level, note again that the relational rights

[43] On the multifunctionality of private causes of action, *see* Andrew S. Gold, The Right of Redress 229 (2020). And with respect to legal concepts generally, *see* Simon Deakin, *Juridical Ontology: The Evolution of Legal Form*, 40 Historical Social Research 170, 180 (2015).

[44] Note that a nesting of smaller modular structures within larger modular structures is not uncommon. *See* Angela D. Buscalioni et al., *Modularity at the Boundary Between Art and Science, in* Callebaut & Rasskin-Gutman, *supra* note 27, at 296 ("An important class of modular systems is that of modules whose inner structure is also modular.").

[45] *See* Smith, *supra* note 38.

and duties of interpersonal morality itself can also be seen in modular terms.[46] For example, the obligation that a promisor owes to a promisee has modular features, carving away at the informational context that promisors would otherwise need to know in figuring out their moral obligations to others. While information costs may sometimes bear on the content of these moral obligations,[47] it is doubtful that this modularity is fully explicable in information cost terms. Irrespective of the reasons why morality has such features, however, the law may still have reasons for adopting legal concepts that mirror a parallel set of moral concepts. If private law doctrine has independent reasons to reflect interpersonal morality, it may then need to take on the modularity of parallel moral norms irrespective of delineation cost and information cost benefits. A failure to do so could result in legal concepts that are not recognizably moral.

Why seek to reflect such moral concepts? One functional reason is if the law is concerned with compliance effects. Where private law obligations are sufficiently close to what citizens understand their interpersonal moral obligations to be, citizens could be more likely to comply with these legal obligations.[48] Alternatively, the law might be motivated by an accommodationist approach.[49] Where private law obligations are sufficiently close to what citizens understand to be their interpersonal moral obligations, this decreases the burden those agents would otherwise experience should they feel compelled to follow laws that they perceive as immoral. In either event, the modularity of the moral norms at issue might be of interest not for its own sake, nor for information and delineation cost reasons, but simply because legal doctrine that retains this modularity would show less of a gap between law and conventional morality. That decreased distance, in turn, could result in better compliance or a smaller burden on moral agents.[50]

Small-scale modularity may also help constitute something intrinsically valuable. For example, obligations that are modular in the right way may be partly constitutive of a special relationship. Consider Philip Pettit's recent work on the virtues. He has argued that friends will often engage in a "standby strategy"

[46] *Cf.* Michael Thompson, *What Is It to Wrong Someone? A Puzzle about Justice*, *in* REASON AND VALUE: THEMES FROM THE MORAL PHILOSOPHY OF JOSEPH RAZ 333, 334 (R. Jay Wallace et al. eds., 2004) (describing a moral relation involving "a peculiar nexus which limits your pursuit of objectives of any kind, even the beautiful objectives of charity and the love of justice."). Thompson appears to be describing a modular structure.

[47] *See* T.M. SCANLON, WHAT WE OWE TO EACH OTHER 189 (1998).

[48] *Cf.* Paul Robinson & John Darley, *The Utility of Desert*, 91 NW. U. L. REV. 453 (discussing this possibility in the criminal law setting); Janice Nadler, *Flouting the Law*, 83 TEX. L. REV. 1399 (2005) (indicating that the perceived legitimacy of a law or legal outcome can influence compliance with unrelated laws).

[49] *See* Seana Valentine Shiffrin, *The Divergence of Contract and Promise*, 120 HARV. L. REV. 708 (2007).

[50] It is also possible that modularity could support more robust sets of values that are attached to each field, values which could be worth advancing in their own right. I thank Paul Miller for emphasizing potential linkages to more robust values, beyond the question of autonomy.

which makes use of modular thought processes.[51] On Pettit's view, a true friend will have a predisposition to help his friend without thinking about it, simply because his friend has made a request. Thus, one should help a friend move from one apartment to another without deliberating about the morality of doing so.[52] On the other hand, when the figurative alarm bells ring, one should stop to deliberate in light of all relevant moral considerations. Should the friend ask for help moving a body instead of moving out of her apartment, it is time for moral deliberation.[53]

Pettit suggests that this standby strategy of moral deliberation in response to appropriate cues (and not otherwise) reflects a modular approach: "When I authorize the rule of such general dispositions in my life I let them govern me like modular, automatic pilots, provided that the red lights don't go on—provided that there are no contextually salient signs that a given situation is exceptional and that following the predispositions might not really be for the best."[54] As he also notes, such a "modular pilot operates more or less autonomously, like the modularized skill revealed in typing and in tying your shoelaces."[55]

What this modularity accomplishes is a kind of deliberative priority that is built into friendships, a priority which means that the one friend will not think "one thought too many" when asked for help by another friend.[56] This deliberative priority, in turn, is part of what makes friendships meaningful for participants in such relationships. When we are friends with someone, part of what makes this relationship valuable is that our friend will help us when we are in need, for the right reasons and in the right way. The reasons for modularity are distinctive in such cases, but, as we will see, they are also suggestive.

Let us return now to interstitial private law, and the field-level modularity under discussion earlier. This standby model offers insights into the operation of the adjudicative process within a complex legal system. Pettit's analysis can help us understand how judges may think in a localized, modular way without completely avoiding larger-scale deliberations where necessary.[57] The standby strategy, moreover, can have multiple applications within legal reasoning.

[51] *See* Philip Pettit, *The Inescapability of Consequentialism*, *in* LUCK, VALUE, AND COMMITMENT: THEMES FROM THE ETHICS OF BERNARD WILLIAMS 41, 45–47 (Ulrike Heuer & Gerald Lang eds., 2012) [*Inescapability*]; PHILIP PETTIT, THE ROBUST DEMANDS OF THE GOOD: ETHICS WITH ATTACHMENT, VIRTUE, AND RESPECT 221–22 (2015) [*Robust Demands*].

[52] *See* PETTIT, ROBUST DEMANDS, *supra* note 51, at 221.

[53] *See id.*

[54] *See id.* at 46–47.

[55] *See id.* at 47.

[56] *See id.* at 221 ("You will be suitably spontaneous and will not have one thought too many to count as a friend."). For the classic discussion of having "one thought too many," *see* Williams, "Persons, Character, and Morality," in *Moral Luck*, *supra* note 41, at 18.

[57] For helpful discussion of this adjudicative approach, *see* Shivprasad Swaminathan, *What the Centipede Knows: Polycentricity and "Theory" for Common Lawyers*, 40 OXFORD J. LEG. STUD. 265, 279 (2020) (describing how judges have a "fragmented vision" in deciding cases).

First, consider how courts resolve ordinary common law disputes. Much of the common law is polycentric in Michael Polanyi's sense, such that courts show a characteristic "blindness to anything and everything other than the case at hand."[58] The result is a "fragmented vision" that, at least in theory, precludes judges from invoking "ultimate values or teleological aims."[59] While it should be evident that courts do not always follow that template, they do so often enough for it to matter. But how can courts manage to be blind in this way—how can they have a fragmented vision—while still occasionally widening their visual horizon to take into account the bigger picture? Pettit's idea of a standby strategy can help explain how this is possible.

A fragmented judicial vision can, however, also work in another way: it can allow judicial focus on the principles central to particular private law fields to the exclusion of their neighbors. Thus, courts applying contract law concepts may deliberate using a contractual lens, and courts applying fiduciary law concepts may deliberate using a fiduciary law lens.[60] As this chapter has sought to show, courts have a fragmented vision with respect to the particular private law field that they determine should apply to a given legal dispute. Even if the court is only trying to do justice between the parties—and even if we assume no macro-level analysis of society-wide effects—the court may still blind itself to otherwise applicable private law principles from adjacent private law fields. It may, likewise, remove the blinders where this seems appropriate (in this regard, consider corporate veil piercing). Once again, the idea of a standby strategy may helpfully indicate how this is possible.

Note the pattern involved. This is a kind of modularity in deliberation, much like the one Pettit describes for friendships. It is also a kind of modularity that can be overcome when the alarm bells go off. Indeed, this standby approach has potential applications in other areas where legal reasoning needs a separation of categories. Thus, it may sometimes hold true when equity intervenes in legal analysis; when equity operates as a safety valve (as opposed to its other modes of operation), courts may avoid equitable reasoning by default in the standard case but know when to apply it in certain exceptional cases.[61] Field-level modularity may not be an isolated case, and it may likewise engage courts in a standby approach, subject to alarm bells in the egregious cases.

[58] *See* Swaminathan, *supra* note 57, at 279 (citing Michael Polanyi, The Logic of Liberty: Reflections and Rejoinders 173–75 (1951)).

[59] *See id* at 279.

[60] On the potential import of a fiduciary lens for judicial reasoning, *see* Gregory Alexander, *A Cognitive Theory of Fiduciary Relationships*, 85 Cornell L. Rev. 767 (2000).

[61] *See* Andrew S. Gold, *Equity and the Right to Do Wrong*, *in* Philosophical Foundations of the Law of Equity 72, 88 n. 69 (Dennis Klimchuk, Irit Samet & Henry E. Smith, eds, 2020) (noting Pettit's argument); Henry E. Smith, *Fusion of Law and Confusion of Equity*, *in* Philosophical Foundations of the Law of Equity 210, 223 n. 57 (Dennis Klimchuk, Irit Samet & Henry E Smith eds., 2020) (same).

Yet, there is also a further insight we can glean from Pettit's account. As noted, field-level modularity may help preserve modular structures at the micro-level. And, as noted, this can cut down on information costs and delineation costs. We are now in a position to see that small-scale modular structures may also help constitute intrinsically valuable relationships, precisely because those small-scale structures are modular. Pettit's analysis suggests a non-legal example—the modularity of loyalty obligations may be part of what makes them a valuable part of certain special relationships like friendships. If a friend automatically deliberated in light of all-things-considered morality, this could damage or even preclude the kind of prioritization in deliberation that helps constitute friendships.[62] But note also that if a friend deliberated in a contractual way, the damage could be, if anything, more severe. It could signal that the friend is acting on her friend's behalf to keep her word, rather than out of loyalty. Depending on the understanding of contract principles, it could also mean that the friend has one thought too many.

This challenge to the loyalty of friends can be transposed to fiduciary relationships. The lawyer or guardian or corporate director who uses a hypothetical bargain analysis to figure out what she ought to do may not seem so loyal—if loyal at all—in comparison to the fiduciary who deliberates in a more modular way. And this suggests another potential justification for interstitial private law. Interstitial private law can decrease the likelihood that fiduciaries will see their loyalty in contractual terms, by more cleanly separating contractual from fiduciary loyalty-based obligations. The resulting non-contract-based deliberative processes, in turn, may be part of why these relationships are intrinsically valuable. In legal settings, the modularity of private law fields may thus help preserve smaller-scale modular structures that partly constitute special relationships.[63]

The challenges to small-scale legal concepts often stem from a certain kind of law and economics scholarship that treats traditional concepts of rights, duties, and remedies as epiphenomenal.[64] Or, they stem from a legal realist perspective on legal concepts, such as the one famously espoused by Felix Cohen in his argument against "transcendental nonsense" in the law.[65] These are external ways of

[62] To be clear, I am not saying that similar deliberative requirements apply to fiduciaries as a matter of law. Theorists' efforts to describe fiduciary loyalty as mandating ways of thinking tend to outstrip what courts actually say.

[63] Note that other forms of reductivism also pose this risk—not just reductivism of one private law field's concepts into the concepts native to another private law field. Breaking legal doctrines and concepts into their component parts (as Hohfeld often does) may also change their meaning. On the possibility that meaning will change if something is seen in terms of its component parts, *see* MICHAEL POLANYI, THE TACIT DIMENSION 18–19 (2009).

[64] For discussion and critique of that approach, *see* Gold & Smith, *supra* note 37.

[65] Felix S. Cohen, *Transcendental Nonsense and the Functional Approach*, 35 COLUM. L. REV. 809 (1935).

thinking about legal concepts, generally coming from outside the legal point of view. Yet reductivist threats to legal concepts can also be internal to the law; they may even come from within private law itself. For example, Gardner recently argued that a contract-based reductivism is a serious threat to certain "strictly relational" legal obligations, most notably those recognized in fiduciary law and family law.[66] If he is right, then it is contract law and its characteristic modes of thought that pose the risk, rather than just an abstract theory of legal concepts. Interstitial private law may be a countermeasure.

Contractarian accounts of fiduciary obligations, however, may not only revise the obligations of neighboring private law fields—qualitatively changing them—they may substantially de-modularize those obligations. This is true for the hypothetical bargain analysis of fiduciary duty espoused by legal economists. Unfortunately, a largely demodularized loyalty doesn't feel much like loyalty at all. That, in turn, could have dramatic effects on the culture of loyalty outside the law if fiduciaries, beneficiaries, and third parties take the courts seriously in their interpretation. Just as efficient breach theory may corrode a culture of promising, the hypothetical bargain account of loyalty may corrode a culture of loyalty.[67] The meaningfulness of relationships built on such obligations could easily be lost or at least curtailed given that the object of the loyalty at issue would no longer be prioritized in the right way.

If interstitial private law limits incursions from one private law field into a neighboring field's territory, it may thus do more than simplify the delineation of each field's doctrines. It may likewise do more than lower information costs for private parties who wish to know which sets of doctrines will apply to their conduct. These boundary-policing rules and standards may also preserve the smaller-scale modularity that operates within each field. That can cut down on legal complexity, but it can do much more. It can also help reinforce intrinsically valuable legal relationships by retaining the right features of the small-scale obligations that help to constitute them.[68]

These reflections are not intended as a last word on field-level modularity in private law. There may well be other benefits to private law's modular features. For example, there are well-recognized linkages between nearly decomposable systems and a system's evolvability. It might be that the partial separation of private law fields is relevant not only for the way those particular fields take root and differentiate, but also for the ongoing evolution of

[66] *See* John Gardner, From Personal Life to Private Law 41–46 (2018).

[67] *Cf.* Shiffrin, *supra* note 49.

[68] A further, related possibility is that this modularization will assist in specialization, so that each module can do whatever it does better. On specialization and legal systems, *see* Smith, *supra* note 20, at 1100–08.

the private law system as a whole. While private law theory tends to focus on a static picture of private law, a dynamic account of private law is also well worth analyzing.[69]

That said, I do not wish to overstate judicial prescience, or even judicial cognizance of these concerns. There could be reasons for the modularity of tort, contract, and fiduciary law, which are not directly concerned with complexity or intrinsic value, let alone the evolvability of systems. These effects could stem from judicial preference *simpliciter*. People may sometimes like to think in a modular way, with or without attendant policy benefits. Consider this account in Robert Musil's lengthy novel, *The Man Without Qualities*:

> We know that our life is ebbing away both outward into the inhuman distances of cosmic space and downward into the inhuman microspace of the atom, while we go on dealing with a middle stratum, the things that make up our world, without troubling ourselves at all over the fact that this proves only a preference for impressions received in the middle distance, as it were.[70]

This perspective suggests a taste for modular thinking, and perhaps it is a taste shared by judges.[71]

Perhaps also the modularity of private law fields is unintended. Courts that think in modular terms when deciding cases are unlikely to devote too much attention to system effects; it might even be self-defeating for them to do so.[72] That is an irony, but the motivations for creating modularity and its desirability are different things. For whatever reasons, interstitial private law reinforces modularity at the field level, and this chapter sketches some potential justifications for this pattern. If there are other justifications for such doctrines, even unintended ones, so much the better.

Note, also, that the subject matter of this chapter could be expanded. Private law's field-level modularity is suggestive of modularity at different scales and concerning different systems. One might fruitfully compare the boundary-policing doctrines that separate private law as a whole—a more macro-level

[69] For further discussion of how to make changes in private law while taking seriously its conceptual structure, *see* Andrew S. Gold & Henry E. Smith, *Restatements and the Common Law*, *in* The American Law Institute: A Centennial History (Andrew S. Gold & Robert W. Gordon eds., 2023).

[70] Robert Musil, 1 The Man Without Qualities 574 (1996).

[71] Query also whether a removal of macro-level (or micro-level) context from our conscious thought is hard to avoid when attempting to understand complex systems. *Cf.* Simon, *supra* note 29, at 207 ("If there are important systems in the world that are complex without being hierarchic, they may to a considerable extent escape our observation and understanding.").

[72] They may, however, be quite cognizant of complexity as a problem. *See* Gold & Smith, *supra* note 37, at 511–12.

module—from public law—another macro-level module.[73] And there is also modularity that impacts different types of law within a larger legal system. Thus, one might compare the boundary-policing doctrines that address the interactions between law and equity.[74] Indeed, it is possible to assess the modularity of private law with respect to systems that are not legal at all. Private law as a modular system has interfaces with custom, and not just with other legal fields.[75] These phenomena are not identical with the interstitial private law that is the central concern of this chapter, but they may well involve similar concerns.

We should likewise be aware that the modularity of private law fields has costs; carving away context can mean you miss out on important information, and it can thus preclude decisions that would be better choices, all things considered. It is also entirely possible that the particular methods selected for policing private law boundaries are poorly chosen or poorly executed in practice. Or, it might be that the separation of private law fields occasionally works to prop up a field that is now obsolete, slowing legal evolution in areas where it is needed. And we should keep in mind that, while the modularity of private law could enhance the system's coherence—if, for example, the narrative coherence of private law does not scale up well—such modularity could instead lead to incoherence if it encourages contradiction in legal principles.

Figuring out how to limit those costs while retaining modularity's benefits is an additional challenge worth facing. Indeed, this consideration may help justify some of the particular mechanisms adopted by this form of interstitial private law, such as the use of equitable safety valves to handle veil piercing, or the adoption of threshold strategies to govern the relation between partnership and contract law. Private law fields may be more or less modular depending on how each field is separated, or when each field prevails over others. Modularity, again, comes in degrees, and there are different ways that it might be achieved.

VII. Conclusion

Interstitial private law helps separate private law fields one from another, while determining which field should prevail in cases of overlap. One major consequence is that these fields are more modular than they otherwise might be.

[73] On the dynamic relationship between private law and public law, *see* Thomas W. Merrill, *Private and Public Law*, *in* The Oxford Handbook of the New Private Law (Andrew S. Gold et al. eds., 2020).

[74] On this topic, compare Samuel Bray's chapter in this volume, on the "Equity will not" doctrines. *See also* Smith, *supra* note 20.

[75] The interactions here may include cases where custom is incorporated into law, as sometimes occurs with tort law. But they may also involve cases where law renders the customary illegal. Cf. Carol Rose's chapter in this volume.

Modularity in the law is best known as a response to complexity, and indeed that is a central reason why this result could be valuable. Yet we have reason to care about field-level modularity even if our primary concern is not with the complexity of systems, delineation costs, or information costs. This is not just because handling complexity can help with other goals, such as advancing the rule of law or providing corrective justice in a more effective way. It is also because modular structures, at both the mid-level and micro-level, can help contribute to the existence and meaning of special relationships and obligations that the law helps constitute. Interstitial private law preserves and reinforces the distinctiveness of private law fields like contract, tort, and fiduciary law—and, if this chapter is right, that distinctiveness is worth having for multiple reasons.

7
Recklessness in Tort

Interstitial Law as Doctrinal Fine-Tuning

*John C.P. Goldberg and Benjamin C. Zipursky**

I. Introduction

This chapter addresses a seemingly haphazard collection of instances in which tort liability turns on *recklessness*. That concept—or one that is typically interpreted in a manner that references it—is particularly prominent in three torts but also pops up in other tort areas.

The most familiar of these is found in modern defamation law. Under *New York Times v. Sullivan*,[1] a public figure suing for libel or slander can prevail only by showing that the defendant published the statement knowing it was false or with reckless disregard for its falsity. Second, and similarly, in common law deceit and in parts of federal securities law, plaintiffs contending that the defendant defrauded them must prove that the defendant knew the misrepresentations were false or acted with reckless indifference to their truth or falsity. Third, to prove the tort of intentional infliction of emotional distress through outrageous conduct (IIED), a plaintiff can prevail by proving that the defendant was reckless as to the risk of causing such distress to them. Finally, courts and legislatures in various situations have adopted a recklessness standard for particular personal injury claims or have defined qualified privileges or safe harbors from liability by reference to a recklessness standard.

In keeping with the theme of this conference, we will pose and sketch an answer to the following question: In what sense, or in what ways, is recklessness an interstitial component of tort law? There are at least three possible answers to this question.

(1) Many scholars have supposed that tort law can fruitfully be organized around three categories: intentional torts, negligence, and strict liability. The validity of this assumption is doubtful.[2] Nonetheless, a modern scholar working

* Thanks to Paul Miller and Ken Simons for very helpful comments.

[1] [1964] 376 U.S. 254.

[2] Kenneth S. Abraham & G. Edward White, Tort Law and the Construction of Social Change 57–70 (2022) (discussing failed efforts to organize tort law along these lines).

John C.P. Goldberg and Benjamin C. Zipursky, *Recklessness in Tort* In: *Interstitial Private Law.* Edited by: Samuel L. Bray, John C.P. Goldberg, Paul B. Miller, and Henry E. Smith, Oxford University Press. © Oxford University Press 2024.
DOI: 10.1093/oso/9780197783627.003.0007

in this vein might argue that attention to the doctrines we have mentioned helps shore up this envisioned framework by locating a heretofore overlooked "fourth planet" in the universe of tort liability standards, thereby aligning tort law with the four-pronged treatment of *mens rea* standards found in the Model Penal Code (MPC).[3]

Even so refined, this project seems unpromising. Conduct standards in tort law don't line up with one another the way that *mens rea* concepts do in the MPC. "Intent" in tort is often far-removed from criminal law's notion of specific intent. And many torts combine intent, fault, and/or strict liability features.[4] For example, trespass to land requires proof of intent to enter or remain on a swath of land. (Thus, a driver that nods off and slides off the road onto private property has not trespassed.) Yet liability for trespass is also strict, in that it arises even for intentional entries made in the mistaken but reasonable belief that the land is the entrant's. Other torts combine aspects of fault and strict liability, as does negligence law, given the objectivity of its breach standard and doctrines such as *res ipsa loquitur*.[5] Finally, there is no reason to suppose that, doctrinally, recklessness occupies a sufficiently prominent place in the tort firmament as to warrant its being treated on par with negligence.

(2) Other jurists draw a very different lesson from the recognition of recklessness's role in tort cases. What these cases show, they argue, is that it is a formalist mistake to suppose that concepts like intent, knowledge, recklessness, or carelessness are well-formed and solid enough to operate as discrete points on a line. In the law, words such as "intended," "knowing," and "negligent" refer not to specific mental states or norms, but instead to vaguely defined probabilities along a spectrum that runs from extremely probable ("intended") to somewhat probable ("negligent"). On this view, to act "recklessly" with respect to a risk of a certain consequence means that the consequence is highly probable, but not quite certain, to happen.

The effort to reduce intention and related concepts to probabilities is no less problematic than the effort to adopt for tort law the MPC's *mens rea* menu. As John Finnis and others have shown, in tort law, the main instance of intending a consequence is acting for the purpose of bringing it about, regardless of whether achievement is probable or improbable.[6] Efforts to recast knowledge, recklessness and negligence exclusively in terms of probabilities are similarly suspect.

[3] U.S. MPC, § 2.02 (ordinarily, persons are not guilty of a crime unless they have acted purposely, knowingly, recklessly, or negligently).

[4] John C.P. Goldberg & Benjamin C. Zipursky, *The Strict Liability in Fault and the Fault in Strict Liability*, 85 FORDHAM L. REV. 743, 748–52 (2016).

[5] *Id.* at 746–48.

[6] John Finnis, *Intention in Tort Law*, *in* PHILOSOPHICAL FOUNDATIONS OF TORT LAW (David G. Owen ed., 1995).

(3) We will argue for a third way in which to make sense of the role of recklessness in tort law. According to this view, recklessness really does operate in tort law *interstitially*. To employ our titular metaphor, courts use recklessness to fine-tune tort doctrine by filling certain gaps that would otherwise exist. While the nuance in recklessness has been noted by other scholars—especially Ken Simons in an article written three decades ago[7]—it is part of the account we are advancing that the concept of recklessness is used principally to fine-tune or craft the boundaries of concepts that play a more central role in tort law.

Complicating our fine-tuning story, however, is the fact that recklessness fills at least two very different gaps in tort law. One is a gap at the edges of "malice," understood as bad faith conduct—that is, mistreatments of others involving dishonesty. Another is at the edges of conduct that is problematic because highly risky: at a certain point, conduct becomes so dangerous, with so little justification, as to indicate that the actor has crossed the line from negligence or even gross negligence to actions that are well beyond the pale.

In sketching our position thus far, we have indicated two kinds of goals for this chapter: the tort scholar's goal of surveying and analyzing the place of recklessness in tort law; and the private law theorist's goal of understanding how to model the interstitial quality of interstitial legal concepts, or at least one important interstitial legal concept. We also hope to make progress on practical questions concerning how and when recklessness concepts should be used in the law of torts. Here we note that one of our principal examples—recklessness in defamation law—is a hotbed of legal activity and debate.

Part II briefly describes the role of recklessness and related concepts in different domains of tort law.

Part III takes a deeper dive into the place of recklessness in *Sullivan*'s actual malice rule, examining both the justification provided for the rule and the particular contours the Supreme Court has given it. Two points are of particular interest to us. One is that, on its face, Justice Brennan's analysis of the chilling effects of liability seems to warrant a no-liability rule. The second is that the form of the limit on defamation liability set by his opinion and the form of recklessness contained within it, include a subjective element that it arguably did not have to include. We argue that the best explanation of both points is that Justice Brennan was setting forth a particular kind of rights-based argument against liability, and the subjectivity of actual malice pertains to fairness-based concerns sounding in the register of abuse of privilege. In this regard, the recklessness prong of *Sullivan*'s rule is quite similar to the recklessness prong of the *scienter* requirement in fraud law. In both contexts, courts use recklessness to capture a special case of misconduct at the edges of intent that involves notions of bad faith

[7] Kenneth W. Simons, *Rethinking Mental States*, 72 B.U. L. Rev. 463 (1992).

or willful blindness, and that would not give rise to liability if liability were limited strictly to intentionally or knowingly uttered falsehoods.

Part IV considers a very different domain of tort law that utilizes the concept of recklessness, namely, the doctrine of implied assumption of risk. In one respect, its role is similar to that found in defamation law—it serves as a boundary for what operates as an important tort defense, allowing tort claims of a certain sort to proceed notwithstanding the defense. In other respects, however, recklessness in this part of tort law operates quite differently. Rather than identifying a special case of bad faith or malice, it marks off conduct that it is so far out of bounds relative to applicable norms and expectations as to warrant responsibility and liability even in domains where there are otherwise plausible reasons to limit both.

We conclude Part V by returning to a broader overview of recklessness in tort law, stepping back to consider general lessons that might be drawn from our inquiry about the interstices of private law.

II. Recklessness in Tort Law

Although criminal law and tort law are both concerned with wrongs, they differ significantly with respect to the role that recklessness plays in each. In the Model Penal Code, recklessness shares star billing with the Code's three other *mens rea* standards: intent, knowledge, and negligence. In fact, Section 2.02(3) makes recklessness first among equals: for any criminal statute that is silent on the *mens rea* requirement for a material element of the offense, courts are instructed to assume the standard is recklessness.[8]

By contrast, recklessness is an outlier in private law generally and tort law in particular. So far as we are aware, it does little work in contracts or property. And its appearances in tort are perhaps best described as notable cameos. Most obviously, "recklessness," in contrast to "negligence," is not the name of a tort. Still, recklessness makes some important appearances in tort law.

A. Defamation

In *Sullivan*, the Supreme Court sharply curtailed the ability of public officials to recover for libel or slander by requiring proof of actual malice, defined as knowledge of the falsity of the misrepresentation made or reckless disregard of its truth or falsity.[9] As the Court made clear four years later, the recklessness prong of

[8] U.S. MPC § 2.02(3).
[9] 376 U.S. at 279–80.

actual malice is not a negligence standard: it is "not measured by whether a reasonably prudent man would have published, or would have investigated before publishing. There must be evidence . . . that the defendant in fact entertained serious doubts as to the truth of his publication."[10]

We discuss in Part III the bases for the adoption of the actual malice standard and its recklessness prong. But it is worth noting initially that it was hardly obvious that the Court's addition of a constitutional overlay on state defamation law—some version of which all of the Justices thought appropriate—would consist of the adoption of this particular limit. Herbert Wechsler's famous brief, which many have credited with influencing the Justices, arguably took no position on the particular rule the Court ought to adopt in order to spare the *Sullivan* defendants from liability.[11] And the Court had available to it less restrictive and more restrictive alternatives. On the less-restrictive side were state court decisions holding that common law conditional privileges to defame were lost upon proof of simple negligence. On the opposite side, several concurring Justices argued that the best position as a matter of principle and policy was a no-liability rule for statements about the official conduct of public officials[12] or for any publication addressing a matter of public concern.[13]

B. Fraud

Under *Derry v. Peek*, liability for deceit requires proof that the defendant uttered a misrepresentation intending or knowing that a person such as the plaintiff would rely on its content, and that the defendant knew the statement was false, did not believe it was true, or was reckless as to its truth.[14] Like Justice Brennan in *Sullivan*, the Law Lords in *Derry* offered further guidance as to when knowledge, lack of belief, or recklessness could be inferred from circumstantial evidence. In the language of Lord Herschell, if the statement in question was "destitute of all reasonable foundation," there would be a basis for concluding that the defendant uttered it while knowing it to be false, or with reckless disregard as to its falsity.[15]

[10] St. Amant v. Thompson [1968] 390 U.S. 727, 731. The Court acknowledged that a defamation plaintiff subject to the actual malice rule can offer circumstantial evidence to prove that the defendant actually entertained serious doubts about the truth of a statement. But it also took pains to limit such inferences, noting for example that a publisher's mere failure to investigate the truth of a statement will not suffice to establish recklessness.

[11] John C.P. Goldberg, *Judging Reputation: Realism and Common Law in Justice White's Jurisprudence*, 74 U. Col. L. Rev. 1471, 1482 (2003).

[12] Sullivan, 376 U.S. at 739 (Goldberg, J., concurring).

[13] *Id.* at 735 (Black, J., concurring).

[14] [1889] 14 App. Cas. 337 (H.L.).

[15] *Id.* at 375.

Nearly a century after *Derry*, the US Supreme Court in its *Ernst & Ernst* decision likewise required proof of scienter for misrepresentations to establish civil liability for securities fraud.[16] Although the Court specifically left open the question of whether recklessness with respect to truth would suffice to establish scienter,[17] its core claim was that liability required a showing of bad faith on the part of the defendant, rather than mere carelessness.[18] Unsurprisingly, lower federal courts have consistently held that recklessness suffices. In one leading formulation, recklessness in this context consists of "'an extreme departure from ordinary care' which presents a danger of misleading buyers or sellers that is either known to the defendant or is so obvious that the actor *must have been aware of it*."[19]

In provisions of the Third Torts Restatement concerning liability for economic harm, one finds a similar definition of scienter. Section 10 requires the maker of the misrepresentation to know or believe it be false, or knowingly to state or imply a basis for the misrepresentation that does not exist.[20] Although this provision does not use the word "recklessness," a comment makes clear that a certain notion of recklessness suffices to establish scienter, namely, recklessness understood as a variant on gross negligence is insufficient, recklessness understood as a statement made "in conscious disregard of a risk that [it] is false."[21] The Restatement is also careful to observe that evidence of carelessness with respect to truth, by itself, is not sufficient.[22]

C. IIED

With two narrow exceptions, Section 46 of the first Torts Restatement did not countenance liability for "pure" emotional distress.[23] Famously, however, this

[16] Ernst & Ernst v. Hochfelder, [1976] 425 U.S. 185, 214 (1976).

[17] *Id.* at 193 n. 12.

[18] *Id.* at 206 (liability attaches only if there is proof defendant "acted other than in good faith").

[19] Sundstrand Corp. v. Sun Chem. Corp., [1977] 553 F.2d 1033, 1045 (7th Cir.) (emphasis added). The SEC in briefs filed with the Supreme Court has described recklessness as "a state of mind closer to conscious intent than gross negligence." "Brief for SEC as Amicus Curiae Supporting Respondents," Central Bank of Denver v. First Interstate Bank of Denver, [1994] 511 U.S. 164. A safe harbor contained in the Private Securities Litigation Reform Act ("PSLRA") for "forward-looking statements" such as financial projections (as opposed to statements of present fact) require plaintiffs suing on the basis of such statements to prove actual knowledge of falsity; recklessness does not suffice. Moshell v. Sasol Limited, 481 F. Supp. 3d 280, 289 (SDNY 2020) (applying 15 USC § 78u-5(c)); *see generally* William H Kuehnle, *On Scienter, Knowledge and Recklessness Under the Federal Securities Laws*, 34 Hous. L. Rev. 121 (1997).. Nonetheless, circuit courts have overwhelmingly permitted some form of recklessness to suffice for scienter in cases not involving forward-looking statements. 3 Thomas Lee Hazen, Treatise on the Law of Securities Regulation § 12:52 (8th ed. 2020).

[20] Restatement of The Law Third, Torts: Liability for Economic Harm § 10 (2020).

[21] *Id.* at cmt. C.

[22] *Id.*

[23] Restatement of The Law, Torts § 46 (1934). The content of Section 46 was presented to the Institute's membership as Sections 45A–45C of Proposed Final Draft No. 1 at its 1934 Meeting. *See* 11

position did not hold. Fourteen years after the Restatement's initial publication, an amended version of Section 46 recognized liability for certain intentionally inflicted emotional distress.[24] A comment to this new version of the section explained that liability under it would typically attach only to conduct "beyond all bounds of decency."[25] In addition, liability was explicitly limited to cases of intentionally inflicted distress.[26]

Still more changes would soon be forthcoming. As it appeared in the Second Torts Restatement (1965)—and as it now appears in the Third Restatement—the black-letter of Section 46 permits recovery for the infliction of severe emotional distress through abominable or outrageous conduct in cases in which the actor was reckless as to the risk of causing it.[27] The Second Restatement's insertion of a recklessness standard into a nominally intentional tort had some support in case law.[28] In his role as Restatement Reporter, Prosser also seemed concerned to find ways to handle situations in which the defendant's outrageous conduct was directed at one person, but ended up distressing another. Still, in a manner resembling *Sullivan*'s initial adoption of recklessness as a feature of its actual malice standard in defamation law, Prosser did not offer much of an argument for adopting recklessness rather than negligence. Presumably, he and others were influenced by case law of the time, which had steadily held that simple negligence causing emotional distress was not actionable unless there was physical contact (the impact rule), or unless the distress directly caused a discrete physical injury such as a heart attack or miscarriage.

D. Recklessness Elsewhere in Judge-Made and Statutory Tort Law

In a manner that might put some readers in mind of the MPC, Sections 1–3 of the Physical and Emotional Harm provisions of the Restatement (Third) of Torts respectively provide definitions of the terms "intent," "recklessness," and "negligence." However, the resemblance to the MPC is only superficial. There is nothing in the Third Restatement that is analogous to the general part of the MPC—that is, nothing like a generic account of the building blocks of all torts.

American Law Institute Proceedings 478–79 (June 30, 1934) (transcript of proceedings of May 11, 1934).

[24] Restatement of the Law, Torts, Supplement § 46 (1948).
[25] *Id.* at cmt. G.
[26] *Id.* at First Caveat.
[27] Restatement of the Law Second, Torts § 46 (1965); Restatement of the Law Third, Torts: Liability for Physical and Emotional Harm § 46 (2010).
[28] *See, e.g.*, Blakeley v. Shortal's Estate [1945] 20 N.W. 2d 28, 31 (Iowa).

Section 2 defines recklessness as an actor's failure to take easily-taken precautions against obvious (or known risks), thus displaying indifference to the realization of those risks.[29] Comment *b* then adds: "while there are general rules exposing persons to liability who cause harm intentionally or negligently, there is no similar general rule subjecting to liability the person who causes harm recklessly."[30] Instead, there are various distinct settings in which state courts or legislatures have employed a recklessness standard of liability, or have held that defendants who enjoy certain defenses from liability grounded in negligence or products liability law forfeit those defenses if they acted with reckless disregard for the safety of persons such as the plaintiff.

A recent example of the first type of decision—a common law decision selecting "recklessness" as a standard of liability—is *Rafferty v. Merck & Co.*,[31] in which the Massachusetts Supreme Judicial Court faced a question of state law that has arisen in the wake of the US Supreme Court's rulings in *Wyeth v. Levine*[32] and *PLIVA, Inc. v. Mensing*.[33] *Wyeth* held that a brand-name drug manufacturer's compliance with federal Food and Drug Agency (FDA) labeling requirements does not preempt state tort law claims by consumers for failure to warn them of risks associated with the drug. As Justice Thomas's *PLIVA* opinion later interpreted *Wyeth*, it was crucial to *Wyeth*'s reasoning that federal law permits brand-name manufacturers to strengthen their warning labels unilaterally (without prior FDA approval), and thus to act as required to fulfill their state-law duties to warn. In *PLIVA*, the Court reached the opposite conclusion with respect to generic drug manufacturers, concluding that, because federal law requires generic drug manufacturers strictly to follow the warnings on brand-name counterparts, a generic manufacturer's use of the brand-name drug's warning label immunizes it entirely from failure-to-warn liability.

Wyeth and *PLIVA* have generated the following question of state tort law: Can the user of a *generic* drug who claims to have been injured by its lack of warnings recover on a failure-to-warn claim brought not against that drug's manufacturer but instead against the manufacturer of the generic's *brand-name counterpart*? On this theory, the brand-name drug's manufacturer would be subject to liability to the consumer of the generic drug for failing properly to warn of a danger

[29] Restatement of the Law Third, Torts: Liability for Physical and Emotional Harm § 2 (2010). One of our core contentions is that there are at least two versions of recklessness at work in tort law—one concerned with bad faith or abuse of right, and the other with unjustifiably dangerous actions. We thus follow Simons in rejecting the assumption underlying Section II that recklessness can be reduced to a single, generic definition. Simons, *Rethinking Mental States*, *supra* note 7, at 482–90.

[30] Restatement of the Law Third, Torts: Liability for Physical and Emotional Harm, *supra* note 29, at cmt. B.

[31] [2018] 92 N.E. 3d 1205 (Mass.).

[32] [2009] 555 U.S. 555.

[33] [2011] 564 U.S. 604.

associated with its brand-name drug—a failure that, by operation of federal law, entailed that the generic drug manufacturer could only adopt the same deficient warning, thereby injuring the consumer.

In *Rafferty*, the Massachusetts court answered this question with a qualified "yes." Crucially, the qualification was expressed in terms of recklessness. In an effort to strike a balance between holding brand-name manufacturers responsible to persons injured because of their failure to adopt appropriate warnings and avoiding the imposition of an undue liability burden on them (particularly given that generic manufacturers are fully immunized), the court held that a consumer suing for injuries caused by her use of a generic drug can recover on a failure-to-warn claim against the counterpart brand-name drug manufacturer only by proving that the latter engaged in conduct beyond mere carelessness. As the Court explained,

> In other types of cases where we have circumscribed liability for public policy reasons, we have nevertheless consistently recognized that there is a certain core duty—a certain irreducible minimum duty of care, owed to all persons—that as a matter of public policy cannot be abrogated: that is, the duty not to intentionally or recklessly cause harm to others. For instance, we have long held in premises liability cases that a landowner owes no duty of reasonable care to a trespasser, Schofield v. Merrill, 386 Mass. 244, 245–246 (1982) . . . . Yet, we have held that a landowner still owes a trespasser a duty to "refrain from wilful, wanton[,] or reckless disregard for the trespasser's safety." [*Id.*] at 245–246. And in cases involving contractual waivers, we have hewed to "the well-established principle of contract law" that "while a party may contract against liability for harm caused by its negligence, it may not do so with respect to its gross negligence" or, for that matter, its reckless or intentional conduct. Maryland Cas. Co. v. NSTAR Elec. Co., 471 Mass. 416, 422 (2015), quoting Zavras v. Capeway Rovers Motorcycle Club, Inc., 44 Mass. App. Ct. 17, 19 (1997).
>
> We have applied this same reasoning in many other types of cases where we have tolerated ordinary negligence but drawn the line at recklessness. In defamation cases, a plaintiff who is a public officer or a public figure cannot recover damages on proof of the defendant's negligence, but can recover if the defendant acted with "actual malice," meaning wilful or reckless disregard of the truth. . . . Similarly, in cases involving sporting events, we have held that athletes and coaches cannot be liable for injuries caused by their negligence, but will be held liable if they act in "reckless disregard of safety." Gauvin v. Clark, 404 Mass. 450, 454 (1989). . . .
>
> In enacting statutes, the Legislature, too, has distinguished between ordinary negligence and reckless conduct, granting immunity or indemnification in

> some situations in claims of negligence but not in claims of recklessness. See, e.g., G. L. c. 21, § 17C (landowner who makes land open to public for recreational use free of charge not liable for personal injuries "in the absence of wilful, wanton, or reckless conduct"); G. L. c. 229, § 2 (railroads not liable for negligence in causing death of trespasser but liable for reckless conduct).
>
> Implicit in both our common and statutory law, then, is a long-standing public policy that, although we may be willing in certain circumstances to excuse ordinary negligence or even gross negligence, reckless indifference to the safety of others takes one outside of the negligence concept and far closer to the level of intentionality.[34]

Other examples of recklessness-based rules can be found scattered throughout tort law. Reckless conduct by a defendant renders inapplicable the traditional all-or-nothing defense of contributory negligence (unless the plaintiff was herself reckless) and even has the same effect in some comparative fault jurisdictions.[35] Good Samaritan statutes typically condition their protection on the good faith of the rescuer, conversely permitting the protection to be surmounted by a showing on recklessness.[36] A provision of the Tennessee Code protects operators of cremation facilities from tort claims for wrongful cremation if the operator has followed the instructions from an heir of the decedent, unless the operator acted maliciously or in a wanton or reckless manner.[37] In many states, common law qualified privileges, such as the common-interest privilege in defamation, are lost if the defendant recklessly discloses false information.[38]

Finally, the Third Torts Restatement, in its comments on recklessness, selects as a key example the role of recklessness in implied assumption of risk doctrine as applied to recreational activities.[39] The Ohio Supreme Court's statement of the majority position is typical: "where individuals engage in recreational or sports activities, they assume the ordinary risks of the activity and cannot recover for any injury unless it can be shown that the other participant's actions were either 'reckless' or 'intentional.'..."[40]

[34] Rafferty, 92 N.E. 3d at 1218–19 (some citations omitted).

[35] Dan B. Dobbs, Paul T. Hayden & Ellen M. Bublick, The Law of Torts § 227 (2d ed. July 2022 update).

[36] *Id.* at § 409.

[37] Thus, Seals v. H & F, Inc. [2010] 301 S.W. 3d 237 (Tenn.), held that a claim by a decedent's mother against an operator required a jury determination as to whether the operator was reckless in relying on instructions from decedent's fourteen-year-old son.

[38] Sandi R. Wilson, *Employer Immunity for Employment References: Maybe, Maybe Not*, 49 So. Car. L.R. 1171 (1998) (discussing South Carolina statutory and common law to this effect).

[39] Restatement of Torts, Third: Liability for Physical and Emotional Harm § 2 cmt. b (Am. L. Inst. 2010).

[40] Marchetti v. Kalish [1990] 559 N.E. 2d 699, 699 (Ohio).

III. Recklessness as the Lower Boundary of Malice

Having offered a brief survey of most or all of the most prominent instances of recklessness in tort law, we now provide more in-depth analysis to help get a better handle on what recklessness means in different tort contexts. The concern of this part is the place of recklessness in the actual malice rule of *New York Times v. Sullivan*.

Justice Brennan's majority opinion in *Sullivan* has much to say about why defamation suits by public officials threaten to undermine rights of free speech and free press guaranteed by the First Amendment. It says relatively little about why this concern points toward the actual malice rule. Indeed, three concurring Justices—Black, Douglas, and Goldberg—offered powerful arguments that a broader no-liability rule is needed. Why, then, did Justice Brennan and the other Justices in the majority settle on actual malice? And what does that tell us about the recklessness prong of that legal standard?

In *Sullivan* itself, Justice Brennan grounded the need for constitutional limits on the common law of defamation in concerns about the chilling effect that the threat of defamation liability might have on media coverage of public officials. Thus, after observing that the "court of history" had declared the *criminal* libel provisions of the Founding era's Sedition Act unconstitutional, he argued that the threat of massive civil judgments had the potential to more seriously chill political speech and media coverage of politics.[41] Rejecting Alabama's argument that the common law's truth defense to civil libel actions sufficiently protected against this effect, Brennan added that defendants concerned about their ability to prove truth (particularly to hostile judges and juries) will "tend to make only statements which 'steer far wider of the unlawful zone.'"[42] Accordingly, his opinion concluded that the federal constitution's guarantees of free speech and a free press:

> require... a federal rule that prohibits a public official from recovering damages for a defamatory falsehood relating to his official conduct unless he proves that the statement was made with "actual malice"—that is, with knowledge that it was false or with reckless disregard of whether it was false or not.[43]

Concurring, Justices Black, Douglas, and Goldberg insisted that this passage concludes with a non-sequitur. In their view, the chilling effect could only be dampened adequately by full-blown immunity. And for this proposition they

41 Sullivan, 376 U.S. at 277–78 (some citations and footnote omitted).
42 *Id.* at 279.
43 *Id.* at 279–80.

could point to solid precedent. Five years earlier, *Barr v. Matteo* had ruled that federal government officials enjoy complete immunity from defamation liability for statements they make in connection with the performance of their official duties.[44] In support of this result, Justice Harlan's plurality *Barr* opinion invoked *Gregoire v. Biddle*, a Learned Hand decision that had relied heavily on a chilling effect rationale:

> The justification for [complete immunity from defamation liability] is that it is impossible to know whether the claim [against the official] is well founded until the case has been tried, and that to submit all officials, the innocent as well as the guilty, to the burden of a trial and to the inevitable danger of its outcome, would dampen the ardor of all but the most resolute, or the most irresponsible, in the unflinching discharge of their duties. Again and again the public interest calls for action which may turn out to be founded on a mistake, in the face of which an official may later find himself hard put to it to satisfy a jury of his good faith. There must indeed be means of punishing public officers who have been truant to their duties; but that is quite another matter from exposing such as have been honestly mistaken to suit by anyone who has suffered from their errors. As is so often the case, the answer must be found in a balance between the evils inevitable in either alternative. In this instance it has been thought in the end better to leave unredressed the wrongs done by dishonest officers than to subject those who try to do their duty to the constant dread of retaliation.[45]

Given *Barr*'s rule and rationale, Justice Goldberg in his *Sullivan* concurrence offered what seems to be a compelling good-for-the-goose, good-for-the-gander argument, quoting the same passage from Hand's *Gregoire* opinion that Justice Harlan had quoted in his *Barr* opinion.[46] Justice Goldberg then added:

> If the government official should be immune from libel actions so that his ardor to serve the public will not be dampened and "fearless, vigorous, and effective administration of policies of government" not be inhibited, Barr v. Matteo . . . 360 U.S. at 571, then the citizen and the press should likewise be immune from libel actions for their criticism of official conduct. Their ardor as citizens will thus not be dampened and they will be free "to applaud or to criticize the way public employees do their jobs, from the least to the most important." If liability can attach to political criticism because it damages the

[44] [1959] 360 U.S. 564. As we discuss later in this section, Justice Brennan dissented from Barr's holding, there favoring a rule of qualified immunity.

[45] *Id.* at 571–71 (quoting Gregoire v. Biddle, [1949] 177 F.2d 579, 581).

[46] Sullivan, 376 U.S. 302–03 (Goldberg, J, concurring).

> reputation of a public official as a public official, then no critical citizen can safely utter anything but faint praise about the government or its officials. The vigorous criticism by press and citizen of the conduct of the government of the day by the officials of the day will soon yield to silence if officials in control of government agencies, instead of answering criticisms, can resort to friendly juries to forestall criticism of their official conduct.[47]

Justice Brennan's opinion for the majority in *Sullivan* never really engaged this precedent- and policy-based argument for absolute immunity. Instead, in one sentence that concludes with a citation to *Barr*, it defended the actual malice "privilege" as "appropriately analogous to the protection accorded a public official when he is sued for libel by a private citizen."[48] No explanation is offered as to why this privilege should be merely "analogous" to, rather than fully symmetrical with, *Barr*'s immunity rule. Instead, Justice Brennan was content merely to note that state courts, in applying the common law of defamation, tended to protect officials from defamation suits by means of a qualified privilege that could be lost on a finding of "malice."[49]

The standard explanation of Brennan's choice is small "p" political and commonsensical. The Court's novel invocation of constitutional law to reshape state defamation law nationwide was a significant exercise of power, and by many measures a piece of judicial activism, albeit one for which there were strong arguments. And Justice Brennan, like Chief Justice Earl Warren, was undeniably at some level a political actor. As such, one would expect him to have taken seriously the argument that the Court would go too far if it entirely shut down state libel law in suits brought by public officials. On this view, the preservation of liability for actual malice cases was what common sense and a minimal sense

[47] *Id.* at 304 (Goldberg, J, concurring). Justice Black's separate concurrence also invoked Barr. *Id.* at 295 (Black, J, concurring).

[48] *Id.* at 282.

[49] *Id.* Justice Brennan focused particularly on Coleman v. MacLennan, [1908] 98 P. 281 (Kan.), probably in part because it was featured in the Harper and James treatise's analysis of defamation law's qualified privileges. 1 Fowler V. Harper & Fleming James Jr., The Law of Torts § 5.27, 451 (1956). At the time Sullivan was decided, both the Harper and James's treatise and William Prosser's treatise maintained that, in the defamation context, state courts predominantly used the word "malice" to refer not to a defendant's subjective desire to harm the plaintiff but instead to defendants who outwardly behaved in accordance with the terms of recognized privileges but did so for purposes other than those that the privileges were meant to serve. *Id.* at 452; William L. Prosser, Handbook of the Law of Torts § 95, 627–28 (2d ed. 1955). An example of such conduct would be that of firm F providing a reference about former employee P to competitor company C, which reference defames P. While F normally would be protected from liability by the "common interest" privilege, if there were evidence that F did not provide the reference in good faith, but instead did so because it was hell-bent on preventing C from getting the benefit of P's talents, the privilege would be lost because "abused." Harper & James, *supra*, at 452. Both treatises added that "malice" of this sort might be inferred from various kinds of circumstantial evidence, including evidence that the defendant knowingly uttered a falsehood, or uttered it believing it to be true but with no reasonable grounds for that belief. *Id.* at 453; Prosser, *supra*, at 629.

of restraint required. And one might reasonably speculate that stopping short of full-blown immunity is how Brennan got all nine Justices to side with the *Sullivan* defendants.

We find this instrumentalist explanation less than fully satisfying because of the focus of Justice Goldberg's concurrence and its undeniable force in identifying a seeming inconsistency in Brennan's analysis. The chilling effect argument seems critical to Brennan's rejection of a negligence standard, but that argument itself depends on the thought that, in politically charged defamation cases, juries cannot be expected consistently to apply such a standard accurately. Justice Goldberg was right that the argument proves too much, for some juries will find actual malice when it is not there.

Needless to say, Brennan appreciated this concern and endorsed special evidentiary and procedural steps to address it. But then one wonders why he did not do so for a somewhat lower standard, like negligence. In this sense, Brennan's selection of these procedural devices only sharpens the question, as did *Barr v. Matteo*. Why did Brennan reject full immunity, which is where the logic of his argument seemed to take him? And if he wanted to appear somewhat less activist but was willing to use procedural devices to ensure the right answer in support of the actual malice rule, why didn't he stop with negligence or gross negligence or something resembling the state privileges found throughout the common law,[50] while perhaps adding layers of judicial and appellate scrutiny?

One can gain insight into the rationale for the actual malice standard by attending to opinions written by Justice Brennan both before and after *Sullivan*. Brennan had dissented from the holding in *Barr*, reasoning that no more than a qualified privilege was appropriate. The need to ensure that federal officials are not harassed by vexatious litigation, he argued, must be balanced against the long-recognized and important common-law right to redress, and this line was appropriately drawn at malice. While there was reason to give officials some extra breathing room to publish defamatory statements, there was no justification for protecting officials who maliciously defame others.[51] A qualified privilege "would, in giving protection against the consequences of his honest mistakes, give [the official] all the protection he could properly claim."[52]

In *Garrison v. Louisiana*, Justice Brennan offered further thoughts on the actual malice rule.[53] A Louisiana district attorney had been convicted of criminal

[50] Interestingly, the Second Restatement of Torts proposed understanding state common law privileges as conditioned by recklessness. In this sense, the path chosen by Brennan was arguably not as distinct from the common law as the language of our text suggests. But the common law of libel and slander in the United States circa 1964 was varied, with different jurisdictions recognizing qualified privileges in both less stringent, more stringent, and quite distinctive ways.

[51] Howard v. Lyons, [1959] 360 U.S. 564, 586–87 (Brennan, J, dissenting).

[52] *Id.* at 588.

[53] Garrison v. Louisiana, [1964] 379 U.S. 64.

defamation based on statements he made at a press conference implying that several state judges were corrupt. The Court ruled that the state's criminal defamation law, as applied to Garrison, was unconstitutional because it permitted punishment for true defamatory statements and for false statements negligently made. According to Justice Brennan, the latter feature of the law was incompatible with *Sullivan*, under which "defeasance of the privilege [to defame] is conditioned, not on mere negligence, but on reckless disregard for the truth."[54] Moreso than in *Sullivan* itself, Brennan explained why, among the possible standards that the Court had considered, actual malice was the right one:

> since "* * * erroneous statement is inevitable in free debate, and * * * it must be protected if the freedoms of expression are to have the 'breathing space' that they 'need * * * to survive' * * *," [*Sullivan*], 376 U.S., at 271—272, only those false statements made with the high degree of awareness of their probable falsity demanded by *New York Times* may be the subject of either civil or criminal sanctions. For speech concerning public affairs is more than self-expression; it is the essence of self-government. The First and Fourteenth Amendments embody our "profound national commitment to the principle that debate on public issues should be uninhibited, robust, and wide-open, and that it may well include vehement, caustic, and sometimes unpleasantly sharp attacks on government and public officials." 376 U.S., at 270.
>
> The use of calculated falsehood, however, would put a different cast on the constitutional question. Although honest utterance, even if inaccurate, may further the fruitful exercise of the right of free speech, it does not follow that the lie, knowingly and deliberately published about a public official, should enjoy a like immunity. At the time the First Amendment was adopted, as today, there were those unscrupulous enough and skillful enough to use the deliberate or reckless falsehood as an effective political tool to unseat the public servant or even topple an administration. Cf. Riesman, Democracy and Defamation: Fair Game and Fair Comment I, 42 Col. L. Rev. 1085, 1088—1111 (1942). ... Hence the knowingly false statement and the false statement made with reckless disregard of the truth, do not enjoy constitutional protection.[55]

[54] *Id.* at 79.

[55] *Id.* at 74–76. Though known today primarily as a sociologist, David Riesman's first academic position was in law. Having earned a law degree from Harvard—from which he graduated three years after Justice Brennan—he clerked for Justice Brandeis and then joined the University of Buffalo law faculty. The cited article is one of three that appeared in the *Columbia Law Review* in 1942. David Riesman, *Democracy and Defamation: Fair Game and Fair Comment II*, 42 Colum. L. Rev. 1282 (1942); David Riesman, *Democracy and Defamation: Fair Game and Fair Comment I*, 42 Colum. L. Rev. 1085 (1942); David Riesman, *Democracy and Defamation: Control of Group Libel*, 42 Colum. L. Rev. 727 (1942). Together, they charted, sometimes in alarmingly resonant terms, the ways in which fascists, particularly Nazi officials, had deliberately engineered campaigns to defame opposition leaders and members of vulnerable groups to rally their political supporters, while also

These passages suggest that the selection of the actual malice rule was not merely the result of an emboldened Supreme Court majority trying to find a politically viable rule and relying on a gestalt sense of what seemed fair. To the contrary, Justice Brennan—even though often inclined to provide instrumentalist deflations of legal concepts—offered a deontologically based understanding of the actual malice rule. The right to speak one's mind on political matters, he reasoned, is grounded in part in a right of self-expression, but more generally in a conception of self-government that envisions citizens exchanging their *authentic* beliefs on political matters. Whether viewed in terms of the value to personal autonomy of self-expression or the value to democracy of political debate, the utterance of lies is unprivileged because lies are neither self-expression nor part of a genuine exchange of views. Nor, for that matter, are reckless falsehoods. For both, the special moral status that applies to the expressions of authentic belief is absent. Indeed, the speech acts of which these are a part are typically manipulations. By contrast, speech that is merely negligent (or even grossly negligent) as to the truth, even though irresponsible, does not—or does not merely by virtue of its negligence—partake of the sort of bad faith that disqualifies it from legal protection.

Our interpretation of the case made by Justice Brennan for actual malice might appear to be, in at least one respect, unremarkable or even obvious. The common law privilege to make fair comment on matters of public concern famously carried with it a malice limitation. Malice was viewed as defeating the privilege, and the usual language of describing it was that one could not "abuse the privilege."[56] In some sense, Justice Brennan did appear to be inserting into (or finding in) federal constitutional law a typical (although not universally recognized) version of the fair comment privilege as found in state common law.

And yet, reading a version of a familiar state-law privilege into the First Amendment was by no means the obvious thing for the Court to do; nor has it been obvious to commentators or subsequent Justices that this is what *Sullivan*

using defamation suits to silence their opponents. Based on the Nazi example and others, Riesman concluded that defamation law is an "important factor[] in the struggle between democracy and fascism." 42 COLUM. L. REV., at 1085. He then canvassed the ways in which different nations had tried to address the problem of the "big lie," concluding that many features of American defamation law left American democracy vulnerable to fascist propaganda techniques.

Justice Brennan's citation of Riesman's work sheds important light on his reasoning. In particular, it suggests he recognized that, because there will always be persons who are evil and savvy enough to say whatever they need to say to secure power, it would be naïve to suppose that democratic governance promises to flourish in a constitutional regime that recognizes an individual right to say *anything* about public officials or political matters. Instead, he concluded that persons must face accountability for smearing others by means of deliberate falsehoods or statements made with utter indifference as to their falsity.

56. Snodgrass v. Cherry-Burrell Corp., [1960] 164 A.2d 579 (N.H.).

did. On our view, Justice Brennan, having gone through the quite significant step of interpreting the Fourteenth and First Amendments to generate rights against overly broad state defamation law, construed them to afford citizens a right against state laws enjoining speakers from expressing their critical views of public officials. The effect of recognizing such a right against the state under the First Amendment was to recognize a privilege as against individuals who might claim to have a right against being described in defamatory terms—a privilege understood as a no-duty rule in the context of a more general setting of legal duty to refrain from making such defamatory statements. A privilege that was commonly generated by the state's common law of defamation itself was understood to be independently generated by the US Constitution.[57]

IV. Recklessness as the Upper Boundary of Limitations on Risk-Based Liability

Tort scholars today are fond of declaring the doctrine of implied assumption of risk doctrine dead. These reports are exaggerated.[58] Indeed, in personal injury litigation between participants in recreational sports, assumption of risk is the governing principle. The California Supreme Court's decision in *Knight v. Jewett* remains a leading case.[59] It ruled that a participant in an informal "touch" football game could not recover from another participant for negligently knocking her over and injuring her. By voluntarily taking part in this sort of activity, the Court reasoned, a participant assumes the risk of being injured by other participants' carelessness. To recover, thus requires, at a minimum, a showing that the defendant caused injury through conduct that was reckless with respect to the risk of causing physical harm to other participants.

Despite its status as a leading implied assumption-of-risk decision, *Knight*'s version of the recklessness standard is narrower than appears to be typical. Here is the key language: "a participant in an active sport breaches a legal duty of care to other participants—i.e., engages in conduct that properly may subject him or her to financial liability—only if the participant intentionally injures another player or engages in conduct that is so reckless as to be totally outside the range

[57] One might interpret *Sullivan* as requiring the recognition of such a privilege in each state's defamation law. While doing so arguably would have the salutary effect of keeping the rights of defamation law itself a matter of state law (albeit constitutionally required state law), it would arguably commit the Court to a deferential approach to the interpretation and application of state defamation law. Casting the privilege as a rule of constitutional law makes sense not only of *Sullivan* but also subsequent Court decisions asserting interpretive authority as to the scope of the privilege.

[58] Kenneth W. Simons, *Reflections on Assumption of Risk* [2002] UCLA. L. Rev. 481, 482.

[59] [1992] 834 P.2d 696 (Cal.); Restatement of the Law Third, Intentional Torts to Persons § 16 cmt. f (Am. L. Inst. TD No. 4, April 1, 2019).

of the ordinary activity involved in the sport."[60] The Michigan Supreme Court's 2018 review of assumption-of-risk cases from across the country suggests that "reckless or intentional" is commonly advanced in a more unqualified form, or one that refers to "reckless disregard of the safety of others."[61] Its analysis merits further attention.

The plaintiff in Michigan's *Ritchie-Gamester* decision was an ice skater who was injured at a public rink when another skater, twelve-year-old Halley Mann, collided with her while she (Mann) was skating backward. The plaintiff sued Mann and others, alleging a serious knee injury caused most immediately by Mann's "careless, reckless, and negligent" conduct. After concluding that the doctrine of assumption of risk for recreational activities would require pleading and proof of conduct that was "intentional or reckless," the Court asked whether proof that the defendant was skating backward without looking behind her could satisfy the latter standard, concluding it could not.

The Michigan Supreme Court provides a useful summary of the reasons for an assumption-of-risk defense. In describing (with approval) other decisions, and in quoting Judge Cardozo's famous "Flopper" opinion,[62] it pointed to the awareness of participants in recreational activities of the risks of injury they may confront and indeed the voluntary choice they make to confront such risks. In affirmatively embracing a recklessness standard, it also articulated the following considerations:

> With these realities in mind, we join the majority of jurisdictions and adopt reckless misconduct as the minimum standard of care for coparticipants in recreational activities. We believe that this standard most accurately reflects the actual expectations of participants in recreational activities. As will be discussed in more detail below, we believe that participants in recreational activities do not expect to sue or be sued for mere carelessness. A recklessness standard also encourages vigorous participation in recreational activities, while still providing protection from egregious conduct. Finally, this standard lends itself to common-sense application by both judges and juries.[63]

Implicit in the court's justification for its rendering of assumption of risk is a reference to various reasons for limiting the scope of the defense. We would summarize those implications as follows. Participants in informal recreational activities are prepared for the possibility that other participants will sometimes be negligent or

[60] *Knight, supra* note 59, at 711.

[61] Ritchie-Gamester v. City of Berkley, (2018) 597 NW2d 517, 521–22 (Mich.) (quoting the decisions of numerous other state supreme courts).

[62] Murphy v. Steeplechase Amusement Co., [1929] 166 N.E. 173 (N.Y.).

[63] Ritchie-Gamester, 597 N.W. 2d at 525.

perhaps even grossly negligent as to others' physical safety, but not for their being reckless. Conversely, they do not understand themselves as potentially responsible for careless conduct that causes injury to others. Indeed, they understand themselves to be at liberty to participate vigorously, even if doing so may generate some unjustified risks of harm. Nonetheless, this does not mean that—on the imagined participant mindset—egregious conduct causing injury goes entirely without accountability. The "recklessness" standard is closely linked to a common-sense conception of recklessness, and what one can fairly expect of others.

Our admittedly cursory review of case law concerning application of the recklessness standard applied in recreational activity settings suggests that it is a demanding but not impossible standard for plaintiffs to meet. Two snowboarding cases from different jurisdictions illustrate the point. In *Angland v. Mountain Creek Resort, Inc.*,[64] the New Jersey Supreme Court permitted the estate of a skier to proceed to trial against a snowboarder (Brownlee) who allegedly ran into the skier, seriously injuring her. Its reasoning displays a conception of recklessness markedly different from the one on display in *Sullivan* or in court discussions of fraud and scienter.

> The record includes Brownlee's several explanations about why he turned and collided with Angland. All of Brownlee's explanations are premised on the existence of a phantom skier who [*sic*] he asserts he was trying to avoid. Plaintiffs, in response, contend that there is no evidence to support Brownlee's claim as to the existence of such an individual and that Brownlee's story is belied by his failure to promptly offer a description of that skier. Although that dispute alone might not be enough for plaintiffs to withstand summary judgment, it is not their only assertion.
>
> In addition, the record includes references to a report prepared by an expert retained by plaintiffs who opined that Brownlee failed to keep a proper lookout, reacted with a panicked stop, made a sudden change of direction, behaved in an unpredictable manner, and failed to readily respond to the unidentified person by taking evasive action in spite of having ample time and opportunity to do so. Those assertions could, if believed by a jury, suffice to support a finding of recklessness.[65]

The Supreme Court of Ohio reached a similar decision in *Horvath v. Ish*,[66] permitting the injured plaintiff's case to go to trial. As in *Richie-Gamester*, the jury would be required on remand to ascertain whether the snowboarder-defendant

64 [2013] 66 A.3d 1252 (N.J.).
65 *Id.* at 1263.
66 [2012] 979 N.E. 2d 1246 (Ohio).

had acted recklessly, but nothing in context smacked of malice, willfulness, or criminality.

In these and other assumption-of-risk cases, recklessness seems to refer to something different than the type of conduct marked off by *Sullivan* as unprivileged or unprotected. There is little suggestion that what renders reckless participants in recreational activities subject to liability for injuring their co-participants is their engagement in conduct that was epistemically deficient because it was completely indifferent to the truth (although there is admittedly a hint of this in *Angland*). Nor does the thought seem to be that recklessness is needed to ensure that the full universe of actors who act maliciously toward others are subject to liability. Instead, these reckless actors are vulnerable to claims because they have acted in a manner that is so dangerous as to be beyond the pale. In this incarnation, an actor who acts recklessly dramatically flouts ordinary expectations, such that even those who have accepted the risk of being injured by grossly negligent conduct are entitled to complain about the actor's stunning irresponsibility.

V. Conclusion

Let us take stock. The domain of recklessness in tort law, as we have sketched it, appears to fall into roughly two categories, perhaps with some leftovers and mixed cases, and perhaps even something resembling a unifying principle between them. In defamation and fraud, recklessness is used to supplement intentionality and knowledge to fill out the concepts of malice and scienter. To use a potentially fraught linear metaphor, courts are willing to expand the latter concepts beyond instances in which the defendant acts with knowledge of falsity but not much further. Recklessness as to the truth marks the borderline.

In the assumption-of-risk context, the analysis appears to proceed from the other direction. Courts and legislatures deem it important to shield defendants from liability for negligence. But they are not willing to eliminate the prospect of liability entirely. Recklessness as to the physical well-being of others marks the borderline, but now by moving "upward" from negligence to cases of conduct that violate even relatively low expectations for how carefully people will or should conduct themselves. Liability under Good Samaritan statutes, landowner liability to trespassers, and the *Rafferty* case discussed in Part II arguably also fit this description.

It is doubtful that this taxonomy covers all cases, and some might be mixtures of the two conceptions we have identified.[67] It is not clear whether the

[67] Ken Simons has isolated three distinct "strands" within the legal concept of recklessness. Simons, *Rethinking Mental States*, *supra* note 7, 482–90. While each of the strands he isolates may not

recklessness that permits an award of punitive damages or that defeats contributory negligence falls into either category. Conversely, the tort of intentional infliction of emotional distress likely includes some cases best characterized as expanding out from intent or knowledge and others that extend up from negligence. Where a defendant is intentionally inflicting emotional distress on someone through extortion or abuse or deeply malicious practical joke, but a third party is the one harmed and seeking damages, courts seem willing to stretch the liability rule if the distress to the third party, though unintended, was a harmful effect as to which the defendant was reckless. From the opposite direction, domains bespeaking gross negligence—as found in the funeral home context—are sometimes deemed actionable as IIED when the gross negligence rises to the level of recklessness.

Our tentatively and roughly drawn distinction between two categories of recklessness cases might seem vulnerable to an obvious objection. Simply put, it is not clear why we are entitled to claim that there are two classes or categories of cases rather than just one. Are we not simply saying that gray is whiter than black and gray is blacker than white? If so, why not just say there are many shades of gray? Why not say that recklessness is at the bottom edge of intentionality and the top edge of negligence, and all of the cases in between are shades of recklessness? The answer, we hope, is borne out by the analysis we have provided.

A close look at *Sullivan* and *Knight* reveals that, while each wields recklessness to fill out the edges of, or fine-tune, certain aspects of tort law, they do so in different ways, on different terms. *Sullivan* says that the right to free speech runs out at the point at which the speaker has nothing to contribute but lies and deceptions. It then adds that a certain kind of speaker—a self-servingly obtuse one—falls within the category of the liar and the dissembler. *Knight* says that voluntary participation in certain recreational activities that already carry with them a risk of physical injury includes acceptance of the possibility that a fellow participant might be somewhat out of control or overly zealous. It then adds that this immunity from liability does not extend to a participant whose dangerous actions are so far out of line with relevant norms and expectations as to indicate appalling indifference to the well-being of others.

Philosophers and lawyers have long debated the precise nature of recklessness and in particular whether or not an actor's subjective awareness of the relevant risks is required for conduct to be reckless. Arguably, the two uses of recklessness we have discussed in this chapter track its subjective and non-subjective renditions. The first version of recklessness—recklessness as quasi-malice—sits

amount to a full-blown, independent conception of recklessness, his analysis suggests that the use of recklessness in American law may in some instances function in ways other than by providing the sort of fine-tuning we describe.

more naturally with conceptions of recklessness that require something like a subjective appreciation of the risk of harm to others. The facts before the speaker "scream" falsity, so much so that any speaker, or at least any speaker who has not culpably cultivated a thoroughgoing indifference to reality, would have some awareness that their statements are very far from the truth. The latter version, by contrast—recklessness as beyond-the-pale-dangerousness—seems to fit more comfortably with fully objective notions of riskiness. The actor—even one who is generally of good will and attentive to the consequences of their actions—may be entirely unaware on the relevant occasion of the unjustifiably massive risks of harm they are generating, and that is part of the problem.

We repair, finally, to the theme of this volume. The word "interstitial" has spatial connotations. In the phrase "interstitial private law," it evokes the idea of spaces between the principal subject-areas of private law. In that spirit, we began this chapter by identifying parts of tort law that do not fit easily into the categories of intentional torts, negligence, or strict liability, and which courts sometimes mark off with the term "reckless" and its cognates. We then elaborated by analyzing specific uses of recklessness: (a) to identify a kind of statement that is sufficiently close to a knowingly false statement to ground an actionable defamation or fraud claim, and (b) to identify conduct that, by virtue of being not only unjustifiably dangerous but especially so, warrants liability even if somewhat less dangerous conduct does not. The former sets a boundary on certain defamation and fraud claims; the latter on the types of risks that can be assumed by injury victims. Of course "boundary," too, is a spatial metaphor, but one perhaps with different connotations than "interstitial." Rather than suggesting points on a continuum with matter in between, it evokes the image of a cell with a nucleus of core meanings, some related meanings hovering around it, and a membrane separating what is in and what is outside of the cell. Things located on the boundary are interstitial in the sense of being situated at the perimeter yet nonetheless marking the edges of the cell, rather than being located outside of it.

8

Equitable Estoppel and Restitution as Interstitial Causes of Action

*Ben McFarlane**

I. Introduction

A conference on interstitial private law provides a chance to look beyond well-established categories such as contract, tort, and property. The purpose of this chapter is to consider two private law causes of action: equitable estoppel[1] and the strict liability restitutionary claim exemplified by that arising on receipt of a mistaken payment.[2] Each cause of action might be seen as relevant to interstitial private law for two main reasons. First, each may be said to be gap-filling, protecting parties who would otherwise be in a no-man's land, beyond the reach of more established categories. Second, each cause of action may be said to have a subsidiary nature, which means it must retreat from the ground covered by contract or property. This raises a wider interstitial question: Do the meta-rules that govern the interaction of different fields of law[3] require these two causes of action to give way to others?

The argument in this chapter is that, to understand the nature and operation of each of equitable estoppel and the restitutionary claim, it is indeed necessary to place each squarely in the realm of interstitial private law. This is not, however, for either of the two reasons just stated. First, equitable estoppel and the restitutionary claim do not simply fill preexisting gaps, areas left vacant by the primary categories of contract, tort, and property, as this would cause incoherence in the law, by undermining the reasons for which those gaps exist. Second, while it is true that each cause of action is, in a sense, secondary, there is no need for a further set of rules that independently limits the operation of equitable estoppel or

* I am grateful to Giorgia Bucaria for research assistance.

1 The focus here is only on equitable estoppel when it functions as an independent cause of action and not when, for example, it simply provides a party with a defense: for a taxonomy of equitable estoppel, *see* B. McFarlane, *Understanding Equitable Estoppel: From Metaphors to Better*, 66 Current Legal Problems 267 (2013).

2 For consideration of which restitutionary claims fall within this model, see Section IV.B.

3 For general discussion of such rules, see Andrew Gold's chapter in this volume.

Ben McFarlane, *Equitable Estoppel and Restitution as Interstitial Causes of Action* In: *Interstitial Private Law*.
Edited by: Samuel L. Bray, John C.P. Goldberg, Paul B. Miller, and Henry E. Smith, Oxford University Press.
 DOI: 10.1093/oso/9780197783627.003.0008

restitution, in order to avoid undermining contract, tort, or property. Rather, the relevant limits on the two causes of action are inherent ones, based on their internal logic.

That internal logic, it will be argued here, rests on the fact that equitable estoppel and the restitutionary claim are interstitial in a specific way: each supplements the operation of contract and property by dealing with particular problems arising from the very legal rules established in those fields. While the two causes of action may seem like upstarts from which the more established categories need protection by higher order rules of priority, in fact each supports those categories, by mitigating dangers arising from legal powers conferred by contract and property. This can be seen both in the form and function of the causes of action. As to form, which will be examined in Section II, rather than recognizing duties to which defendants are subject, each of the causes of action recognizes what may be called a primary liability: a liability, to the making of a court order in the claimant's favor, which does not arise because of the defendant's breach of a preexisting duty. This is why the claims do not fill gaps in the network of duties established by contract, tort, and property; they instead have a different form. It will be argued that this form is related to the particular function equitable estoppel and the restitutionary claim play in mitigating the practical effects of primary legal rules that confer legal powers. That function will be examined in Section III. It will be argued that this supplemental nature of the causes of action is characteristic of many substantive equitable doctrines, which play the vital (and interstitial) role of dealing with problems that the law itself creates. Some of the practical implications of this analysis will be considered in Section IV, which considers some of the inherent limits on the availability of the two causes of action. It will be argued there that these limits, which depend on the interstitial nature of the causes of action, remove the need for any meta-rule regulating their relationship with contract or property. It will be argued by way of conclusion that a failure to grasp this particular interstitial nature of equitable estoppel and the restitutionary claim risks bringing incoherence to private law and, ironically, will undermine precisely the established rules that the two causes of action, properly understood, support.

II. Form: Liabilities

The notion of a liability-imposing rule is important in the following analysis, which adopts the definition provided by Stephen Smith in part of his seminal work on private law:[4]

[4] *See* S. Smith, *A Duty to Make Restitution*, 26 CAN. J.L. & JURISPRUDENCE 157, 162 (2013). See further S. SMITH, RIGHTS, WRONGS, AND INJUSTICES: THE STRUCTURE OF REMEDIAL LAW (2019).

> duty-imposing rules and liability-imposing rules have different forms: duty-imposing rules tell citizens how to act (and how others should act towards them), whereas liability-imposing rules (or more strictly 'liability to orders-imposing rules') tell citizens what the state may do to them (and what they may cause the state to do to others).

It may also be useful to distinguish between primary and secondary liabilities. In his work on remedies, Smith argues that the commission of a tort, or a breach of contract, gives rise not to a duty (such as a duty to pay damages) but rather to a liability (such as a liability to be ordered by a court to pay damages).[5] As it arises only on a breach of a duty, such a liability can be seen as secondary.[6] It is also possible for the law to recognize primary liabilities, which arise without the need for the claimant (C) to show any breach of duty by the defendant (D). One example occurs where an innocent misrepresentation by D causes C to enter into a contract with D. C's equitable power to rescind the contract correlates to a liability of D, even though D has committed no wrong against C. It will be argued that two further examples of primary liabilities are provided by each of equitable estoppel, when operating as a cause of action, and the strict liability restitutionary claim arising, for example, in the case of a mistaken payment.

A. Equitable Estoppel

When equitable estoppel operates as a cause of action, the term "estoppel" is misleading: D is not merely prevented from asserting the truth of some matter of fact or law, which may then assist C in establishing some other cause of action; rather, D is instead subject instead to an independent claim by C. Consider so-called promissory estoppel: the term is close to being oxymoronic. If D makes a promise to C, such as a promise, for example, to leave D's land to C in D's will, then an estoppel that prevents D from denying, as against C, the making of the promise is both redundant (as C can prove the fact of the promise in any case) and unhelpful (as the mere fact of D's having made a promise is not, in itself, sufficient to give C any independent cause of action against D).[7]

[5] *See, e.g.*, S. Smith, *Duties, Liabilities, and Damages*, 125 HARV. L. REV. 1727 (2012). This view as to the effect of a tort or a breach of contract is controversial, but nothing in the analysis in this chapter depends on its validity.

[6] Adopting the distinction between primary and secondary rights often attributed to Austin's analysis: *see* LECTURES ON JURISPRUDENCE OR THE PHILOSOPHY OF POSITIVE LAW, Vol. II, ch. XLV, 761–64 (Campbell ed., 5th ed. Rev., 1911).

[7] As noted by Gaudron J in Waltons Stores v. Maher (1988) 164 CLR 387, 459, "[b]ecause common law or evidential estoppel operates by precluding the assertion of facts inconsistent with an assumed fact, the assumption must necessarily be as to an existing fact and not as to a future event."

So, when equitable estoppel operates as an independent cause of action, it ceases to be a true estoppel.[8] The standard language used in such cases, in England at least, is that, once the relevant facts have occurred, an "equity" arises, and the court must decide how D is to satisfy that equity of C.[9] There is, therefore, a distinction between the "equity by estoppel" arising before the court order[10] and the rights C may acquire as a result of that court order. That term "equity by estoppel" is dangerous if it suggests that the type of right acquired by C is the same, and has the same effect on third parties, whenever an equitable estoppel arises, irrespective of the content of the promise by D on which the claim depends.[11] Nonetheless, the reference to an "equity" is consistent with the view that, on D's promise and C's reliance, the prospect of C's detriment does not impose an immediate duty on D; rather, D is under a liability to be ordered by a court to provide C with some relief. It is similar to the term "mere equity"[12] that is used, for example, where C has an equitable power to set aside a transaction under which C has transferred a right to D, but has not yet exercised that power:[13] again, D is under no immediate duty to C.

I have argued that a primary liability model provides the best way of understanding the form of claims in which equitable estoppel operates as a cause of action.[14] Certainly, in such cases, it is very difficult to say that D is under an immediate duty to C, arising before any court order.[15] This is consistent with the fact that, when deciding how best to satisfy an "estoppel equity," the court must take into account the circumstances then prevailing, including relevant changes of circumstances after the time of C's reliance.[16] Hoffmann LJ (as he then was) expressed the point memorably, and influentially,[17] when considering

[8] As noted by, *e.g.*, McFarlane, *Understanding Equitable Estoppel, supra* note 1, 271–77; and Lord Leggatt in Guest v. Guest [2022] UKSC 27, [2022] 3 WLR 911 at [155].

[9] *See, e.g.*, Crabb v. Arun DC [1976] Ch. 179, 198–99; Guest v. Guest, *supra* note 8, at 10.

[10] Land Registration Act 2002, s. 116(a).

[11] *See* B. McFarlane, *Proprietary Estoppel and Third Parties after the Land Registration Act 2002*, CLJ 667 (2003).

[12] *See, e.g.*, Land Registration Act 2002, s. 116(b).

[13] *See. e.g.*, Mortgage Express v. Lambert [2016] EWCA Civ. 555, Ch. 93 at 16 (2017).

[14] *See, e.g.*, McFarlane, *Understanding Equitable Estoppel, supra* note 1; and *Equity and the Justification of Private Rights, in* JUSTIFYING PRIVATE RIGHTS 229–32 (S. Degeling et al. eds., 2020). *See*, too, Smith, *Rights, Wrongs, and Injustices, supra* note 4, at 270–71; A. Robertson, *Justifying Liabilities and Duties, in* JUSTIFYING PRIVATE RIGHTS (S. Degeling et al. eds., 2020).

[15] As Robertson, *supra* note 14 points out at 213, given the range of factors influencing what a court may order D to do, it is impossible to say that D is under a duty to C prior to a court order, as it would be impossible for D to know how to fulfill that duty.

[16] *See, e.g.*, Habberfield v. Habberfield [2019] EWCA Civ. 890; Guest, *supra* note 8, at 74. Note too that C's enjoyment of countervailing benefits in the period between C's reliance and the court's determination may mean that D's liability has been exhausted: *see, e.g.*, Sledmore v. Dalby (1996) 72 P. & C.R. 196.

[17] Hoffmann LJ's analysis was relied on, for example, by Lord Walker and Lord Neuberger in Thorner v. Major [2009] UKHL 18, [2009] 1 WLR 776 at [52]–[57] and [101] and by the majority in Cowper-Smith v. Morgan [2017] SCC 61, [2017] 2 SCR 754 at [26] and [28].

the difference between a contractual claim and an equitable estoppel. In the former case, D's promise imposes an immediate legal duty on D that "subject to the narrow doctrine of frustration, must be performed come what may," and so must, for example, be one which was intended to impose such a duty; in contrast, equitable estoppel:[18]

> does not look forward into the future and guess what might happen. It looks backwards from the moment when the promise falls due to be performed and asks whether, in the circumstances which have actually happened, it would be unconscionable for the promise not to be kept.

B. Restitution

Stephen Smith argued, in my view persuasively, that in the type of restitution claim arising where C makes a mistaken payment to D, a liability-imposing rule operates. As Smith notes,[19] this is certainly reflected in much of the language used by the *Restatement Third: Restitution and Unjust Enrichment.*[20] Similarly, Ames described implied or quasi contracts as "really equitable liabilities, upon which the common law assumes to grant a remedy."[21] As Smith shows, a liability can be contrasted with cases where D is under an immediate duty to C, arising on the occurrence of particular facts, such as the conclusion of a contract. A key consequence of such a duty is that D can then be said to have acted wrongfully if breaching it; whereas if a set of facts (such as a mistaken payment) give rise only to a liability, then D cannot be said to commit a wrong by, for example, failing to return the value of the mistaken payment: after all, as Smith notes, D may be unaware not only of C's mistake, but also of the fact that the payment came from C.[22]

If this restitutionary claim is seen as depending on a primary liability of D, this may assist in understanding the change of position defense. The judicial recognition of this defense played a critical role in overcoming previous limits to the scope of the restitutionary claim, such as the "mistake of law bar."[23] One explanation of the defense sees it as following from the fact that the content of D's duty depends on the extent of D's enrichment at C's expense, so that as D is

[18] Walton v. Walton (April 14, 1994, CA).

[19] S. Smith, *The Restatement of Liabilities in Restitution*, in THE RESTATEMENT THIRD: RESTITUTION AND UNJUST ENRICHMENT: COMPARATIVE AND CRITICAL ESSAYS (C. Mitchell & W. Swadling eds., 2013), esp. note 27.

[20] *See, e.g.*, AMERICAN LAW INSTITUTE, RESTATEMENT THIRD, RESTITUTION AND UNJUST ENRICHMENT § 1 (2011), at §5 (1).

[21] J.B. Ames, *Purchase for Value without Notice*, 1 HARV. L. REV. 1, 3 (1887).

[22] Smith, *Rights, Wrongs, and Injustices*, *supra* note 4, at 243–45.

[23] See the analysis of Lord Goff in Kleinwort Benson v. Lincoln City Council [1999] 2 AC 349, at 372.

disenriched by a change of position, the sum that D must pay C is reduced.[24] As Stevens has pointed out,[25] however, this analysis does not fit well with the practical operation of the defense: it is not wholly linked to the extent of D's enrichment as there are some disenrichments that do not count for the purposes of the defense, as when D acts with knowledge of C's mistake.[26] Indeed, courts have been reluctant to pin the scope of the defense to the specific question of enrichment and have instead identified the central question as being whether it would be, at the time C's claim is determined, "inequitable in all the circumstances to require [D] to make restitution, or alternatively restitution in full."[27] Indeed in *Australian Financial Services v. Hills*,[28] the High Court of Australia expressly drew a link to the approach adopted when equitable estoppel operates as a cause of action, noting the need to assess matters at the point of C's claim, and to take into account circumstances arising after D's receipt of the payment from C in order to evaluate what the need to avoid unconscionable conduct requires of D. This "backward-looking" approach aligns squarely with a liability-based analysis and with Hoffmann LJ's description, noted in Section IIA, of the operation of equitable estoppel as a cause of action.

III. Function: Dealing with Problems the Law Itself Creates

A. Equitable Estoppel

It was noted in Section I that, when operating as a cause of action, equitable estoppel may be seen as interstitial in the particular sense of filling a gap in the protection afforded by the law to C. This view was certainly adopted by Lord Briggs in *Guest v. Guest*.[29] The case concerned a very common fact pattern for such cases: D, a farmer, promises C, one of D's children, that C will inherit D's farm (or a substantial part of it), and, as a result, C works on the farm, for low wages, for a number of years, before the parties fall out and D makes clear that the promise will not be honored. It has been recognized that, where C can show that a sufficiently clear promise was made, and C would now suffer a detriment

[24] *See, e.g.*, P. Birks, Unjust Enrichment 208–09 (2005).

[25] R. Stevens, The Laws of Restitution 356 (2022).

[26] *See* Lord Goff in Lipkin Gorman v. Karpnale Ltd. [1991] 2 A.C. 548 at 580; Cressman v. Coys of Kensington Ltd. [2004] E.W.C.A. Civ. 47; [2004] 1 WLR 2774 at [21] and [41].

[27] Lord Goff in Lipkin Gorman v. Karpnale Ltd. [1991] 2 AC 548 at 580; Dextra Bank & Trust Co Ltd v. Bank of Jamaica [2002] 1 All ER (Comm.) 193 at [38]; Australian Financial Services v. Hills [2014] HCA 14, (2014) 253 CLR 560 at [27] (French CJ) and at [77][93] (Hayne, Crennan, Kiefel, Bell & Keane JJ). *See* too Restatement Third §65.

[28] [2014] HCA 14, (2014) 253 CLR 560 at [23] (French CJ) and at [85]–[88] (Hayne, Crennan, Kiefel, Bell & Keane JJ).

[29] [2022] UKSC 27 [2022] 3 WLR 91.

as a result of C's reasonable reliance on that promise were D to be wholly free to go back on it, an equity arises.[30] Lord Briggs stated that, in such cases, the courts have "recourse to equitable principles" to provide a remedy for C as:[31]

> [o]ne of the principal functions of equity is to put right injustice to which the law is otherwise blind, by restraining the rigid application of legal rules where their implementation would be unconscionable.

Lord Briggs then identified two legal rules "engaged" on the facts: the first being "that a promise is not enforceable unless it is made part of a contract" and the second that "a person is free to change his will until he dies (or loses mental capacity to do so)."[32] The question then is what it means to "restrain the rigid application" of those rules. On one view, the scope of the rule is cut down, so that particular situations are recognized in which a promise *can* be enforced despite not being in a contract, and a party *can* be prevented from changing his will. This is consistent with the view, noted in Section I, that equitable estoppel plays a gap-filling role, correcting deficiencies in the coverage of primary rules of contract or property. On the different view, preferred in this chapter, those rules are instead left intact, but their practical application is mitigated in specific circumstances. That second view recognizes the crucial difference between on the one hand, correcting a rule and, on the other, modifying its practical effect.[33]

The difference between the two views can be seen by contrasting the approach of Lord Briggs, who gave the majority judgment in *Guest*, and that of Lord Leggatt, who dissented.[34] For Lord Briggs, it seems, where a gap in the common law would otherwise cause injustice, equity can "fill the lacuna."[35] If the "lacuna" in *Guest* is seen as being the lack of a duty of D to perform D's promise to C, then the role of equity is to recognize and enforce such a duty. Indeed, Lord Briggs links this to the use of the term "estoppel," stating that:[36]

> [t]he perhaps quaint word "estoppel" encapsulates the notion that the equitable wrong which has been threatened or done is the repudiation of the promise where it would be unconscionable for the promisor to do so. So the equitable

30 *See, e.g.*, Thorner v. Major [2009] UKHL 18 [2009] 1 WLR 776.
31 [2022] UKSC 27 [2022] 3 WLR 911, at [4].
32 *Id.*
33 Indeed, it is notable that the determination of the majority in Guest did not in fact involve either enforcing D's promise as though it were contractual, or preventing D from changing his will: *see* Guest at [101]–[05].
34 Lord Stephens agreed with Lord Leggatt; Lady Rose and Lady Arden agreed with Lord Briggs.
35 [2022] UKSC 27, [2022] 3 WLR 911 at [5].
36 [2022] UKSC 27, [2022] 3 WLR 911 at [4].

> remedy is to restrain, or stop or "estop" the promisor from reneging on the promise.

While at one point expressing less certainty about the appropriateness of the term "wrong" in this context,[37] Lord Briggs later states that "it is the repudiation of the promised expectation which constitutes the unconscionable wrong."[38] On Lord Briggs's approach, therefore, the starting assumption is that, where an equitable estoppel claim is made out, a court should order D to put C in the position C would have been in had the promise been performed, although there may be cases where D can show that the need to avoid unconscionable conduct by D can be met by means of a lesser remedy.[39]

This can be contrasted with Lord Leggatt's approach, which keeps more clearly in mind the distinction between equitable estoppel and contract. He makes the important point that, as applied in England, equitable estoppel does not simply allow detrimental reliance to act as a substitute for consideration and thus to make a promise legally binding.[40] This is amply evidenced by the fact that there are a number of other requirements for an enforceable contract, beyond consideration, which are also absent in such a claim. For example, an estoppel claim can arise even if C cannot show that D's promise was intended to be legally binding,[41] and even in the absence of the formalities required for a valid contract to dispose of an interest in land.[42] As Lord Leggatt put it:[43]

> The doctrine [proprietary estoppel] does not and could not sensibly have as its aim the enforcement of promises which do not satisfy the requirements of the creation of legal obligations. A [proprietary estoppel] claim is not a form of contract lite.

The disagreement between Lord Briggs and Lord Leggatt may seem to be merely a local one, but it reflects a wider debate as to the nature and operation of equitable estoppel that has important implications for our understanding of contract law, and has raged quite fiercely in relation to the role of what is now §90 of the Restatement (Second) of Contracts. It shows how our understanding of

37 [2022] UKSC 27 [2022] 3 WLR 911 at [9]: "The equitable "wrong" (if that is the right word) is not the making of the promise in the first place."

38 [2022] UKSC 27 [2022] 3 WLR 911 at [53].

39 [2022] UKSC 27 [2022] 3 WLR 911 at [75].

40 *See* too McFarlane, *Equitable Estoppel as a Cause of Action: Neither One Thing Nor One Other*, *in* Contracts in Commercial Law (S. Degeling et al. eds., 2016).

41 *See, e.g.*, Walton, *supra* note 18.

42 *See, e.g.*, Farrar v. Miller [2018] EWCA Civ. 172 at [59] and the extrajudicial analysis of Lord Neuberger, *The Stuffing of Minerva's Owl? Taxonomy and Taxidermy in Equity*, CLJ 537, 546 (2009).

43 [2022] UKSC 27, [2022] 3 WLR 911 at [183].

a key private law concept, such as contract, can be shaped by our analysis of an apparently less important doctrine, such as equitable estoppel. It also raises the broader question of the relationship between common law and equity, and whether we take seriously the language used by the courts in developing doctrines such as equitable estoppel.

On one view, then, consistent with the approach of Lord Briggs, equitable estoppel operates to correct a problem with a common law rule that denies the existence of a duty on D to perform a promise, where one or more requirements of an enforceable contract are absent. A consequence, embraced by some scholars[44] but only dealt with indirectly by Lord Briggs, is that equity thus contradicts the common law position. This view lies behind those analyses of the rule in Section 90 of the Restatement of Contracts that consider it as shedding light on the nature of contract law as a whole.[45] One response, evident in Lord Briggs's approach, is then to emphasize "the discretionary approach to a remedy"[46] and the "flexible conscience-based discretion"[47] preferred by equity, thus preserving some distance between the practical outcomes where D's promise is contractually binding and where instead its breach constitutes only an "equitable wrong."[48]

On the second view, consistent with the approach of Lord Leggatt,[49] equitable estoppel instead operates to mitigate the practical effect of particular primary rules but does not challenge the validity of those rules. It does not deny the basic point that D's promise to C does not impose an immediate duty on D; it rather recognizes that there may also be circumstances in which D's promise, when coupled with C's detrimental reliance, may impose a liability on D. Factors that might on the first view be said to show the flexibility of equity can instead then be seen as based on the "backwards-looking" nature of the liability: a court has to look at the facts as a whole and ask what is *now* required of D to avoid the particular form of unconscionability, which consists of leaving C to suffer a detriment as a result of C's reasonable reliance on D's promise. On this view, equity is not contradicting the primary legal rules as to when a promise can give rise to an immediate duty. Indeed, by dealing with a particular practical injustice that may

44 *See, e.g.*, P. Atiyah, *When Is an Enforceable Agreement Not a Contract? Answer: When It Is an Equity*, 92 LQR 174 (1976).

45 *See, e.g.*, D. Farber & J. Matheson, *Beyond Promissory Estoppel: Contract Law and the "Invisible Handshake,"* 52 U. CHICAGO L. REV. 903 (1985); E. Yorio & S. Thel, *The Promissory Basis of Section 90*,101 YALE L.J. 111 (1991); R. Barnett, *The Death of Reliance*, 46 J. LEGAL EDUC. 518 (1996). *Contrast, e.g.*, R. Scott, *Hoffmann v. Red Owl Stores and the Myth of Precontractual Reliance*,161 OHIO ST. L.J. 71 (2007).

46 [2022] UKSC 27, [2022] 3 WLR 911 at [30].

47 [2022] UKSC 27, [2022] 3 WLR 911 at [53].

48 Note that a similar role is played by the final sentence of §90(1): "The remedy granted for breach may be limited as justice requires."

49 *See* too P. Millett, *Crabb v. Arun District Council—A Riposte* 92 LQR 342 (1976), responding to Atiyah, *supra* note 44.

arise through the operation of those rules, it is supporting the generality of those rules, and, by helping to deal with a possible objection to them, is contributing to the validity of their adoption by the legal system.[50] Equity can thus be seen as dealing with a risk that arises from the very fact that rules of property law give D a power to make a testamentary gift to C. The presence of such a power, while usefully promoting D's autonomy, creates the risk that C may reasonably rely, and even structure his whole life, on a belief that D will exercise that power in a particular way. Where D bears sufficient responsibility for that belief, there may then be circumstances where the prospect of C's suffering a detriment as a result of C's reliance justifies a court in making an order against D. A liability of D may thus be necessary, not to alter the rules of contract or property, but to help support them by mitigating a practical injustice they would otherwise cause. As will be discussed further in Section IIIB, this function is one that is characteristic of equity and is also consistent with a primary liability model.

B. Restitution

It was noted in Section II that Ames, in the passage cited there, referred to implied or quasi contracts—terms used to describe what are now more commonly labeled as restitutionary claims—as *equitable* liabilities.[51] Cardozo also referred to the action for money had and received as "equitable in origin and function";[52] but the concern here is only with the role of the claims, not their jurisdictional place of birth. In his analysis of restitutionary claims as liability based, Stephen Smith referred to justifications of such claims that "suppose that the rules governing defective transfers are intended to fix a problem that the law, in particular, the law of property, has itself created or at least authorised."[53] He then cites as an example of such an argument my suggestion that, where, for example, a restitutionary claim arises on a mistaken payment by C to D, liability is "justified at one remove. The function of the principle . . . is to mitigate the effects on C of other legal rules."[54] Smith links this justification to the form of the restitutionary claim by suggesting that, while it would be inappropriate for the law to fix a problem of its own making by imposing a duty on D, the approach adopted instead is the following:[55]

[50] *See, e.g.*, M. Harding, *Equity and the Rule of Law*, 132 LQR 278 (2016); McFarlane, *Equity and the Justification of Private Rights*, *supra* note 14.

[51] Ames, *supra* note 21.

[52] Atlantic Coast Line Railroad Co v. Florida (1935) 295 U.S. 301, 309.

[53] Smith, *supra* note 19, at 246.

[54] *Id.* at 246–47, citing B. McFarlane, *Unjust Enrichment, Rights, and Value*, *in* Rights and Private Law 581, 607 (D. Nolan & A. Robertson eds., 2012).

[55] Smith, *supra* note 19, at 247.

> for the law, or more strictly the courts, to fix the problem themselves. Interpreted as liability rules, the rules governing defective transfers provide a means by which citizens who have been disadvantaged by the rules governing the passage of title can approach the courts for relief. It is as if the law says to citizens: 'Here are the rules governing property transfers. They work well most of the time, but in rare cases they lead to undesirable results. When that happens, come to us and we will fix the problem.'

Soon afterwards, Smith briefly notes the connection such a model suggests between restitutionary liability and equity, noting that:[56]

> unjust enrichment law is equitable in the sense that it is meant to provide relief for, broadly speaking, *legal* injustices . . . From the perspective of the liability model, unjust enrichment law is equitable in the core sense that it provides a corrective to other laws.

When previously suggesting that the liability principle applying in the mistaken payment case is justified at one remove, I had not then made the link to the form of the principle, as imposing a liability rather than a duty, nor to the similarity with the broader notion of equity.[57] Smith's insights on those points, I believe, are very valuable, and can strengthen such an approach to understanding the reasons for particular restitutionary claims.

In considering the link to equity, it is important to note the specific sense in which equity is seen as a secondary system, correcting primary outcomes. This is consistent both with Maitland's description of equity as supplementary, as a gloss on legal rules,[58] and with Henry Smith's analysis of equity as a form of meta-law, as rules about rules.[59] On such views, it is not the case that equity fills gaps by simply giving a different answer to the very question already tackled at common law; as seen in relation to equitable estoppel in Section IIIA, the equitable intervention rather accepts, and indeed *depends on*, the relevant common law rule.[60] Such views can, therefore, meet the objection that the necessary gap-filling can be carried out by simply altering the offending common law rules, so that equity is redundant.[61]

[56] *Id.* at 249.

[57] Although *see* B. McFarlane, *Equity and the Justification of Private Rights*, *in* JUSTIFYING PRIVATE RIGHTS (S. Degeling et al eds., 2020) for consideration of the link to equity.

[58] F. MAITLAND, EQUITY; ALSO, THE FORMS OF ACTION AT COMMON LAW: TWO COURSES OF LECTURES 9 (A. Chaytor & W. Whittaker eds., 1909).

[59] H. Smith, *Equity as Meta-Law*, 130 YALE L.J. 1050 (2021).

[60] For the application of such an analysis to the trust, and to equitable assignment, *see* B. McFarlane, *The Persistence of Equity: Lessons from the Trust*, *in* EQUITY TODAY: 150 YEARS AFTER THE JUDICATURE REFORMS (B. McFarlane & S. Elliott eds., 2023).

[61] Note the argument here is that such secondary intervention is characteristic of equity; it is not that equity can *only* intervene in such a way. For example, the extension of breach of confidence to

Consider, for example, restitutionary claims depending on the mistaken transfer of a right. In *Cressman v. Coys of Kensington (Sales) Ltd.*,[62] for example, auctioneers, when selling C's title to a car, failed to comply with C's instruction to retain the valuable registration mark also held by C. As a result, when buying the car, D also acquired title to that mark and successfully registered as its holder. D attempted to rely on this registration to resist a restitutionary claim of C:[63] as D had acquired the mark consistently with the governing statutory scheme, how could his acquisition or retention of it be an *unjust* enrichment? As Mance LJ pointed out, however, that objection was misguided: the claim was in fact founded on D's holding of the right.[64] The claim was not that the statutory rule—recognizing that the registered party was the holder of the mark—was too general in its application, and should not be applied where there had been a lack of consent from the vendor of the mark; rather the claim was that, while D did have title to the mark, D could nonetheless be ordered to pay to C the value of that right, given that lack of consent. So, the generality of the statutory rule, while forming a crucial part of the justification of the claim, is not itself challenged, denied, or corrected by the claim. Rather, the rule is left intact, but a specific practical consequence arising from its application is reversed or remedied.[65]

A crucial point, in a case such as *Cressman*, and indeed in any case where a strict liability restitutionary claim arises on the mistaken transfer of a right, is that there are good reasons for the primary rules, often rules of property law, which hold that, C's mistake notwithstanding, the transfer of C's right to D is valid. These reasons take into account the position of third parties who, for example, are then able to rely on a register in ascertaining the current holder of a particular right. The restitutionary claim does not deny the validity of those reasons, but instead simply mitigates, as between C and D, a particular practical effect of their operation.

This can be seen as a form of interstitial intervention that, as noted by Henry Smith in his examination of equity as meta-law, can be vital in helping to justify the content, and generality, of those primary rules which, for example, reduce information costs for third parties by allowing a transfer to be valid even where

play the role, in some cases, of a tort protecting privacy shows how equity has also adopted a genuinely gap-filling role: for discussion *see* J. Goldberg & H. Smith, *Wrongful Fusion: Equity and Tort, Equity and Law: Fusion and Fission* (J. Goldberg et al. eds., 2019).

62 [2004] EWCA Civ. 47 [2004] 1 WLR 2775.

63 The claim was in fact brought by the auctioneers, who had taken an assignment of C's claim.

64 [2004] EWCA Civ. 47, [2004] 1 WLR 2775 [24].

65 Note that even if a court were to impose a duty on D to return the mark itself to C, this would not be inconsistent with the statutory scheme, as C would acquire the mark only on D's compliance with the court order, and the completion of any registration requirements.

a mistake has been made.[66] More broadly, the restitutionary claim can help to promote a coherence across private law: a significant purpose of recognizing C as having a particular legal power, such as the power to enter a contract with D, or to transfer a right to D, is to promote C's autonomy, by extending the range of legally valid decisions C can make. In cases, however, where there is a defect in C's reasoning process, such as a mistake, the exercise of the power (while it is, for good reason, still valid) does not promote C's autonomy: the possibility of the restitutionary claim against D provides some recourse that can limit the damage to C in such a case.

It should be noted that the restitutionary claim could still be seen as having such a function if it had a different form: even if the claim depended on a duty of D to C, rather than a liability, it would retain its secondary nature as it would not contradict the position that C's right had indeed been transferred to D. The difficulty with a duty model of the restitutionary claim, however, lies in explaining why *D*, who need not be responsible for C's mistake, should be under a duty to C. If the claim is seen as requiring the same type of fully bilateral justification as is often present in relation to duties recognized in the laws of contract, tort, and property, then problems arise: Why should C be able to *demand* that D pay C the value of the mistakenly transferred right? If, however, the claim is seen as depending instead on a liability of D to an order of a court, made in C's favor, responding to a problem arising from the operation of a legal power, and attempting not to find something due to C from D, but rather to balance the interests of the two parties, then some of those difficulties can be avoided.[67]

IV. Limits: Internal or External?

It was noted in Section I that there is a question of whether particular meta-rules are needed to coordinate the interaction of equitable estoppel and the restitutionary claim considered here with better-established areas of private law. The argument made in this section is that there is no need for such external, higher-level rules in this context,[68] as the inherent limits of the two causes of action, flowing from their form and function, adequately deal with the legitimate concern not to undermine the law of contract or of property.

66 Smith, *Equity as Meta-Law*, *supra* note 59.

67 Note in particular the discussion in Section II.A of the change of position defense.

68 This is not to suggest that such rules are never relevant to either cause of action; the point is rather that they are not required in order to protect contract or property. For consideration of some of the general limits on equitable claims, see Samuel Bray's chapter in this volume.

A. Equitable Estoppel

In England, the current position, contrasting with the broader approaches in American and (probably) Australian law,[69] is that an equitable estoppel claim based on a promise made by C to D can give rise to a cause of action only where D's promise is to give C a right in relation to land, or some other property.[70] This limit seems somewhat surprising: it might be thought that D should be given more, not less, protection from claims that may lead to D's losing a right in relation to land, as shown by, for example, the additional formality requirements that apply to contracts for the sale or other disposition of an interest in land.[71] It is true that, in practice, claims arise most often in this context as, in the absence of such a formality requirement, it may be possible for C to fit a claim within the confines of contract law.[72] Nonetheless, the English limit gives rise to arbitrariness: if, for example, C is a landowner who incurs costs following D's non-contractual promise to take a lease of C's land, it seems that C has no equitable estoppel claim against D, even though D would potentially have such a claim against C if D had similarly relied on C's promise to grant the lease.[73] Certainly, in Australia, a key case with just such facts revealed the arbitrariness of the limit[74] whereas in England such a case has not been considered at the very highest level.[75]

It is difficult to see English law's limit on the ability of equitable estoppel to operate as a cause of action as an internal one, required by the very nature of the cause of action. After all, if the aim of the doctrine is to prevent the unconscionability arising where D's refusal to honor a promise leaves C to suffer a detriment, why is the outcome any less unconscionable if that promise is to do something other than to give C a right in relation to land or other property?[76] One explanation is that the limit is an external one, required in order to prevent the claim undermining the law of contract.[77] Such a view, by itself, does

[69] For discussion of the somewhat unclear position in Australia, *see* A. Robertson, Three Models of Promissory Estoppel, 7 J. EQUITY 226 (2013).

[70] *See, e.g.*, Lord Walker in Thorner v. Major [2009] UKHL 18 [2009] 1 WLR 776 at [61]. This is why, in English law, the form of equitable estoppel giving rise to a cause of action is generally referred to as proprietary estoppel.

[71] *See* Law of Property (Miscellaneous Provisions) Act 1989, s. 2.

[72] Note that the doctrine of consideration has been interpreted more flexibly in England than in the United States, which again lessens the need in English law for a general cause of action in equitable estoppel: for discussion, *see* B. McFarlane, *The Protection of Pre-contractual Reliance: A Way Forward?*, 9(2) OUCLJ 95 (2010).

[73] *See, e.g.*, B. McFarlane & P. Sales, *Promises, Detriment, and Liability: Lessons from Proprietary Estoppel*, 131 LQR 610 (2015).

[74] Waltons Stores, *supra* note 7.

[75] Brewer Street Investments Ltd. v. Barclays Woollen Co. Ltd. [1954] 1 QB 248 (CA) is perhaps the closest example but was decided well before the promise-based strand of proprietary estoppel came to prominence.

[76] *See* McFarlane & Sales, Promises, Detriment, and Liability, *supra* note 73.

[77] *See, e.g.*, Denning LJ in Combe v. Combe [1951] 2 KB 215 (CA) at 220.

not explain why contract law should be seen as the sole means of giving effect to certain promises, but not others. In other words, why are contracts relating to property not undermined by the possibility of an equitable estoppel claim?[78] Certainly, if there is in fact a binding contract between the parties, there are no grounds for an equitable estoppel claim;[79] but this does not come from any arbitrary prioritization of contract law. Rather, it depends on an inherent limit to the equitable estoppel claim. The claim depends on C's showing a detriment that would result from C's reliance on D's promise, but the acquisition of a contractual right is a powerful countervailing benefit that prevents C's establishing such detriment.[80] Moreover, an equitable estoppel claim cannot give C a remedy that requires D to do more than would be required by a successful contractual claim based on D's promise: even if the extent of C's reliance exceeds the value of D's promise, it cannot be unconscionable for D to put C in the position C would have been in had the promise been honored.[81]

The better view is that there are no external limits—that is, limits unrelated to the internal logic of an equitable estoppel claim—which should restrict the scope of such a claim in order to regulate its relationship with contract. The inherent function of the claim, however, as dealing with certain problems to which the law itself gives rise, should provide some limits on the type of promises capable of giving rise to an equitable estoppel claim. One influential statement of the Australian position is that an equitable estoppel claim can be based on D's promise where that promise is to make a change in the parties' legal relationship, by creating or extinguishing a right.[82] While this limit has been questioned,[83] it can be related to the analysis in Section IIIA. The existence of D's power to initiate a change in legal relations with C, while justifiable overall, necessarily creates particular risks: D may abuse such a power by making a promise to C to exercise the power, reasonably understood by C as seriously intended, on which C then reasonably relies in such a way that C would now suffer a detriment were D wholly free to go back on the promise. In such a case, the "shock to the conscience of the court"[84] justifying the imposition of a remedy is not the mere fact of detriment: given there is no general duty to avoid causing (intentionally or

[78] Note one response would be to argue that equitable estoppel should never operate as a cause of action, even where the promise relates to D's property (*see, e.g.*, STEVENS, *supra* note 25, at 276–85). This would however require a significant reworking of the existing law.

[79] Gordon v. Havener [2021] UKPC 26; Lloyds Bank v. Carrick [1996] 4 All ER 630 (CA).

[80] *See* B. MCFARLANE, THE LAW OF PROPRIETARY ESTOPPEL 4.121–4.124 (2d ed., 2020).

[81] *See, e.g.*, Parker v. Parker [2003] EWHC 1846 (Ch) [210]; AMERICAN LAW INSTITUTE, RESTATEMENT SECOND: CONTRACTS § 90 (1981).

[82] *See* Brennan J in Waltons Stores, *supra* note 7, at 425.

[83] *See, e.g.*, W v. G, 20 FAM. LR 49 (1996); and A. Robertson, *Three Models of Promissory Estoppel*, 7 J. EQUITY 226 (2013).

[84] To use the phrase of Lord Walker in Cobbe v. Yeoman's Row Management Ltd. [2008] UKHL 55 [2008] 1 WLR 1752 at [92].

carelessly) economic loss to another, it is hard to say that there is a general duty to avoid causing loss through induced reliance.[85] Rather, intervention is required to prevent D taking unfair advantage, as against C, of a particular primary legal rule. Contrary to the analysis of Lord Briggs in *Guest*,[86] in a case where D makes a promise to leave D's property to C, the relevant rules are not those of contract law, or succession law, which deny that D is under a duty to C to perform D's promise, as these are purely negative in their application to the facts. Rather, the relevant rule is the one conferring on D the power to make the disposition to C at all: it is that rule that creates the risk of C's suffering a detriment as a result of reliance on D's promise to exercise the power. It is true, however, that in preventing that rule, in specific circumstances, from causing a practical injustice to C, equitable estoppel does—consistently with Harding's analysis of one of the key purposes of equity[87]—avoid a situation which would not only be detrimental to C, but could also undermine more general confidence in legal institutions such as contract law and the law of succession.[88]

B. Restitution

Birks described the law of unjust enrichment as "the law of all events materially identical to the mistaken payment of a non-existent debt."[89] The term "enrichment" suggests that, if injustice is also present, the claim may be available whenever there is a simple factual, or economic, gain of D at C's expense.[90] The analysis in this chapter, in contrast, takes a relatively narrow view of a key aspect of the material event in such a case:[91] it is rather the fact that a particular *legal* event—the payment—has occurred, which inherently involves, as two sides of the same coin, both a legal plus to D and a legal minus to C.[92] That pattern is also

[85] M Spence, Protecting Reliance: The Emergent Doctrine of Equitable Estoppel (1999) argues for the existence of such a duty. For difficulties with the view, *see, e.g.*, A. Robertson, *Estoppels and Rights-Creating Events: Beyond Wrongs and Promises, in* Exploring Contract Law (J. Neyers et al. eds., 2009).

[86] [2022] UKSC 27 [2022] 3 WLR 911 at [4].

[87] M. Harding, *Equity and the Rule of Law*, 132 LQR 278 (2016).

[88] For the argument that equitable estoppel plays such a role, *see* B. McFarlane, *Equitable Estoppel as a Cause of Action: Neither One Thing nor One Other, in Contracts in Commercial Law* (S. Degeling et al. eds., 2016); and *Proprietary Estoppel: Undermining the Law of Succession?, Current Issues in Succession Law* (B. Haecker & C. Mitchell eds., 2016).

[89] Birks, *supra* note 24, at 3.

[90] Note that such a broad analysis of the necessary connection between C and D was rejected by Lord Reed in *Investment Trust Companies v. Revenue and Customs Commissioners* [2017] UKSC 29 [2018] AC 275, at [57].

[91] The analysis here is consistent with the approach set out in more detail in McFarlane, *Unjust Enrichment, Rights, and Value, supra* note 54.

[92] Note that this formulation is narrower than that of Lord Reed's in ITC (*supra* note 90). Lord Reed's view requires a transfer of value that may occur even in the absence of a legal event. The

visible in cases where, for example, C transfers a right to D, or where C makes a payment to X, which discharges a debt D owed to X, or where C makes a contractual agreement with D. In such cases, the relevant legal event depends, at least in part, on C's exercise of a power. If then there is some flaw in the basis on which C exercised that power, a liability may be imposed on D, to reverse, as far as possible, the effects on C and D of C's exercise of that power. On this view, the mistaken payment example does not generalize to a principle that is prima facie applicable in a case where, for example, C improves D's property in the mistaken belief that the property belongs to C,[93] or where C mistakenly makes a payment to X, who as a result makes a payment, which X would not otherwise have made, to D. In the first case, the effect of C's action, in improving D's property, does not depend directly on the positive operation of a primary legal rule; and in the second case, while C's payment to X was, factually, a but for cause of D's receipt, it was not part of the same legal event as D's receipt, which depended directly on the exercise of a power by X, not by C.[94] On this view, the core aim of the liability principle evident in the mistaken payment case is the mitigation of the practical effects, as between C and D, of a primary legal rule that directly involves a change in the legal position of each of C and D.

It should be noted that this narrow model is directed to ascertaining cases where D can come under a liability to C as a result of a flaw in C's consent to the exercise of a power, even where that flaw is wholly unilateral, as in the case of the mistaken payment. It does not, therefore, deny the possibility of restitutionary claims arising for different reasons, as when, for example, work is done by C for D on the basis of a shared condition that later fails.[95] As persuasively argued by Stevens,[96] it should though be noted that, given they arise for a different reason, there is no basis for assuming that such restitutionary claims should operate in the same way as the claim arising in the case of a mistaken payment. It seems, for example, that the change of position defense—seen in Section IIB to be key to

formulation is also, to that extent, narrower than Stevens's suggestion that a "performance" between C and D is required: *see* STEVENS, *supra* note 25, at 36–50, although the gap with Stevens's suggestion is narrowed by the fact that, if C's performance of a service discharges a contractual duty of C to D, it can be seen as a legal event (*see, e.g.*, Whittington v. Seale-Hayne (1900) 82 LT 49, discussed by STEVENS, *supra* note 25, at 70).

93 Note that in English law it is clear that no strict liability restitutionary claim arises in such a case: *see, e.g.*, the analysis in Blue Haven Enterprises Ltd v. Tully [2006] U.K.P.C. 17. The situation in the United States is different: *see* RESTATEMENT THIRD, *supra* note 20, § 10. For discussion, *see* B. McFarlane, *Rights and Value; Means and Ends, in* THE RESTATEMENT THIRD: RESTITUTION AND UNJUST ENRICHMENT: COMPARATIVE AND CRITICAL ESSAYS 13–15 (C. Mitchell & W. Swadling eds., 2013).

94 See re Byfield [1982] Ch 267.

95 *See, e.g.*, Cobbe v. Yeoman's Row Management Ltd [2008] UKHL 55, [2008] 1 WLR 1752.

96 STEVENS, *supra* note 25, at 9–10, Ch. 7 and 359–60.

the operation of the strict liability claim arising in the mistaken payment case—does not apply in cases involving the failure of a shared condition.[97]

On this narrow model, the "secondary" nature of the strict liability restitutionary claim is evident from its scope: it operates only where there is some primary legal rule which determines the mutual effect, on C and D, of particular facts. This primary rule thus provides the critical link between C and D, providing, unlike broad terms such as "enrichment at the expense of," the "compelling nexus"[98] between the parties which is a crucial part of the justification of D's coming under a liability to C. As a result, some of the suggested external limits on the scope of the restitutionary claim, applied to deny liability where there is a prima facie unjust enrichment of D at C's expense, are redundant. For example, it has been suggested that, to avoid undermining well-established rules of property law, there must be a bona fide purchaser defense to the restitutionary claim.[99] Such a defense is needed if it is assumed that there can be a prima facie liability of D even when D acquires a right from X, rather than directly from C.[100] In contrast, on the narrower view preferred here, if, for example, X steals cash from C and then uses that cash to buy goods from D, who is bona fide, there is no need for D to establish a defense to the restitutionary claim considered here as that claim does not arise: there was no power exercised by C that caused both a legal gain to D and a legal loss to C. Such an analysis explains why D is not liable and does not rely on the unjustified premise that the rules of property law must displace those of unjust enrichment: after all, as is clear in cases such as *Cressman*, the fact that D has acquired a particular right does not prevent D's also being under a restitutionary liability to C.

When limits on a cause of action are seen as external, depending not on the inherent logic of the cause of action, but rather on a different basis, such as the need to protect a different area of law, it may be sensible to see those external limits as themselves subject to exceptions: the reasons for them may be outweighed, in some cases, by other factors. For example, in *International Energy Group v. Zurich Insurance*,[101] D, an employer, had liability insurance with C for six of the twenty-seven years in which an employee, later diagnosed with mesothelioma, had worked for D. Under the special tort rules developed at common law

[97] *See, e.g.*, Goss v. Chilcott [1996] AC 788 and Haugesund Kommune v. Depfa ACS Bank [2010] EWCA Civ. 579 [2012] QB 549. Contrary to the suggestion of Robert Goff J in BP Exploration Co (Libya) Ltd v. Hunt (No. 2) [1979] 1 WLR 783 at 800 and 804, the ability of D to deduct expenses incurred "in, or for the purpose of the performance of" a contract with C, when facing a claim for repayment of a sum paid by C when that contract is later frustrated, is best seen as a limited statutory rule applying only under section 1(2) of the Law Reform (Frustrated Contracts) Act 1943 rather than as an application of a general change of position defense: *see, e.g.*, STEVENS, *supra* note 25, at 141–42.

[98] To use the language of Goulding J in re Byfield [1982] Ch. 267, at 276.

[99] *See, e.g.*, BIRKS, *supra* note 24, at 240–44.

[100] *Id.* at 89.

[101] [2015] UKSC 33 [2016] AC 509.

in such cases, D was liable in full for the employee's illness as the employment covered some part of the period of the employee's exposure to asbestos, and it was impossible to know which part of the employee's exposure had caused the illness. C paid D under the policy for D's full liability, but then claimed back a proportion of that amount, by way of a contribution from D. Such claims to a contribution had been permitted as between different employers, where each had employed a victim for particular periods. The difficulty for C, however, was that it had a contract with D, and that insurance contract seemed to impose a duty on C to pay to D the full sum of D's liability.

The minority in the Supreme Court[102] found in C's favor by interpreting the contract so that C's duty had only been to pay D a proportionate sum, based on the period of D's insurance with C. This avoided any conflict between the content of C's contractual duty to D and C's restitutionary claim arising from the payment in full to D. The majority,[103] however, found that it was possible, in limited circumstances, to allow a restitutionary claim even if it related to payments that were due under a contract between the parties. Speaking for the majority, Lord Mance stated that:[104]

> I do not accept that there is any absolute bright-line principle . . . whereby equity must refuse to recognise a right of contribution between parties to a contract which according to its terms involves a particular result . . . There is a general rule to that effect, but it is subject to exceptions.

This approach is consistent with that of Burrows.[105] On Burrows's view, cited by the majority, where an enrichment acquired by D at C's expense is owed by C to D under a valid legal obligation, such as a contractual duty, any prima facie injustice arising as a result of, for example, C's having made a mistake, will be "normally outweighed by the fact that the defendant is legally entitled to the enrichment."[106] However, there may be exceptions: cases where the "prima facie injustice constituted by there being an unjust factor is not outweighed by the defendant's legal entitlement to the enrichment."[107] On Burrows's view, to decide whether such an exception arises, a court must carefully consider the policies

[102] Lords Neuberger, Sumption, and Reed.
[103] Lords Mance, Clarke, Carnwath, and Hodge.
[104] [2015] UKSC 33 [2016] AC 509 [68].
[105] Now of course himself a member of the Supreme Court.
[106] A. Burrows, *The Law of Restitution* 88–89 (3d ed., 2011), cited by Lord Mance in Zurich Insurance at [68]. *See* too C. Mitchell et al. eds., *Goff and Jones on Unjust Enrichment* (10th ed., 2022), at [2-01], stating that "the defendant can escape liability if another legal rule entitles him to keep the benefit, and this rule overrides the rule generated by the law of unjust enrichment which holds that the defendant should make restitution."
[107] A Burrows, The Law of Restitution (3d ed., 2011), 88–89, cited by Lord Mance in Zurich Insurance at [68].

involved. Adopting that view, the majority in *Zurich Insurance* held that allowing recovery to C was permissible, given the change in the law that "for the first time ever, imposed liability on the basis of risk, rather than the probability, that negligence during the insurance period led or contributed to the illness." This required the law to "redress the unjust and wholly anomalous burden which would otherwise fall on any particular insurer with whom insurance was only taken out for part of the total period of exposure by the insured."[108] In contrast, Lord Sumption, for the minority, stated that "The suggestion that equity can partially adjust the result of this injustice by requiring the insured to repay to the insurer part of the insurance moneys which the latter was contractually obliged to pay him, is contrary to basic principles of law."[109]

The view of Lord Mance is similar to his analysis in the *Cressman* case, discussed in Section IIB. There is, however, a crucial difference between the two sets of facts. In *Cressman*, the restitutionary claim responded to the practical injustice caused by the operation of the rule that D had acquired title to the registration mark, but it did not contradict the operation of that rule by denying that D held that mark. In contrast, in *Zurich Insurance*, the terms of the contract between C and D must (in the absence of the contract's being set aside, frustrated, or terminated) determine whether D was entitled to retain the value of the payment received from C. To find otherwise is not to mitigate the practical effect of the primary rules of contract law, but is rather to modify the rules themselves. Indeed, the majority changed those primary rules by recognizing a situation in which an unexpected change in the law can be used, in effect, as grounds for altering the content of a contractual duty. However, if there is a need to alter the rules of contract law in this way, it should be applied directly, rather than by means of a supposed interstitial gloss.

Indeed, later courts have been reluctant to apply the majority's approach. It is notable that a judge in one such case was Leggatt LJ (now Lord Leggatt), who cited academic criticism[110] of the majority's approach in *Zurich Insurance* and went on to state that "allowing an equitable principle or restitutionary claim to override a valid and binding contract should in my view be regarded as an absolutely last resort, if not counsel of despair."[111] This is consistent, of course, with his approach in *Guest*, discussed in Section IIA, to the relationship between equitable estoppel and contract: just as a restitutionary principle should not deny the existence of D's valid contractual entitlement to a payment, nor

[108] [2015] UKSC 33 [2016] AC 509 [77].

[109] [2015] UKSC 33[2016] AC 509 [113].

[110] Citing R. Merkin, *Insurance and Reinsurance in the Fairchild Enclave*, 6 LS 302 (2016); K. Krishnaprasad, *Unjust Enrichment in the* "Fairchild Enclave," 80 MLR 1150 (2017); and R. Stevens, *The Unjust Enrichment Disaster*, 134 LQR 574, 597–98 (2018).

[111] Equitas Insurance Ltd. v. Municipal Mutual Insurance Ltd. [2019] EWCA Civ. 718, [2020] QB 418 [145].

should equitable estoppel contradict the absence of a contract by imposing, as a standard response, a duty to perform a promise.

On the view taken in this chapter, the minority view in *Zurich Insurance* should be preferred. The denial of the restitutionary claim where D has a continuing contractual entitlement as against C to the benefit acquired by D is not the result of a meta-rule operating as an external limit that may, as a result, be subject to exceptions. Rather, it is a consequence of the fact that a claim that has a secondary purpose, of mitigating the practical impact of a primary legal rule, is inherently unable to contradict the operation of such a rule. Recognizing a liability of D to be made to pay the value of a right to C does not contradict the legal event of C's transfer of that right to D; but recognizing such a liability in a case where D has an unconditional entitlement, as against C, to such a benefit would simply contradict the primary rule establishing that entitlement.[112]

V. Conclusion

It may be thought that the type of restitutionary and equitable estoppel claims examined here have an "apparently second order vacuum filling role."[113] In considering the relationship between those claims and more established categories such as contract, tort, and property, as when considering interstitial private law more generally, it is important to be aware that some gaps do not need to be filled. If a set of rules is to operate in a secondary, or supplementary way, it should not simply contradict a primary rule that, as a matter of design, does not extend to a particular set of facts. If a change to that primary rule is required, it should be made directly, rather than through the subterfuge of a secondary rule. Careful attention must therefore be paid to the form of C's claim in order to see if it is really seeking to modify a primary rule, rather than to leave that rule intact and instead modify the effects of its application as between C and D.

The argument made here is that equitable estoppel, when operating as a cause of action, and the type of restitutionary claim exemplified by the case of a mistaken payment are each examples of claims that have the characteristically equitable, and interstitial, function of mitigating the practical impact on C, as against D, of particular primary rules. The claims are thus "second order" without filling a vacuum left by a primary rule. They share a purpose of mitigating the impact

[112] *See* too Stevens, *supra* note 25, at 88–89. Stevens notes there that the position can be different where an agreed condition for a payment has failed (*see, e.g.*, Roxborough v. Rothmans Pall Mall Australia Ltd. [2001] HCA 61, (2001) 208 CLR 516), as the claim then has a basis (the parties' agreement), which is different from that of the strict liability restitutionary claim examined in this chapter.

[113] R. Stevens, *Is There a Law of Unjust Enrichment?*, *in* Unjust Enrichment in Commercial Law 11, 23 (S. Degeling & J. Edelman eds., 2008), in relation to restitutionary claims.

on C, as against D, of particular primary rules. As a result, the inherent scope of the claims is limited: they do not respond, even prima facie, to all cases where C would suffer a detriment were D to go back on a promise on which C has reasonably relied, or to all cases where D has benefited at C's expense and such enrichment may be seen as unjust. If the claims are given an appropriately narrow scope, reflecting their purpose as mitigating the practical effect of particular legal powers conferred by primary legal rules, there is then no need to apply an external limit to their operation, by more or less arbitrary rules as to the ranking of particular types of claims. Indeed, such rules, which suggest a tension between equitable estoppel and restitutionary claims on the one hand, and rules of contract or property on the other, are misleading: far from being dangerous upstarts which need to be limited in order to preserve the more traditional categories, the two causes of action play a vital role in mitigating the practical problems of powers established by those primary rules, and thus form an important part of the arguments to be made in justifying the very existence of those powers.

9

The Concept of Personality in Private Law

*Paul B. Miller**

I. Introduction

How is private law structured? What are its bedrock categories? How does the legal-semantic development and use of legal concepts shape these categories? What is involved in theorizing about, or in deliberating (authoritatively and otherwise) on, the semantics of legal concepts and categories? What is involved in isolating the normative upshots of a legal concept (i.e., in deriving actionable normative guidance from law)?

To think these questions worth pursuing is to recognize that law has certain formal requisites and aims (for instance, coherence) and certain substantive ones (for instance, practical reasonableness) in its provision of normative guidance. Not everyone thinks the pursuit worthwhile, especially in the United States, because of long-entrenched skepticism that legal concepts do the work they are purported to do (i.e., providing effective, authoritative guidance). But scholarship in the New Private Law affirms the questions and has set about answering some of them.[1]

The New Private Law is an American scholarly movement, shaped subtly by modes of thought characteristic of common law traditions. One of the "tells" is our tendency toward departmentalism: an emphasis on parts and relative neglect of the whole of private law. The subject matter of this volume—*interstitial* private law—might thus strike American and other common lawyers as curious. Interstitial doctrine transects and modulates concepts and categories that might otherwise—*qua* our habitual departmentalism—be analyzed in isolation.

* I am grateful to participants in the Interstitial Private Law Workshop at the Notre Dame Rome Global Gateway and to audience members of the Private Law Workshop at the London School of Economics for their feedback; I am also grateful to Chris Essert, Andrew Gold, Rachel Leow, Eva Micheler, Manish Oza, and Henry Smith for detailed comments.

[1] On methodology and the New Private Law, *see* Paul B. Miller, *Juridical Justification of Private Rights*, *in* JUSTIFYING PRIVATE RIGHTS (Michael Crawford, Simone Degeling & Nicholas Tivieros, eds., 2020); and Paul B. Miller, *The New Formalism in Private Law*, AM. J. JURIS. 175 (2021). For exemplification, *see* THE OXFORD HANDBOOK OF THE NEW PRIVATE LAW (Andrew S. Gold, John C.P. Goldberg, Daniel B. Kelly, Emily Sherwin & Henry E. Smith eds., 2020).

Paul B. Miller, *The Concept of Personality in Private Law* In: *Interstitial Private Law*. Edited by: Samuel L. Bray, John C.P. Goldberg, Paul B. Miller, and Henry E. Smith, Oxford University Press. © Oxford University Press 2024.
DOI: 10.1093/oso/9780197783627.003.0009

Attention to what is interstitial requires one to confront common law private law as a *system*.

But where might a common lawyer begin in examining interstitial concepts that enable our law to function as a system? I here follow in the footsteps of common lawyers of old,[2] taking inspiration from the architecture of civil law systems. With the civil law as muse,[3] we may again ask: Which of our juristic categories are bedrock? What concepts are found within or across them? How are they meant to figure in practical deliberation undertaken by the law's addressees? Must a legal concept be developed and invoked in a direct and sustained way (in the manner of codal development of the meaning of words and phrases) to figure in the conceptual structure of a legal system and/or as a background or foreground concept in legal deliberation and decision-making? If not, how might a legal concept developed incrementally nonetheless cohere? And: what are some differences between, and relationships amongst, legal concepts that structure *legal thought* (i.e., that reflect organized thought, or patterns of thought, about law), and those that structure *legal decision-making* (i.e., those that are directly justiciable)?[4]

I presently consider these questions selectively, drawing inspiration from the most basic architectural feature of civilian thought: its tripartite division of the law of *persons*, *property*, and *obligations*.[5] The tripartite structure reflects an ordering by *object* of laws, such that laws are understood as bearing primarily upon *either* persons, resources, or obligations. But these objects are not coequal. The legal concept of a *person* is *primordial*. One must have a concept of personhood if one is to have a sensible concept of property and obligation. This often ignored point should be obvious: posited law is, after all, made by and for persons, to guide, instruct, cajole and admonish us such that we might survive and flourish in community in ways suited to our nature and circumstances.[6] These

[2] *See, e.g.*, Henry of Bracton, On the Laws and Customs of England 1569 (1968); William Blackstone, *Commentaries on the Laws of England* 1765–69 (1979); and Peter Birks, ed., English Private Law (2001).

[3] In invoking civil law as a muse, we may take it as an occasion for elucidating common law concepts and categories, but it should not be supposed that the learning will be one way. Indeed, legal personality—like other interstitial concepts—lies in the background of mature legal systems, and thus in the recesses of legal thought; it seems likely to have been invoked, analyzed, and developed in sporadic and incremental ways in both common law *and* civilian systems.

[4] On the difference between categories that encompass concepts for "thinking" and "deciding," respectively, *see* Hanoch Dagan, *Doctrinal Categories, Legal Realism, and the Rule of Law* (2015), U. Pa. L. Rev. 1889, 1910–11 (2015).

[5] Derived from the tripartite structure of Roman law—*personae*, *res*, *actiones*—found in Gaius's *Institutes* and Justinian's *Digest*. For detailed discussion, *see* Jakob Stagl, *Institutional Scheme of Roman Law*, *in* Oxford Classical Dictionary (online: https://doi.org/10.1093/acrefore/9780199381135.013.8054).

[6] As a conceptual matter, the law construes persons as authors and addressees, much as it elaborates terms on which persons are to interact. In turn, given that systems of posited law are meant to supply authoritative normative guidance to individuals amenable of such guidance, normative

truisms are reflected in presuppositions embedded in concepts of property and obligation: namely, that property regulates *relationships between persons in respect of claims upon resources*, and that obligations regulate *relationships between persons* in respect of the integrity of one's person, property, and undertakings.

In this chapter, I aim to show that, though it has been developed incrementally—and, most often, *impliedly* as a concept assumed by *legal thought* rather than *explicitly* as a justiciable concept in *legal decision-making*—the common law nonetheless knows of a coherent concept of personality.[7] I will also argue that the concept of personality found at common law is best viewed as *interstitial*: it is a concept that is assumed by, while also joining or modulating the application of, other legal concepts. My primary task is one of elucidation. I aim to show that, as a conceptual matter, the law must and does construe persons, just as it elaborates terms of interaction. In turn, given that systems of posited law are constructed normative systems meant to guide beings or entities amenable of normative guidance, I will suggest that the normative primordiality of legal personality is implied by the nature of law. Law could have no author or object were it not made by, and in contemplation of, persons. And, furthermore, it should not be supposed that posited law simply takes persons as found. Instead, it offers its own renderings. Ours is a distinctively *juridical* concept of personality: one that is essential to the structure and organization of law, but that also (and in consequence) has important moral and other social consequences downstream of the law.

I will argue that legal personality has three primary facets: *legal agency*; *entitlements and burdens premised on possession of recognized interests*; and *legal status*. The concept is evolving and has changed through adjustment of these facets. However, *contra* reductive accounts that emphasize one over others, I argue that each is salient. One cannot truly understand legal personality without noticing each facet of the concept and the relationships between them.

The analysis will unfold as follows. In Part II, I explain that legal personality connotes agency and encompasses specific legal capacities. In Part III, I elaborate the sense in which legal personality also encompasses possession of recognized moral interests, the latter grounding the ascription of legal entitlements and burdens to persons. And, in Part IV, I explain that legal personality includes legal statuses, including *threshold statuses* (e.g., legal personhood and citizenship) as

primordiality is entailed by the nature of law: law is at once an artifact of public practices of practical reasoning by individuals with capacities for practical reason and is relied upon as a guide to conduct by these individuals. *See generally* John Finnis, *The Priority of Persons*, *in* INTENTION AND IDENTITY: COLLECTED ESSAYS, VOL. III (2011).

[7] The concept coheres in the rough-and-ready sense that, despite being developed incrementally, its various facets are consistent with one another and prove adaptive, functionally, where facets are interdependent in legal reasoning. For more on coherence, *see infra* note 40.

well as *nominate statuses* (e.g., being a minor or a bankrupt). Throughout, I illustrate integration of the three facets and show how they underpin interstitial functions served by the concept of personality. Part V concludes.

II. Legal Personality as Agency

For nearly a century at common law, and increasingly in civilian thought, legal personality has been conceived in terms of the *legal agency* of individuals (i.e., beings or organized groups).[8] By "legal agency,"[9] I mean an individual's legally recognized innate or acquired capacity for intentional action (a capacity that encompasses consciousness, rationality, and free will). Legal persons *qua* their legal agency are treated as conversable agents;[10] that is, they are treated as persons whose words and other actions can be attributed to them by others on the basis of their capacity for intentional action.[11]

A. Agency, Intentionality, and Practical Reason

Agency typical of human beings encompasses a variety of mental faculties, some rational and others sub-rational; in turn, a narrower but still varied set of faculties are integral to human *moral* agency, some rational (e.g., practical reason) and others sub-rational (e.g., the moral-affective capacity for empathy). I will not comment here on what might be typical of human agency in terms of the integration of these faculties, but I should not be understood to suggest that the law focuses exclusively on rational faculties and intentional action. Some standards of legal fault are arguably premised on moral culpability linked to sub-rational faculties (e.g., depraved indifference), and certain limits on the legal personality of artificial persons are impliedly rooted in the recognition that they lack these faculties. But I leave these considerations to one side.

[8] *See, e.g.*, Bryant Smith, *Legal Personality*, 37 YALE L.J. 283 (1928); Gerald J. McGinley, *Roman Law and Its Influence in America*, 3 NOTRE DAME L. REV. 70 (1927).

[9] "Legal agency" is often referred to as "legal capacity," but because the latter also denotes specific capacities (e.g., the capacity to contract) for which we lack a ready synonym, I here mean by referencing "legal capacity" to denote specific legal capacities, these being modes of intentional conduct recognized or provided for by law.

[10] Philip Pettit introduces the phrase "conversable agent" in order to explain the sense in which groups can achieve agency, but the notion supports the broader invocation advanced here. *See* Philip Pettit, *The Conversable, Responsible Corporation*, *in* THE MORAL RESPONSIBILITY OF FIRMS (Eric W. Orts & N. Craig Smith eds., 2017).

[11] *Id.* at 17: "[one is] an agent when, in normal, unrigged circumstances, [one] maintains certain purposes, forms reliable representations of its environment, and acts reliably so as to satisfy [one's] purposes according to those representations."

I set them aside because the core of legal agency is grounded on a capacity for practical reason. By this I mean possession of rational faculties requisite to practical deliberation, judgment, and action.[12] Practical reason is a capacity to discern and to be guided by norms. It includes the ability to recognize that one is subject to a norm, to identify and deliberate appropriately with applicable norms, and to form and to realize intentions for action that evince reasoned abidance of applicable norms. A capacity for practical reason is assumed by, and implicated in, all normative interaction, and hence all normative systems meant to realize normative order.

Practical reason, like any capacity, can be exercised well or poorly. Where it is exercised well, we say that an individual and/or their behavior is *practically reasonable*, insofar as their deliberation and/or behavior evinces reasoned appreciation of and intentional compliance with dispositive practical reasons derived from applicable norms. Where it is exercised poorly, we say that an individual and/or their behavior is *practically unreasonable*, insofar as their deliberation and/or behavior reflect a defect of practical reasoning or will (e.g., a failure to notice applicable norms, error in deriving practical reasons, or inconstancy in forming intentions in conformity with them). Importantly, the capacity implies a critical posture. A practically reasonable person demonstrates practical wisdom in discerning the practical reasonableness (moral soundness) of a norm, and likewise in discerning and responding reasonably to the practical unreasonableness (moral deficiency) of a norm.

Of course, the law does not (because it cannot) count on perfectly practically reasonable behavior; the guidance it supplies can prove effective among those who are occasionally or even reliably practically unreasonable, provided that the law's aims depend on mere behavioral conformity, and that lawmakers have accounted for different motivations for conformity. However, the law *does* count on its addressees having a capacity for practical reason, and so a capacity to be guided by law.[13] *This* is the presumption that underlies and shapes the law's attribution of legal agency to persons (and, where untenable, it is the untenability of the presumption that moves the law to focus on others facets of legal personality).

Legal persons *qua* legal agents are, in virtue of their practical reason, treated as capable of generating, identifying, deliberating with, acting in compliance or conformity with, and appraising the conduct of others in light of laws and other norms. It is through practical reason that legal persons prove *conversable*

[12] *See generally* JOHN FINNIS, NATURAL LAW AND NATURAL RIGHTS (1980); John Finnis, *Foundations of Practical Reason Revisited*, 50 AM. J. JURIS. 109 (2005); JOSEPH RAZ, PRACTICAL REASON AND NORMS (1975); and JOSEPH RAZ, THE AUTHORITY OF LAW (1979).

[13] On the importance of the law accounting for the well *and* the badly motivated, *see* YUVAL FELDMAN, THE LAW OF GOOD PEOPLE (2018).

participants within normative social practices (that is, participate directly in normative economies—legal, moral, and customary—that obtain in social practices, devising, critiquing, communicating, experiencing, internalizing, feeling, enforcing, calling out, or calling for the enforcement of norms, hence experiencing conduct within these practices as *salient*, normatively).

It is in this light that one might see wisdom in Hobbes's analysis of legal personality in terms of *authorship* and *accountability*. A legal person is, Hobbes suggests, one deemed to fit to author, and in that sense to "own," their legally consequential words and deeds and thus to bear legal accountability for them. The normative economy established by law is premised upon (because it constitutes) relationships of accountability: it promises that an impartial accounting will be given of the actions of legal persons-*cum*-agents upon reasonable demand. Hence, legal agency is part of what it means to be a legal person, even if it is not the whole of it, and even if the requisites of legal agency are neither necessary nor sufficient as requisites for legal personality.

B. Agency and Capacity

Reflection on non-focal persons is instructive of how the law treats rationality as a requisite of legal agency and how it modulates ascriptions of legal agency. We tend to think of rationality as a requisite of agency in a holistic sense, influenced by our familiarity with the focal case of a legal person: a cognitively mature and intact human being. Philosophers might usefully differentiate practical from theoretical reason and rational from sub-rational faculties. But where faced with cognitively mature and intact human beings, the law contents itself with holism: it attributes legal agency to individual adult human beings on the supposition that we enjoy rationality requisite to full normative conversability.

However, when one considers how the law construes other persons—artificial persons and cognitively immature or impaired human beings—one finds ample evidence of its willingness to disaggregate rationality and to differentiate forms of standing implied by normative conversability. Here, the law frames legal agency in terms of specific legal capacities. Differentiation of legal capacities is linked directly to the law's need to identify in individuals (especially in case of doubt) the rational faculties requisite or otherwise pertinent to a particular kind of legally significant conduct. Hence, the law might isolate legal capacities to inherit and own property, to contract, to execute a will or to provide consent, to initiate a civil suit, and so on. For instance, corporations are treated as persons of inherently limited legal capacity, with the drawing of these limits being based (in part) on their nature. Natural persons, by contrast, may be subject to assessments of competence to exercise various legal capacities and/or to legal presumptions of incompetence.

Note also that the manner of exercise of different legal capacities varies. *All* legal capacities properly so-called are active: they contemplate communicative conduct, in word or deed, within social practices enabled or governed by law.[14] What this is involves will depend on how the law construes the capacity and its object(s), but it is through the exercise of legal capacities that legal agency becomes real, with the person encountered as fully or partly normatively conversable within a legal system.

C. Agency, Status, and Representation

As noted, the three facets of legal personality—legal agency, the ascription of entitlements and burdens premised on recognized interests, and legal status—intersect. One point of intersection, to be discussed in Part IV, lies in status-based presumptions about the legal capacities of persons. These presumptions can be constraining or enabling. For instance, minors are, in virtue of that status, denied many legal capacities afforded to adults. In turn, married persons are, in virtue of the status of marriage, granted the privilege of exercising certain joint legal capacities (e.g., of filing taxes jointly). Legal statuses are thus a mechanism through which legal capacities, and hence legal agency, can be ordered.

In respect of adult natural persons, the default position (subsequent to reversal of the immoral withholding of legal personality from women and enslaved persons) is ascription of the status of *full legal agency*. That is, individual adult natural persons are presumed to enjoy all legal capacities ascribed to persons generally, and their conduct is presumed to have been undertaken personally, with each bearing their own legal person through the exercise of various capacities.

Of course, this is but a default position, and so it sometimes yields. Minors are denied various legal capacities, subject to limited exceptions. In turn, cognitively impaired adults might be subject declarations of incompetence, which will limit the scope of agency afforded to them.

Natural persons subject to status-based or ad hoc declarations of incompetence are thereby precluded from full enjoyment of legal agency. However, they

[14] I thus dissent from the suggestion, made first by MacCormick and since echoed by Kurki, that legal persons have "passive" as well as "active" capacities. As I shall explain in Part III, below, what they call passive capacities are best understood as denoting a person's having moral interests that are recognized at law. *See* Neil MacCormick, Institutions of Law: An Essay in Legal Theory 77–99 (2007); and Visa A.J. Kurki, A Theory of Legal Personhood 91–125 (2019).

can receive many of the benefits associated with exercise of withheld capacities through devolution of same upon a fiduciary. As I have explained elsewhere, all fiduciary mandates are representative: underlying enabling law allows a grantor[15] to confer authority upon a fiduciary who, under the mandate and subject to its terms, exercises powers upon the footing of devolved legal capacity.[16] Fiduciary mandates thus enable the extension of legal personality by substitution: fiduciaries personate (bear the legal person of) the grantor, whether devolved capacities are exercised in the grantor's interests or for advancement of the interests of a person or pursuit of a cause designated by the grantor.[17]

Fiduciary representation involves personation in a distinctive way in respect of artificial persons. The legal personality of artificial persons is a contrivance: the law plays a direct constitutive role in establishing requisites of personality of artificial persons in a way that is not true of natural persons. The law is here not disciplined by, nor is it merely selectively responsive to, extralegal facts about given properties of *these* persons as candidates for attribution of legal personality. As I have argued elsewhere, corporations and other personified organizations achieve "real"[18] personality through purposive conduct that is directly attributable to them, usually through certain requisites of agency achieved through mechanisms of representation that the law itself provides (e.g., decision-making structures that foster a collective form of practical reason).[19] However, while the law can endow them with requisites of legal agency, artificial persons do not have a conventional or natural moral claim to legal recognition of their personality akin to that held by natural persons. The legal personality of organized groups is, then, not just constitutively artificial; it is also derivative, being dependent on reasoning by analogy to the focal case of the legal personality of cognitively mature and intact natural persons. Because the attribution of legal capacities to natural persons is premised on rationality, an artificial person can sustain ascription of these capacities where mechanisms of representation enable decision-making under conditions that approximate pertinent cognitive functions of a natural person.

[15] The grant may be original or delegated; for instance, the grant of a fiduciary mandate to a guardian may be made by partial and conditional delegation by the state of a *parens patriae* jurisdiction.

[16] Paul B. Miller, *Fiduciary Representation*, in FIDUCIARY GOVERNMENT (Evan J. Criddle et al. eds., 2018).

[17] Miller, *supra* note 16. *See also* Paul B. Miller, *The Fiduciary Relationship*, *in* PHILOSOPHICAL FOUNDATIONS OF FIDUCIARY LAW (Andrew S. Gold & Paul B. Miller eds., 2014).

[18] Real, in a social ontological sense: corporations are perceived as social actors and realize agency as participants in social practices.

[19] Paul B. Miller, *Corporations*, *in* THE OXFORD HANDBOOK OF THE NEW PRIVATE LAW (Andrew S. Gold et al. eds., 2020).

III. Legal Personality and the Ascription of Entitlements and Burdens

In contemporary common law systems, there is a tendency to think about legal personality reductively in terms of legal agency. Thus, the narrow ambit within which debates over corporate personality have tended to take place.[20] But legal personality has other facets. When the law ascribes personality, it sometimes does so by treating an individual as a legal agent. But it sometimes does so by treating them as having interests that warrant (i.e., that justify and orient) legal entitlements and burdens, whether or not the individual has the requisites of legal agency.

The notion that the law treats individuals as legal persons by deeming them fit for the ascription of legal entitlements and burdens should be familiar. It was expressed influentially, if clumsily, more than a century ago by Frederick Maitland who said that the law "treats the corporation very much as it treats the man. Like the man, the corporation is a right-and-duty-bearing unit."[21]

A. Personality and the Bearing of Legal Entitlements and Burdens

Maitland's emphasis on the ascription of entitlements and burdens has a certain bottom-line-oriented appeal. It sidesteps legal agency and hence hard questions about whether corporations *really* are agents, and if so, of what kind. It effaces differences between natural and artificial persons, treating each as equivalent objects of the law's ascriptions. And it focuses attention on what the hard-nosed think is the most (maybe the *only*) pertinent question about legal personality: Who or what is recognized at law as a right-holder, duty-bearer, power-holder, and/or liability-bearer?

One ought not to question interest in bottom-line matters. But one may and one should question a reductive depiction of legal persons as passive objects ("units") of ascriptions and the related suggestion that legal personality is but a conclusion that follows from the ascription legal entitlements or burdens. The former begs questions about the natural, normative, and conceptual substrata of ascriptions of legal entitlements and burdens to persons, including those going

[20] Consider the emphasis on agency in the discussion of corporate personality in CHRISTIAN LIST & PHILIP PETTIT, GROUP AGENCY: THE POSSIBILITY, DESIGN AND STATUS OF CORPORATE AGENTS (2011), but note that it has deep roots: see Smith, *Legal Personality*, *supra* note 8; Arthur Machen, *Corporate Personality*, 24 HARV L. REV. 253 (1910) & 347; John Dewey, *The Historic Background of Corporate Legal Personality*, 35 YALE L.J. 655 (1926); and Max Radin, *The Endless Problem of Corporate Personality*, 32 COLUM L REV 643 (1932).

[21] F.W. Maitland, *State, Trust and Corporation* 63 (David Runciman ed., 2003).

to their suitability. The latter belies the complexity of the concept of legal personality (i.e., that it encompasses more than a tallying of ascriptions made by lawmakers of individuals). Maitland offers insight, but if read literally he leaves us with a thoroughly denuded notion: one according to which a "person" is but an empty vessel for normative ascriptions.[22]

I don't think that this interpretation of Maitland is the best one. But it seems to be increasingly popular, and in some contemporary work it is commingled with a casual positivism[23] and nominalism. Consider work that treats legal personality as a contingent bundle of rights: a placeholder for varying sets of rights, duties, powers, and liabilities that may be attributed by law to different objects, be they humans, animals, entities, things, forms of artificial intelligence, or features of built or natural environments.[24]

I have suggested that this reading of Maitland and resultant theories of legal personality are casually (one might say crudely) positivistic. Yet I have also framed our present task as a positivistic one of conceptual elucidation. Lest it be thought that there is any inconsistency, note that our aims and method diverge from those content with casual positivism. Notably, the present account is developed in recognition that received conceptions of legal personality are inherently normative, at once reflecting and calling for normative judgment (i.e., reflecting and calling for moral judgments about morally salient characteristics of natural persons and groups). It does not imply reductivism or nominalism in any direction. Rather, it treats legal personality as a compound concept with a focal conceptual and normative sense rooted in the capacity for flourishing of cognitively mature and intact human beings.

B. The Juridical Constitution of Personality: Horizontal and Vertical Dimensions

To be recognized as a legal person is, in part, to be treated as having a distinctive set of moral interests valued by law as judged by its aims.[25] This implies being treated as a beneficiary of the normative guidance that the law supplies (e.g., that one is among those whom a particular law is meant to protect, counsel, enable,

[22] Consistent with increasingly popular nominalistic accounts. *See*, for instance, Peter A. French, *The Corporation as a Moral Person*,16 Am. Phil. Q. 207, 208 (1979)) ("a juristic person may be defined as any entity that is a subject of a right"). For criticism of Maitland's analysis of corporate personality, *see* Eva Micheler, Company Law: A Real Entity Theory (2021).

[23] As contrasted with jurisprudentially sophisticated positivist thought of the sort exemplified in, for example, the work of H.L.A. Hart, Joseph Raz, and Leslie Green.

[24] *See* Kurki, *A Theory of Legal Personhood*, *supra* note 14. For criticism of the nominalism implicit in bundle of rights models of property, *see* Henry E. Smith, *On the Economy of Concepts in Property*, 160 U. Pa. L. Rev. 2097 (2012).

[25] Léon Michoud, La Notion de Personnalité Morale (1899).

or constrain). But legal persons do not exist in contemplation of law merely by its attributions *alone*, as if occupying normative locations fixed by declaration.

To understand how legal personality is constituted through legal recognition of the moral interests of individuals, one will need to think *horizontally* across the three facets of the concept, noticing their relationships. And one will need to think *vertically*, asking what grounds the ascription of legal entitlements and burdens to persons as a matter of the posited morality of law.[26]

Starting with the *horizontal dimension*, note that some entitlements and burdens are ascribed to persons irrespective of whether they have requisites of legal agency. For instance, it is commonplace to ascribe rights and even limited liabilities to children and cognitively impaired adults. This facet of their legal personality is usually borne by a fiduciary who asserts standing to assert ascribed entitlements and/or to answer for ascribed burdens *derivatively* (i.e., for or on behalf of the beneficiary).

Equally, however, ascriptions of certain legal entitlements and burdens contemplate other facets of legal personality. In preview of Part IV, consider first the connection between *legal statuses* and the ascription of entitlements and burdens. Some legal statuses are responsive to legal incapacity and include the ascription of a fixed set of legal entitlements while modulating different structural responses to the status-bearer's incapacity (for instance, the status of minor brings with it a suite of protective entitlements). Others structure the ascription of entitlements and burdens without any deviation from default presuppositions about the legal agency of the bearer (for instance, the modern status of marriage affirms the equal and independent legal agency of both spouses while establishing new rights, duties, powers, and liabilities between them).

Consider, next, connections between *legal agency* and the ascription of legal entitlements and burdens. That there are connections should be plain simply because the very idea of legal agency encompasses practices of ascribing legal entitlements and burdens. Legal systems are, after all, normative systems, establishing normative economies of social interaction the currency of which consists in entitlements and burdens borne by, and exchanged between, persons acting upon their legal agency.

We turn now to the *vertical dimension*: Upon what considerations of fact and value are ascriptions of legal entitlements and burdens grounded? And in what sense do these judgments imply recognition by legal officials of an individual *as a person*?

These questions are overlooked in recent work on legal personality, which tends to ignore grounding considerations. It is *au courant* to say that a legal person is just whomever or whatever a lawmaker designates as such. But

26 On posited morality, *see* Miller, *Juridical Justification of Private Rights*, *supra* note 1.

whatever appeal casual positivism might have for those averse to normative questions, it comes at too high a cost. To ignore grounding considerations is to efface or distort the nature of legal entitlements and burdens as *norms* situated within *normative systems* meant to shape *normative practices* (i.e., practices that necessarily involve practical deliberation about how we ought to govern ourselves, treat one another, and live lives of meaning and purpose). We shall thus put them back on the table below.

C. The Interests of Persons as Grounds for the Ascription of Legal Entitlements and Burdens

To ascribe a legal entitlement to an individual is to make a value judgment about the importance of their interests as a matter of natural and/or social ontology (i.e., as a matter of kind of being or entity that they are, with a view to context-sensitive understanding of their basic needs and capacity for flourishing or, in the case of groups, their contribution to communal flourishing). The significance of these judgments permeates but also transcends positive law; it is a way in which we as members of political communities recognize someone as an object of moral concern.

The ascription of burdens is more complicated, for it is underlain by assumptions about accountability that are hard to sever from legal agency. However, one might argue that the judgments upon which these ascriptions rest reflect not merely recognition of agency and its requisites, but also wider moral interests in being treated as responsible in ways connoted by full normative conversability.

Given that the ascription of legal entitlements and burdens is an important facet of legal personality, it is important to say more about how the value judgments underlying these ascriptions are or might be grounded.

The posited morality of law is characteristically thin and unsystematic.[27] Working piecemeal, the law typically embeds value judgments expressed in broad and general terms, asserting the importance of the moral interests of one in respect of whom an ascription is made. Put simply, ascriptions of legal entitlements and burdens are made on the footing of a person having moral interest(s) that render the ascriptions morally intelligible.

Of course, the nature and salience of specific moral interests will vary depending whether an individual is a natural or an artificial person. Natural

[27] *See generally* Miller, *Juridical Justification of Private Rights*, *supra* note 1. On the thinness and relative simplicity of moral reasoning in private law, *see also* Andrew S. Gold & Henry E. Smith, *Sizing Up Private Law*, 70 UTLJ 489 (2020).

persons have a (naturally) capacious set of moral interests capable grounding a wide array of legal entitlements and burdens; artificial persons have a more circumscribed set of moral interests (interests that vary by their objects, governance, constitution, and capacity). Recognizing that legal officials will (at a meta-evaluative level) differ on the salience of interests that might ground entitlements and burdens, one might parse things by differentiating moral interests that are cognizable relative to personal goods (constituents of personal flourishing) from those cognizable relative to common goods (constituents of communal flourishing).

In respect of natural persons, where grounding considerations are addressed at all in contemporary scholarship, they are usually presented in a perfunctory and reductive way. Often, common goods are ignored, and autonomy is picked out as the sole personal good to which law is responsive. This sort of normative reductivism is aligned with the interpretive reductivism, noted earlier that equates legal personality with legal agency. The combined result is something like the following account, meant to fill in the vertical dimension of the ascription of legal entitlements and burdens to persons:

- law is made by and for natural persons;
- the most normatively important fact about natural persons is our rationality;
- the law treats this fact as pivotal in positioning autonomy as the exclusive moral foundation of legal personality; and
- the ascription of specific legal entitlements and burdens to persons is grounded on the autonomy interests of natural persons.

We may call this *the simple view of the morality of legal personality*. By extension, the simple view supports the following account of a moral basis for the ascription of legal entitlements and burdens to artificial persons:

- law is made by and for natural persons;
- groups, entities, and nonhuman beings have no *innate* capacity for rationality, and hence no innate moral status such as might *compel* legal "recognition" of their personality;
- groups of natural persons might develop simulacra of individual human rationality via modalities of representation and/or group agency;
- where so, the law may rationally treat a group as a person by artifice, ascribing it legal personality subject to constraints of sound analogical reasoning (i.e., the need to establish robust correspondence between natural and artificial persons in respect of the latter's rational faculties analyzed relative to its ascribed purposes); and

- the ascription of legal entitlements or burdens to artificial persons is grounded morally in the autonomy interests of the natural persons by or for whom they were formed.

Notice that on this extension of the simple view, the relevant moral interests of an artificial person are just the autonomy interests of natural persons, reposed in it by proxy for enhancement of their autonomy.

i. Artificial persons

The reductive equation of legal personality with legal agency has been buttressed by scholarly preoccupation with artificial persons, especially corporations. Much of the scholarship on legal personality within the last century focuses on corporate personality and the "endless problems"—metaphysical, moral, social, political, and juristic—that it is believed to present.[28] A preoccupation with corporations has nurtured reductive thinking about legal personality generally, for it seems that organized groups can warrant personhood only if that they evince analogues of human rationality.[29]

But suppose we resist the pull of the simple view, and stubbornly ask again: What kinds of moral interest might an artificial person have in the ascription of legal entitlements and burdens? While I think it doubtful that an artificial person can have moral interests of its own, we may set that question aside, for they clearly can have *derivative moral interests* (i.e., interests attributed to them as proxy for the interests of natural persons).

With this in mind, I observe that the simple view captures an important truth: artificial persons can have autonomy interests enjoyed by proxy for natural persons. Corporations, for instance, have autonomy interests in the free exercise of legal capacities that they are fit to bear in pursuit of lawful objects. The autonomy interests of corporations are traceable to those of their constituents as reflected in choices made by the latter to join, invest in, work for, or otherwise associate with a corporation.

But the simple view also misses much. It misses the fact that natural persons have moral interests other than autonomy interests, and that the law is responsive to these other interests, too, in ascribing legal entitlements and burdens to artificial persons. And it misses the fact that autonomy interests are morally important as matter of instrumental as well as inherent value, insofar as

[28] Radin, *The Endless Problem of Corporate Personality*, *supra* note 20. For a different perspective, *see* Paul B. Miller, *Corporate Personality, Purpose, and Liability*, *in* Research Handbook on Corporate Purpose and Personhood (Elizabeth Pollman & Robert B. Thompson eds., 2021).

[29] For discussion of similar tendencies of thought in connection with proposals to ascribe legal personhood to artificial intelligence, *see* Gerhard Wagner, *Robot, Inc.: Personhood for Autonomous Systems?*, 88 Fordham L. Rev 591 (2019).

it is through autonomous decision-making that natural persons realize a plurality of goods in our states of being, relationships, associations, and prosocial behavior.

The first point is particularly important in thinking about the kinds of moral interests that an artificial person might bear for—and by analogy to—natural persons. Leading theories of the good encompass different dimensions of human flourishing. The normativity of human goods is such as to foreground and orient autonomous choice, providing measures by which we understand our own actions and those of others as well as evaluate conduct as sound (practically reasonable) or unsound (practically unreasonable). We needn't attempt to exhaustively list or decide between competing accounts of moral interests that reflect the normativity of human goods. It suffices to say that in addition to autonomy interests, they include dignitary interests (e.g., interests in respect for our person), welfare interests (e.g., our interest in health and prosperity), epistemic and spiritual interests (e.g., our interest in discerning truth and finding meaning), and our relational interests (e.g., our interest in loving and in being loved, in forging bonds of solidarity, in providing and in being provided for). Artificial persons are by their nature unfit to bear certain of these interests and variably fit to bear others. But they are plainly fit to bear interests that natural persons might have in objects lawfully pursued through organizations (e.g., relational interests in charitable work done through a non-profit, or epistemic and spiritual interests in a foundation established to support religious formation, to provide education, or to support science).

Of course, artificial persons are not mechanisms for the expression or realization of every kind of human moral interest. There are limits to our ability to cogently project moral interests upon corporations and other artificial persons. In every case, lawmakers must confront the question a given artificial person is fit to bear a moral interest and associated legal entitlement or burden. Assessment of fitness involves legal, moral, and analytical judgment in consideration of (a) the legal nature of the entity, entitlement and/or burden; (b) the mechanism(s) through which the entity achieves legal agency; and (c) the identity and nature of the entity's lawful purposes and associated purposive conduct viewed in social context. For instance, in light of these considerations, corporations are by their nature unfit to bear dignitary interests, or welfare interests premised on embodiment. Hence, the law's refusal to countenance absurdity in protecting corporations from emotional distress, invasion of privacy, abduction, or battery. The interests underlying these entitlements cannot by cogently assigned to, or otherwise located in, an artificial person. As I will explain in Part IV, the same sort of analysis explains the preclusion of artificial persons from certain legal statuses and status-mediated entitlements and burdens (e.g., marriage and citizenship).

ii. Natural persons

It is less difficult to appreciate that ascriptions of legal entitlements and burdens are made of natural persons on the basis of their having a plurality of moral interests. As noted, natural persons vary as to whether they have the requisites of legal agency. And, as also noted, the ascription of certain legal entitlements and burdens turns on which legal capacities a person has (where they are of less than full capacity, and so of diminished agency). Nevertheless, acknowledging these complexities, it remains true to say that the analysis of natural persons' moral interests and associated entitlements and burdens is less awkward than in respect of artificial persons.

For natural persons, lawmakers may avoid (often strained) analogical reasoning and contemplate directly the kind(s) of moral interests that are, or should be, recognized as enjoyed by human beings in innate entitlements and burdens and/or in the possession of normative powers enabling the undertaking or alienation of acquired entitlements and burdens. Building on the sketch of categories of moral interest provided above, I shall here comment briefly on three things: first, the value of autonomy as grounds for the ascription of certain entitlements and burdens to cognitively mature and intact natural persons; second, the limited significance of autonomy interests in grounding the ascription of entitlements and burdens to natural persons whose rational faculties are impaired or immature; and third, how other kinds of moral interest—welfare, dignitary, epistemic, and relational—ground the ascription of entitlements and burdens to natural persons in private law.

First, private law plainly treats autonomy as a personal good, invoking specific autonomy interests as grounds[30] for the ascription of some entitlements and burdens to natural persons (especially, but not only, those involving the exercise of normative powers). It is plausible that private law treats autonomy as inherently valuable; however, it is equally plausible that it also treats autonomy as instrumentally valuable. Private law recognizes the instrumental value of autonomy when it enables or protects freedom in the pursuit of goods that can only, or best, be realized through autonomous choice (for instance, goods such as loving companionship, fostered through marriage, or provision for the flourishing others, effectuated by donative transfers).

Second, as emphasized earlier, the good of autonomy and a concern for autonomy interests can little explain the law's ascription of entitlements and

[30] Whether in an exclusive or contributory way. A moral interest is the exclusive ground of an entitlement or burden where it supplies justificatory practical reasons that are necessary and sufficient to support the entitlement or burden. It is a contributory ground where it, along with other moral interests, supplies justificatory practical reasons for an entitlement or burden none of which is alone sufficient to support the entitlement or burden. It may also be that, for some entitlements and burdens, justification is overdetermined (i.e., supported by more than one, and perhaps several, sufficient justificatory practical reasons).

burdens to natural persons whose rational faculties are still maturing or have lapsed. The general posture of private law here is protective, being focused on enabling sound custodial care and administration. Many entitlements ascribed to natural persons with impaired or immature rational faculties are responsive to their welfare, epistemic, and dignitary interests (for instance, their interest in being kept in good health, in being provided with educational and other developmental support, in being treated with respect). The law treats natural persons of diminished capacity as human beings who deserve support for their flourishing, even as autonomy is less central to their flourishing than to that of others.

Finally, even in respect of cognitively mature and intact persons, private law reveals concern for a plurality of moral interests. For example, legal burdens of respect for the remains of deceased persons are grounded on dignitary interests borne by the now-deceased or by their survivors. In turn, entitlements to physical integrity protected by tort are grounded on a wide array of moral interests, including welfare and dignitary interests, in addition to oft-invoked autonomy interests. Complexity in the posited morality of law here reflects genuine moral-existential complexity of natural persons' suffering from torts.

IV. Legal Personality as Legal Status

A. Status and Personality: A Common Narrative

It is sometimes suggested that the concept of legal personality at common law has changed markedly over time, such that older notions dominated by *status* have gradually been displaced by a newer one that positions *agency* as central.[31] This narrative treats the evolution of the concept as a microcosm of wider social, economic, political, and legal changes associated with the rise of liberalism; changes that Henry Maine memorably argued reflect a transition from status to contract as a basic precept of legal, economic, and social ordering.[32]

On this account, law has produced different figures of the "person."[33] The person of times past is a natural person hemmed in by fixed positioning within a social order defined by social norms, conveyed and sustained partly through imposed legal statuses (e.g., those of feudal property systems). By contrast, the person of post-Enlightenment liberal democracies is an independent rational actor; a natural person who, unburdened by status, forges their own social

[31] For critical discussion, *see* Manfred Rehbinder, *Status, Contract, and the Welfare State*, 23 STAN. L. REV. 941 (1971).

[32] HENRY MAINE, ANCIENT LAW (1861) (1906).

[33] That is: someone for whom the social ordering wrought by law is meant to be intelligible, and whose actions are intelligible as ordered by law.

identity and enjoys moral personality understood in terms of self-determination, underlain by a new concept of legal personality defined in terms of legal agency.

This narrative has proven enduring because it resonates with wider narratives about social progress. It is in the genre of triumphal stories and, like most good tales, it is compelling because it offers glimmers of truth. Legal systems are iteratively constructed normative systems, which means that, like the political communities that sustain them, they are often in flux in respect of their normative commitments and aspirations. Legal concepts, by implication, are often up for contestation and revision. And this has been true of the concept of legal personality. For instance, legal statuses associated with feudal property became defunct along with those systems, with moral criticisms of the statuses largely mirroring the moral case for restructuring land law.[34] In turn, personal and family statuses (notably, those that sustained slavery and coverture) changed through reforms shaped by moral critique. The effect of reform of these legal statuses was long overdue freedom for those formerly subject to now-defunct status ascriptions.

This said, the triumphal narrative is also in important respects false. Specifically, it is false in its contrastive representation of status and agency.[35] The presentation of status and agency in opposing terms is probably well-motivated. Collective experience of morally wicked disabling statuses commands attention. If this experience were representative as an indication that *all* legal statuses are unjustly disabling, one might think (or hope) reliance on status something mostly overcome. But that supposition is wrong. If one attends more closely to the use of legal statuses at common law, one finds not evidence of the emergence of a new concept of legal personality that leaves status designations behind but, rather, the substitution of new legal statuses for old ones, redefinition of retained statuses, and removal of fetters on the attainment or ascription of statuses.[36]

B. The Nature of Legal Status

Granting that legal statuses continue to be prevalent, it remains to consider their general characteristics, how they are attained or ascribed to persons, and how they interact with other facets of legal personality.

[34] For historical analysis of feudal and other legal statuses, *see* Sir John Baker, *Status and Legal Personality*, *in* Sir John Baker, The Oxford History of the Laws of England, Vol. VI (2003).

[35] As also emphasized in Jeremy Waldron, One Another's Equals: The Basis of Human Equality (2017).

[36] For critical discussion, *see* Katharina Isabel Schmidt, *Henry Maine's "Modern Law": From Status to Contract and Back Again?*, 65 Am. J. Comp. L. 145 (2017). *See also* John Gardner, From Personal Life to Private Law 45 (2018).

I have commented already upon a tendency to think about legal personality reductively in terms of legal agency at common law. There is a similar habit of thinking about legal personality reductively in terms of status in civil law. Statuses were foundational in Roman law and they have for centuries figured prominently in codal development of the law of persons in civilian jurisdictions.[37] Understandably if unfortunately, codal specification of statuses can seem exhaustive of legal personality in civil law if consideration is not given to other facets of the concept that arise by implication from its appearance in the law of property and obligations.

Partly because of the troubled and divergent historical development of legal statuses in common law and civilian legal systems, it easy to err in theorizing them. So let us make a fresh start.

Put most abstractly, a status is a defined position held by persons, places, or things within a normative system (legal, moral, and otherwise). Statuses supply fixed points in the organization of a normative system that enable one to more readily locate the bearer for the purposes of the system's effective operation. The effective functioning of any complex normative system is at risk of being bedeviled by complexity. Modern legal systems are extraordinarily technically complex, with this complexity being compounded by exogenous complexity in social contexts that shape, and are meant to be shaped by, law. Legal systems must economize on information in order to supply effective normative guidance. They do so partly through the structural formality of legal rules,[38] for instance, by organizing norms and enabling doctrines through various modular legal forms of holding, transaction, relationship, and association.[39] Legal statuses make their own contribution to the structural formality of law. Legal statuses attributed to persons enable the bearer and others to more readily understand and act in ways responsive to the bearer's normative positioning within a legal system.

Persons are typical bearers, but legal statuses can be borne by places (e.g., protected conservation areas) and things (e.g., patented inventions). Thus, legal status and legal personality are not correlative concepts. Indeed, our relationships to our natural and built environments are mediated by a myriad of legal statuses ascribed to places and things, much as our relationships with others are mediated by legal statuses ascribed to or acquired by persons.

[37] *See generally* P.W. Duff, Personality in Roman Private Law (1938).

[38] On structural formality in law, *see* Miller, *The New Formalism in Private Law*, *supra* note 1.

[39] *See* Henry E. Smith, *On the Economy of Concepts in Property*, 160 U. Pa. L. Rev. 2097 (2012); Henry E. Smith, *Modularity in Contracts: Boilerplate and Information Flow*,104 Mich L. Rev. 117 (2006); and Henry E. Smith, *Modularity and Morality in the Law of Torts*, 4 J. Tort L. 1 (2011). See also Andrew S. Gold, "Private Law's Choice of Private Law" in this volume.

C. Types of Legal Status

As noted, legal persons are among the bearers of legal statuses; in turn, legal status is a key facet of the concept of legal personality. In order to better understand the significance of legal statuses to legal personality, we may distinguish *threshold statuses* from *nominate statuses*. As I will explain, *threshold statuses* are determined as a matter of public law even as they operate transversally, across private and public law. *Nominate statuses* may originate in public or private law and may operate transversally or more narrowly (e.g., within a statute that establishes a status for specific legislative purposes).

The most important *threshold status* is that of personality as such: that is, whether one is treated as eligible for legal personhood. That legal personality is a threshold status is easy to miss because eligibility is assumed for natural persons: in most jurisdictions, a human being is recognized as a legal person by government before or upon a live birth. The importance of this status should be plain upon reflection on its denial to some, including women and slaves. Exclusion from legal personhood was enormously consequential, only in part because it meant presumptive legal ineligibility to bear *nominate statuses* (e.g., of citizenship or marriage).

Legal personality is a threshold status for candidates for artificial personhood, too. Most legal systems closely regulate the ascription of legal personality to nonhuman beings and entities precisely because it can have unforeseen, unwelcome implications. Downstream implications include decisions made by other lawmakers about artificial person's eligibility for nominate statuses, legal agency, and fitness for the ascription of legal entitlements and burdens.

Threshold statuses are often regulative in respect of other facets of legal personality. The determination that a candidate is not a legal person is usually dispositive of questions whether they have interests of the sort that the law recognizes in persons. Thus, those who insist that the unborn are not legal persons often mean, in denying the threshold status, to foreclose arguments that they unborn have non-derivative dignity and welfare interests in protection from intentional infliction of harm. In contrast, consider efforts to establish that places or animals are eligible for legal personhood. These arguments—which sometimes ignore or deprecate other protective legal statuses for places and animals—impliedly recognize the significance of legal personality as a threshold status. The arguments aim to elevate the legal position of a purported candidate for personhood (e.g., animals generally, or an endangered species, or an ecosystem) by having it designated a legal person.[40]

[40] Some animal rights activists are critical of advocacy of legal personhood for animals, emphasizing that the moral status of animals and associated moral claims that animals have for protection must be put on a different footing. *See* Richard L. Cupp, *Focusing on Human Responsibility*

I have emphasized the threshold status of legal personality, partly in view of its singular importance, and partly to highlight the duality of the concept: legal personality is at once a legal status and a locus for, and composite of, other ascriptions made of persons at law, including subordinate statuses. But there are other threshold statuses. For instance, citizenship and immigration statuses; these have a profound impact on the treatment of persons within legal systems. Other threshold statuses—some involving mutable, others immutable, characteristics of natural persons, and many embedding contentious normative judgments—include age, sex, race, ethnicity, and tribal membership. These statuses may be defined under, and/or invoked by, laws conditioning access to government resources or programs, eligibility for reserved privileges, rights, and powers, and susceptibility to reserved duties, liabilities, and disabilities.

Nominate statuses have certain general characteristics of legal statuses: they fix the normative position of the bearer within a legal system and, like threshold statuses, enable uniformity in the law's treatment of the status-bearer. Nominate statuses are nevertheless distinctive in that they (a) are conditioned on, and subject to modulation through the operation of, threshold statuses; and (b) arise within and serve purposes largely peculiar to nominate categories of legal rules. Unlike threshold statuses, they may have limited or no impact on other parts of the law. And while threshold statuses are pervasively interstitial in effect, nominate statuses are interstitial only in respect of select nodes or interstices between nominate categories of legal rules.

The characteristics of nominate statuses may best be appreciated by illustration. Consider status-based designation of certain roles and relationships as fiduciary.[41] Fiduciary status structures the incidence of fiduciary liability rules and guides the formation and performance of fiduciary mandates. Status-based identification of fiduciary relationships makes it easier for the parties and third parties to know that their interactions will be subject to fiduciary impositions. It operates primarily within equity's regulation of fiduciaries but, given that fiduciary mandates are normally exercised via disparate power-conferring rules (e.g.,

Rather Than Legal Personhood for Nonhuman Animals, 33 PACE ENVTL. L.J. 517 (2016); and Richard L. Cupp, *Cognitively Impaired Humans, Intelligent Animals, and Legal Personhood*, 69 FLA. L. REV. 465 (2017). On claims of personhood in respect of land, ecosystems, and other features of our natural environment, *see* Christopher D. Stone, *Should Trees Have Standing? Toward Legal Rights for Natural Objects*, 45 S. CAL. L. REV. 450 (1972); and Gwendolyn J. Gordon, *Environmental Personhood*, 43 COLUM J. ENVTL. L. 49 (2018).

41 *See* Paul B. Miller, *The Idea of Status in Fiduciary Law*, *in Contract, Status, and Fiduciary Law* (Paul B. Miller & Andrew S. Gold eds., 2016); and Paul B. Miller, *The Identification of Fiduciary Relationships*, *in* THE OXFORD HANDBOOK OF FIDUCIARY LAW (Evan J. Criddle, Paul B. Miller & Robert H. Sitkoff eds., 2019).

those of contract, property, trust, guardianship, corporate, and partnerships law), fiduciary statuses can have wide interstitial effects.

Finally, I want to emphasize that both types of legal status modulate other facets of legal personality (legal agency and the ascription of legal entitlements and burdens). Certain statuses—including those that have earned ignominy—are disabling, altering default presuppositions about natural persons' suitability for legal agency by precluding the bearer from all or some legal capacities. Others are enabling, enhancing the legal agency of their bearer (e.g., the status of being a licensed professional). In turn, legal statuses often embed special or reserved legal entitlements and burdens, driving the law's ascription of same with the status reflecting lawmakers' normative judgment that interests of the bearer are worthy of special protection, treatment, or concern.

V. Conclusion

Private law—like all posited law—is made by and for those most naturally identified as persons: human beings. But it does not simply take persons as found; rather, it offers its own renderings. Given that private law is for and about persons, it is curious that private law theorists have been more concerned with the structure of jural relations and a miscellany of norms and enabling doctrines than with these renderings. Despite this, if we are to understand private law, we must come to understand how it construes persons.

I have argued here that, despite the fact that at common law, unlike in civil law, the law of persons is not an explicit category of legal rules, we do have a concept of legal personality. That we do is easily missed. We live in a time in which entrenched nominalism about legal concepts and anti-realism about moral concepts have left us with fragmentary *conceptions* of personality. A casual positivist who has imbibed deeply from adjacent wells of legal nominalism and moral anti-realism might think that references to "legal personality" in our laws betray inherent instability in their referent(s), consisting in nothing more than a hodgepodge of different ascriptions made of different objects (persons, places, things, animals) declared "persons."

I have challenged all of this. I claim that the concept of legal personality found at common law is reasonably coherent.[42] I suggest that its coherence is a product

42 Coherence here being pragmatic rather than scholastic: the various facets of the concept are not always engaged by law at once, but their functional coherence can be inferred by attending to cases in which all facets of the concept are engaged and relied upon in legal reasoning without evident difficulty (as where, for example, a court must acknowledge, at once, that a person is subject to a disabling status that limits the agency of the bearer while generating special entitlements for the bearer and burdens for others).

of the fact that extensions of the concept have been typically (not perfectly) disciplined as a matter of analogical reasoning by recourse to a focal exemplar (cognitively mature and intact natural persons). And I argue that the concept of legal personality consists in three facets—legal agency (and its requisites), the ascription of legal entitlements and burdens, and legal statuses—each of which makes reference to, and is integrated with, the others.

10

Understanding the Rules of Attribution in Private Law

*James Penner**

I. Introduction

The attribution of one person's act to another is a legal phenomenon that occurs across private law. This chapter presents a survey or overview of the rules by which attribution occurs. Because of the variety of these attributions, and the contexts in which they occur, it is not clear that there is a univocal concept of attribution in private law. However, following this survey, I shall argue that what I call rules of "relationship attribution," which focus on the particular relationship the parties are in, provide insight into the phenomenon of attribution.

II. Representation

At first glance, it would appear that an inquiry into the concept of representation[1] would provide illumination in understanding the concept of attribution.

* Thanks to Michael Bridge, Lusina Ho, Duncan Horne, Pey-Woan Lee, Kelvin Low, Timothy Chan, Weiming Tan, Christian Witting, Hu Ying, and the contributors to this volume for comments and discussion. I am particularly grateful to Cheng-Han Tan for detailed comments on an earlier draft, and to Paul Miller and Henry Smith for searching comments on the penultimate draft.

[1] The modern *locus classicus* of a conceptual analysis of representation is Hannah Pitkin's 1967 *The Concept of Representation*: H.F. Pitkin, The Concept of Representation (1967). For a survey of the book's impact, *see* S. Dovi, *Hannah Pitkin, The Concept of Representation, in* The Oxford Handbook of Classics in Contemporary Political Theory(J.T. Levy ed., 2015); for an essay that anticipated some important features of Pitkin's analysis, see A.P. Griffiths & R. Wollheim, *How Can One Person Represent Another*? 34 Proceedings of the Aristotelian Society, Supplementary Volumes 187–224 (1960). *See also* J. Kalhat, *Varieties of Representation*, 91 Philosophy 14–37 (2016); and P.B. Miller, *Fiduciary Representation, in* Fiduciary Government 21–48, 35–37 (E.J. Criddle, E. Fox-Decent, A.S. Gold, S.H. Kim & P.B. Miller eds., 2018). I think it is fair to say that while Pitkin illuminates many features of the concept of representation, her chief concern is that of representation in the political context. The most relevant chapter for our purposes concerns not what Pitkin calls "Descriptive Representation" (ch. 4) or "Symbolic Representation" (ch. 5), both examples of X "Standing For" Y, but her chapter 6, which is entitled "Representing as "Acting For": The Analogies." This is a wide-ranging analysis of the language employed to speak of the case where one person "represents" another, and some of her analysis anticipates what I shall say here. Toward the end of the chapter she reaches something of a conclusion (at 139):

James Penner, *Understanding the Rules of Attribution in Private Law* In: *Interstitial Private Law*. Edited by: Samuel L. Bray, John C.P. Goldberg, Paul B. Miller, and Henry E. Smith, Oxford University Press. © Oxford University Press 2024.
DOI: 10.1093/oso/9780197783627.003.0010

One immediately thinks of an agent, whose act in entering into a contract for their principal is, one might say, attributed to their principal just because the agent *represents* their principal. But despite this first glance plausibility, we shall see that the concept of representation provides limited insight into the legal phenomenon of attribution.

In its broadest formulation, the relationship of representation exists between persons when one person in some sense "stands for" another. The basic idea is that the knowledge, acts and so forth of the representor are for some purposes attributable to the "representee," here meaning the person represented, such that the legal standing or practical position of the representee is affected. But this notion of representation is broad, and it covers very different sorts of case. In particular, enlarging upon a typology I have used before,[2] we must distinguish three different modes or types of representation: acting "as," acting "for/for the benefit of/in the interests of," and acting "on behalf of or in the place of."

A. Acting *as* Another

Our first case is not really a case of representation at all, but I discuss it because of the extensive way in which the word "represent" may be used. A true representation is essentially relational: there is something or someone that is represented, and there is something or someone which represents that thing or person. By contrast, "acting as" is simply constitutive of the identity or nature of a given thing. For example, I do not represent myself when I speak. I speak, and this may tell you a great deal about me, but my speech is not a representation of myself, although we do say on occasion that I represent myself, as when I appear in court as a litigant in person. But there is one case in private law, in company law, which is of importance here. In a general meeting of the shareholders of a company, the shareholders together act *as* the company. Although it would not be a solecism to say that together they "represent" the company, this is not a true *relational* representation, for their acts are not

From the chaos of the many analogies and adverbial expressions, and the many implications of each, three major ideas emerge: the idea of substitution or acting instead of; the idea of taking care or acting in the interest of; and the idea of acting as a subordinate, on instructions, in accord with the wishes of another. None of the three, by itself, turns out to be a satisfactory equivalent of the idea of representing.

[2] J.E. Penner, *Trustees and Agents Behaving Badly: When and How Is "Bad Faith" Relevant?*, *in* Fiduciaries and Trust: Ethics, Politics, Economics and Law 121–48 (M. Harding & P.B. Miller eds., 2020), 136–38; J.E. Penner, *Private Law Offices*, 70 UTLJ 299, 301–02 (2020).

distinct from the company's acts but are identical with them. The shareholders are not acting as agents of the company, performing acts that are attributed to the company. The shareholders act in their own right as individual members of the company, its shareholders, but because of the decision-making process (voting their shares), their acts just are those of the company.[3] Because they do not act as agents of the company, they are not in a fiduciary relationship with the company or inter se.[4] It is disputed whether and in what circumstances a company's board of directors acts *as* the company rather than merely as (co)-agents of the company.[5]

B. Acting for/for the Benefit of/in the Interests of Another

The trustee-beneficiary relationship is, perhaps, the clearest example of this notion of representation.[6] Trustees hold title to property under the rules of the general law and the terms of the trust with the purpose of benefitting the beneficiaries, thus acting in the interest of the beneficiaries. Advisory relationships also fall into this category. Solicitors advising clients provide that advice for/for the benefit of their client, or in the interests of their client. But trustees or advising solicitors do not act *as* their beneficiaries or advisees, nor do they act *on their behalf*, in the sense that their acts are attributed to their beneficiaries or advisees. Trustees and advising solicitors cannot by their acts alter the rights, duties, or powers of their beneficiaries or advisees with respect to third parties. Thus it is not a solecism to say that trustees or solicitors "represent" their beneficiaries or advisees, or at least those persons' interests, and this notion of "representation" is genuinely relational. So just as in the company law case discussed above, acting for/for the benefit of another is not a case of genuine attribution, so we need not discuss it further.

[3] For an overview of the historical conceptual change from treating the shareholders *as* the company, as equivalent to a kind of partnership, to treating the company as a distinct legal personality, *see* P. Ireland, *Property and Contract in Contemporary Corporate Theory*, 23 Legal Studies 453, 457–65 (2003).

[4] Although there are rules preventing the "oppression" of minority shareholders.

[5] P. Watts, *Directors as Agents—Some Aspects of Disputed Territory*, *in* Agency Law in Commercial Practice 97–117 (D. Busch, L. Macgregor & P. Watts eds., 2016).

[6] Trustees can be agents as well as trustees, but they are not so simply in virtue of their trusteeship. *See* J.E. Penner, The Law of Trusts 2.29–2.34, ch. 11 (12th ed., 2022). In this chapter I shall not discuss the fiduciary relationship per se, except briefly in Part III.A, for fiduciary law essentially restricts the valid exercise of a fiduciary's powers vis-à-vis her principal. It does not have as far as I can tell, its own rules of attribution when those powers are validly exercised. For the treatment of fiduciaries as representatives of their principals, *see* Miller, *Fiduciary Representation*, *supra* note 1.

C. Acting on Behalf of Another—a True Case of Attribution

This case might be called "representation with attribution." The classic example here is, of course, the agent: the agent's acts, entering into contracts with third parties, are attributed to their principal, such that the principal is the counterparty, not (generally)[7] the agent. Note the difference with trustees. A trustee acts in its own name, albeit for the benefit of the beneficiaries, but not on behalf of, or in the place of, the beneficiaries.

D. Nonrepresentative Legal Relationships

As with any concept, it is important not to be promiscuous with its application.[8] Although a very important legal relationship, the marriage relationship is not one where (nowadays) the partners represent each other. While some aspects of the parent-child relationship are representative, for example where a parent consents to a surgical procedure on behalf of her child, parents do not in general represent their children any more than children represent their parents. In particular, just in virtue of the relationship itself, parents and children are not trustees of, agents of, or fiduciaries to each other.[9] Contractual counterparties generally serve each other's interests by discharging their contractual obligations, so in that sense act for or for the benefit of or in the interests of their counterparty, but they don't represent each other. For this reason the contractual employee-employer relationship is not, of its essence, a representational relationship either. An employee simply provides services for their employer.

Another case of what might be called "promiscuous" attribution is its use in saying that such-and-such and act is "attributable" to a person's role in a legal relationship. Not all of a person's acts are significant for the performance of obligations or the exercise of powers within a particular legal relationship. Those acts that do fall within the relationship can be said to be attributed to the person's role in the relationship. So, considering an employee, one might say that those acts of theirs that fulfill his contractual obligations are attributed to the performance of his contract. This terminology is also used of trustees. The "rules of attribution" here concern *which acts* the trustee undertakes qua trustee, and which not. To take a simple example, a trustee has an indemnity in respect of the trust

[7] For example, in the case of an undisclosed principal; see P. WATTS & F. REYNOLDS, BOWSTEAD AND REYNOLDS ON AGENCY 9–12 (2018). *See also* C.-H. Tan, *Implied Terms in Undisclosed Agency*, 84 MODERN L. REV. 532–52 (2021); C.-H. Tan, *Undisclosed Principals and Contract*, 120 LAW QUARTERLY REV. 480–509 (2004).

[8] *See, e.g.*, the explosion of the use of "fiduciary" in the context of US law: E.J. Criddle, P.B. Miller & R.H. Sitkoff eds., THE OXFORD HANDBOOK OF FIDUCIARY LAW (2019).

[9] See further Penner, *Private Law Offices*, *supra* note 2, at 303–07.

assets for all expenses it properly incurs in its execution of the trust, and the law must determine which of the expenses the trustee incurs falls into this category.[10]

The preceding discussion shows that, given the breadth of the concept of representation and its various manifestations in legal doctrine, we should hesitate to identify any univocal concept of representation in the legal context. Rather, we must try to clarify the various kinds of rules of attribution themselves, and notice their different purposes and functions.

III. A Survey of Attribution Cases

A. Agency and Delegation

We have identified the most prominent case of attribution in private law, that of agency. Strictly speaking, an agency relationship only arises where a person, the "principal," grants or confers authority to or upon another person, the "agent." Generally the authority is an authority to conduct the affairs of their principal, in particular to enter into contracts on the principal's behalf. Principals are also said to *have authority* over their agents in the sense of normally having the power to provide instructions to their agents, with which their agents must comply.[11] The power to appoint agents, to confer authority upon them, is one of the central cases of the facilitative side of the law as Hart would describe it;[12] acting through a legal agent extends a person's own "agency" (in the philosophical sense). Another clear case of a legal relationship of attribution is the grant of a power of attorney, to act, for example, on behalf of an incapacitated person. The property transactions engaged in by the attorney are attributed to that person—they count as dispositions of that person's property. Powers of attorney can also be given to extend the agency (in the philosophical sense) of a grantor who is not incapacitated, but who simply wishes to delegate some of their affairs to another for practical reasons (because, e.g., they are embarking upon a six months' journey into the wilderness).

The idea of delegation is very much akin to, if not identical to, a principal's conferring upon an agent or similar person to act on her behalf, as we just saw where a person confers a power of attorney upon another to look after their affairs because they will be incommunicado for some time. But powers of

[10] *See generally* PENNER, LAW OF TRUSTS, *supra* note 6, at 2.29. For a nice decision on this issue, *see* Bennett v. Wyndam (1857) 23 Beav. 521, where the court held that the trustee had recourse to his indemnity where he was vicariously liable for injuries arising from the felling of trees on an estate.

[11] In the case of a gratuitous agency, the agent may choose not to act at all, though if they choose to act they must comply with the instruction: WATTS & REYNOLDS, BOWSTEAD ON AGENCY, *supra* note 7, at 6–28.

[12] H. HART, THE CONCEPT OF LAW 27 (1994).

delegation, or the conferral of authority upon another, may be restricted for those who hold powers for the benefit of or on behalf of another. In the case of fiduciary powers, where an agent or trustee has powers to act that require their exercising judgment so as to choose that course of action that in their opinion best serves the interests of their principal or beneficiaries, standardly the principle of *delegatus non potest delegare* applies, that a power conferred upon someone requiring the exercise of that kind of judgment may not delegate the exercise of that power to another. An exception is made for what are called "ministerial acts," which require no exercise of judgment. One example will suffice. A trustee of a trust that holds rental properties may delegate the task of collecting the rents to a third party, as fulfilling this task requires no judgment on the part of the delegate.[13]

Beyond these clear cases, there are a host of other relationships of attribution that can only be described as quasi-agency cases, which are a miscellany. Part of the problem here is the different ways in which people use the term "agent." Many employees have "quasi"-agential functions just to the extent that their actions implicate their employer's legal relations with third parties, although these cases occur outside the context of legal agency relationships strictly speaking. The following list is probably not exhaustive.

B. Spokespersons

The spokesperson for an individual, collective, or company, who answers press queries and makes announcements, speaks on behalf of them, and so their speech may be attributed to the individual, collective, or company for the purposes of, for example, the law of defamation.

C. Knowledge or Information

A second example, essentially the flipside of the last, might be called representation for the purpose of attributing knowledge or information. This raises a continuing and difficult question of company law in particular—whose knowledge or receipt of information may be attributed to a company? Which employees or officers of a company are the appropriate ones upon which to serve documents in the making of a legal claim, and so on.

[13] *See, e.g.*, PENNER, LAW OF TRUSTS, *supra* note 6, at 2.28, 8.41–8.45.

D. Custody

The right to possession of tangible personal property (i.e., goods and chattels) may be attributed to another in cases of what the law calls "custody." Where an employee possesses, say, a laptop owned by their employer, the employee has in law the right to exclusive possession just in virtue of their having taken factual possession of the laptop. This right is attributed to their employer for the purposes of the law of conversion. It is the employer who has the claim against the converter, not the employee. It is also important for the passing of title by delivery. In many cases, in order for title to tangible property to be acquired, factual possession must (generally) be acquired. When an employee obtains factual possession of a chattel, their right to possession is attributed to his employer and, conversely, where the employee delivers possession to a third party, their loss of the right to exclusive possession equally disposes of their employer's right to possession.[14] Custody is thus best defined as an "attributed right to possession."

E. Employee Performance of an Employer's Obligations

In many cases where an employee discharges their obligations to their employer, they also discharge their employer's obligations to third parties. Among a multitude of examples, consider the case of an employer engaged to do building works. When its employees complete the job, thereby discharging their obligations to the employer, they also thereby discharge the employer's obligations to its counterparty under the building contract. The employees' actions here are agent-like in some sense[15] but not in the strict legal sense.

F. Vicarious Liability or Respondeat Superior

A final example comes from the law of torts. Leow has recently provided a thorough survey of the law in England and Wales governing "vicarious liability," which shows how until relatively recently what was attributed to the employer was the employee's tortious act, whereas now the reigning orthodoxy is that what is attributed is the employee's own liability for the wrong.[16] Either way, this is a clear case of attribution.

[14] M. Bridge, Personal Property Law 39–40 (2015).
[15] *See, e.g.*, R. Stevens, The Laws of Restitution 157 (2023).
[16] R. Leow, Corporate Attribution in Private Law ch. 4 (2022).

IV. What the Rules of Attribution Attribute

As we have seen from this survey of examples, it seems that a variety of things may be attributed to a person, natural or legal. With these examples in hand, we can investigate this variety, and in doing so we will look at the important distinction between a person's acts that amounts to the exercise of legal powers and those which do not. We must also consider the attribution of rights and capacities.

A. "Natural" Acts and the Exercise of Legal Powers

We must first distinguish between what I shall call "natural powers" to perform "natural acts" and the exercise of "normative powers," such as the powers to make an agreement with others or to transfer title to property.[17] The latter are "powers" in the Hohfeldian sense of that term.[18] What "natural powers" and "natural acts" refer to is a person's entire realm of agency in the philosophical sense, *minus* the exercise of normative powers. So we run, climb, eat, have a conversation, investigate the natural world, concentrate on a problem, change our minds, and so on. These are all things a non-incapacitated person can normally do. Here we are typically concerned with acts that a person has a "liberty" to do in the Hohfeldian sense of that word.[19] The use of "natural" here is stipulative. By using it I do not mean to imply that our normative powers are not natural. As language-using creatures we are naturally capable of attending to norms, and can devise new norms limited only by our imagination, for example, in devising agreements with others, inventing a new game, or inventing new systems of measurement. So our normative powers are just as natural to us are the "natural" powers in the sense I have stipulated. With respect to normative powers, we typically have a Hohfeldian liberty also to exercise Hohfeldian legal powers, for example, to exercise our legal power to enter into an agreement with others. Thus we are concerned with two kinds of things a person might have a liberty to do, and so there are, in turn, two things the law may attribute to Y, the natural acts of *X*, where no legal powers are exercised; and the acts of *X* which constitute the exercise of a legal power.

[17] *Id.* at 32 makes what I think is the same distinction using a different terminology.

[18] W.N. Hohfeld, *Some Fundamental Legal Conceptions as Applied in Judicial Reasoning*, 23 Yale L.J. 16–59 (1913–14). For discussion, *see* J.E. Penner, *The Problems with Powers*, *in* Property Rights: A Re-Examination (J.E. Penner ed., 2020).

[19] *See* Hohfeld, *Fundamental Legal Conceptions*, *supra* note 18. For discussion, *see* Penner, Property Rights, *supra* note 18, at ch. 3.

We have already seen a number of examples of both of these. A spokesperson's speaking is a natural act, as is the employee's doing work that discharges his employer's contractual obligations, as is a tort that is attributed to another under the doctrine of vicarious liability; committing a tort is not the exercise of a legal power, though it has, of course, legal consequences.[20] As to the exercise of legal powers, an agent's entering into a contract on behalf of his principal is a clear case of the exercise of a legal power.

B. Rights and Capacities

The law may also attribute certain rights of one person to another, the classic example being custody, where the right to exclusive possession of a chattel that an employee has is attributed to the employer.

As to capacities, the law could, but as far as I know in private law in fact does not, attribute the capacity of one person to another. As a matter of positive law, where P lacks capacity to enter into a contract, P cannot extend or enlarge his capacity by employing an agent with that capacity. Thus under the company law ultra vires doctrine a company is not bound by contracts which were capable of being formed by its directors or agents with powers to enter into those contracts personally but which the company itself lacked by not being provided for in its "objects" provisions. But there is nothing in principle that would prevent the law from attributing capacities.

V. The Metaphysics of Attribution and "Relationship Attribution"

Addressing the rules of attribution presents us with some "philosophical" issues, if I can put it that way. These issues are "metaphysical" in the sense that they raise questions about how we can or should conceive of what the rules of attribution are attributing. Different problems arise in the case of natural acts and legal rights on the one hand and the case of the exercise of powers on the other, so each must be dealt with in turn. The claim of this section is that the concept of "relationship attribution" provides insight into these cases.

[20] PENNER, PROPERTY RIGHTS, *supra* note 18, at 71–73; John Harrison, *Immunity Rules*, *in* WESLEY HOHFELD A CENTURY LATER: EDITED WORK, SELECT PERSONAL PAPERS, AND ORIGINAL COMMENTARIES 386, 392–94 (Shyamkrishna Balganesh, Ted M. Sichelman & Henry E. Smith eds., 2022). I assume it is common ground among theorists that liability for a breach of a "non-delegable duty" concerns the primary liability of the duty ower and is not a species of vicarious liability or respondeat superior. It therefore does not involve a rule of attribution.

A. Attributing Natural Acts and Legal Rights

As we have seen in Parts III.E and III.F, the law may choose between attributing the act of an employee to their employer under the principle of *qui facit per alium facit* per se ("he who acts through another acts himself") or choose to attribute the employee's own liability to the employer via the notion of "vicarious liability." The former view has been regarded as ill-judged because it imports a fiction into the law: How could the employee's act *be* the employer's act? But there are reasons for thinking this objection is too quick.[21] Consider our attitude toward games. When a player scores a goal, in football say, the goal (qua the rules of the game)[22], we might say, is "attributed" to the team for the purpose of determining which team wins the game. That is, it is first the player's goal (the player has a Hohfeldian liberty to gain a goal for themself), which is then assigned to or attributed to the team. But surely it is better simply to say that a player, by putting the ball in the net, *scores for the team*.[23] We should treat this rule as "constitutive," "constitutive," of the game of football. By parity of reasoning, it is constitutive of the employment relationship that an employee's acts carried out in the course of fulfilling his obligations under the contract of employment are those of its employer, not in the sense that the "employer" fictitiously acted itself, but in the sense that it was the employer's agency (in the philosophical sense) that was extended by the relationship. This is also why its employees' carrying out work for it under their contract of employment can discharge its obligations to a third party. The same logic applies to the attribution of the employee's right to possession in cases of custody. These rules of attribution, which I shall call rules of "relationship attribution," are ones where the nature of the relationship itself determines which of a person's acts and states are constitutive of the relationship and thus attributable to the other party or parties to the relationship.

B. Attributing Wrongful Acts

Now the possibility of attributing A's acts to B will always raise some tricky borderline cases, in particular in the case of wrongful acts. It seems acceptable that an employee's negligent carrying out of their contractual duties causing loss to a

[21] See the helpful discussion in R. Stevens, Torts and Rights 259–67 (2007).

[22] For a closely similar line of thought, *see id.* at 261. I should add that we can of course count up the goals that Pele scored over the course of a season or over the course of his career, treating them as *his* goals, but the point here is that the identity of the player is irrelevant so far as the rules of scoring in the game goes. All that is relevant is that he was a member of the team, was properly on the pitch, was not offside, and so forth.

[23] By "team," I do not mean some metaphysically problematic entity that exists apart from the players. See Part V.B.i.

third party will be reasonably attributed to their employer, because the negligent act occurred in the course of the employee's carrying out, or at least trying to carry out, what their duties required of them. On the other hand, it is more difficult to justify holding an innocent employer liable for an act that is not authorized under the terms of the contract, does not discharge any obligation under the contract, and which may indeed amount to a breach of that contract. But the fact that there are borderline cases of this kind simply shows that there can be uncertainty about what the best rules are for making the relationship itself most valuable, and hence justifiable for all concerned.

We have discussed the case of spokespersons, above. Clearly speech can be attributed to another person, and this is important in the law of defamation[24] and deceit.[25] In such cases we have a particular rule of attribution whereby a certain kind of natural act is treated as the act of another. Notice that in this case this is not the attribution of any liability of the speaker.[26] I would also argue that this is perfectly understandable under the "relationship attribution" analysis. It is part of what being a spokesperson is that the speech is attributable to the person spoken for.

C. Attributing the Exercise of Legal Powers

Here I will argue that rules of "relationship attribution" apply equally well to explain the attribution of the exercise of legal powers. But here the issues are significantly different, and this has largely been a result of disputes in the realm of company law.

i. Attributing the exercise of legal powers: Three alternative analyses

It is trite law that, A being P's agent, A's exercise of the power to contract with C within A's authority and with the intention that the contract be for P rather than a contract entered into on A's own account binds P, that is, creates a contract between P and C. What concerns us here is the following question: vis-à-vis C, the third party, *whose* power to enter into contracts, A's or P's, is in question? There are three options. One might say that A exercises A's own legal power to enter into a contract, but the law attributes the *results* of that exercise to P, the results being the rights and obligations of a counterparty under the contract. Or one might say that A exercises P's powers, in which case P is *ipso facto* the party under the contract. The third option is to apply a "relationship attribution" analysis.

24 Stevens, Torts and Rights, *supra* note 21, at 246–47.

25 *Id.* at 256.

26 *See* Egger v. Viscount Chelmsford [1965] 1 QB 248 (CA).

On the first view, the agency relationship would appear to effect an immediate and automatic transmission or assignment of A's rights and powers under the contract, and a similarly automatic undertaking by P to fulfill A's liabilities under the contract. This view seems overly complicated and could not explain the case where the contract is not assignable, though it has had some adherents.[27]

Now consider the second view that seems, I think, to be something of the orthodox view, viz that it is P's own powers that A exercises. This alternative is problematic in its own right. We can illustrate the possible problem here by first returning to the case of natural acts. When A, a natural person, strikes X and the law attributes A's wrongful act to P, also a natural person, it would be a fiction to say that P himself struck X.[28] This shows that, at least in the case of natural acts, the attribution does not turn on finding that A exercised any natural power to commit a natural act of P's, such that P themself acted.[29] The point here is that If we can attribute A's striking X to P without A's claiming that he exercised P's own physical powers and capacities to commit a natural act, it seems unmotivated (in the philosophical sense) to take a different line when the case concerns legal powers, here insisting that A exercised P's power to contract.

The obvious motivation for saying that A exercises P's powers where the powers happen to be legal rests upon a view about the nature of companies, viz that companies, while having no natural powers to commit natural acts, do have legal powers. Furthermore, since a company can only act via natural persons, for a company even to have *legal* relations with others is just to say that its legal relations with others must turn on the legal powers that it itself has. But this argument, if it is an argument, proceeds too quickly. Let me begin with an observation.

As a matter of normal discourse, it is arguably analytic of a power that the powerholder themself may exercise it *without* the help of third parties.[30] Here we see the clear connection between power-holding and capacity. A child has no power to consent to an operation; the power to consent is that of its parent. An incapacitated person has no power to sell her property, though her power of

[27] For a discussion of this "transmission of rights" thesis, *see* Tan, *Undisclosed Principals*, *supra* note 7, at 497.

[28] Although if the agent was instructed by her principal to act in such a way, the *attribution* of the act seems straightforward.

[29] Leaving aside the philosopher's much-loved science fiction examples, for example, where P has a device that allows him to make A use his natural power to strike X.

[30] Of course the exercise of legal powers necessarily *involves* others, for example, in the case of a transfer of property; and even necessarily involves others also exercising a power, for example, in the case of contract formation. (For a persuasive argument that the power to contract is one that must be *jointly* exercised by the contracting parties, *see* Irina Sakharova, *Understanding the Power to Contract* (Ph.D thesis 2021, on file with the author.) This is so simply because powers change legal relations, and legal relations always involve at least two persons. Seeing this shows one way in which Hohfeld's scheme of jural relations is misconceived. *See* PENNER, PROPERTY RIGHTS, *supra* note 16, at 75–79.

attorney holder has. But on the orthodox view, there is, I think, supposed to be a contrast between these cases and that of a legal person like a company. The idea is that companies are special, in that they have legal powers but cannot exercise them themselves, but only by "proxy" as it were, through the acts of others. This strikes me as mysterious. It suggests that we draw a sharp distinction between the parent-child case and the incapacitated owner-power of attorney holder case just for the sake of some theory about companies.

ii. Company law and the relationship analysis

These thoughts gain support from Lord Hoffmann's view in *Meridian Global Funds Management Asia Ltd v. Securities Commission*[31] that one should not look behind the attribution rules themselves to try to answer metaphysical questions about the nature of companies, in this case the question "whose" power is being exercised. Accordingly, one should say that when an agent enters into a contract within the scope of his authority with the intention to contract for his principal, a company, the result will be that the company is the proper counterparty to the contract, *and say no more than that, for saying anything more will entangle us in bad metaphysics.* The relationship attribution analysis we applied first to games, a version of which I think can be extracted from *Meridian*, counsels us to treat the rules of agency likewise, as constitutive of the relationship we call "agency:" What does the law say is the result of A's entering into and concluding a contract with C where A is P's agent? The law tells us what that is—a contract between P and C—and there is no point in speaking about whether it was A's power to contract the exercise of which is then attributed to P, or A's exercise of P's powers to contract, whose exercise resulted in the contract in which P, not A, is the party. We should just say that P's conferral (or rather, in the case of companies, P's agent's conferral) of authority upon A provides A with a power to create contracts between P and C.

Let me emphasize that these thoughts do not turn on the special case of companies, but rather that the case of companies brings out a feature of the dialectic *if*, but only if, you think that the rules of attribution in agency cases should be understood as rules which apply on the same basis to cases where companies are concerned as well as cases where only natural persons are concerned. The basic argument is that if you want to treat A's exercise of a power as the exercise of P's power, the second analysis I considered in Part V.B.i, you seem to have to distinguish the exercise of a person's natural powers, simply acting as an agent in the philosophical sense, from the case of exercising legal powers, for in the former case the idea that A exercises Company P's power or capacity to do something

[31] [1995] 2 AC 500.

physical, like strike X, or indeed for A to undertake any natural act that, say, discharges the company's contractual obligation, seems fanciful.

Distinguishing the cases in this way allows you to say that companies "really do" have legal powers, though they have no natural powers to commit natural acts. But this seems unmotivated. If the law attributes acts of A to P in the same way whether the persons are natural or legal, what we want to say both about A's exercise of natural powers to commit natural acts and A's exercise of legal powers is that in certain circumstances, so the rules say, we will treat P as "implicated" in what A has done on the basis of the nature of the relationship between them, just as we "implicate" the team when an individual player puts the ball in the net. In terms of legal powers, all we need say is that A has a power to create legal relations between P and C. Hence the superiority of the relationship attribution analysis—it doesn't entangle one in bad metaphysical questions.

None of this, I should add, commits me to a version of the "fiction" theory of the corporation. (In my view it was unfortunate that Lord Hoffmann linked his correct assertion that a company is constituted by the applicable rules of attribution[32] with the terminology of "persona ficta."[33]) Companies are no more fictions than games are fictions.[34] But it may be the case that some company law theorists are committed to the view that a company, as an "artificial" person, has itself powers, not just legal powers but the ordinary "physical" powers of a natural person.[35] Let me explain.

[32] Meridian, *supra* note 31, at 507A.

[33] *Id.* at 506B.

[34] Leow attributes to Lord Hoffmann in Meridian a fiction theory of the company (LEOW, CORPORATE ATTRIBUTION, *supra* note 16, at 29). For reasons I have given in the main text, I think this is wrong. Some entities are constituted by rules. To say this of a company is not to say that it is a fiction, but to identify its nature. By contrast, Leow says her account is non-fictional, but as far as I can tell this simply means that we need not modify the rules of attribution that apply between natural persons to apply them between companies and natural persons. That might be one definition of "non-fictional," but it is not a helpful one. All it tells us is that we don't need to bend the rules where companies are concerned. It doesn't say anything about the nature of corporate personality beyond the fact that we apply the rules governing private law equally to natural and artificial legal persons. More worryingly, Leow seems to embrace her own fiction, or at least her own mystery, when she speaks of the company acting "personally" or exercises its "own powers." See the discussion in *infra* note 35. In any case, I am baffled by this entire talk about corporations being "real" or "fictional." Although there were a number of flaws in the details (see P.M.S. Hacker, *Definition in Jurisprudence*, 19 PHILOSOPHICAL QUARTERLY 343–47 (1969)), I thought Hart had put paid to this nonsense debate many years ago: H.L.A. Hart, H. L. A. ESSAYS IN JURISPRUDENCE AND PHILOSOPHY ch. 1 (1983).

[35] Rachel Leow may be one such theorist. Leow has recently proposed what might be called a "unitary theory" of attribution rules by which the knowledge, acts, or liabilities, and so forth of X are attributed to Y. (LEOW, CORPORATE ATTRIBUTION, *supra* note 16. *See also* R. Leow, *Equity's Attribution Rules*, 15 J. OF EQUITY 35–62 (2021).) Leow sets out her main thesis as follows (LEOW, CORPORATE ATTRIBUTION, *supra* note 16, at 3, my italics):

> The central argument of this book is that attribution turns . . . on the allocation and delegation of the *company's* powers to act.

Let me begin by offering a few quotes to give a sense of what Leow means by a company's *own* powers (all parenthetical pinpoint cites to LEOW, CORPORATE ATTRIBUTION, *supra* note 16):

iii. Companies and the Philosophy of "Shared" or "Joint" Agency

Many theorists have been concerned with the idea of shared or joint agency (hereafter just "joint agency"), the agency of teams, orchestras, legislatures and so on, a kind of agency that arises from the coordinated activity of natural individuals. And the question would be whether the phenomenon of joint agency leads us to think that a separate agent, dependent upon the agency of individuals, but distinct from it, arises. Two of the most prominent theorists in the field, Margaret Gilbert and Michael Bratman both deny that their accounts posit metaphysically suspect entities, such as a distinct "group agent" of some kind.[36] But on one reading of Gardner's account of joint agency, teams, orchestras, legislators and so on are themselves genuine agents, albeit "artificial ones."[37] It would seem that we could easily add companies to this list of genuine, albeit artificial agents.

> Attribution involves treating *this* act of *this* individual as *this* company's. [13, italics original]
>
> This chapter advances a non-fictional account of attribution which connects act, individual, and company. It argues that attribution turns on the internal allocation and delegation of the company's *own powers* to act under the company's constitution. When these powers are properly exercised by those to whom they have been allocated or delegated, *the company acts personally*. This involves no fiction, *only the application of ordinary legal concepts*. [14, my italics]
>
> Whether [corporate personality] is 'fictional' or 'real' is not particularly helpful in this context. *The crucial point is that ordinary concepts applicable to human persons become potentially applicable to companies. Like human persons, companies possess an array of powers which they may exercise. When a company exercises them, it acts personally.* This involves no legal fiction. It just requires the application of the tools that the law already has; tools it has had all along. . . . [The company's] powers are allocated and delegated through the company's constitutional documents to groups or individuals. When they are exercised, *the company acts personally*. This is not a fiction; it is just how the company acts. [30–31, my italics]

As you will see from the second and third quotations, Leow wishes to put forward a non-fictional account of corporate attribution. But though she refers to the "fiction" versus "real" theory of corporate personality, I don't see any place in which she lets us know, beyond the passages above, what she thinks makes an account a non-fictional one.

36 Gilbert says that her theory does not "posit any metaphysically suspect group mind." M. Gilbert, Joint Commitment: How We Make the Social World 119–20 (2013); *see also* 9–10. In my view, Gilbert would equally deny that her analysis posits any metaphysically suspect "group personality." M. Bratman, Faces of Intention (1999), holds his account to be "broadly individualistic" and "reductive" in spirit (at 108, 129) and says we "should not appeal to an attitude in the mind of some superagent" (at 111; *see also* 122–23). Paul Miller's "integretave" approach to corporate personality, while superficially opposed to a "reductive" approach, does not, in my view, posit any metaphysically problematic notions of the corporation, and is essentially in keeping with Gilbert's and Bratman's approach to joint agency. *See* P.B. Miller, *Corporations, in* The Oxford Handbook of The New Private Law 341–60 (A.S. Gold, J.P. Goldberg, D. R. Kelly, E. Sherwin & H.S. Smith eds., 2020). *See also* P.B. Miller, *Corporate Personality, Purpose and Liability, in* Research Handbook on Corporate Purpose and Personhood 222–39 (E. Pollman & R. Thompson eds., 2021); while Miller speaks of a corporation's "personality," "agency," and "capacity," I think he successfully avoids invoking any metaphysically troubling notions of these concepts, and I would argue that his analysis is compatible with what I say in the text to this part.

37 *See* J. Gardner, *Reasons for Teamwork*, 8 Legal Theory 495–509 (2002); J. Gardner, Law as a Leap of Faith 61–65 (2012).

Here are two of Gardner's examples that give the gist of the nature of his claim on this reading.

> The team has reasons to act that are distinct from those of any of its individual members, although whether it conforms to or acts on the strength of those reasons is entirely a function of what its members do and why. In short, the team is an agent, and a rational agent, but not (in Kant's sense) an autonomous agent.[38]
>
> [T]he concerted agency is not completely fictitious; the members of legislative institutions do typically perform much of their work as a team, and in that respect they are to be regarded as natural concerted agents akin to orchestras and football teams. Second, there is nothing wrong with a legal fiction of concerted agency, if by that phrase we mean simply that the law attributes actions by one agent (an official) to another agent (an institution) under norms that make the former a representative of, and hence an agent who acts on behalf of the latter. For there are artificial concerted agents, and many are creatures of law. It does not follow from the fact that they are creatures of the law that they do not exist or that they are not agents. On the contrary, it follows from the fact that they can perform actions with legal effect, such as legislating, that they do exist, and that they are agents.[39]

Here I shall claim that if these passages are read to support the claim that a company, say, is some kind of actual agent with genuine (albeit artificially created) natural and legal powers, then on that reading Gardner's views must be rejected, for that reading would convict Gardner of committing one or both of two fallacies, the fallacy of composition and the fallacy of equivocation. Following an exploration of this reading, I will show that Gardner would almost certainly have rejected it, though he may be accused of some unclarities in his claim that a team or legislature is an "agent."

We can approach this question by considering a case of a joint agency where no legal personality is involved, the case of a sole proprietor and his plumbing business. His business consists in his business assets, his stock in trade, his rights in his business premises, his business bank account (as opposed to his personal assets, his television, residential premises, personal bank account) plus the "nexus" of contracts with his employees, customers, suppliers, lenders, bankers, and so on. How these property rights are employed and how these contracts go, that is whether the contractual obligations under them are discharged, breached, frustrated and so on, will determine whether the business is a success. The success

[38] Gardner, *Teamwork*, *supra* note 37, at 507.
[39] Gardner, Leap of Faith, *supra* note 37, at 65.

of the business therefore, and obviously, turns on the actions of all of the players involved, acting with regard to their natural powers to commit natural acts and in exercising their legal powers. But simply because all of these players have these ordinary and legal powers it does not follow that the business itself has all these powers. To conclude (without more) that the business does have them is to commit the fallacy of composition, attributing properties of something's parts to the thing as a whole, here attributing attributes or properties of the members or constituents of a thing, the humans engaged in it, to the thing itself, here the organized activity of a number of persons that constitutes the business. This criticism would apply in particular to Gardner's claim that "The team has reasons to act that are distinct from those of any of its individual members." It is not clear to me what it means to say that a team has reasons, unless this is just a *façon de parler*,[40] a way of saying that as a member of a team the *players* have reasons that they would not have but for their being members of the team. So it is perfectly all right to say, "Tottenham Hotspur has a reason to find a new keeper as the one they have now is inept." By parity of reasoning, the business has no reasons of its own, though all the persons involved in the business have reasons they would not have but for the business. In order to avoid this critique one would need to show that the organization in question, the team or the business, somehow *inherits* the properties of its constitutive parts, but as far as I can see there is no reason to think that that is possible in these cases. It would seem that this reasoning applies just as much to that concerted activity we call a "company."

We can now turn to the fallacy of equivocation. No one denies that concerted action by natural individuals, when they act as members of a football team, orchestra, or legislature, has real world effects, including effects recognized, facilitated, and regulated by law, effects that would not be realized were the individuals not engaged in these kinds of concerted action. So in that sense, teams, orchestras and legislatures have "agency," in that their existence *as* teams, orchestras, and legislatures, as cases of concerted action by natural individuals, contributes to the effects that the actions of their members bring about. And the same goes for the plumbing business I have described. In the same way we can say that the institution of money has agency, in that it obviates, or at least markedly diminishes, the resort to the more costly alternative of credit, allowing individuals to pursue transactions that would otherwise be more costly, so as to release, as we might say, "pent-up" demand.[41] In this way the liquidity function

[40] For another example of this "philosophical" use of "*façon de parler*," *see* M.R. Bennett & P.M.S. Hacker, Philosophical Foundations of Neuroscience 62–63 (2003), about how our speaking of "the mind" is to speak of a range of active and passive powers of the intellect and will.

[41] For an analysis of the nature of money and payment systems and their importance as legal institutions, *see* James Penner, *Tracing and Payment Systems*, *in* Law at the Cutting Edge: A Festschrift in Honour of Dame Sarah Worthington, DBE, KC (Hon) FBA, 221–42 (Sinéad

of money promotes and facilitates market activity. The institution of money therefore has real world effects, but money is not itself an agent in the way that natural individuals are agents. Thus, that a business or money has agency in the first sense, contributing to real world effects, does not mean that it ipso facto has agency in the second sense, the sort of agency we attribute to natural persons. To say so would be to commit the fallacy of equivocation over the meaning of agency, treating the agency of money as equivalent to the agency of natural individuals. So I think this critique properly applies to Gardner's claim that "it follows from the fact that they can perform actions with legal effect, such as legislating, that they do exist, and that they are agents." To put the point facetiously, if agency were attributed to something just because it had real world effects, a tornado would be an agent. Of course I am *not* suggesting an equivalence between natural phenomena and concerted human activity, only that having "real world effects" cannot be a sufficient test for agency in the sense in which we apply that to natural persons, who are self-moving, language-using creatures who are responsive to reasons and can coordinate their activities with others.

Returning to the case of companies, one can note that the deed of settlement companies that were the immediate forerunners of modern companies were able to achieve many of the functions of companies, though not of course all. These "companies" were, of course, trusts. But the legal facility that is the trust has no legal personality. Nothing can be attributed, in particular ordinary or legal powers, to it *as such*. This should tell us that when we are discussing modern, incorporated, companies, there is no *need* to hold that the company itself is an agent itself with ordinary and legal powers, albeit ones that can only be exercised by proxy, *just because it is a legal entity*.

But we should not attribute this reading of the texts I have cited to Gardner, for elsewhere Gardner has adopted[42] Anthony Kenny's capacious notion of agency.[43] Kenny recognizes a hierarchy of agency, rising from "natural agency, through living agency, through voluntary agency, to the summit of intentional agency."[44] Kenny gives the following examples of each:

> Natural agency: the action of acqua regia on gold;[45]
> Living agency: a plant's roots growing hairs to collect moisture;[46]

Agnew & Marcus Smith eds., 2024); more generally *see* C. Desan, Making Money: Coin, Currency, and the Coming of Capitalism (2014).

[42] J. Gardner, *Reasons and Abilities: Some Preliminaries*, 58 Am. J. of Jurisprudence 63, 67 (2013).

[43] A. Kenny, The Metaphysics of Mind ch. 3 (1989).

[44] *Id.* at 38.

[45] *Id.* at 33.

[46] *Id.* at 38.

Voluntary agency: where a dog chooses to follow a scent rather than responding to his master's call;[47]

Intentional agency: the agency of language-using creatures to choose to act for reasons.[48]

As far as I know, Kenny never considered the agency of joint agency. But on Kenny's account Gardner is clearly correct to say that teams, legislatures, and so on are agents just to the extent their existence has real world effects. But Gardner appears not to have applied Kenny's hierarchy of agency correctly to the case of joint agency as he describes it. In the first quotation above,[49] Gardner says both that a team has (presumably its own) reasons for acting but that the team, though a rational agent, is not "in Kant's sense" an autonomous agent. It seems to me that these claims are contradictory. An "autonomous agent" in Kant's sense is one which does not merely respond to its heteronymous desires and impulses, but one that can choose to act on the basis of reasons. So I do not see what sort of agent Gardner is describing, for it seems to equivocate between treating the team as a merely voluntary agent and an intentional agent. In any case, I would argue that Gardner's discussion does not provide any support for the idea that an unincorporated business, or a company with legal personality, has any natural or legal powers of its own.

This is not a paper on linguistic hygiene. I am not concerned to upend the perfectly sensible *façon de parler* that a company's agents exercise the powers of a company, as that is a perfectly useful shorthand for saying that a company's constitution, bylaws, objects and so on, may restrict what its agents effectively may do in acquiring property, entering into contracts, and so on. It is a way of saying that the "company's powers" may not be coextensive with the powers of its individual agents. But it is, I have submitted, mystifying to treat the company as a real actor or agent in the way natural individuals are agents.

D. The Attribution of "Mentalities"

I use "mentalities" as a compendious term for knowledge, intentions, and so forth. It is orthodox to think that these mentalities are attributed, in particular in the case of companies, when we speak of whether so-and-so's knowledge is to form part of the company's "directing mind and will." But we can draw again upon *Meridian* and the relationship attribution analysis, using the example of

[47] *Id.* at 37–38.

[48] *Id.* at 38–40.

[49] Text to *supra* note 38.

deceit. I have no difficulty with the idea that a principal or employer, whether a company or not, may be liable in appropriate circumstances when their employee or agent commits the tort of deceit. But it does not seem to me to be necessary for a finding of this that we need to attribute two separate things to the principal or employer, first, the employee's or agent's deceitful statement; and second, his state of mind (the intention to deceive another). It would be better, to my mind, simply to attribute the wrongful act of deceit (intention and all), or the liability for it. I should say the same in the case of attributing the "mistake" in the case of a mistaken payment where the mistake is one made by an employee or agent. Indeed, generally, post-*Meridian* it is not clear that knowledge or other mentalities should, as such, ever separately be attributed to a company or other principal. Post-*Meridian*, the question should always be whether it is appropriate to attribute the act (or in the case of a wrong, the liability for it) to the principal, whether a company or not. So, to take another example, it seems to make no sense to ask whether an employer, whether a company or not, should be liable for knowing receipt by inquiring whether knowledge of the circumstances of the receipt should be attributed *following* a finding of receipt on its behalf. The question is first whether, in principle, the knowing receipt by *this* employee or agent *counts* as knowing receipt by the employer or principal, or whether the receipt by this employee or agent does not so count; in the latter case the employer or principal should be treated as an innocent non-bona fide purchaser of the asset if no consideration is given (an innocent volunteer), or a bona fide purchaser if consideration is given. Whether it counts or not is a matter of the general *Meridian* point about the nature of the relationship that obtains between the parties in question. Thus, one first decides as a matter of principle whether P should ever be bound by this act, liability, etc., of A, given their relationship. As a matter of principle, where A murders a third party, the standard response is "no." By contrast, the crime of "manslaughter" has been accepted as "attributable."[50] The next question is which members of the set of those in a relationship to P, for example where P is a company, its directors, its agents, its employees, and so on, are those whose acts, liabilities, and so on, are capable of being attributed to the company, on the basic assumption that this should vary from case to case based on the policy of the underlying rule, for example, the rule against defamation, deceit, the rule providing for restitution of a mistaken payment, and so on. Applying the resulting rule of attribution to the facts will require showing that the act in question meets the requirements of falling under the underlying rule, including any necessary mental element, for example, an intent to deceive.

[50] The Corporate Manslaughter and Corporate Homicide Act 2007.

VI. Conclusion

It may seem only too obvious that the attribution to X of something of Y's, whether Y's natural acts, Y's exercise of Y's powers, or Y's liabilities, turns on the finding of some relationship between them. We do not attribute any of those to random strangers. But I hope that the foregoing has shown that attending to the various relationships themselves provides some insight into the rules of attribution in private law. We can conclude with something of a summary.

First, one must distinguish basic rules of the identity of any legal relationship from the relationship attribution rules, though the latter form a special part of the nature of the relationship. Rules of identity simply determine the nature of a thing that is constituted by rules, such as a game, or a company. According to Lord Hoffmann in *Meridian*, a company's rules of identity are coextensive with the rules that attribute the acts of natural individuals to the company. But that cannot be right, since a company cannot come into existence but for its creation under the relevant statutes, and they will determine its character, its identity as it were. In the same way individuals are not able to determine the rules of identity that determine other legal relationships recognized in private law, such as contracts, trusts, agency relationships, bailments, and so on. It is the law that does that. Once the company is formed, however, I think Lord Hoffmann is correct. Anything further that shapes the particular company in question is a matter of how the rights of, the natural acts of, and the exercises of legal powers by natural individuals determine its course, and this is true of all the other legal relationships just mentioned.

The rules of attribution are found in many areas of private law as, outside the law of tort, private law is facilitative, allowing individuals to enter into legally significant relationships. In such relationships it is, at the most general level, necessary that the behavior of the individual participants is relevant for determining the legal position of the other participants. Rules of attribution are just a special case of these rules but a special case of great importance.

11

General Customs and Legal Institutions

The Short, Sad Example of Racially Restrictive Covenants in the United States

Carol M. Rose

I. Introduction: Customs Reasonable and Unreasonable, Local and Universal

Shirley Jackson's famous story, *The Lottery*,[1] describes an annual festival in a fictional contemporary community: all the village's families gather on the festival day to draws lots, and the "winning" lot has a black dot. The family that draws it then selects a member to be stoned to death by all the rest of the villagers.

In this customary practice, one could imagine other possibilities for selecting the annual victim: community members might lure a passing stranger for the annual sacrifice. Alternatively, the person could be chosen by the village elders or the village chief, and if we are to draw inferences from the history of witchcraft, this person is likely to be a middle-aged or elderly woman with no male protectors, perhaps irascible or mentally ill, or perhaps outspoken vis-à-vis the neighbors or the local pastor.[2]

By comparison, this lottery among the ritual's participants seems more democratic and egalitarian than the alternatives, and in that sense a preferable customary practice. Moreover, all the community members come to the lottery voluntarily, perhaps illustrating their wish to signal acceptance of the community's ritual, or perhaps to strive for the esteem of fellow community members.[3]

How should legal institutions deal with this community's ritual? Blackstone's *Commentaries on the Laws of England* remains a primer for the legal management of custom. Blackstone made short work of widespread or universal

[1] Shirley Jackson, *The Lottery*, New Yorker, June 26, 1948, available at https://www.newyorker.com/magazine/1948/06/26/the-lottery.

[2] Carol F. Karlsen, The Devil in the Shape of a Woman: Witchcraft in Colonial New England (1987).

[3] Eric A. Posner, Law and Social Norms 5 (2000), 18–22 (signal); Richard H. McAdams, *The Origin, Development, and Regulation of Norms*, 96 Mich. L. Rev. 338, 366–86 (1997) (esteem).

Carol M. Rose, *General Customs and Legal Institutions* In: *Interstitial Private Law*. Edited by: Samuel L. Bray, John C.P. Goldberg, Paul B. Miller, and Henry E. Smith, Oxford University Press. © Oxford University Press 2024. DOI: 10.1093/oso/9780197783627.003.0011

customs, asserting that these simply constituted the common law of England. He then described special customary practices as localized deviations from the ordinary common law—and this lottery would certainly count as that—but he also laid out several criteria for their legal viability. In the Blackstonian canon, the law would recognize local customs if they were time-honored ("ancient)," continuous, undisputed ("peaceable"), reasonable, certain, obligatory ("comusable"), and consistent with other customs.[4]

Clearly the sticking point here is reasonableness; it is hard to imagine that unmotivated ritual murder would ever count as reasonable. But if Jackson's lottery flunks reasonableness, it is not because the participants choose the victim by lot. On the Blackstonian criteria, a customary lottery for some other purpose could easily be unobjectionable. The problem is the overarching meta-custom that demands an annual human sacrifice—the driving customary goal that deploys a lottery in its service. Jackson's lottery exemplifies an instance of a layered customary practice, part of which is unobjectionable—the use of lots—but the other part clearly reprehensible, and certainly illegal in Blackstone's calculus.

This chapter will explore the role of law in a different set of layered customary practices, a dyad not so overtly violent as Jackson's lottery, but one that evolved from legal acceptability to illegality over the first half of the twentieth century in the United States. This customary set consisted of a goal of residential segregation, as enforced through the means of restrictive real estate covenants. Just as in Jackson's tale, where the simple method of choice by lots was not the problem, so too the use of restrictive covenants in general was not problematic in residential communities; but their use for *racial* exclusion was the critical issue.

An important difference from Jackson's murder-through-lottery, however, is that over several decades, the enforcement of segregation through real estate covenants spread far beyond merely local practice; instead, covenants came to be used widely throughout the United States for the purpose of residential segregation. Blackstone did not bother to enumerate tests for very widespread customs, but if his account was correct that general customs would count as common law, enforcement of segregation through racially restrictive covenants could have qualified as newly generated common law.

Refining the Blackstonian observation, Henry Smith draws on information theory to argue that a general custom may indeed become law if it is relatively simple and formal, so that a variety of actors may understand and use it.[5] Here

[4] 1 Bl Comm *67–78.

[5] Henry E. Smith, *Custom in American Law: A Vanishing Act*, 48 Tex. Int'l L.J. 507, 508 (2013). Smith develops a theme from his other work illustrating a tradeoff between informational intensity and audience size/heterogeneity; thus smaller and more close-knit groups use highly complex directives to organize activities, whereas larger and looser groups require simpler directives. *See* Henry E. Smith, *The Language of Property: Form, Context, and Audience*, 55 Stan. L. Rev. 1105

too, residential racial covenants certainly met those criteria, however objectionable they may be in hindsight; they simply forbade specific racial groups from owning or using properties in specific areas, and they were well understood both by those who used them to exclude and those whom they targeted for exclusion.

In spite of the content, then, segregation through racial covenants seemed to meet the criteria for legal recognition as a general customary practice. But the dyad of segregation-through-covenants lost legal acceptance just as these covenants became especially dominant, a phenomenon that suggests that legal institutions may police general customs as well as local ones. The aim of this chapter is to explore the evolution of that policing phenomenon.

The chapter will illustrate that the relationship between law and custom was dynamic in the case of racial covenants, with law reinforcing custom and vice versa for several decades, as the use of covenants for racial discrimination became more and more commonplace. But the chapter will argue—contrary to Blackstone's implication—that the very spread of racial covenants made them *more* susceptible to legal policing rather than less so; ubiquity itself turned legal attention to the problems that these restrictions created. Nevertheless, one aspect of racial covenants' dynamic relationship to law lives on in unfortunate ways. This chapter will further argue that even though law and custom ultimately diverged with respect to covenants as an instrument for segregation, the decades of their legality played an essential role in fortifying the underlying meta-custom of residential segregation, a customary pattern that is now only gradually receding.

II. Customary Functions, Potential Pathologies

Racially restrictive covenants exemplified a custom gone bad, but the law supports a variety of customary practices that are not only unobjectionable but quite useful. Blackstone discussed the relation of custom to law almost entirely in the context of local groups, and many customs do apply within specialized or close-knit groups, whose members know one another or at least are familiar with the group's usual practices. In tort law, customary practice can help to define standards of care showing non-negligence, historically with special significance for the medical profession;[6] or in contract, customary

(2003); see also Smith's influential article with Thomas Merrill, *Optimal Standardization in the Law of Property: The Numerus Clausus Principle*, 110 Yale L.J. 1 (2000).

[6] Stephen G. Gilles, Rule-Based Negligence and the Regulations of Activity Levels, 21 J. Legal Stud. 319 (1992), 345–48; for a more critical view, *see* James F. Blumstein, *Medical Malpractice*

trade practices can help to define the parties' probable understandings of an agreement.[7]

Many customary practices can help to solve scenarios that are recognizable within game theory. A very old example was the practice of "stinting," that is, rationing individual families' livestock access to a common meadow in order to prevent overgrazing—a custom that solved a community's multiple-person Prisoners' Dilemma or Tragedy of the Commons problem.[8] Similarly, a custom of taking turns or tossing a coin can solve the so-called Battle-of-the-Sexes games, a name that describes situations in which persons wish to do things together but have different preferences about which things to do.[9] Elinor Ostrom's work on common property regimes has generated a burgeoning literature on "the commons," much of which applauds the ways in which prosaic customary practices resolve issues that would otherwise shatter long-lasting communities and their economic livelihoods.[10]

Nevertheless, some customary practices have problematic aspects, even where legal institutions may treat them as "reasonable." Chief among those aspects are their reinforcement of inequitable hierarchy, their externalities to third parties, and their stickiness or inertia. To begin with hierarchy, some customary practices give precedence to one subgroup over others as part of a largely unexamined meta-custom of rank. Gender relations come to mind: for example, if, as some argue, physical possession is the focal point that solves an implicit hawk/dove game in property relations,[11] then we are likely to see a pattern of male-dominant ownership. More subtly, in other hawk/dove or battle-of-the-sexes games, turn taking or coin tossing is often *not* the customary solution; instead brothers may have greater access than their sisters to education, food, and health care.[12] One finds other one-sided customary outcomes in the context of

Standard-Setting: Developing Malpractice Safe Harbors as a New Role for QIOs, 59 VAND. L. REV. 1017, 1026–31 (2006).

[7] *See, e.g.*, Elizabeth Warren, *The Trade Usage and Parties in the Trade: An Economic Rationale for an Inflexible Rule*, 42 U. PITT. L. REV. 515 (1981).

[8] Robert McC Netting, *What Alpine Peasants Have in Common: Observations on Communal Tenure in a Swiss Village*, 4 HUMAN ECOL. 135, 139 (1976).

[9] Carol M. Rose, *Game Stories*, 22 YALE J.L. & HUMAN 369, 378–82 (2010). This article notes the excessively macho names attached to standard game theory matrices and suggest alternatives, for example, substituting "Lunch Date" for Battle of the Sexes, "Quilting Bee" for Stag Hunt, and "Too Many Cooks" for Hawk/Dove.

[10] ELINOR OSTROM, GOVERNING THE COMMONS: THE EVOLUTION OF INSTITUTIONS FOR COLLECTIVE ACTION (1990).

[11] *E.g.*, ROBERT SUGDEN, THE ECONOMICS OF RIGHTS, COOPERATION, AND WELFARE 94 (1986), cf. Carol M. Rose, *Psychologies of Property (and Why Property Is Not a Hawk/Dove Game)*, *in* THE PHILOSOPHICAL FOUNDATIONS OF PROPERTY LAW (J.E. Penner & H.E. Smith eds., 2013).

[12] Hanna Papanek, *To Each Less Than She Needs, From Each More Than She Can Do: Allocations, Entitlements and Value*, *in Persistent Inequalities* 167 (Irene Tinker ed., 1990); Robert Sugden, *Contractarianism and Norms*, 100 ETHICS 768, 779–82 (1990).

ruling and subordinate castes,[13] or, in the case of fishing communities, established and newcomer fishers.[14] Are such customary practices "reasonable"? Blackstone himself discussed varying localities' practices of widows' inheritance, all assuming the background of an unequal status of coverture; he apparently had no qualms about the overarching background norm of gender inequality.

Another problematic aspect of commons organization concerns negative externalities. Many environmental problems emerge from customary practices, for example, the custom from my childhood of raking autumn leaves to burn at the curbside, without regard for or even knowledge of the effect on air pollution.[15] Robert Ellickson's well-known book, *Order Without Law*,[16] devotes most of a chapter to another example: in the nineteenth century, whalers' customs were accepted by courts in the handful of incidents in which they were litigated. Whalers adopted several practices to identify which whaling vessel could claim ownership of a whale harpooned at sea, ranging from a rule of relatively simple possession (i.e., roping the slain animal to the vessel) in the case of more easily hunted right whales, to "iron holds the whale" for the larger, faster, and more dangerous sperm whales. The "iron holds" rule rewarded the first whaling crew to take the risk of harpooning and weakening the animal, even when others completed the kill. These variations in customary practices not only smoothed disputes among whalers but also rewarded effort, and they permitted whalers to engage more efficiently in what was then a very profitable hunt. But the efficient hunting customs were imbedded in a meta-custom of taking ocean resources without limit; indeed, nineteenth-century whaling practices quickly devastated whale populations. Thus whaling customs entailed negative common pool externalities that undermined the enterprise itself—and this is of course without regard to more modern concerns about animal welfare.[17]

Inertia is a version of a negative externality over time periods, such that some customary practices resist needed adaptation to changed conditions. Ostrom and her colleagues have celebrated the durability of customs that successfully manage commons problems in many venerable communities. But as Arun Agrawal has astutely noticed, this scholarship has paid little attention to external changes that can disrupt customary communities, such as population pressure, market penetration, and new technology.[18] Other scholars, such as Brigham

[13] See, for example, the class distinction in Niger between the descendants of slaves and the so-called nobles: Thomas Kelley, *Unintended Consequences of Westernization in Niger: Harming Contemporary "Slaves" by Reconceptualizing Property*, 56 AM. J. COMP. L. 999 (2008).

[14] James M. Acheson, *The Lobster Fiefs: Economic and Ecological Effects of Territoriality in the Maine Lobster Industry*, 3 HUMAN ECOL. 183, 187 (1975).

[15] Carol M. Rose, *Surprising Commons*, BYU L. REV. 1257 (2014), explores the unwitting character of many environmental problems.

[16] ROBERT C. ELLICKSON, ORDER WITHOUT LAW: HOW NEIGHBORS SETTLE DISPUTES (1991).

[17] *Id.* at 191–206.

[18] Arun Agrawal, *Commons Resources and Institutional Sustainability*, *in* THE DRAMA OF THE COMMONS 41, 56–58 (Elinor Ostrom et al. eds., 2002).

Daniels, have argued that simply using a resource for a long time without running out is not necessarily an appropriate measure of success, since newer resource use practices might be more productive; he gives several examples, including water law in the American West, in which earlier commons management has stifled response to evolutionary change.[19] Even the much-decried enclosure movement in England could serve as an example. The centuries-long custom of scattering individual plots solved problems of distribution, stability, and strategic behavior among the participants in the common fields.[20] But over time and with improved transportation, larger markets, and changes in product values, it appeared that these same fields might be used more productively in other ways, particularly for more modern specialized agriculture. However sympathetic the village communities may have been, one might also ask whether their customary agricultural practices, so helpful in solving some kinds of collective action problems, did not also lock the participants into outdated practices that reduced the capacity for innovation.[21]

The lesson is that localities' or specialized groups' customary practices may be very useful in organizing the affairs of the group, but those customs may exhibit at least the three problems suggested above: hierarchy, externality, and inertia. This is not to say that legal institutions are necessarily free of these problems; after all, just to cite some of the examples above, legal institutions supported coverture, ratified whalers' practices, and even today succumb to gridlock in dealing with western water law. One difference, however, is that legal institutions have built-in procedures for change, and sometimes very rapid change. Courts can repudiate past precedent, and legislatures can undo or prohibit practices that once were allowed. The saga of racially restrictive covenants illustrates this institutional capacity, though it will also point to the persistence of the customary practices beyond their era of legal support.

In this chapter, in discussing racially restrictive residential covenants, I will be examining a set of customary practices that were not local or specialized, but rather generalized through a larger political regime—the type that Blackstone might have called the "custom of the country" or common law. I hope to show

[19] Brigham Daniels, *Emerging Commons and Tragic Institutions*, 37 Envtl. L. 515, 520–22, 541, 554–59 (2007).

[20] Henry E. Smith, *Semicommon Property Rights and Scattering in the Open Fields*, 29 J. Legal Stud. 131 (2000); Donald [Dierdre] McCloskey, *The Persistence of the English Common Field*, *in* European Peasants and Their Markets 73, 113–19 (William N. Parker & Eric L. Jones eds., 1975).

[21] Smith, *supra* note 20, at 160–61; Dan Bogart & Gary Richardson, *Property Rights and Parliament in Industrializing Britain*, 54 J. L. & Econ. 241 (2011); Carl J. Dahlman, The Open Field System and Beyond: A Property Rights Analysis of an Economic Institution 106–08, 167–78 (1980); *cf.* J.M. Neeson, Commoners: Common Right, Enclosure and Social Change in England 1700–1820, 19 (1993) (stressing viability of common field agriculture; social and economic disruption with enclosure).

that the typical problems of local customs can crop up in those much more widespread customary practices. But there are some differences, and residential racial restrictions illustrate two particularly important features that may distinguish general customary practices from more localized customs. First, general customs and law may have a much more reciprocal relationship than is the case with local customs: that is, law builds on general custom and general custom builds on law in a mutually reinforcing pattern. But second, the very generality of a custom may be a factor in an ultimate divergence between law and custom—a reason why a custom comes to be considered dangerous and unacceptable. Nevertheless, despite the intertwining of law and general customs, aspects of general customary practices, like local ones, may live on long after law ceases to support them.

This chapter, however, will not argue that legal recognition of general custom is always or even often pathological. I use the example of racial covenants only as a cautionary tale to warn that customs and norms themselves are not necessarily benevolent, and that their fixation in law can make them even more objectionable. In the case of racially restrictive covenants, the objections fall into all three rubrics of hierarchy, externality, and inertia.

III. Early Days of Racial Residential Restrictions—Weak Customs, Uncertain Law

When looking to the past, one finds an ambiguous picture of white Americans' views and customs about residing near people of other races. Enslaved Africans arrived almost with the first European settlers in North America; during the long years of slavery, white slave owners in the countryside lived near their African American slaves, albeit generally in very different kinds of quarters, as slave quarters were generally rude shacks or barracks. Perhaps more surprisingly, in urban areas too in those years, people of different races in in the United States often lived close by one another.[22] In one pattern both before and after the abolition of slavery, servants and service personnel commonly lived near their white employers. In Washington, DC, for example, wealthy white homeowners built and lived in the big houses facing the streets, while their Black servants occupied the ally houses out back, a pattern that lasted well into the twentieth century.[23] In another common pattern among much poorer persons, free Blacks lived in the same neighborhoods with some whites, although those neighborhoods were often in the most blighted sections of the city, as in

22 Jeannine Bell, Hate Thy Neighbor: Move-In Violence and the Persistence of Racial Segregation in American Housing 11–13 (2013).

23 Chris Myers Asch & George Derek Musgrove, Chocolate City: A History of Race and Democracy in the Nation's Capital 179–80, 253–55 (2017).

the notorious and polyglot Five Points area in New York, which housed all kinds of new arrivals and others with little wealth and few options.[24] In something of a contrast, Chinese immigrants in San Francisco and elsewhere clustered into communities of their own, in no small part to escape the hatred and attacks of white residents.[25] Indeed, one might speculate that local "Chinatowns" could have accustomed white Americans to think that persons of other races should live in separate areas.[26]

If there was any customary practice running through these patterns, it was thoroughly *racist* but not necessarily or even frequently *segregationist*. To be sure, many white people could live peaceably near people of other races, but generally only so long as social and class distinctions were obvious to all. This pattern was particularly true in the South, where it was clearly understood, even long after the Civil War, that African Americans could not possibly claim social equality with whites.[27] Where social distinctions were not so clear, however, white residents put more effort into physical segregation. In a chilling early nineteenth-century preview of what would later be called "move-in violence," when an African American schoolteacher in Boston considered moving to a better neighborhood, the white neighbors vowed either to drive her out or to tear down the house.[28]

In the last years of the nineteenth century, greater urbanization muddied previously familiar relations and well-understood social distinctions, and some white property owners turned to legal means to initiate or enforce residential segregation. A few white owners tried to use nuisance law to keep out Black neighbors, but even Southern courts rejected the argument that a person could be a nuisance simply because of his or her race.[29]

But another potential legal device emerged in the nineteenth century: covenants "running with the land." These covenants appeared first in the context of leases, aimed at assuring that rights and obligations of landlords and tenants would continue even if new parties took over a leasehold or underlying property. American property owners began to deploy running covenants in the context of sales as well, and some white owners used these relatively new

[24] Gilbert Osofsky, Harlem: The Making of a Ghetto, Negro New York *1890–1930*, 9–12 (2d ed., 1971).

[25] Ronald Takaki, Strangers from a Different Shore 115–18 (rev. ed. 1998).

[26] This was the view of Robert C. Weaver, The Negro Ghetto 22 (1948).

[27] Thomas Lee Philpott, The Slum and the Ghetto: Neighborhood Deterioration and Middle-Class Reform, Chicago 1880–1930, 119 (1978).

[28] Leon Litwak, North of Slavery: The Negro in the Free States, 1790–1860, 169–70 (1961). For "move-in violence," *see* Bell, *supra* note 22.

[29] Rachel D. Godsil, *Race Nuisance: The Politics of Law in the Jim Crow Era*, 105 Mich. L. Rev. 505 (2006); Richard R.W. Brooks & Carol M. Rose, Saving the Neighborhood: Racially Restrictive Covenants, Law, and Social Norms 31–34 (2013).

instruments not only to control land uses of given properties but also to prevent sale or occupancy by unwanted racial groups.[30]

Like covenants generally in this later nineteenth century era, racial covenants initially affected only single lots or small numbers of residences in a handful of new developments. African Americans were to become the dominating targets, but in West Coast cities, covenants against Asians appeared even earlier. One of these was a rather crude single-lot restriction in San Francisco, prohibiting occupancy of the property by "Chinamen." This covenant was challenged in federal court in the case *Gandolfo v. Hartman* (1892), where the trial court invalidated the covenant as a violation of the Fourteenth Amendment's Equal Protection clause, or alternatively, as a violation of the United States' treaty with China.[31] Because of this alternative ground, and because the case was never appealed beyond the trial court level, *Gandolfo* left private racial residential covenants in an ambiguous constitutional status. The conventional interpretation of Fourteenth Amendment rights soon came to require "state action"—rights violation by some governmental entity—and courts in later challenges to private racial restrictions either ignored *Gandolfo* or treated it with barely disguised contempt. Still, the constitutional matter was unclear for a few decades after *Gandolfo*.[32]

Constitutional law was not the only issue, however. Private law also presented potential pitfalls for racial residential covenants in the later nineteenth and early twentieth centuries. Courts in property cases were suspicious of all kinds of running covenants since these devices purported to bind future owners as well as the persons who had created them. The courts often spoke disapprovingly of covenants as "restraints on alienation," and they imposed several tricky limitations aimed at assuring that any running covenants had lasting value to land and that future buyers would know about them.[33]

Thus, at the turn of the nineteenth century to the twentieth, neither customary practice nor law was entirely settled on the issue of residential racial segregation. In spite of widespread racist attitudes, and in spite of the cascade of segregationist laws that followed the Supreme Court's permissive treatment of legal segregation in *Plessy v. Ferguson* (1896),[34] many white persons were still willing to live in the vicinity of racial minorities—but generally only when the latter were clearly marked as inferiors.

Both custom and law came into sharper focus in the first decades of the twentieth century, however, as earlier urbanization trends gained momentum.

[30] Maureen E. Brady, *Turning Neighbors into Nuisances*, 134 Harv. L. Rev. 1611, 1620–24, 1647 (2021).

[31] Gandolfo v. Hartman, 49 F. 181 (Cir. Ct. S.D. Cal. 1892).

[32] Brooks & Rose, *supra* note 29, at 51–54.

[33] *Id.* at 50–62, 78–93.

[34] Plessy v. Ferguson, 163 U.S. 537 (1896).

Until that time, the vast majority of African Americans had lived in the rural South, first in slave quarters and later, for many, in whatever kind of farm hovels they could piece together. But at the turn of the century, increasing numbers of African Americans migrated to cities to escape the brutal racial oppression of the Southern countryside. In the early years of this "great migration," some went to Southern cities, but many also flooded into urban areas in the Midwest and Northeast, following lines of latitude to Washington, DC, Baltimore, and New York; or to St. Louis and Chicago and slightly later Detroit. Still later waves went to Los Angeles, Oakland, and Seattle.[35]

Quite aside from their initial poverty and the rural manners of many, these new migrants were not known personally to white urban residents, and they were not under white domination, as they had been in the rural South. But greater minority autonomy seemed to stoke white animosity. Symptomatic of the changes in white attitudes was a case in Illinois about a final resting place: a Chicago cemetery corporation had changed its burial policy to white-only in 1907, and thereafter claimed that it could not bury a deceased African American—whose family members were already interred there—because the white customers would "kick" too much.[36] Meanwhile, racial tensions boiled over in several cities in the early 1900s. Whether due to a fear of violence or not, more white citizens began to look for ways to keep themselves separated from the influx of African American migrants.

One can trace an emerging general customary norm of residential segregation to these decades, and an effort to engage the law was very much entwined with that larger evolving norm, albeit with mixed results. Nuisance law had proved unavailing, but Baltimore passed a racial zoning ordinance in 1910, and other cities followed. Somewhat surprisingly, however, given its approval of other segregation laws in the then-recent past, the Supreme Court in *Buchanan v. Warley* (1917) struck down Louisville, Kentucky's racial zoning as a violation of the Fourteenth Amendment; apparently racial zoning trenched too deeply on individuals' right to buy and sell property.[37] By ruling out zoning, *Buchanan* marked a watershed in the still-uncertain relationship between law and custom. While general customary norms were building among white persons to favor residential segregation, earlier cases on nuisance law, together with *Buchanan*'s ruling against governmentally enforced racial zoning, substantially narrowed the possibilities for legal enforcement of residential segregation.

[35] Louise Venable Kennedy, The Negro Peasant Turns Cityward 9, 29 (1930); *see also* Isabel Wilkerson, The Warmth of Other Suns: The Epic Story of America's Great Migration (2010).

[36] People ex rel. Gaskill v. Forest Home Cemetery Co., 101 N.E. 219, 220 (Ill. 1913).

[37] 245 U.S. 60 (1917). The Court did not rely on equal protection but rather on substantive due process, implicitly distinguishing property ownership from other subjects in which the Court upheld segregation.

Meanwhile events outside the law, notably violence or threats of violence, showed ever-sharper white rejection of racial mixing. In Chicago, when the Black real estate entrepreneur Jesse Binga attempted to move to then-all-white Hyde Park, his house was bombed seven times.[38] Close-knit immigrant communities in urban areas were especially known for forcefully rejecting any impending influxes of African Americans. Meanwhile, in towns all over the Midwest, signs informed African Americans that they should not let the sun set on them there.[39] Two years after the *Buchanan* case, an especially vicious race riot broke out in Chicago, initiated when a Black youth drifted into a lakefront beach area that white people thought was theirs alone. The riot raged on for ten days, leaving thirty-eight deaths and much destruction, evidently convincing many residents that white and Black persons could not share the same space.[40]

The Chicago riots may have fixed white people's view that it was dangerous to live near African Americans. But what was to be done? For those who eschewed violence, could law play a role, now that neither public law (in zoning) nor undifferentiated private law (in nuisance) were available legal levers? What about more explicit private law? The Supreme Court's vehement defense of property in *Buchanan* suggested that one legal tactic might remain, even though it was relatively narrow: the property law device of residential restrictive covenants, which had been sporadically deployed in the nineteenth century but saw sharply increasing use after 1900. Could race be added to residential covenants? The test was to come in newly emerging types of real estate development.

Prior to 1900, residential areas grew up largely lot-by-lot, but with the turn of the century, high-end "community builders" began to buy up large areas in outlying urban areas or just outside city boundaries; they then divided the land into individual lots, installed streets and infrastructure, and invited new residents to build their own houses. To assure all buyers that a given subdivision would retain the character intended for it, these "high class" developers expanded covenants as legal devices, creating packages of covenants in the form of deed restrictions. The restrictions could be highly specific: they usually limited construction to single-family residences, required certain setbacks and building styles, and imposed limitations on outbuildings, types of decoration, and plantings; they sometimes designated minimum construction costs, and they often added other regulations relating to appearance and upkeep.[41] By around 1915, yet another

[38] DOUGLAS S. MASSEY & NANCY A. DENTON, AMERICAN APARTHEID: SEGREGATION AND THE MAKING OF THE UNDERCLASS 35 (1993).

[39] JAMES W. LOEWEN, SUNDOWN TOWNS: A HIDDEN DIMENSION OF AMERICAN RACISM (2005).

[40] MASSEY & DENTON, *supra* note 38, at 26–35; STEVEN GRANT MEYER, AS LONG AS THEY DON'T MOVE NEXT DOOR: SEGREGATION AND RACIAL CONFLICT IN AMERICAN NEIGHBORHOODS 30–36 (2000).

[41] MARC A. WEISS, THE RISE OF THE COMMUNITY BUILDERS: THE AMERICAN REAL ESTATE INDUSTRY AND URBAN LAND PLANNING 45–46 (1987).

covenant requirement appeared in these packages: residences in the new communities could not be sold to or used by members of the "African or Negro race," or more generally, those who were not "Caucasian."[42]

Covenants restricting race soon spread beyond well-to-do subdivisions and filtered into more middle-class developments. Moreover, a different type of racial covenant emerged in older and often less upscale urban white neighborhoods, many not far distant from areas of African American expansion.[43] These white urban neighborhoods were already built out, so that their residents could no longer avail themselves of restrictions written into the initial deeds. But by the 1920s, enterprising individuals and "neighborhood improvement associations" began to circulate petitions through which groups of owners promised for themselves and their "heirs and assigns" not to sell or rent to African Americans.[44]

In close-knit urban ethnic neighborhoods, a credible threat of violence put up a virtual fence to keep out other minorities; these neighborhoods did not bother with restrictive covenants.[45] But in looser-knit but respectable middle-class white neighborhoods, racial covenants, whether included in a broader package of subdivision controls or gathered among neighbors in single-purpose petitions, provided a relatively safe, civilized, and ostensibly legal way to maintain segregation without resorting to violence. Indeed, the appearance of legality was an essential element in the burgeoning growth of racially restrictive covenants.[46]

Through racial covenants, legal institutions could respond to and reinforce an emergent custom of residential segregation, in a manner that did not depend on violence in close-knit communities. But initially, this legal response, too, was hesitant. With new real estate practices, covenants running with the land themselves were becoming increasingly common and evolving into quite complicated forms. But could the evolution of the covenant form add the critical layer of *racial* restriction? Private law constrained covenants of any sort that attempted to bind future owners simply because they bought a particular piece of property. One private law doctrine required that covenants "touch and concern land," whereas racial covenants applied to personal characteristics rather than land uses. Another worrisome property doctrine required that any restraints on alienation be "reasonable," among other things meaning that they not apply to large swaths of people. Then there was the messy business of constitutional constraints, not so clear in the early twentieth century. The old *Gandolfo* case had ruled that

42 *Id.*; Robert M. Fogelson, Bourgeois Nightmares: Suburbia 1870–1930, 95–103 (2005); Helen Monchow, The Use of Deed Restrictions in Subdivision Development 47–50 (1928).

43 Colin Gordon, *Dividing the City: Race-Restrictive Covenants and the Architecture of Segregation in St. Louis*, J. Urban Hist. 1 (online, May 26, 2021), at 10.

44 Brooks & Rose, *supra* note 29, at 80–83, 106–07; Massey & Denton, *supra* note 38, at 35.

45 Rose Helper, Racial Policies and Practices of Real Estate Brokers 74 (1969).

46 Brooks & Rose, *supra* note 29, at 17; Philpott, *supra* note 27, at 185, 189–91.

racial covenants violated the Fourteenth Amendment, even though it had given an alternative ground for the ruling, and even though it was only a district court opinion that was never ratified by a higher court.[47]

Despite these uncertainties, however, Louisiana's highest court approved racially restrictive covenants in a 1915 case.[48] Two years later, the US Supreme Court's rejection of racial zoning in *Buchanan v. Warley* raised hopes among some, and fears among others, that racial covenants would go the way of racial zoning as a violation of the Fourteenth Amendment. But this did not occur. Several state supreme courts soon followed Louisiana's lead, ruling that the Fourteenth Amendment applied only to acts by governmental agents or bodies—the already-familiar "state action" doctrine—whereas, they said, racial covenants were created by private parties and hence outside the scope of the amendment.

Private property law constraints on covenants too were more or less brushed aside in these cases. California's Supreme Court put up a show of taking property law traditions seriously, ruling in 1918 that a racial prohibition on *sales* was an unreasonable restraint on alienation—but then held that a racial prohibition on *use* was acceptable.[49] This meant that a racial covenant could not stop an African American from buying a house—but the buyer could not then live in that house. Other influential state Supreme Court decisions around the same time came from Missouri and Michigan, both giving considerable leeway to racial restrictions. Michigan's court followed California in prohibiting racial restrictions against sales but not those against use, while Missouri's Supreme Court permitted racial restrictions on both sale and use.[50]

IV. Racial Covenants Take Hold as Custom—and Law

These legal developments in the state courts played out over the backdrop of newly evolving real estate practices, including not only the new subdivision developments but also a corresponding professionalization of the real estate industry. As the various elements of that industry became increasingly organized and specialized, financial institutions joined developers and brokers in promoting racial restrictions that would shield their white clients from what they saw as a threat to property values.[51] Within a dozen years after 1915, efforts to keep white neighborhoods segregated clearly had become a customary practice among these professionals, whether through covenants or professional practice.

[47] BROOKS & ROSE, *supra* note 22, at 51–52, 56–62, 87–91.
[48] Queensborough Land Co. v. Cazeaux, 60 So. 641 (La. 1915).
[49] Los Angeles Inv. Co. v. Gary, 186 P. 596 (Cal. 1919).
[50] Porter v. Barrett, 296 N.W. 532 (Mich. 1925); Koehler v. Rowland, 205 S.W. 217 (Mo. 1918).
[51] WEISS, *supra* note 41, at 19–46.

By the early 1920s, the developers of Palos Verdes Estates in Los Angeles referred to racial covenants as part of the "usual restrictions." Meanwhile, the newly formed National Association of Real Estate Boards (NAREB) included in its 1924 statement of Realtor Ethics the provision that a real estate broker should not introduce into a neighborhood "members of any race or nationality ... whose presence will clearly be detrimental to property values. ..."[52]

The national realtors' organization apologized for this proviso in 2020,[53] but it is worth repeating that in 1924 and decades thereafter, this directive was described as an *ethical* responsibility for real estate brokers. White purchasers were the chief clientele for these real estate professionals, and the professionals regarded it as a duty to maintain the property values of their customers. One well-known real estate text drew the obvious conclusion for African Americans: they "must recognize the economic disturbance which their presence in a white neighborhood causes" and forego expanding beyond their own "established district[s]."[54]

One sees in these developments a reciprocal reinforcement between law and practice, perhaps most clearly visible in a 1926 case in the Supreme Court, together with its aftermath. In *Corrigan v. Buckley*, the Court declined to review a lower court ruling upholding a racial covenant in the District of Columbia, stating that there was no constitutional basis for jurisdiction under either the Fifth or the Fourteenth Amendment.[55] Although the ruling was merely jurisdictional, it seemed to settle the view that racial covenants were legal as private matters rather than state action, and thus not subject to the Fourteenth Amendment's requirement of equal treatment. Real estate professionals exulted that racial covenants were now "constitution proof," while NAREB came out with a model covenant by petition that was based on *Corrigan*'s restrictions, and the Chicago Real Estate Board added a pamphlet entitled "Choose Your Neighbors."[56]

During these years, an emergent general custom of residential segregation thus birthed a secondary customary practice: the deployment of racial covenants to enforce segregation legally both in new developments and in older white neighborhoods. As constitutional concerns faded, private law constraints on racial covenants too fell away, receiving at most perfunctory and dismissive

[52] FOGELSON, *supra* note 42, at 15 ("usual restrictions"); HELPER, *supra* note 45, at 201, 221 (NAREB code). NAREB is now the National Association of Realtors (NAR); "realtor" is a trademarked name.

[53] *NAR Apologizes for Housing Discrimination*, THE REAL DEAL: REAL ESTATE NEWS, November 20, 2020, available at https://therealdeal.com/national/2020/11/20/national-association-of-realtors-apologizes-for-housing-discrimination/.

[54] STANLEY L. MCMICHAEL & ROBERT F. BINGHAM, CITY GROWTH AND VALUES 182 (1923).

[55] Corrigan v. Buckley, 271 U.S. 323 (1926).

[56] BROOKS & ROSE, *supra* note 29, at 121.

notice. The *Corrigan* case involved a covenant by petition, one of those that were gathered among neighbors along the block, and it thus lacked the formal ex ante relationship of landlord-tenant or buyer-seller that had earlier been required of running covenants. In *Corrigan* itself, the defending seller was one of the original signers, but other cases enforced petition covenants against successor parties, without questioning whether the covenants met the private law requirements to run to later owners who had not personally agreed. Over the next few years, racial covenants by petition, whatever their formal failures, were uniformly enforced by injunction so long as they were recorded, on the theory from equity jurisprudence that even remote parties knew or should know about matters of record. Similarly, courts smoothly sidelined any references to the private law doctrines that cabined restraints on alienation.[57]

So acceptable had racial covenants become that by 1927, the Michigan Supreme Court could enforce residential racial exclusion as customary practice even under a covenant that made no mention of race, but rather barred "persons whose ownership or occupancy would be injurious to the locality." The court ruled that this provision could properly be read as excluding an African American couple, since this had been the long-standing practice and understanding in the subdivision, adding that evidence showed that the couple's presence would "materially diminish the value of the neighboring property."[58] A few years later, the Maryland Supreme Court similarly implied that racial covenants had become the legal instantiation of residential segregation. It upheld a residential racial covenant with the remark that after the Supreme Court's *Buchanan* case had overturned racial zoning—inexplicably in the Maryland court's view—"all agree [that] something ought to be done."[59]

By the early 1930s, then, real estate practitioners routinely deployed racial covenants in new subdivisions, and they routinely encouraged white neighbors in existing homes to create these covenants by petition—and the courts routinely upheld them. The next chapter in the emergence of racial restrictions came from what may seem an unlikely source: Franklin Roosevelt's New Deal, beginning in 1933.

One of the Roosevelt administration's early priorities was to revive the flagging banking system and with it the moribund housing industry. Many figures from the newly professionalizing real estate industry joined the administration, and they brought with them their views about the negative impact of racial mixing on property values. One early New Deal measure was the creation of the Homeowners Loan Corporation or HOLC, which was tasked with making

57 For example, Meade v. Dennistone, 196 A.330 (Md. 1938).
58 Schulte v. Starks, 213 N.W. 102 (Mich. 1927).
59 Meade v. Dennistone, *supra* note 57, at 333.

direct mortgage loans to homeowners. As part of its assessment of risk for lending, the HOLC created maps of several cities, assigning the colors green, yellow, and red to different areas, ostensibly based on the level of risk. Minority and transitional neighborhoods were generally colored red for high risk, giving rise over time to the nickname "redlining" for any practice that denied services to minority areas.[60]

The HOLC itself did lend in minority areas, but the agency that ultimately displaced it, the Federal Housing Administration (FHA), was much more restrictive.[61] The FHA was created in 1934; it did not make loans directly, but instead insured banks against defaults on homeowner mortgages. Actual defaults would of course use up FHA funds and diminish the availability of FHA insurance and ultimately mortgage lending, and so the FHA too had concerns about the riskiness of borrowers. Among those concerns was the ever-growing conventional view that racial mixing in a neighborhood would pose a threat to property values. The FHA's *Underwriting Manual* listed racial covenants among the positive features that assessors should seek out when they determined the eligibility of new housing for FHA mortgage insurance. In turn, developers and builders routinely included racial covenants in deeds, sometimes even referring specifically to the FHA guidelines.[62]

By the time that a housing boom began at the end of the Second World War, covenants against African Americans, and Asians too in the West, had become standard practice across the country. In 1944, the American Law Institute (ALI), a prestigious association of jurists, legal academics, and leading attorneys, issued a so-called *Restatement of Property Law*, detailing what were supposed to be the best legal practices in courts across the nation. The ALI's *Restatement* asserted that in American property law, racially restrictive housing covenants were acceptable as "reasonable" restraints on alienation, in spite of their application to a very large segment of the population.[63]

Thus by the mid- to late 1940s, racially restrictive covenants had become a recognized legal device throughout much of the nation, deployed to support a now-pervasive customary norm of residential racial segregation. This general customary norm rested on the widespread belief that integration would undermine housing values, and major legal and governmental institutions amplified this belief. Law and custom reinforced each other to support residential segregation across the states; as Detroit historian Thomas Sugrue wrote,

[60] Brooks & Rose, *supra* note 29, at 108.

[61] Price V. Fishback et al. (Federal Reserve Bank of Chicago Working Paper No 2022-01), *New Evidence on Redlining by Federal Housing Programs in the 1930s*, available at https://papers.ssrn.com/sol3/papers.cfm?abstract_id=4001970.

[62] Brooks & Rose, *supra* note 29, at 108–10.

[63] American Law Institute, Restatement of Property 4, § 406 and cmt. l and m, 2411–12 (1944).

white Americans had come to believe that they had a right to live in segregated neighborhoods, and that this supposed right would be protected by government and by the courts.[64] Leading legal figures and institutions supported that belief.

This is not to say that the racial covenants and residential segregation were universally approved; African American newspapers like the *Chicago Defender* and the *Pittsburgh Courier* had long railed against racial covenants as demeaning and unfair. Indeed, almost since the NAACP's founding, its attorneys had fought racial covenants on a constitutional basis, even though to no avail in the courts. Individual attorneys did manage to chip away at covenants, especially those established by neighborhood petitions, using small-potatoes grounds like invalid signatures and failure to include spouses, or on the equitable ground that neighborhood change had made the covenants valueless. But a rhetorical disadvantage of such cases was the implicit acknowledgment that more artfully written racial covenants would have been legal. As to ordinary African Americans looking for housing, a common refrain was that they did not want to be "pioneers"—or worse "law breakers."[65] Thus the victims of housing segregation themselves recognized that racial covenants had become a legally supported practice, however much they detested and sometimes contested these covenants and the larger segregationist practices they enforced.

By the mid- to late 1940s, racially restrictive covenants were widely deployed to shore up an ever-broader customary norm favoring residential racial segregation. As such, they had clearly come to exhibit the critical characteristics that Henry Smith details for customs that may be incorporated into general property law. Residential racial covenants, ubiquitous in their support of residential segregation, were relatively simple (or as Smith would say, "stripped down"), and their function and effects had come to be very widely understood.[66]

The argument of this chapter, however, is that legal incorporation was not simply a one-time event or a one-way street; instead, customary practice influenced legal actors, and legal actors in turn bolstered a wider custom. The unfortunate saga of racial covenants is an especially blatant example of a reciprocal relationship that nurtured and cultivated residential segregation, but once one sees it here, one can see similar reciprocal relationship of law and custom in many other areas. Most auto drivers drive on the right in the United States and many other countries. Traffic laws then require it. Auto manufacturers then

[64] Thomas J. Sugrue, *Crabgrass Politics: Race, Rights, and the Reaction against Liberalism in the Urban North, 1940–1964*, 82 J. Amer. Hist. 551, 564 (1995).

[65] Clement E. Vose, Caucasians Only: The Supreme Court, the NAACP, and the Restrictive Covenant Cases (1959); Brooks & Rose, *supra* note 29, at 52–55, 116–17, 126–31; Helper, *supra* note 45, at 90 ("pioneer"); St. Clair Drake & Horace R. Cayton, Black Metropolis: A Study of Negro Life in a Northern City 199 (1945) ("law breaker").

[66] Henry E. Smith, *Community and Custom in Property*, 10 Theoret. Inquiries in Law 5, 20, 22–23 (2009).

produce cars that facilitate driving on the right. Drivers then take the right lane all the time. A mirror image occurs in countries where custom, reinforced by law, induces drivers to take the left lane.

But with respect to racially restrictive covenants, despite the important role of law and government in furthering a general pattern of residential segregation, law and custom began to diverge. This occurred around the same time that the ALI's imprimatur clearly brought racial covenants into the general legal canon. Paradoxically enough, the very ubiquity and seeming acceptability of racial covenants contributed to their downfall.

V. Law Corrals Custom, Custom Slips under the Rails

By the end of the Second World War, several factors converged to undermine what had seemed previously to have become almost unassailable legal support for racial covenants. In the mid-1940s, several judges, including the distinguished Roger Traynor of the California Supreme Court and Henry Edgerton on the DC Circuit, wrote minority opinions reflecting the NAACP's argument that judges should consider the larger social costs of upholding the residential racial covenants that spread across wide swaths of urban areas. Fresh reminders of Nazi racism let opponents of racial covenants beam an especially harsh light on the damage done by a now-pervasive pattern of segregation at home, especially when African American and Asian veterans could not find housing outside ghetto conditions. Foreign policy officials worried that racial covenants were ripe fodder for growing Cold War propaganda touting the hypocrisy of America democracy.[67]

Amidst these rumblings of a change in the legal assessment of racial covenants, in 1948 the US Supreme Court took up the issue. Whatever the omens, real estate interests thought that the existing law was on their side in support of racial residential covenants. But instead, the case illustrated the ability of legal institutions to make a sharp break. Fortified by a barrage of amicus briefs from civil rights organizations as well as the Department of Justice—itself influenced by State Department concerns over America's Cold War image—the Court decided in *Shelley v. Kraemer* that judicial enforcement of racially restrictive covenants was state action after all, despite covenants' origin in private agreements. As state action, said the Court, judicial enforcement was unconstitutional under the Fourteenth Amendment's Equal Protection clause.[68]

[67] VOSE, *supra* note 65, at 64–68, 163–210; BROOKS & ROSE, *supra* note 29, at 136–39, Fairchild v. Raines, 151 P.2d 260, 267 (Traynor conc. CA 1944); Mays v. Burgess. 147 F.2d 260 (Edgerton diss. DC 1945).

[68] 334 U.S 1. (1948).

Shelley was controversial among lawyers not only because of its break with most existing precedent, but also because of its breadth. Indeed, the ruling appeared to obliterate the distinction between private and governmental action, thus threatening to impose constitutional constraints on such ordinary private law matters as contracts, torts, and wills. This extraordinary sweep turned out to be a weakness over a longer run, however, and *Shelley* was not to have much impact as precedent for subsequent law. Richard Brooks and I have argued that *Shelley* might have proved a much stronger precedent if it had focused on *general custom* as a version of state action, treating covenants as legal enforcers of widespread customary practices of segregation. But neither our view nor other limiting strategies have revived *Shelley* as much more than a rhetorical legal precedent.[69] Nevertheless, however clumsily, *Shelley* did show that legal institutions can police their own creations. Even though many courts and administrators had long and eagerly embraced racial covenants, these widely accepted and hitherto-legal racial covenants were still subject to the Supreme Court's higher-level legal scrutiny.

Even so, much of the larger customary practice of residential segregation itself lingered past *Shelley*'s legal policing of covenants. Some commentators hoped that *Shelley*'s blow to racially restrictive covenants would bring about the end of residential segregation as well. It was not to be. For a time, many real estate professionals thought that *Shelley* could be overturned, or at least that it might be undone by several different workarounds. But in 1953, the Supreme Court ruled in *Barrows v. Jackson* against one of these workarounds—that is, suits for damages against covenant-breaking white sellers rather than injunctions against minority buyers.[70]

After *Barrows*, racial covenants entered a twilight zone in which they were *legal* but *not legally enforceable*. New racial covenants tapered off, but references to older racial covenants still appeared in title documents. More important, the larger customary practice of residential segregation had become too entrenched to vanish. Opportunistic "blockbuster" real estate entrepreneurs made a business of transitioning urban neighborhoods from white to minority. They introduced a few minority members into white neighborhoods, then bought up white-owned properties at panic prices, and finally sold at high prices to other minority buyers while the white former owners fled to the suburbs—a process that resegregated metropolitan areas into minorities at the center and whites in the suburbs. Blockbusters' terrible reputation has seen some revision in recent years, because to their credit, these brokers did increase housing opportunities

[69] Brooks & Rose, *supra* note 29, at 140–45, 160–66.

[70] Barrows v. Jackson, 346 U.S. 249 (1953).

for minorities,[71] but the cost was continued if reconfigured housing segregation along with greater white fear of integration. For decades, most other real estate brokers eschewed blockbusting practices as unethical, and instead they "steered" customers to neighborhoods of the customers' own race. As even one advocate of housing desegregation acknowledged in the early 1960s, the supposedly reputable brokers were probably only trying to make their customers comfortable.[72]

Finally, the Fair Housing Act of 1968 underscored the breach between custom and law, outlawing not only racially restrictive covenants but blockbusting and steering as well, along with several other real estate practices that supported housing segregation.[73] Hereafter, the wider custom of racially segregated housing has had little explicit legal support, and increasing numbers of legal obstacles.

Nevertheless, the wider custom of residential segregation has persisted, albeit gradually softening in many cities and at least some suburbs. Ostensibly neutral legal devices have arguably taken the place of racial restrictions—for example, large lot or "exclusionary" zoning on the public side, and perhaps golf course communities or other expensive housing amenities on the private side.[74] Attitudes left over from once-legal housing discrimination still appear in what would appear to be unconscious decisions, such as the low-ball appraisals given to houses owned by African Americans,[75] not to speak of the continuing and dispiriting instances of opposition to integration and even move-in violence.[76]

What role did racially restrictive covenants play in the continued if now weaker pattern of residential segregation? These covenants were prevalent only for a forty-year period, roughly between 1915 and 1955, but they left behind a stout and widespread informal customary norm of residential segregation that is diminishing only somewhat today. Several factors described earlier in this chapter were at play: First, from the outset, racial covenants piggybacked on other trends, particularly the ever-growing use of deed restrictions in new developments, along with the increasing professionalization of real estate practice. Racial covenants became part of a standard package of restrictions, promoted by real estate professionals whose chief customer base was white, and who thought that it was their duty to protect those customers' property values. Second, racial covenants were picked up by governmental as well as private

[71] Brooks & Rose, *supra* note 29, at 135–36,189–90, 208–09; Dmitri Melhorn, *A Requiem for Blockbusting: Law, Economics, and Race-Based Real Estate Speculation*, 67 Fordham L. Rev. 1145 (1998).

[72] US Commission on Civil Rights (1962) *Hearings: Housing Washington* 416 (testimony of Marvin Caplan).

[73] 42 U.S. Code Secs. 3601–19.

[74] Lior Jacob Strahilevitz, *Exclusionary Amenities in Residential Communities*, 92 Va. L. Rev. 437 (2006).

[75] Alexandria Burris, *Black Homeowner Had a White Friend Stand In for 3rd Appraisal. Her Home Value Doubled*, Indianapolis Star, May 16, 2021, 1.

[76] Bell, *supra* note 22.

financial agencies, all of which deployed them as part of their efforts to stabilize housing values. These factors solidified a widespread belief—even what came to be called a self-fulfilling prophecy—that housing integration would undermine property values.[77]

Another and perhaps more subtle factor was a distinction between types of racial covenants, a distinction that would lead to housing segregation on a very wide scale. Racial covenants structured as deed restrictions in new subdivisions were formally correct, and they were relatively understated insofar as they were simply one of several constraints on new owners. The covenants created by neighborhood petitions, on the other hand, were aimed at race and race alone. Aside from their overtly discriminatory purpose, the petition covenants were comparatively shaky legally as well.[78] Moreover, as historian Colin Gordon has observed in the case of St. Louis, the covenants by petition were most prevalent in older urban neighborhoods already in the path of minority expansion—indeed in areas that colored red on the 1930s housing agency maps—unlike the newer developments further out.[79]

Because of this combination—critical location together with frequent formal flaws—these petition-based covenants were easier targets for minority lawyers and their clients than were the covenants in new subdivisions. As each set of petition covenants fell, it created a new wave of panic in the next white neighborhood, together with flight to the all-white suburbs. The result was a pattern of residential segregation on the scale of whole jurisdictions, with white residents in the suburbs and minorities in central cities, often with limited economic opportunity, political influence, or access to adequate public services.[80]

Thus the past legality of racial covenants cast a shadow over the future, leaving behind a general informal custom of residential segregation even after legal support faded away. It is a shadow that is only beginning to lighten in the present day.

VI. Conclusion

The saga of racially restrictive covenants has some lessons for the relationship between widespread customs and law—lessons that one might not expect from Blackstone's offhand comment that general customs become the common law.

First, widespread customs can have some of the same major pathologies that may be present in local customs, that is, hierarchy, externality, and inertia. In the

[77] CHARLES ABRAMS, FORBIDDEN NEIGHBORS: A STUDY OF PREJUDICE IN HOUSING 173 (1955).

[78] BROOKS & ROSE, *supra* note 29, at 82–84.

[79] COLIN GORDON, PATCHWORK APARTHEID: PRIVATE RESTRICTION, RACIAL SEGREGATION, AND URBAN INEQUALITY 50 (2023).

[80] *Id.* at 115.

case of racially restrictive covenants, the most obvious was their reinforcement of a racial hierarchy. Equally obvious were the negative externalities that racial covenants imposed on ghettoized minorities, reducing minority opportunities not only for housing but also for employment and public services that were available to white residents. The inertia of racial covenants has been most discernable in the continued fears that white residents have about loss of property value with integration.

Second, law can play a significant role in magnifying embryonic practices to the point of general custom. When confronted with racial covenants, initially a newly minted device to segregate residential areas, judges and administrative bodies gave a green light to successive expansions of prior covenant law. Legal acceptability encouraged real estate professionals to deploy these covenants for their chief clientele, that is, white residents, while discouraging minorities from seeking housing where they would have to play the role of "pioneers."

But third, the arc of racial covenants contradicted the airy Blackstonian comment that universal custom itself is law. Instead, the ubiquity of racial covenants ultimately drew legal scrutiny and opened a breach between law and custom. Racial covenants showed that the more general a custom becomes, the more it becomes inescapable but also more vulnerable. If the custom causes damage, a wider range causes even more, and inescapable damage draws observation, criticism, and demand for reform. A few scattered discriminatory housing projects, without more, would have seemed a distasteful oddity, but ubiquitous discrimination became a matter of social, economic, and political concern. Moreover, as one sees in the case of racial covenants, insofar as a general custom takes on the instruments of law, it also enters a different realm, one in which formal institutions and criteria take on new relevance. Legal institutions initially narrowed the enforcement of residential segregation to racial covenants, ruling out nuisance and zoning. Greater reliance on racial covenants certainly increased their reach over time, but that same increased reach made them more susceptible to legal policing. *Shelley v. Kraemer* may have been an awkward case of legal scrutiny, but it was predictable that both constitutional law and property law would eventually come to bear more heavily on racial covenants precisely because they were so pervasive.

By now, the breach is complete between law and racial covenants. But this leads to the fourth point: the divergence of law from custom does not necessarily erase customary practice. This is well-known in the case of local customs.[81] But it is also true of more general customary practices, even extreme ones. Honor killings are an example: despite relatively recent illegality, they are still

[81] Ellickson, *supra* note 16; Shitong Qiao, Chinese Small Property: The Co-Evolution of Law and Social Norms (2018).

widespread in some parts of the world, leading to murders that one might compare to Shirley Jackson's story of the annual village lottery.

Jackson's customary lottery was fictional, local, presumably illegal, and as far as we know, never actually in existence. Racial covenants promoted a custom of housing discrimination that was in many ways a contrasting case to Jackson's lottery: real, increasingly widespread, and for a time legally acceptable. Over time, residential segregation became a general custom that survived even when legal enforcement was no longer available.

This chapter does not mean to assert that legality alone created residential segregation in the United States, but legality did matter. Legal enforceability empowered racial covenants, and thus powerfully reinforced an emergent meta-custom of residential segregation—one that has been so difficult to overcome. Without legal racial covenants, Americans of different races would undoubtedly have come into conflict over residential uses; but for a few critical decades, the legal acceptance of racial covenants helped to solidify a wider customary practice of segregation, and with it, the loss of an earlier opportunity to learn that property values need not—and should not—be linked to race.

The saga of racially restrictive covenants thus suggests caution about the Blackstonian view that general custom is law. Instead, it suggests that law has its own structure and concerns, and even if law tolerates or even reinforces a general custom for a time, it may ultimately reject the general custom as sharply as the local one. Nevertheless, the saga also suggests that law is not all-powerful in the face of contrary custom; general customs like local ones may have considerable inertia, particularly those that may once have been accepted. On a happier note, however, the reversal of legal support for racial covenants does appear to have gradually altered customary norms favoring housing segregation, and even to have undermined patterns of residential segregation itself. One may hope that the remaining elements of those patterns continue to dwindle into nonexistence.

12

The Threat and Promise of Collateral Benefits for Private Law's Coherence

*Zoë Sinel**

I. Introduction

The presence of interstitial concepts in private law—concepts that connect, surround, and demarcate core private law doctrines—supports claims that private law forms a coherent domain. The most promising place to look for interstitial private law phenomena is the law of civil remedies. Remedial doctrines like mitigation, remoteness, and causation traverse the more bounded or modular parts of private law. Indeed, in contrast to the subject silos of property, tort, and contract that make up the traditional first-year law curriculum, the upper-year course in remedies boldly claims to offer a picture of private law's unity and consistency as it tackles doctrines that apply to all private law causes of action.

Of all the boundary-crossing remedial doctrines, the one with the largest ambit is the compensatory principle, encapsulated in the Latin maxim *restitutio in integrum*, applying whenever money is awarded in response to losses suffered due to a tort or a breach of contract. According to this principle, the aim of compensatory damages is to restore the plaintiff to her original position. In the law of tort, this means putting the plaintiff in the position she occupied before the tort; in the law of contract, this means putting the plaintiff in the position she would have been in had the contract been performed. Implicit in the principle of *restitutio in integrum* is the thought that the plaintiff should be made neither *worse* nor *better* off consequent a remedial response to a tort or breach of contract; her world should simply be restored. This operation of *restitutio in integrum* is what John Gardner refers to as the "built-in conservative feature" shared by the law of torts and the law of contracts in their damages assessments: both "aim to put the plaintiff's life back on its previous track."[1] Private law, we might say, is united by

* Thank you to Joanna Langille, Anne Schuurman, participants at the University of Western Ontario's Faculty Workshop, and participants at the Interstitial Private Law Workshop for their helpful comments on earlier drafts. I am particularly grateful to Paul Miller and Henry Smith for their insightful feedback.

[1] John Gardner, From Personal Life to Private Law 165 (2018).

Zoë Sinel, *The Threat and Promise of Collateral Benefits for Private Law's Coherence* In: *Interstitial Private Law*. Edited by: Samuel L. Bray, John C.P. Goldberg, Paul B. Miller, and Henry E. Smith, Oxford University Press.
 DOI: 10.1093/oso/9780197783627.003.0012

virtue of its remedial role in erasing the consequences of private injustices by returning parties to their ex ante positions, making it as if the tort never occurred or the contract was never breached.

Despite its near universality in private law, the compensatory principle's operation is not without its skeptics. Some argue that it is inconceivable that a payment of money can really make it as if a plaintiff had never suffered a personal injury.[2] Others claim that contract law's expectation measure restores a plaintiff to a better position than she was in before the breach by giving her something she did not yet have.[3] And remedial doctrines relating to the likelihood of a future loss occurring that is, doctrines that permit a court to alter a lump sum award to adjust for future contingencies, both positive and negative—necessarily leave a plaintiff either over- or undercompensated.[4]

But this is not a chapter about these usual doubts, nor is it a chapter directly on the compensation principle itself. Rather, it takes as its object an often ignored, but nonetheless significant, doctrine regarding the treatment of collateral benefits,[5] what is known in the United States as the collateral source rule,[6] in England as the collateral recovery rule,[7] and in Canada as the collateral benefits rule.[8] This rule governs the potential deductibility of benefits received by the plaintiff from sources other than the defendant.[9] I will argue that it is this rule that is the true interstitial remedial principle as it operates at the

[2] Scott Hershovitz, *Treating Wrongs as Wrongs: An Expressive Argument for Tort Law*, 10(2) J. Tort Law 405 (2017).

[3] Lon Fuller & William Perdue, *The Reliance Interest in Contract Damages* (pts. 1 & 2), 46 Yale L.J 52 (1936).

[4] For example, if the unfortunate future loss does occur, the plaintiff will only receive a percentage of what it would take to fully compensate her (that is, if there is a 40 percent chance that she will develop a future negative contingency, she will receive only 40 percent of the total value of that loss), but, if the loss does not occur, then any percentage she receives is a pure windfall (she will receive 40 percent of the value of the future loss that she never ends up suffering). *See* Schrump v. Koot [1977] 18 OR (2d) 337 (CA).

[5] Albert Averbach, *The Collateral Source Rule*, 21 Ohio State L.J. 231 (1960), calling the collateral source rule one of the "most important damage rules." And Richard Lewis has called it "a neglected and yet important area of compensation law," stating that "[t]he questions posed by collateral benefits . . . lie at the heart of any compensation system, and constitute the key to its future direction." (R. Lewis, *Deducting Collateral Benefits from Damages: Principle and Policy* (1998) 18(1), Leg. Stud. 15, 15–16.)

[6] Authorities suggest that the collateral source rule in the United States originated in The Propeller Monticello v. Mollison, 58, 152 (1854); however, the term "collateral source" itself came later in Harding v. Townshend, 43 Vt. 536 (1871).

[7] Shearman v. Folland, (1950) 1 ER 976 (AC).

[8] IBM v. Waterman, 2013 SCC 70.

[9] More specifically, they are benefits that do not come from the defendant *and* are not the defendant's payment of damages for the loss in question. In the leading Supreme Court of Canada case, IBM v. Waterman, *id.*, for example, the disputed collateral benefit (a retirement pension) flowed from the defendant (IBM).

boundary between contract and tort and performs a key interstitial function of maintaining this boundary's integrity.[10]

The chapter focuses on the most established instantiation of the collateral benefits rule: the interaction of contracts of private insurance with damages for personal injury. Here, the collateral source rule permits a plaintiff to recover monetary payments in respect of his tort from *both* his insurer and his tortfeasor. The rule's operation, therefore, appears to place the plaintiff in a better position than he would have been in had he never been wronged at all. On the basis that it violates the principle of *restitutio in integrum*, many have advocated the rule's abolition.[11] They argue that private law remedies are meant to compensate the plaintiff for her wrongfully caused losses, and, thus, to the extent that the plaintiff receives more than she needs to make good these losses, the damages award is unjustified. I reject these abolitionist arguments as they are premised on a misunderstanding of the compensatory principle. The articulation of the proper interpretation of the compensatory principle allows us not only to uncover (or recover, as the case turns out to be) the best justification for the collateral source rule, but also provides insight into the important interstitial role it plays.

II. The Challenge of Collateral Benefits

In *IBM v Waterman*,[12] a leading recent collateral benefits case, Justice Cromwell of the Supreme Court of Canada offers a plausible definition of these benefits as well as a snapshot of the problem they pose:

> A collateral benefit is a gain or advantage that flows to the plaintiff and is connected to the defendant's breach. This connection may exist either because there is a 'but-for' causal link between the breach and the receipt of the benefit or because the benefit was intended to provide the plaintiff with an indemnity for the type of loss caused by the breach. The problem raised by collateral

[10] My argument that the two types of transactions (tort, on the one hand; and, and the insurance contract or gift, on the other) should be kept distinct can be seen as a position in favor of a kind of modularity. See Andrew Gold's contribution to this volume, "Private Law's Choice of Private Law," for an argument about the benefits of such modularity, in particular, the reinforcement of values specific to each distinct sphere or module.

[11] *Unreason in the Law of Damages: The Collateral Source Rule* 77(4) HARVARD L. REV. 741 (1964); John G. Fleming, *The Collateral Source Rule and Loss Allocation in Tort Law*, 54(4) CALIFORNIA L. REV. 1478 (1966); P.S. Atiyah, *Collateral Benefits Again*, 32 MLR 397 (1969); Victor E. Schwartz, *Tort Law Reform: Strict Liability and the Collateral Source Rule Do Not Mix*, 39 VAND. L. REV. 569 (1986); James Branton, *The Collateral Source Rule*, 18 ST. MARY'S L.J. 883 (1987); Lewis, *supra* note 5.

[12] IBM, *supra* note 8.

benefits is the question of whether they should be deducted from the damages otherwise payable by the defendant on account of the breach.[13]

Collateral benefits are compensating advantages received by the plaintiff that are connected to the defendant's breach, but they are not damages. They are benefits that flow to the plaintiff from a third party as a consequence of the defendant's breach.[14] The paradigm instance of the operation of the collateral source rule and the focus of this chapter is a payout from private insurance for personal injury.[15] Other examples of collateral benefits are gifts,[16] sick or disability pay,[17] pensions,[18] and other employment and social benefits.[19] In cases in which pri vate insurance is the collateral benefit, if the insurance proceeds are not deducted from the plaintiff's award, the plaintiff appears to be overcompensated; she appears to receive a "bonanza"[20] or a "windfall."[21] However, if the contractual benefit is deducted, then the plaintiff seems to sacrifice her contractual entitlement for the benefit of the defendant. To illustrate, consider the 1874 English case *Bradburn v. Great Western Railway*.[22] Here, the plaintiff was injured in an accident caused by the defendant's negligence and as a result was unable to work. Following the accident, the plaintiff received a sum of money from his private insurer that seemed to compensate him for this lost income. Baron Pigott of the

13 *Id.* at [15].

14 For reasons outlined in note 9, it is more accurate to say that these benefits *usually* flow from a third party.

15 Bradburn v. The Great Western Railway Company (1874) LR 10 Exch 1; Cunningham v. Wheeler (1994) 113 DLR (4th) 1; The Propellor Monticello, *supra* note 6. The focus on private insurance payouts is justified because not only are these the paradigm cases, with all other examples (except for gift) treated as either analogous to private insurance payouts and therefore nondeductible or disanalogous to them and therefore deductible, but also it is here that we see most starkly the tension the collateral source rule poses for tort and contract.

16 Redpath v. Belfast and County Down Railway, [1947] NI 167; Parry v. Cleaver, [1970] AC 1; Cunningham v. Harrison, [1973] QB 942; Boarelli v. Flanagan (1973) 36 DLR (3d) 4, 8 (per Dubin JA); Burke .v Byrd 188 F Supp 384 (1960); Cunningham, *supra* note 15, at 41.

17 Turner v. MOD (1969), 113 SJ 685; Chan v. Butcher, [1984] 4 WWR 363 (BCCA); Hussain v. New Teplow Mills, [1988] AC 514; Ratych v. Bloomer, [1990] 1 SCR 940.

18 IBM, *supra* note 8. In Guy v. Trizec Equities Ltd. (1979), 99 DLR (3d) 243 (SCC), Justice Ritchie found that contributory pension benefits should not be deducted. See also Hewson v. Downs, [1970] 1 QB 73.

19 Jorgenson v. Jack Cewe Ltd., [1980] 1 SCR 812 establishes that no deduction is made at common law for unemployment insurance benefits; however, section 45 of the Employment Insurance Act (S.C. 1996, c. 23) provides legislated subrogation. According to this section, the plaintiff who receives benefits and is also awarded damages covering the same period of unemployment must pay the Receiver General the overpayment of the benefits. In MB v. BC, [2003] 2 SCR 477, welfare benefits were held to be deductible. Courts in the past have treated these benefits as nondeductible.

20 Fleming, *supra* note 11, at 1478. Fleming calls the collateral source rule in American accident law an "oddity" because the rule permits "no reduction . . . on account of benefits received by the plaintiff from other sources, even though they have partially or wholly mitigated his loss." According to Fleming, its "sting" lies in the fact that the plaintiff "may ordinarily keep both the damages as well as the collateral benefit and thus turn his plight into a bonanza."

21 Ratych, *supra* note 17, at 962 (McLachlin J [as she then was]).

22 Bradburn, *supra* note 15.

Court of the Exchequer maintained that, nonetheless, the plaintiff did not have to set off his private insurance proceeds against the defendant's damages. This is the operation of the collateral source rule: funds received from a collateral source are not considered in setting the quantum of the defendant's liability.

Most who comment on the above situation advocate the abolition of the collateral source rule on the basis that it violates the fundamental principle of all compensatory damages awards, the principle of *restitutio in integrum*.[23] This principle is set out most famously by Lord Blackburn in *Livingstone v. Rawyards*:

> [W]here any injury is to be compensated by damages, in settling the sum of money to be given in reparation of damages you should as nearly as possible get at that sum of money which will put the party who has been injured, or who has suffered, in the same position as he would have been in if he had not sustained the wrong for which he is now getting its compensation or reparation.[24]

According to the usual gloss of this passage, through a defendant's damages payment, a plaintiff should be put in a position ex post that is equivalent to her position ex ante. And, crucially, this payment should make the plaintiff no better and no worse off: "tort damages are designed to compensate . . . not to overcompensate."[25] In the 1990 Supreme Court of Canada case *Ratych v. Bloomer*, Justice McLachlin (as she then was), gives judicial voice[26] to these worries of overcompensation:

> the purpose of awarding damages in tort is to put the injured person in the same position as he or she would have been in had the tort not been committed, in so far as money can do so. The plaintiff is to be given damages for the full measure of his loss as best that can be calculated. But he is not entitled to turn an injury into a windfall.[27]

[23] Joel K. Jacobsen, *The Collateral Source Rule and the Role of the Jury*, 70 Oregon L. Rev. 523 (1991); Steven B. Hantler, Victoria E. Schwartz, Cary Silverman & Emily J. Laird, *Moving Toward the Fully Informed Jury*, 3 Georgetown J.L. & Public Policy 21 (2005), 24–25, for the argument that the collateral source rule allows a victim to be made "more than whole."

[24] Livingstone v. Rawyards Coal Co. (1880), 5 App Cas 25, at 39 (HL (Sc)) (Lord Blackburn).

[25] Law Commission, *Damages for Personal Injury: Collateral Benefits* 2 (Law Com No 147, 1997).

[26] Justice McLachlin's skepticism about the collateral source rule is notable. She wrote for the majority in Ratych, *supra* note 17, a decision in which the plaintiff's already received employment benefits were deducted from the defendant's damages. And again, in Cunningham, *supra* note 15, a case with similar facts to Ratych but where the employment benefits were not deducted, McLachlin J criticized the nondeductibility of collateral benefits in her dissent. The majority distinguished Cunningham from Ratych on the ground that the plaintiff in the former, in contrast to the latter, could show that he had "paid for" the benefits. And, finally, in IBM, *supra* note 8, Chief Justice McLachlin joined Justice Rothstein in his stinging dissent that interpreted the pension benefits flowing to Mr. Waterman as not coming from a collateral source at all because they flowed from the same contract, the breach of which was the object of the claim.

[27] Ratych, *supra* note 17, at 962. See also Corey J in Cunningham, *supra* note 15, at 7: "the plaintiff is not entitled to double recovery for any loss arising from the injury."

The perceived threat is clear. If compensatory damages are intended to compensate a plaintiff for the losses he suffers following a tort, and yet if a plaintiff's private contract of insurance *already* seems to have made good those losses, how can a rule like the collateral source rule, a rule that ignores the effect of compensatory advantages, be justified? In other words, if the plaintiff has already been made whole, has been restored materially to his ex ante position, then there remains no loss upon which to ground the defendant's obligation to compensate the plaintiff.

When forced to choose between the collateral source rule and the compensatory principle, most academics and legal commentators have sacrificed the former for the latter.[28] Even those few scholars who steadfastly defend the collateral source rule, for the most part, accept that this defense necessitates the sacrifice of the compensatory principle. They view the collateral source rule as an exception to the rule set out by the compensatory principle—as a qualification of private law's general rule that damages should make the plaintiff whole and nothing more.[29] The consensus is that we must choose between the compensatory principle and the collateral source rule. But this chapter takes a different approach and rejects the terms of the ultimatum. On my defense, the collateral source rule is a natural implication of the compensation principle, not a threat or an exception to it.

III. Leading Justifications of the Collateral Source Rule

Leading justifications for the nondeductibility of insurance payouts accept that the collateral source rule operates as an exception to the compensation principle. In other words, defenders of the rule do not dispute how the rule's detractors characterize the problem, namely, that the collateral source rule runs afoul of

[28] See note 11 for criticisms of the rule. Others, however, have nonetheless defended it: For a grudging defense, see Richard C Maxwell, *The Collateral Source Rule in the American Law of Damages*, 46 MINN. L. REV. 669 (1961). For more robust defenses, see Thomas F. Lambert Jr., *The Case for the Collateral Source Rule*, 9 INSURANCE L.J. 551 (1966) (argues in favor of the collateral source rule on the basis of its role in deterrence); Michael Krauss & Jeremy Kidd, *Collateral Source and Tort's Soul*, 48(1) U. LOUISVILLE L. REV. 1 (2009) (defends collateral source rule from the perspective of corrective justice); Daniella Murynka, *Collateral Benefits Revisited: A Case Comment on IBM Canada Ltd. v. Waterman*, 53 ALBERTA L. REV. 243–57(2015); James Boyd, *Collateral Benefits: Defending the Causal Rationale*, 76 U. TORONTO FACULTY L. REV. 92 (2018).

[29] As Justice Cromwell acknowledges,

> The principle that the defendant should compensate the plaintiff only for his or her actual loss is not, on its own, an answer to the problem. There are exceptions to the strict application of this principle, the most important of which is the exception for private insurance and other benefits which, for this purpose, are considered analogous to private insurance.
>
> (IBM, *supra* note 8, at [16])

the compensatory principle.[30] The rule's defenders accept that the plaintiff is overcompensated, but argue that, for a variety of reasons, she deserves to be. As James Branton argues,

> For those who view it objectively, the question becomes, as between a wrongdoer and an innocent victim, who is to get the alleged 'windfall'? Is it to be the wrongdoer who doesn't have to pay because the victim has insurance coverage, is it to be the first-party insurance carrier who has been paid to provide the insurance, or is it to be the person who has been injured as a result of the negligence of the wrongdoer? Perhaps there are those who would line up on the side of the wrongdoer or the company that has been paid premiums for providing coverage, but it is unlikely. One without an interest in the issue would almost certainly line up on the side of the innocent victim.[31]

Collateral source rule defenders argue that the *defendant* should not be the beneficiary of the plaintiff's prudence. The idea here is that, yes, there is a windfall, but, as between the innocent victim of the tort and the blameworthy tortfeasor, this windfall should go to the plaintiff.[32] Given that the plaintiff paid premiums for her insurance policy, why should the defendant receive the benefit of the plaintiff's prudent investment? As the English Court of Appeal put the point in *Shearman v Folland*,

> If a wrongdoer were entitled to set-off what the plaintiff was entitled to recoup or had recouped under his policy, he would, in effect, be depriving the plaintiff of all benefit from the premiums paid by the latter and appropriating the benefit to himself.[33]

Lord Reid echoes the above sentiment in *Parry v. Cleaver*, stating that the "real and substantial reason" for disregarding accident insurance moneys was that the

[30] As the authors of the Law Commission frame the issue:

> The key difficulty in this area of law resides in the conflict between the fundamental principle that . . . tort damages are designed to compensate but not to overcompensate, and a set of policy arguments favouring overcompensation. . . . This paper is primarily concerned to establish whether the case law resolution of the tension between the principle against double recovery and the policy arguments for it is in need of amendment. (Law Commission, *supra* note 25, at 2)

[31] Branton, *supra* note 11, at 889. See also Grayson v. Williams, 256 F.2d 61, 65 (10th Cir. 1958): "If there must be a windfall certainly it is more just that the injured person shall profit therefrom, rather than the wrongdoer shall be relieved of his full responsibility for his wrongdoing."

[32] Victor Schwartz has criticized this argument as inapplicable when the tort involved is one of strict liability on the basis that the defendant is not really to blame: Victor E. Schwartz, *Tort Law Reform: Strict Liability and the Collateral Source Rule Do Not Mix*, 46 MINNESOTA L.R. 669 (1961).

[33] [1950] 1 All ER 976, 978. Quoted with approval by the Supreme Court of Canada in Cunningham, *supra* note 15, 399–400 (Cory J).

plaintiff "has bought them and that it would be unjust and unreasonable to hold that the money which he prudently spent on premiums and the benefit from it should enure to the benefit of the tortfeasor."[34]

We might call this justification the *unjust benefit rationale.* At its core is the thought that, by not deducting the insurance payout from the defendant's damages, the court prevents an unjust enrichment from arising. If the defendant were to receive the benefit (the deduction), he would be enriched at the plaintiff's expense (the premiums the plaintiff has paid), and there would be no juristic reason for this enrichment. To put the point somewhat differently, we would *not* say that the plaintiff *intended* the payment of premiums to be for the benefit of the defendant. She intended this payment to be for her own benefit. In this way, the collateral source rule's verdict of nondeductibility prevents an unjust enrichment from occurring.[35]

It bears noting that, even according to the unjust benefit justification of the collateral source rule, the plaintiff remains overcompensated. The implicit justification of the operation of the collateral source rule that it prevents the occurrence of an unjust enrichment does not, on its own, remove the worry of the plaintiff's double recovery. This is because the situation prevented is not a true situation of unjust enrichment. In the orthodox law of unjust enrichment, the plaintiff's deprivation and the defendant's corresponding enrichment are one and the same.[36] In cases regulated by the collateral source rule, the defendant's enrichment does not correspond in a one-to-one way with the plaintiff's deprivation. The plaintiff's deprivation is the cost of the premiums—the money that the plaintiff prudently expended on securing and maintaining his private insurance. The defendant's enrichment is the saved expense of the damages award or the amount of the insurance payout.[37] In other words, the plaintiff is deprived of the cost of the contract, its price, while the defendant is enriched to the extent of the ultimate value of the contract, the

[34] Parry, *supra* note 16, at 588.

[35] This rationale is at work in the distinction mentioned about between Ratych and Cunningham. In the former, the court could not find a "deprivation" of the plaintiff by virtue of which the defendant was enriched. By contrast, in Cunningham, *supra* note 15, the plaintiff was found to have "paid for" his employment benefits by making sacrifices to his overall pay. In my opinion, the fact that the plaintiff has "paid for" the benefit is not determinative of the question of deductibility. Rather, what payment signals is that this benefit is the subject of a separate contractual obligation. Notably, gifts, the second paradigm case of where the collateral source rule operates, are not deductible, and it is the characteristic feature of a gift that it is not paid for. Hence, whether something is paid for or not cannot answer the question of whether it is deductible.

[36] *See* Mitchell McInnes, *The Measure of Restitution*, 52 UTLJ 163 (2002) and Mitchell McInnes, *Restitution, Unjust Enrichment and the Perfect Quadration Thesis*, 7 RESTITUTION L.R. 118 (1999).

[37] Thus, one possible solution is for the defendant to pay the plaintiff's paid premiums—for the defendant to bear the cost of the insurance that now redounds to his benefit. This solution has not, as far as I know, been judicially endorsed.

amount of the policy itself. This is analogous to saying that the plaintiff's deprivation is the cost of the lottery ticket while the defendant's "corresponding" enrichment is the jackpot.

This first set of justifications for the collateral source rule concerns the distributive question of who deserves the windfall as between the plaintiff and the defendant. It accepts without question that there is a windfall to be had and looks for justifications for its falling where it does. Clearly, if we accept that this is the right way to look at the situation, the victim of a tort who has paid for the benefit should receive it over the perpetrator of the wrong that occasioned the loss in question. Another potentially complementary set of justifications looks at the windfall less as a boon that is deserved or not but rather as either a stick or a carrot that can promote or deter desirable or undesirable behavior, respectively. Plaintiffs, we are told, should be motivated to take the prudent course of taking out insurance.[38] To deduct collateral benefits would disincentivize this socially responsible behavior.[39] Defendants, we are further reminded, would be less deterred against committing torts if they did not have to shoulder the full burden of liability.[40]

To conclude, most leading defenses of the collateral source rule choose to sacrifice the linchpin of private law liability, the compensation principle, for the sake of what they consider to be more distributionally just or efficacious results. I argue that this sacrifice is far from necessary and indeed is based on a misinterpretation of the compensatory principle.

IV. Out with the Old and In with the Older

Recall that the problems for the collateral source rule began with the thought that allowing a plaintiff to receive tort compensation and insurance proceeds amounted to double recovery. Collateral source rule abolitionists advocated the priority of the compensation principle, while collateral source rule defenders granted that, on the basis of an assortment of policy reasons, the principle should give way. Both the arguments for and against the collateral source rule accept without criticism the premise that, by not deducting a plaintiff's insurance payout, the plaintiff stands to be overcompensated for the losses that she suffered

[38] Stephen Shavell has argued in a somewhat different vein that if the awards are too high that the plaintiff would be deprived of incentives to take reasonable precautions to avoid injury and in fact would create incentives for victims to either cause losses themselves or fabricate them. SHAVELL, ECONOMIC ANALYSIS OF ACCIDENT LAW 237, 237 (1987).

[39] See Lambert, *supra* note 28.

[40] Richard Posner argues that making defendants internalize the full costs of their torts is necessary to achieve the deterrence. RICHARD POSNER, ECONOMIC ANALYSIS OF LAW (9th ed., 2014).

as a result of the defendant's tort.[41] In what follows, I challenge this premise and argue that a receipt of a collateral benefit does not overcompensate the plaintiff. According to my view, the operation of the collateral source rule is not a threat to *restitutio in integrum.*

Advocates on both sides of the collateral source rule debate are predisposed to view its operation as leading to double recovery due to a basic misunderstanding of the compensatory principle. This misunderstanding, in turn, arises out of a particular picture of tort law, according to which tort law is an institutional mechanism designed to address interpersonally caused material setbacks. This picture is now arguably the dominant paradigm in private law. According to this conception of private law, a principal role of private law is to allocate the losses following a private wrong or injustice fairly and efficiently (as well as to prevent these losses from occurring in the first place).

In contrast to this distributive and instrumental approach, we might choose instead to view private law as a coherent and unified phenomenon, undergirded by interstitial concepts. On this more traditional approach, we focus on the separateness of private law's bipolar relationships.[42] It is the relationship of the plaintiff and the defendant, a relationship that begins either voluntarily (through contract) or involuntarily (through tort or unjust enrichment) and ends with either the performance of the contract or the judicial award of a remedy. This relationship's exclusivity, I argue, is a grounding, unifying, and true interstitial concept of private law. A consequence of this exclusivity of the relationship between the plaintiff and the defendant is that actions of third parties are irrelevant to the relationship itself—that is, an action of a third party cannot change the normative form or content (the rights or duties) that make up the relationship between the plaintiff and the defendant.[43] The parties, so understood, relate wholly and exclusively through the transaction between them.

On this transactional account, it is the wrongful disruption of the rightful relationship between the plaintiff and the defendant and its restoration that are the focus of the compensation principle and its ideal of *restitutio in integrum.* The focus is *not* on the plaintiff's material position before and after the defendant's wrong or breach. Thus, the compensatory principle is not primarily about undoing deleterious consequences of an unfortunate event but about correcting a wrongful transaction. The compensatory principle is not essentially about the

[41] I have heard anecdotally that some American defenders of the rule argue that the plaintiff is actually not materially better off, because as a practical matter this "extra" money goes to pay the plaintiff's legal fees given that costs are not generally awarded in many American jurisdictions.

[42] *See* Ernest J. Weinrib, The Idea of Private Law (1995).

[43] This idea of privity is clearly expressed in the doctrine of *res inter alios* (or, in its full form, *res inter alios acta, aliis nec nocet nec prodest* (a thing done between some does not harm or benefit others)). According to this Latin maxim, a contract cannot affect the rights of one who is not a party to the contract. It is private law's way of saying, "Mind your own business!"

material repair of the plaintiff but rather the *normative* repair of the disrupted relationship between the plaintiff and defendant.[44] *Restitutio in integrum* does not mean that the plaintiff, understood in isolation, should be put materially back in the position she was in before. Rather, it means that the relationship between the *plaintiff and the defendant* that was disrupted by the defendant's wronging of the plaintiff needs to be corrected, restored to a rightful relationship. Of course, part of what it means to correct a wrong is to repair the deleterious consequences of that wrong, but this material reparation is parasitic on the normative repair that is the justification for the court's order of compensation. Often to effectuate this normative repair, material repair is necessary, but this empirical reality does not mean that we should identify normative repair with one of its phenomenal manifestations.

If we understand the parties' relationship as exclusive and transactional, then the compensatory principle and the collateral source rule cannot be characterized as rule and exception, respectively, but rather as manifestations of the same principle regarding the relational character of private law. Because the object of reparation is the exclusive relationship between the plaintiff and the defendant and not just the material standing of the plaintiff herself, the argument about double recovery misses the mark. The plaintiff cannot be put in a better position by virtue of the payout from the insurer. This is just what she is owed under the insurance contract upon the satisfaction of the triggering condition that is the defendant's tort. This payout can in no way (unless the insurer is operating on behalf of the defendant)[45] restore the relationship of the defendant and the plaintiff to their pre-wrong positions. In the relational or transactional picture that I endorse, the defendant's action of reparation undoes (rationally responds to) the defendant's anterior breach of duty. Thus, a collateral reparative action that does not come from the defendant or is not effectuated on his behalf cannot rationally respond to—cannot undo—the injustice that is the plaintiff's ground of complaint. The defendant (or someone acting on the defendant's behalf) must pay the damages to the plaintiff for this relationship to be restored.[46] According to our revised understanding of *restitutio in integrum*, because it is the discrete transaction itself that needs to be corrected, the defendant cannot drop out of the picture; he is a necessary element to the rectification of the injustice that he perpetrated.[47]

44 Ernest J. Weinrib, *The Gains and Losses of Corrective Justice*, 44(2) DUKE L.J. 277 (1994).

45 For an in-depth analysis of what it means to act on behalf of another, see James Penner's contribution to this volume. Also see Andrew Gold, *Delegation and the Continuity Thesis*, 40 L. & PHIL. 645, 648–52 (2021).

46 For more on this point, seeZoë Sinel, *Is Personal Injury Law Personal?*, 6 J. TORT L. 145 (2013).

47 Krauss & Kidd, *supra* note 28. The authors argue that the corrective justice tenet of making whole does not explain the collateral source rule, but that corrective justice's other central tenets of correlativity and personality do. In a nutshell, they argue that because wrongdoing requires the defendant's agency, so too does the remedy.

The current justifications for the collateral source rule rely on considerations that are external to the transactional relationship between the plaintiff and the defendant (the plaintiff's moral desert, the defendant's turpitude, the plaintiff's prudence, the defendant's fear of sanctions). As such, they conceive of the interaction between the collateral source rule and the compensatory principle as one of relative pros and cons judged against an instrumental criterion for private law's nature. These justifications implicitly rely on a non-relational understanding of private law, according to which the aim of damages is to compensate the plaintiff for harm. If the goal is harm compensation and harm compensation is divorced from the question of wrong correction, then anything that ameliorates this harm obviates the need for the defendant's obligation to pay compensation. The defendant's obligation, if it remains, must be justified on different grounds. Given this distributional understanding of tort law, it is no surprise that, from this perspective, the defenses of the collateral source rule justify the defendant's continued obligation on the basis of relative moral desert, general deterrence, or specific deterrence. Thus, whether the collateral source rule is endorsed or criticized, its operation, according to leading accounts, leads to double recovery. By contrast, on our revised, relational understanding of the compensation principle, we can begin to see that there is no problem of overcompensation posed by the collateral source rule because we now can understand that there are two separate relations at issue when it operates.

Indeed, a relational understanding of the collateral source rule already exists, dating back to its nineteenth-century justification: the *causal rationale.*[48] The causal rationale receives its most famous expression in *Bradburn v. Great Western Railway Co*:

> I think that there would be no justice or principle in setting off an amount which the plaintiff has entitled himself to under a contract of insurance, such as any prudent man would make on the principle of, as the expression is, 'laying by for a rainy day.' He pays the premiums upon a contract which, if he meets with an accident, entitles him to receive a sum of money. *It is not because he meets with the accident, but because he made a contract with, and paid premiums to, the insurance company, for that express purpose, that he gets the money from them. It is true that there must be the element of accident in order to entitle him to the money; but it is under and by reason of his contract with the insurance company, that he gets the amount;* and I think that it ought not, upon any principle of justice, to be deducted from the amount of the damages proved to have been sustained by him through the negligence of the defendants.[49]

[48] See Boyd, *supra* note 28, for a defense of the causal rationale on historical and logical grounds.
[49] See Bradburn, *supra* note 15 (Pigott B.) (emphasis added).

The language of causation, however, is infelicitous. Both the insurance contract and the wrong are necessary causes of the plaintiff's insurance payout: but for the plaintiff's insurance contract, he would not receive the insurance payout. And, equally, but for the defendant's wrong, there would be no insurance payout. For this reason, the causal rationale was rejected by courts who lamented the semantic flailing about encouraged by arguments that something was a "*causa sine qua non*" rather than a "*causa causans*."[50] Rather than throw out this promising relational rationale, I suggest we change our terms. Better terminology relies on a conceptual distinction between two kinds of causative events: reasons that lead to results, on the one hand; and conditions that lead to consequences, on the other. It is not the *defendant's wrong* but rather the contract with the insurer that is the reason for the insurance payout. When something is a reason for a result, the connection between the two is necessary and non-arbitrary: the result flows from the reason for it. The result is constituted by the reason for it. When something is a condition of a consequence, on the other hand, the connection between the two is arbitrary. Anything can serve as either the condition or the consequence. When we make a contract for an owed sum and I say, "Pay me the money you owe me by next Thursday," the condition, "next Thursday" is not necessarily connected to the obligation (payment of the owed sum)—its only connection is achieved through the posited terms of the contract.[51]

We can understand the insurance contract as the *reason for* the insurance payout. Part of what it means to have an insurance contract is that, when its terms are met, you receive insurance. Only the basis of a valid insurance contract can result in an insurance payout. The defendant's wrongful injuring of the plaintiff is the *condition* of the insurance payout. In theory, what triggers the payout could be any condition stipulated by agreement, not just the defendant's wrong. As Baron Pigott explains, "It is true that there must be the element of accident in order to entitle him to the money; but it is under and by reason of his contract with the insurance company, that he gets the amount."[52] Because it identifies the relationships between the relevant entities as separate and does not view a private law action as an opportunity to distribute the costs of accidents, the causal

50 *Causa causans* is the immediate cause, or the last cause in a sequence of causal events. A *causa sine qua non* is a necessary or an inevitable cause.

51 A further potentially helpful philosophical distinction is that between results and consequences. Consequences are eventualities that follow an action and that are also causally connected to it. Results are causal constituents of action. They do not follow an action; they are part of it. (See John Gardner, *Obligations and Outcomes in the Law of Torts, in* Relating to Responsibility: Essays for Tony Honoré (P. Cane & J. Gardner eds., 2001).) We might say that the plaintiff's receipt of insurance benefits is the result of the insurer's contractual performance while his receipt of insurance benefits is the consequence of the plaintiff's suffering a wrong at the hand of the defendant. The plaintiff's recovery of damages from the defendant is the result of the plaintiff's suffering a wrong at the hand of the defendant.

52 Bradburn, *supra* note 15.

rationale can provide a coherent picture of the joint operation of the collateral source rule and the compensatory principle. One way to understand cases of nondeductible advantages flowing from a collateral source is that they simply reflect the operation of the doctrine of privity. Here we find the idea, endemic in private law, that a thing done between others does not harm or benefit others: *res inter alios acta* (*aliis nec nocet nec prodet*).[53] A contract made between the plaintiff and a third party cannot affect the legal rights and duties of the tortfeasor and the plaintiff. Analogously, if upon breach of contract the innocent party enters into another contract with a third party and makes up for all the losses on the first breached contract, these gains are not considered when damages for breach of the first contract are calculated. The rights of the innocent party on the first contract are separate from the rights of that party under a subsequent beneficial contract.

V. To Deduct or Not to Deduct

On our revised understanding of the compensatory principle, the principle is concerned with correcting unjust transactions, not with allocating the deleterious effects of these transactions in accordance with a comparative criterion of moral desert or distributive efficiency. Our corresponding revised understanding of the collateral source rule is that the plaintiff is entitled to both the payment of the defendant's damages award and her insurance payout because they are separate transactions. As separate transactions, they generate obligatory action that is specific to that transaction. Only the defendant's payment of damages to the plaintiff can address the defendant's wrongful interference with the plaintiff; only the insurer's payment of the contractually owed premium to the insured plaintiff can satisfy the insurer's contractual obligation to the insured plaintiff. This transactional lens explains why the plaintiff's receipt of insurance proceeds, even if they do seem to make it as if the plaintiff suffers no loss as a result of the defendant's tort, should not affect the defendant's obligation to pay compensatory damages in tort.

Yet sometimes actions that ameliorate the plaintiff's losses *do* get set off against the defendant's damages. Why? While the preceding section offered an explanation of the nondeductibility of compensating advantages, this section attempts to offer a principled understanding of why in certain circumstances they might be deducted.

The remedial doctrine of mitigation is the most obvious example of when the amelioration of the plaintiff's loss disentitles the plaintiff from receiving

[53] On this maxim, see *supra* note 43.

compensatory damages for that loss from the defendant. Following a tort or a breach of contract, the plaintiff cannot recover compensation for losses that flow from the tort or the breach that he in fact avoided or should have avoided through his reasonable efforts. The evidentiary burden is on the defendant to establish that the plaintiff either did mitigate his loss or ought to have. Why, then, does a plaintiff's ex ante mitigatory behavior of purchasing private insurance not count as mitigation for the purposes of reducing the defendant's damages when a plaintiff's ex post mitigatory behavior does?[54]

The transactional lens we employed to understand why collateral benefits are not deductible can also help us distinguish the doctrine of mitigation from the operation of the collateral source rule. When a plaintiff sues his defendant for compensatory damages that flow from a bodily injury she has suffered at the hand of the defendant, she seeks compensation for losses that flow from the defendant's violation of her right that the defendant not interfere with her bodily integrity. By contrast, the money payment that comes from the insurer is *not* directed at these losses *qua* consequential losses. Rather, the payment is simply the satisfaction of the plaintiff's right to the payment as a term of her contract. If the insurer refused to pay out the plaintiff's policy, the plaintiff could sue not only for the loss of the policy—the sum due under the contract—but also for any losses that flow from the defendant's breach of contract.[55] These losses, just like the consequential losses that flow from the defendant's tort, are subject to the limiting doctrines of remoteness and mitigation. To the extent that they are ameliorated, they are not suffered and so cannot ground a claim in damages. The insurance payout does *not* ameliorate the losses the plaintiff suffers following the defendant's tort; rather, this payout is merely the satisfaction of the plaintiff's

[54] Daniella Murynka, one of the few scholars to tackle this issue directly, offers the following explanation (Murynka, *supra* note 28, at 256–57):

> Although it is reasonable to impose a requirement to mitigate avoidable losses on plaintiffs who have notice of breach, it would require too much of plaintiffs to demand as a matter of law that they secure substitute performance in advance of breach. In other words, a plaintiff should not be precluded from claiming losses that could have been insured against. A perfect mirror between collateral benefits and mitigatory benefits therefore does not exist.

This explanation strikes me as satisfying as a matter of intuition, but not as a matter of logic. We often require plaintiffs to have performed ex ante mitigative behavior in order to claim for certain losses. If I fail to wear a seatbelt and then am in a car crash caused by the defendant's negligence, but the injuries I suffer are due (in part) to my failure to wear a seatbelt, I cannot claim compensation for these injuries from my defendant. (Although I can of course recover damages for injuries that I would have suffered regardless of my failure to take a safety precaution. One could argue that in this situation the defendant simply did not *cause* the plaintiff's loss. In these scenarios, the doctrines of causation and mitigation are hard to distinguish.) That it demands too much of a plaintiff to take out accident insurance prior to a wrong cannot be the explanation for the different treatment of collateral benefits and mitigatory acts.

[55] Whether these losses are considered too remote is governed by the principle in Hadley v. Baxendale (1854), 9 Exch 341, 355; 156 ER 145, 151.

contractual right and the insurer's contractual duty.[56] Because it does not compensate for *losses*, it cannot discharge the defendant's duty with respect to these losses.[57]

In other situations, however, it does appear that the payment of money does make good the plaintiff's loss, leaving her in the same position she would have been in had the wrong not occurred. These are situations in which the payment is meant to *indemnify* the consequential losses suffered by the plaintiff.[58] Here, the losses suffered by the plaintiff are consequential losses that have been fully compensated by a party that is not the defendant. In these situations, the courts tend either to deduct the collateral benefit from the defendant's damages award, award the third-party payer a right of subrogation against the defendant, or impose a trust on the damages award given to the plaintiff to hold on behalf of the third-party payer.

Consider the following excerpt from Justice McLachlin's dissent in *Cunningham v. Wheeler*. In this case, the plaintiff was injured when he was hit

[56] Here I follow Robert Stevens's helpful distinction between damages that are awarded for the consequential losses one suffers as a result of a rights infringement and damages that are intended to be a substitute for the value of the right itself. (Robert Stevens, Torts and Rights 60–61 (2007)). Limiting doctrines like mitigation apply to consequential damages. I must mitigate my consequential losses; however, I am under no duty to mitigate with respect to the objects of substitutive damages. The defendant could not argue, for example, after blowing up my Porsche, that it was unreasonable of me to have such an expensive car. He could argue, however, that it was unreasonable for me subsequently to refuse to go to work because I allegedly could not get there as a result of my refusal to rent a less fancy rental car. Similarly, the defendant cannot say that it is unreasonable of me, when he smacks me upside the head and my jaw shatters, to have such birdlike bones, but he could argue that my refusal to undergo surgery, a refusal which led to further time away from work, was unreasonable.

The insurance payout does not address the consequential losses that the plaintiff suffered. The payout represents the value of his right under the contract. If the insurer breached its contract of insurance with the insured (the plaintiff) by not paying out its premium consequent the triggering event of the defendant's tort, the plaintiff would be entitled to sue the insurer for the agreed sum under the contract. The plaintiff's receipt of the insurance proceeds is just the receipt of his contractual entitlement under the contract of insurance. It is not a remedy, in other words, for the plaintiff's losses following the tort. In Stevens' terminology, the damages are substitutive, not consequential. By contrast, if we are looking at the plaintiff's lost wages that he suffers as a result of the tortious injury, these are losses that are the consequence of the defendant's tort. The plaintiff is under an obligation to mitigate this loss—that is, he cannot turn down a job that he could reasonably do. These losses flow from the tort committed, but the compensatory damages that are awarded to ameliorate them do not substitute for a stand-alone right the plaintiff has against the defendant.

[57] For commentary on the doctrine of avoided loss where there is a similar confusion between damages that are a substitute for the right infringed and damages that compensate for losses that flow from an infringed right, *see* Zoë Sinel, *Rights, Wrongs, and Injustices: The Structure of Remedial Law by Stephen A Smith (Review)*, 72 UTLJ 125 (2022), 134

[58] This thought is mainly in line with KD Cooper's suggestion that whether a collateral benefit should be deducted or not turns on whether the benefit was intended to indemnify the very loss complained of:

> It will be contended that there is a crucial distinction to be made in this respect between benefits which are intended to compensate a specific pecuniary loss (which should be deducted); and benefits intended for other purposes, such as to compensate non-pecuniary loss, (which should not be deducted).
>
> (*A Collateral Benefits Principle*, 49 Canadian Bar Rev. 501, 502 (1971))

by a car. During the time he was unable to work due to his injuries, he received disability benefits from his employer pursuant to the terms of a collective agreement with the employer. Justice Cory, writing the Supreme Court of Canada's majority opinion, argued that the plaintiff had "paid for" the benefit through the collective bargaining process that offset some of the plaintiff's salary against benefits promised under the collective agreement. Justice McLachlin considered the idea that the plaintiff's contribution could play such a role as illogical:

> As a matter of logic, the fact that a plaintiff may lose the benefit of having made a contribution does not affect the fact that, to the extent a loss is made good by the plan, the plaintiff in fact suffers no parallel loss recoverable against the defendant under tort principles. Tort law says the plaintiff who is prevented from working by an injury caused by the defendant's negligence may claim any lost earnings from the defendant. *If the earnings have not been lost because they continued under an employment plan, then the plaintiff has suffered no loss of earnings. So logic dictates the plaintiff can recover nothing on account of lost earnings.*[59]

Justice McLachlin's logic is sound. If a loss is ameliorated or never arises in the first place, then there is no loss left for the defendant to fix. This explains why a plaintiff who mitigates her loss by finding a new job following her wrongful dismissal cannot claim lost income, since, by definition, she has not suffered that loss consequent the defendant's wrong.

Sometimes the reason that we do not deduct compensatory advantages from a defendant's damages award is that these advantages only contingently address the plaintiff's consequential losses suffered at the hands of the defendant's tort. The essence of the received benefit is that it forms the subject matter of a stand-alone claim that the plaintiff has against the third party (that is, her rights under her insurance contract). If the insurer were to withhold payment on the plaintiff's claim, she could sue the insurer for breach of contract and her remedy would be the award of the contractually stipulated sum. Although the remedy is monetary, it is not an award that compensates for loss; it is not damages. Rather, it is a remedy that substitutes for the right infringed: the loss of the value of the contract.

Sometimes, however, the collateral benefit does indemnify the plaintiff's loss, and does so in a non-contingent way. In these situations, the plaintiff can still claim against the defendant for her consequential losses, but we rightfully see these awards as leading to overcompensation in a way we do not in

[59] Cunningham, *supra* note 15, at 381–82 (emphasis added).

the situations of private insurance articulated above. In these situations, if a plaintiff recovered her full losses from her tort-defendant and then sued her insurer for these same losses in a contract claim, she would receive nothing as there would be no loss remaining for the insurer to indemnify—the condition of the payout is the plaintiff's loss and this condition would be absent. But if the plaintiff receives money from her insurer first, then the plaintiff-insured's rights as a matter of law remain intact despite receiving indemnity from the insurer. In other words, despite being fully indemnified, this indemnification, because it does not come from or on behalf of the defendant, does not expunge the defendant's obligation to the plaintiff. A fully indemnified plaintiff can then demand compensatory damages from a defendant for her own sake, that is, not for the sake of the person that has indemnified her loss. A court, however, might view this demand as akin to an abuse of rights. The plaintiff is standing on her rights to sue in a situation in which the insurer has indemnified the plaintiff's loss.

In this light, one promising way to understand the collateral source rule is as an evidentiary rule that normally prohibits the defendant from raising the existence of a collateral benefit in order to reduce his damage award.[60] It is possible to think that in situations in which a fully indemnified plaintiff demands compensation from her defendant, the court will not allow the plaintiff to rely on such an evidentiary rule since to do so would have the effect of compensating the plaintiff for a loss that she did not in fact suffer. The plaintiff, in other words, cannot use the collateral source rule to stop the defendant from leading evidence of what are essentially non-collateral benefits. Moreover, in these situations, the loss suffered now belongs to the indemnifier of the loss, who has effectively discharged a debt owed by the defendant to the plaintiff. Just as is the case in joint liability of tortfeasors, the third party should be entitled to claim contribution from the defendant for the loss that it incurred. Subrogation, in these scenarios, is thus properly understood as an equitable principle that operates to prevent the court from creating an unjust enrichment.[61]

[60] As Rebecca Levenson explains, "the collateral source rule plays both a substantive and an evidentiary role. The evidentiary function of the rule is to determine what evidence pertaining to collateral sources may be introduced at trial for the jury to consider when deciding the defendant tortfeasor's liability.... The common law collateral source rule prevents the defendant from presenting evidence that the claimant possessed insurance to the jury before the verdict" (*Allocating the Costs of Harm to Whom They are Due: Modifying the Collateral Source Rule*, 160 U. Pennsylvania L. Rev. 921, 924–25 (2012)).

[61] This is in part an answer to an additional concern about the collateral source rule which asks why subrogation is automatic with property claims but not personal injury. Part of the answer to this concern is that personal injury insurance contracts are not seen as indemnity insurance (or traditionally were not). They did not compensate the plaintiff for the losses she suffered consequent a tort, but were instead more like life insurance, non-indemnity contracts. Property insurance, by contrast, is indemnity insurance. You are insured for the value of the losses you suffer.

VI. Conclusion

Through this exploration of the collateral source rule and its interaction with the ostensibly unifying compensatory principle, we can see the true nature of private law's unity and coherence. What unifies private law is not its emphasis on repairing wrongful losses but rather in correcting wrongful transactions. When the transactions are separate, private law correctly treats them as irrelevant to one another for the purposes of damages assessment through the operation of the collateral source rule. Given that losses are singular, however, if a compensating advantage is intended to and does eliminate the loss a plaintiff suffered, while she may still claim this loss against her defendant, the law makes it so that she claims it not on her own behalf but on behalf of the party to whom the loss has now shifted, the third party. The collateral source rule thus provides the important interstitial function of maintaining the boundary between different heads of liability.

If we think about the compensation principle as an ameliorative and allocative principle, one that concerns the curing of loss or harm, then we must either reject the collateral source rule or rescue it through an appeal to policy. By contrast, if we understand the compensatory principle as concerned with discrete transactions and their rectification, that is, as concerned with exclusive relations of injustice, then the doctrine remains coherent and unified.

Index

For the benefit of digital users, indexed terms that span two pages (e.g., 52–53) may, on occasion, appear on only one of those pages.